Judaism

2nd Edition

by Rabbi Ted Falcon, Ph.D. and David Blatner

D0891249

for
dummies®
A Wiley Brand

Judaism For Dummies®, 2nd Edition

Published by: **John Wiley & Sons, Inc.**, 111 River Street, Hoboken, NJ 07030-5774, www.wiley.com

Copyright © 2019 by John Wiley & Sons, Inc., Hoboken, New Jersey

Published simultaneously in Canada

No part of this publication may be reproduced, stored in a retrieval system or transmitted in any form or by any means, electronic, mechanical, photocopying, recording, scanning or otherwise, except as permitted under Sections 107 or 108 of the 1976 United States Copyright Act, without the prior written permission of the Publisher. Requests to the Publisher for permission should be addressed to the Permissions Department, John Wiley & Sons, Inc., 111 River Street, Hoboken, NJ 07030, (201) 748-6011, fax (201) 748-6008, or online at http://www.wiley.com/go/permissions.

Trademarks: Wiley, For Dummies, the Dummies Man logo, Dummies.com, Making Everything Easier, and related trade dress are trademarks or registered trademarks of John Wiley & Sons, Inc. and may not be used without written permission. Fitbit is a registered trademark of Fitbit, Inc. All other trademarks are the property of their respective owners. John Wiley & Sons, Inc. is not associated with any product or vendor mentioned in this book.

LIMIT OF LIABILITY/DISCLAIMER OF WARRANTY: THE PUBLISHER AND THE AUTHOR MAKE NO REPRESENTATIONS OR WARRANTIES WITH RESPECT TO THE ACCURACY OR COMPLETENESS OF THE CONTENTS OF THIS WORK AND SPECIFICALLY DISCLAIM ALL WARRANTIES, INCLUDING WITHOUT LIMITATION WARRANTIES OF FITNESS FOR A PARTICULAR PURPOSE. NO WARRANTY MAY BE CREATED OR EXTENDED BY SALES OR PROMOTIONAL MATERIALS. THE ADVICE AND STRATEGIES CONTAINED HEREIN MAY NOT BE SUITABLE FOR EVERY SITUATION. THIS WORK IS SOLD WITH THE UNDERSTANDING THAT THE PUBLISHER IS NOT ENGAGED IN RENDERING LEGAL, ACCOUNTING, OR OTHER PROFESSIONAL SERVICES. IF PROFESSIONAL ASSISTANCE IS REQUIRED, THE SERVICES OF A COMPETENT PROFESSIONAL PERSON SHOULD BE SOUGHT. NEITHER THE PUBLISHER NOR THE AUTHOR SHALL BE LIABLE FOR DAMAGES ARISING HEREFROM. THE FACT THAT AN ORGANIZATION OR WEBSITE IS REFERRED TO IN THIS WORK AS A CITATION AND/OR A POTENTIAL SOURCE OF FURTHER INFORMATION DOES NOT MEAN THAT THE AUTHOR OR THE PUBLISHER ENDORSES THE INFORMATION THE ORGANIZATION OR WEBSITE MAY PROVIDE OR RECOMMENDATIONS IT MAY MAKE. FURTHER, READERS SHOULD BE AWARE THAT INTERNET WEBSITES LISTED IN THIS WORK MAY HAVE CHANGED OR DISAPPEARED BETWEEN WHEN THIS WORK WAS WRITTEN AND WHEN IT IS READ.

For general information on our other products and services, please contact our Customer Care Department within the U.S. at 877-762-2974, outside the U.S. at 317-572-3993, or fax 317-572-4002. For technical support, please visit https://hub.wiley.com/community/support/dummies.

Wiley publishes in a variety of print and electronic formats and by print-on-demand. Some material included with standard print versions of this book may not be included in e-books or in print-on-demand. If this book refers to media such as a CD or DVD that is not included in the version you purchased, you may download this material at http://booksupport.wiley.com. For more information about Wiley products, visit www.wiley.com.

Library of Congress Control Number: 2019945778

ISBN 978-1-119-64307-4 (pbk); ISBN 978-1-119-64308-1 (ebk); ISBN 978-1-119-64311-1 (ebk)

Manufactured in the United States of America

SKY10032041_121621

Contents at a Glance

Table of Contents

CHAPTER 3: A Never-Ending Torah: The Unfolding of a Tradition 35

CHAPTER 4: A Path of Blessing: Judaism as a Daily Practice 47

Introduction

We're amazed by how many people have become interested in Judaism in recent years. Some people interested in Judaism are in search of meaningful connections to the past. Some have a hunger for deeper understanding and ritual, a longing for something precious to pass on to their children, something nourishing and loving to live by. For many Jews (and non-Jews, too) this has meant exploring the rich tapestry of Judaism — some discovering the religion for the first time, others re-examining the lost or forgotten traditions from their youth.

For non-Jews, perhaps this interest follows an increasing awareness of the significance of Judaism as the source and inspiration for both Jesus and the "Old Testament." People seem to have a greater openness these days to appreciating the depth of Judaism without seeing it as a threat to other faiths.

For Jews, perhaps this resurgence of interest stems from a community recovering from Holocaust horrors and rediscovering that the faith and practice still exist. Certainly, much of the interest seems to come from the increasing realization that Judaism has much to offer in the mystical, meditative, and spiritual realms.

About This Book

The problem facing many people interested in Judaism is that the vast majority of Jewish books on the market today either tackle one particular subject in great depth (such as 300 pages just on the holiday of Sukkot), or they approach Judaism from an orthodox perspective ("These are the 613 things you *should* do if you know what's good for you"). We don't find anything wrong with either of these approaches, but we want to offer something different. We believe that even a subject as deep and important as Judaism can be fun to read about. And the more you find out about the subject, the more fun it is.

With that in mind, we offer you *Judaism For Dummies*. Wherever you're coming from — whether you're interested in the religion or the spirituality, the culture or the ethnic traditions — this book offers you a glimpse into Judaism that you've never seen before, one that helps you appreciate what all the excitement is about.

Even better, we've packaged all this great information in easy-to-read chapters that are organized in easy-to-access chunks.

Conventions Used in This Book

We use practices throughout this book that might take some getting used to. First, when we discuss dates, we don't use BC and AD, because they're based on Christian theology. Instead, we use BCE ("Before the Common Era") and CE ("in the Common Era").

We also do our best not to assign a gender to God. As we describe in Chapter 2, Judaism makes it very clear that God is neither male nor female. However, when we feel that something is being lost by not using masculine or feminine pronouns, we leave them in.

Additionally, to help you navigate this book as you begin to navigate the world of Judaism, we use the following conventions:

>> *Italic* text highlights new words and defined terms. We italicize Hebrew words when we first define them and then use regular font for subsequent appearances of the term.

>> **Boldfaced** text indicates keywords in bulleted lists and the action part of numbered steps.

>> Monofont text highlights a web address.

Pronouncing Jewish Words

You can't read about Judaism without bumping into the Hebrew language, and we include a lot of Hebrew throughout this book. However, there are a few things you need to know about reading Hebrew. For example, the Hebrew language is read right-to-left.

Cha, Kha, Ha!

Hebrew doesn't have a "ch" sound, like the English words "chew" or "lunch." The sound just doesn't exist!

On the other hand, English doesn't have that guttural, throat-clearing sound like the Scottish make when they say "Loch Ness" (like saying "ha" down in your throat instead of in your mouth), and Hebrew does. In most cases we *transliterate* ("spell out the way it sounds") this "kh" sound. However, for a few words that are better known, such as "Chanukkah" and "challah," we use "ch" because that's how they are usually spelled. Even though we spell them using "ch," you should use the guttural sound when you see words such as "Chanukkah" or "challah."

Yiddish — that Eastern European mixture of Hebrew, German, and Slavic languages — *does* have the English "ch" sound, and every now and again, we include words that use this sound (like "boychik" and "kvetch"). In these few instances, we let you know which pronunciation to use.

You say Tomato, I say Tomaso

There is one letter in the Hebrew alphabet that Ashkenazi Jews have traditionally pronounced "sav" and Sephardi Jews have pronounced "tav." The result is that many words can be pronounced correctly in two ways. For example, *Shabbat* and *Shabbos* are both correct. Modern Israeli Hebrew follows the Sephardic tradition (with the hard "t"), but many descendants of Eastern European Jews prefer the softer "s" sound.

In this book, we almost always use the Modern Israeli pronunciation. If you're more comfortable with "bris" (rather than "brit"), "Shavuos" (rather than "Shavuot"), or "B'reishees" (rather than "B'reisheet"), don't call our publisher and complain — just swap them in your head.

Also note that Israelis tend to place the emphasis of a word on the last syllable, where Westerners tend to place it on an earlier syllable. So, you hear "Shah-vu-*oht*" instead of "Sha-*vu*-ohs," or "mah-*zahl* tov" instead of "*mah*-zel tov."

Pronouncing vowels

Hebrew vowels are pronounced almost like Spanish or Japanese vowels: the *a* is said "ah," *o* is "oh," *e* is "eh," *i* is "ee," and *u* is "oo." For example, *Magen David* (the star of David) is pronounced "mah-*gehn* dah-*veed*," and *Tikkun Olam* ("the repair of the world") is pronounced "tee-*koon* oh-*lahm*." Whenever possible, we include pronunciation keys throughout the book.

About the translations

Translating one language into another always requires interpretation and compromise. The translations of Hebrew that you see in this book — which are either our own or came from traditional Jewish sources — may be significantly different than those in other books. If you find two different translations for the same text, there's a good chance that both are true, depending on your perspective, and that there are lessons to appreciate from both versions.

Foolish Assumptions

When writing this book, we assumed that our readers didn't know anything about Jews and Judaism. Toward that end, we explain all the rituals, ideas, and terms that you need to know in a way that you can understand, even if you're reading about these things for the first time.

In fact, when it comes to Judaism, being a "dummy" isn't just tolerated — it's actively encouraged, and has been for over 2,000 years. Each spring, during the holiday called Passover (see Chapter 25), Jews around the world reread a book called the *Haggadah*. The book tells the story of how the Hebrews escaped Egyptian slavery about 3,300 years ago, and it supplements the tale with a bunch of other poems, songs, and fables, including one about the following four children:

>> The "Wise" child searches for depth and meaning in the Passover story, trying to find hidden connections and spiritual truths in the holiday.

>> The "Wicked" child, whose rebellious nature requires detailed explanations for everything, demands that the holiday's rituals be relevant in his or her own life.

>> The "Simple" child just smiles, saying, "Tell me what to do and I'll do it." This child wants to know how but not why, and finds deep comfort in the rituals themselves.

>> The "dummy" that the title of this book refers to is the fourth child. This child hungers for knowledge but doesn't know where to begin. The *Haggadah* describes the fourth child only as the "One who doesn't know enough to ask a question."

Centuries of rabbis have taught that *all* these children live within each of us, and that you must celebrate them all — and especially the dummy inside.

This book is designed for all four of your inner children. Sometimes you may say, "Listen, I just want to know how this ritual is done." So we describe rituals and give you step-by-step instructions. Other times you may want to stomp your feet and say, "What is this tradition? How is it relevant to me?" That's good! Sometimes everyone needs to express some rebelliousness, so we discuss those things in the book, too.

If you're a wise and worldly searcher with a longing for connection, you'll also find jewels in each chapter of this book. Ultimately, we hope you read the book from the open and honestly curious perspective of the dummy's "beginner's mind," which makes you available for deeper learning.

How This Book Is Organized

In order for you to get the most out of the book quickly and efficiently, we've broken it down into parts, each with its own theme.

Part 1: What Jews Generally Believe

We begin by exploring the different groups within the Jewish community, like Ashkenazi and Sephardic, and denominations, like Orthodox, Reform, and so on. Then we target two of the most important issues in Judaism — God and Torah — before discussing the basic practices and ethical foundations of Judaism, like the kosher laws, what happens in worship services, and what Judaism says about war and the environment. Part I ends with a look at the ancient (and really cool) practices of Jewish mysticism (usually called *Kabbalah*).

Part 2: From Womb to Tomb: The Life Cycle

In Part 2 we discuss how Judaism honors and celebrates the major stages of life with rituals, including the *bris* (circumcision and naming for boys), *brit bat* (welcoming and naming for girls), Bar and Bat Mitzvahs, weddings, and funeral rites.

Part 3: An Overview of Jewish History

You can't understand Judaism (or even Western civilization) without knowing something about Jewish history. But that doesn't mean that the history has to be boring! In Part 3 we delve into the highlights and the low points — from the Biblical stories to modern day — focusing on what you need to know and why you need to know it.

Part 4: Celebrations and Holy Days

Okay, so it's Chanukkah again (or Passover or Sukkot, or whatever) — how do you "do it right"? In Part 4 we explore every major Jewish holiday, from the weekly Shabbat to the weeklong Sukkot. If you want to know what, where, when, why, how, or who, this is the place to look.

Part 5: The Part of Tens

If you've only got time for a quickie, make sure to put a bookmark at the beginning of Part 5. We include a list of people you should know about, plus answers to common questions about Judaism.

Part 6: Appendixes

If you're in a heated debate with a Jewish person, you'd better know the differences between "shlemiel" and "shlemazl," and between "tukhis" and "tsuris." Don't worry, we cover all this in the Appendixes, along with a quick easy-in/easy-out guide to prayers and blessings and a list of resources to consult for additional information.

Icons Used in This Book

In order to highlight some important bits of information, we use the following icons throughout the text.

TIP

The information next to this icon tells you things that can lead to a deeper understanding of or a more fulfilling experience with Judaism.

REMEMBER

This icon highlights ideas you should keep in mind as you explore or practice Judaism.

CONTROVERSY

Wherever you see this icon you find some disagreement in the Jewish world.

ANECDOTE

This icon warns you of a more personal story hidden in the text. Read at your own risk.

CAUTION

The text next to this icon will help you steer clear of any road blocks you may run across as you read about or experience the faith.

WORDS OF WISDOM

This icon highlights some of the many important Jewish teachings from the last few millennia.

Where to Go from Here

This book is a reference, meaning that you don't need to read it from cover to cover. (Though you're certainly welcome to do just that.) We wrote the chapters as self-contained packets of information. So for example, if you're heading to a Jewish wedding, you can jump right to Chapter 9; if you were invited to a Passover seder, dive right into Chapter 25.

Of course, many of the core ideas in Judaism — the themes that we come back to time and time again throughout the book — are all covered in Part I, so you may want to peruse that part first.

As an added bonus, we invite you to check out our online resources about Judaism. Check out our detailed calendar of Jewish holidays as well as our list of ten important Jews you should know at www.dummies.com/extra/judaism; and feel free to visit our website at www.joyofjewish.com. And because we believe that Judaism is like a conversation that continues forever, send an e-mail to authors@joyofjewish.com.

1

What Jews Generally Believe

IN THIS PART . . .

You'll find out why you can never be sure someone is Jewish (or not) just by how they look. Plus, you'll get the skinny on all the details about *being* Jewish, like is it a race or a tribe? Is it a religion or a practice? Do you have to believe in God? And what's all this about meditation and the kabbalah? That stuff isn't Jewish, is it?

IN THIS CHAPTER

» Understanding the difference between Ashkenazi and Sephardi Jews

» Exploring the wide spectrum from Orthodox to Reform (and beyond)

» Playing the "Who's a Jew" game

Chapter **1**

That's Funny, You Don't Look Jewish: Who's a Jew and Why

We used to think we could tell if someone was Jewish just by looking at them. We each grew up in very different times and very different places in America, but we both developed the same notion of what being Jewish meant: Small stature (but often slightly overweight), large nose, dark wavy or curly hair, dark eyes . . . you can't really explain it in print — it's more like a feeling. "Hey, is that guy Jewish?" "Oh yeah, no doubt about it." You just know!

Then we went to Israel. It took about five seconds for each of us to realize that what we thought was "Jewish" was just one small segment of a much bigger picture — like finding out that kissing isn't all there is to love. We saw blond Jews, Middle-Eastern Jews, Asian Jews, Black Jews, Latino Jews, Jews who looked like Arnold Schwarzenegger, and Jews who looked like Britney Spears. Boy, we had a lot to learn!

The Jewish Tribe

Judaism isn't a race or even a particular culture or ethnic group. A little over 15 million Jews are spread around the world, including about 6 million in the United States and about 5 million in Israel — so Judaism obviously isn't "a nation." And, if you're anything like us, you know more Jews who don't believe in God or practice Jewish observances than those who do, so being Jewish doesn't even necessarily have to do with religion.

REMEMBER

So what *does* it mean to be Jewish? Here are the basics:

>> **Being *Jewish* (being "a *Jew*") means you're a Member of the Tribe (an M-O-T).** The tribe started with a couple named Abraham and Sarah more than 4,000 years ago, it grew over time, and it's still here today. You can become an authentic part of the Jewish tribe in two ways: by being born to a Jewish mother or joining through a series of rituals (called *converting*). Some folks think there are other ways of becoming a Jew, too; we cover that issue later in this chapter.

>> ***Judaism* is a set of beliefs, practices, and ethics based on the Torah (see Chapter 3).** You can practice Judaism and not be Jewish, and you can be a Jew and not practice Judaism.

What's in a name?

The word "Jewish" doesn't appear in the Bible at all. For example, the folks who came out of slavery in Egypt in the Book of Exodus (see Chapter 11) were called "Hebrews" or "Children of Israel," and they each belonged to one of the 12 tribes of Israel. Ten of the 12 tribes were dispersed by the Assyrians in the eighth century BCE (see Chapter 11), but the tribe of Judah and the smaller tribe of Benjamin remained as the Southern Kingdom known as Judea until early in the sixth century BCE.

TIP

When Judea fell to the Babylonians, and the people were taken into exile, they became known as the Judah-ites (*Yehudim*), since they were the people of Judah (*Yehudah*). In Hebrew, the name *Yehudim* persists today and simply means "Jews." The religion they practiced was later called "Judah-ism" — which became "Judaism." We prefer to pronounce this word "Judah-ism" rather than "Jude-ism" or "Judy-ism" — which makes it sound like you're talking about Judy Garland.

Jews far and wide

The Jewish people have always tended to fan out across the known world. Evidence indicates that even centuries before Jesus, Jewish communities inhabited the North African and East African coasts, Europe, and Asia. Jews were among the first people to come to the Americas from Europe in the fifteenth and sixteenth centuries. Some evidence suggests that there was at least one Jew aboard the ship with Columbus. (Some people suspect that Columbus himself was a Jew, perhaps because Jews were kicked out of Spain in 1492.)

Everywhere the Jews went, their population grew through intermarriage and conversion, and — most importantly — they kept their basic religion while adopting the culture and norms of the local area. That's why up to 20 percent of Jews descended from European ancestors have blue eyes, and why some Jews are Black, Hispanic, or Asian. It's also why a Jew from New York looks and acts different than a Jew from Bombay, but each one could probably fumble along with most of the other's Shabbat service (see Chapter 18).

Similarly, Jewish food, music, and humor from Iraq and Yemen is much more Arabic in nature than the Spanish flavor of Jews from Brazil and Argentina, which is different than the borscht soup and klezmer music of Jews from Europe. They even all speak Hebrew with different dialects! Jews just don't fit any consistent set of stereotypes or expectations.

And yet, all Jews are inextricably linked together simply by being Jewish. Perhaps it's a common practice and belief in Judaism; perhaps it's a common sense of history, or a shared sense of being an outsider from the broader culture. Or perhaps it's a deep, innate feeling of connection to the tribe.

Who decides if you're Jewish?

Two years after the new government of Israel came to power in 1948, it passed the Law of Return, which states that anyone born of a Jewish mother or anyone who has converted to Judaism can move to Israel and claim citizenship. This immediately re-ignited a controversy that began much earlier and continues to this day: Who gets to say whether or not someone is really Jewish?

Whether someone practiced Judaism wasn't an issue for citizenship, because Israel was founded for the most part by secular Jews. But what about people born Jewish who had been raised as Christians or Muslims, or who practiced another religion? Some say you have to not only identify yourself as Jewish, but also not practice any other religion. Others say that religion has nothing to do with it and point out that the Nazis killed thousands of people who were Jewish by birth but practiced some other religion. Each year Israeli courts consider cases arguing over whether someone is or is not Jewish.

BLACK AND JEWISH

In most synagogues in the world, it's rare to see someone of African descent. Sure, there's the occasional convert, like Sammy Davis Jr., but on the whole, Jews tend to be either white- (European) or olive-skinned (Middle-Eastern). However, there are over 100,000 Black Jews around the world, including many Jews from Ethiopia who were air-lifted to Israel between the late 1970s and early 1990s. The Ethiopian Jews, who were largely cut off from the rest of world Jewry for millennia, practiced a form of Judaism that hadn't changed since pre-Talmudic times. Note that while these people are some-times called "Falashas," that name has become somewhat derogatory, and "Ethiopian Jews" or "Beta Israel" ("House of Israel") is preferable. In addition, some African-Americans call themselves Black Jews, Hebrews, or Israelites. Many Black Jews are very observant of ancient rituals and traditions, read and write Hebrew, and have identified themselves as Jews their whole lives.

CONTROVERSY

And what about people who convert? Technically, someone who converts to Juda-ism is no different from someone who was born Jewish. However, not everyone sees it that way. In the next section, we discuss the various denominations of Judaism, including the Orthodox Jews who refuse to acknowledge the conversion of anyone converted by a Reform or Conservative rabbi.

Many people say, "I'm half Jewish" (if one parent is Jewish) or "I'm a quarter-Jewish" (if one grandparent is Jewish). Traditional Jews argue that either you're Jewish or you're not. To them, if your mother's mother was Jewish, then your mother is Jewish, and if your mother is Jewish, then you're Jewish. Among Reform and Reconstructionist Jews, if only your father is Jewish and you were raised Jew-ish, then you're considered Jewish, too.

After all, it's a small world

Jews have long spread out to the corners of the world, so significant Jewish com-munities (over 100,000 people) live in France, Australia, Argentina, and South Africa. In America, most people think all the Jews live in big cities like New York (where there are over 1.5 million Jews). But many also live in the "Wild West" states like Wyoming, the deep south states like Louisiana, and everywhere in-between.

In fact, not only do far more Jewish people live outside of Israel than within today, it has been this way for over 2,500 years. And no matter where they live, most Jews today identify with one of two groups: Ashkenazi and Sephardi.

Ashkenazi

The descendants of Jews who, until around 1900, lived anywhere from northwest Europe (like France and Germany) to eastern Europe (including Russia, Ukraine, and Lithuania) are usually called *Ashkenazi* (pronounced "ahsh-ke-*nah*-zee;" *Ashkenazim* is plural). The majority of Jews in the world are Ashkenazi.

Sephardi

The descendants of Jews who lived in Spain up until the 15th century are called *Sephardi* (seh-*far*-dee; *Sephardim* is plural). After the expulsion (see Chapter 14), these Jews traveled to North Africa, Italy, the Ottoman Empire (Turkey), and back to the Middle East. Of course, many Jews started out in those areas (never having traveled as far as Spain to begin with), but they're generally called Sephardi anyway. You also hear Jews from the Middle East called *Mizrachi* ("from the East;" remember that Hebrew has no "ch" sound, so this is the guttural "kh" sound).

Over the past 500 years, the Sephardim primarily interacted with Muslims, especially African and Arab Muslims. Today much of their culture (music, language, liturgical melodies, food, festival customs, and so on) is based on those cultures. The Ashkenazim, on the other hand, mostly interacted with European Christian cultures, resulting in a very different ethnic feeling.

Although Israel was founded primarily by Ashkenazi Jews, more than half of Israelis have always been Sephardim. However, the very different cultures have caused a number of difficulties. Many Ashkenazi Jews mistrust Sephardi Jews and think they've "ruined" Israel, and vice versa. Fortunately, as time goes by, things seem to be getting better.

Major Branches of the Tree

When we say that Judaism is a set of beliefs and practices, we're glossing over one key point: Judaism encompasses a lot of different sets of beliefs and practices! In some ways, you can see Judaism as a tree with many branches; there's a common trunk and root system, but each sect or denomination is off on its own branch, and in many cases, each synagogue is on its own little twig.

Most Jews see the biggest branches of the tree as Orthodox, Conservative, Reform, and Non-Religious — plus, they might add a few others, like Ultra-Orthodox, Modern Orthodox, Reconstructionist, Renewal, and Humanistic. On the other hand, some traditional Orthodox Jews see it differently: To them, Orthodoxy is the whole tree, and what everyone else is doing is something else — maybe a whole other tree, but certainly not practicing Judaism.

The basic difference between the groups is that while the Orthodox believe that the Torah (both written and oral; see Chapter 3) was literally given by God to Moses, word for word, more liberal Jews tend to believe that the Torah and *halakhah* (Jewish law) may have been Divinely inspired, but were expressed by humans influenced by their own time and place.

Orthodox Jews

When you hear the term "Orthodox Jew," you probably think of a man in a long black coat, with long locks of hair over his sideburns, a big beard, and a black hat. But in reality, there are dozens of different styles within Jewish Orthodoxy, each of them with a different culture, educational philosophy, leadership model, and set of policies. True, many of them do, in fact, wear black hats and coats, but many others — typically called Modern Orthodox Jews — almost always wear modern dress, and you might not be able to even tell them apart from non-Jews.

However, all Orthodox Jews technically accept the Torah as the word of God. So although you can see a massive cultural difference between the Orthodox Jew who wears a *shtreimel* (the black fur hat worn by some Ultra-Orthodox) and the Orthodox Jew who wears jeans and a T-shirt, most people would find it extremely difficult to discern a difference between their religious beliefs and observance.

Liberal Jews began calling more observant Jews "Orthodox" (which literally means "correct belief" or "proper doctrine") in the late 19th century as a somewhat derogatory term. But to the Orthodox, there's no spectrum of "less Orthodox" and "more Orthodox," so the term didn't really mean anything to them. Nevertheless, the word stuck.

However, most people make a distinction between "Modern Orthodox" Jews (who engage in many aspects of modern, secular culture) and "Ultra-Orthodox" Jews (sometimes called *haredi* or "black hats," who tend to insulate themselves from modern culture). You can always find exceptions, though! Chabad (which we discuss in Appendix A) falls somewhere between the two.

All the black clothes

We know you're dying to ask: "Why do some Orthodox Jews wear all that black?" The simple answer is that they're in mourning for the destruction of the Second Temple more than 1,900 years ago. However, that doesn't explain *what* they wear. Although some "black hat" Orthodox communities (like Chabad Lubavitch and the Mitnagdim; see "Hasidim and Mitnagdim," later in this chapter) wear somewhat modern black suits, others — especially Hasidic Ultra-Orthodox — consciously try to resist modern influences. Their long black coats, black hats, white stockings, and old-style shoes are a way to hold on to the old eastern European culture of the 18th century. Traditional women don't have the same dress codes, but they do tend to dress more modestly (see Chapter 4).

Ultra-Orthodox Jews set themselves apart in other ways, too. Many Ultra-Orthodox Jews minimize their contact with the "outside world," so they usually don't have televisions in their homes, they tune their radios to religious programming, they don't go to movies, and at least one group has ruled that its members shouldn't use the Internet.

For many people, these restraints seem extreme. On the other hand, think of it this way: How much pornography do you want your family exposed to? For some folks, much of the secular world is pretty pornographic and offensive, and they wonder "Why even be tempted by it?"

Different groups, different interpretations

Even in a relatively small Jewish community with few Orthodox Jews, you might find several Orthodox synagogues. Two reasons explain this: First, the Orthodox have to be able to walk to the synagogue on Shabbat (see Chapter 18); second, each Orthodox congregation has its own particular culture, ideas, interpretations, and style.

For example, one Orthodox rabbi may say that the biblical commandment "Don't round off the corner of your beard" means don't cut the *earlocks* (the hair that grows to the side of the forehead). Another rabbi says, "No, the commandment means that men should not shave." A third rabbi may chime in with this interpretation: "You can't shave with an instrument with a single cutting edge, but you can use a rotary-blade shaver."

Similarly, some groups are staunch Zionists (supporters of a Jewish state of Israel), and others don't believe that Israel should exist (because the Messiah hasn't come yet). Some believe that their children should get a secular education as well as a religious education, and others say that only a religious education is important. Some will socialize with non-traditional Jews or visit a non-Orthodox synagogue, and others refuse.

As we explain in the next two chapters, there is no ultimate authority for Judaism; so each Jew must decide whom and what to follow.

Hasidim and Mitnagdim

A "who's who" of all the different Orthodox groups and their doctrines would fill a small book by itself. However, they all basically fall into one of two types: *Hasidim* and *Mitnagdim* (also pronounced "misnagdim" by many Ashkenazi Jews). Because the word "Hasidim" (plural of "Hasid") is pronounced with the "kh" sound at the back of the throat, like the Scottish "Loch Ness," some people spell it Chasidism.

Hasidism was a movement founded in the 18th century by the Ba'al Shem Tov (see Chapter 28), focusing on sincere, joyful, and intense prayer — including ecstatic dancing, singing, and storytelling as a way to connect with God. Shortly after 1760, when the Ba'al Shem Tov died, Hasidism splintered into a number of other groups, like Chabad Lubavitch, Belzer, Satmar, and Breslov (which all still exist today).

Hasidism appeared at a time when traditional Judaism focused on an ascetic, scholarly approach to Torah and Talmud (see Chapter 3). Most rabbis of the time insisted that only learned, critical, and erudite study was important, in contrast to the simple and sincere devotion of Hasidism. Elijah ben Solomon Zalman, known as the Vilna Gaon, was the driving force behind these ascetic Jews, who became known as *Mitnagdim* (which literally means "opponents"); he even went so far as to prohibit interactions with the Hasidim, fearing that their ecstatic worship and lack of intellectual focus was a danger to Judaism.

Fortunately, by the end of the 19th century, most of the antagonism subsided, especially as the two groups formed a common front against religious reformers and anti-Semitism. Since then the Hasidic and Mitnaggid movements have greatly influenced each other. There are still differences, though. While the Mitnagdim tend to focus on the head of a particular *yeshivah* (school), the Hasidim tend to focus on their particular *rebbe* (what they call their rabbis), who acts almost as a guru does in some Eastern traditions. Mitnagdim tend to base their study on Talmud and halakhah, and Hasidim tend to study the writings of their rebbe (and his rebbe, and so on, as well as other traditional texts).

Breakaway denominations

How does Judaism deal with the fact that times and people change? Traditional Jews tend either to avoid the changes or — more commonly — to apply established interpretations of Torah, Talmud, and previous halakhah to modern issues. However, in the early 19th century, many Jews began to rethink this position, arguing that these sources weren't actually Divine after all, but rather very human responses to Divine inspiration. If the Torah, Talmud, and halakhah are human creations, these reformers reasoned, then they should be inspected, judged, and understood to be affected by their particular time and place of creation.

REMEMBER

These folks weren't saying that the traditional texts had no meaning; they still studied Torah, Talmud, and halakhah, but they insisted that some passages were more meaningful for particular timeframes than others, and that individuals are responsible for finding what's relevant in their own time.

These groups are usually lumped together under the umbrella of "Liberal Judaism," although there is a wide spectrum of belief and observance among the groups. The best-known groups are Reform, Conservative, Reconstructionist, Renewal, and Humanistic. Most of these groups are American and — to a lesser degree — European movements. They do exist in Israel, where they're gradually becoming more established.

Reform

Reform Judaism (it's Reform, not Reformed!) — probably the largest Jewish group in America — rests on the idea that all Jews have the responsibility to educate themselves and make decisions about their spiritual practice based on conscience rather than simply relying on external law. In Reform Judaism, the Torah, Talmud, and halakhah are necessary resources, but Reform Jews tend to focus on social and ethical action based on the writings of the Prophets rather than the ritual observance of the Torah and the halakhah of the Talmud.

Unfortunately, many Jews today associate the Reform movement — which outside of North America is usually called Progressive or Liberal Judaism — with empty and meaningless services, or congregations that want to retain a sense of being Jewish without actually following any practice other than the Passover seder and Friday night services. We won't deny that some groups are like this, nor that the Reform movement of the 1950s and 1960s often lacked a sense of spirituality, but the Reform movement has changed radically in recent decades. Today, many Reform congregations are deeply committed to a living and evolving sense of Judaism and Jewish spirituality.

Reform Jews tend to strip away what they consider to be unessential elements of Judaism in order to more closely observe the kernel of the tradition. For example, when the movement began in the early 19th century, Reform synagogues started seating men and women together, pretty much dropped the dietary laws, and encouraged instrumental music at Shabbat services. Clothing customs — like yarmulkes and prayer shawls — were discouraged (though today growing numbers of Reform Jews wear them).

In 1972, the Reform movement became the first Jewish movement to ordain women as rabbis. Although the Reform movement, which is currently the fastest-growing group in American Jewry, continues to innovate, it has also started to embrace more traditional practices, as reflected in the 1999 revision of the basic principles of Reform Judaism.

Conservative

The Conservative Judaism movement (which is often called Historical Judaism in Europe, and is called *Masorti* in Israel) always reminds us of the fable of the Three Bears, in which Goldilocks said, "That one was too soft, that one was too hard, but this one is just right!" Since the late 19th century, many Jews have felt that the Reform movement went too far in its rejection of traditional observance, but also that Orthodox communities were unrealistic in their restrictions regarding modern life.

Conservative Jews tend to respect many Jewish laws, like keeping kosher, observing Shabbat and other religious holidays, and performing daily prayers. At the same time, they agree with the Reform movement that halakhah has its basis in history and therefore needs to be reconsidered in each age. Conservative rabbis ruled that when Jews live too far from a synagogue, they can drive there (but they encouraged walking when possible), and some wines and cheeses that were ruled kosher for Conservatives have not been accepted by Orthodox Jews.

Conservative synagogues have sometimes been perceived as being inconsistent on Jewish legal issues. Some people have accused Conservative Jews of hypocrisy because their rabbis appear to tend toward Orthodox practices while the congregants appear to tend toward Reform practices. But we know of Conservative congregations that are virtually indistinguishable from Modern Orthodox groups, so you just can't tell without walking in, sitting down, and seeing for yourself.

Conservative Judaism flourished during the 20th century and was, for a long time, the largest Jewish movement in the United States. However, some reports indicate that its size has been shrinking in recent years as many Conservative Jews find themselves increasingly drawn to Reform, Renewal, or Orthodox congregations. (People who were offended when the Conservative movement began ordaining women rabbis in 1985 were especially drawn to the Orthodox community.)

Reconstructionist

When the 17th-century Jewish philosopher Baruch Spinoza announced that God was not a separate being but rather nature itself, the Jewish community was so outraged that they excommunicated him, declaring that no other Jew could even talk with him, much less read his writings. Skip ahead 300 years and you find the 20th-century theologian Mordecai Kaplan taking Spinoza's theories even further. The result? A group of Orthodox rabbis excommunicated him and burned the prayer book that he had published.

Today, no one remembers the names of those book-burning rabbis, but every philosophy student in the world reads Spinoza, and Kaplan is the founder of the fourth major Jewish movement: Reconstructionist Judaism.

Kaplan was a Conservative rabbi, and during his long tenure at the Conservative rabbinical seminary, he began to teach that God wasn't a Being, but rather the natural, underlying moral and creative force of the universe, the force that creates order and makes for human happiness. He also taught that each generation of Jews had the obligation to keep Judaism alive by "reconstructing" it — not by stripping away the practices and words like the Reform movement, but by reinterpreting them, in order to find new meanings that are relevant for the time.

Reconstructionism, as a separate movement, developed in the late 1920s but didn't establish a rabbinical school until 1968. Today the movement counts about 100 congregations. Reconstructionist congregations tend to see the rabbi as a facilitator and a valuable resource, but not necessarily the leader; they encourage a lot of lay participation and creative reworking of both ritual and worship.

Renewal

Jewish Renewal sprang from the philosophies of Martin Buber and Abraham Heschel (see Chapter 28), as well as the "Neo-Hasidic" teachings of Reb Shlomo Carlebach and Reb Zalman Schachter-Shalomi. It teaches that people can draw wisdom from a variety of diverse sources, including Hasidism, Kabbalah, feminism, the Prophets, environmentalism, and the writings of the ancient rabbis.

Renewal focuses on a welcoming, egalitarian, hands-on approach to Jewish worship and community. It encourages mixing both traditional and feminist ideals. What's more, Renewal congregations have embraced lessons from diverse spiritual traditions, such as Eastern philosophy and both Eastern and Jewish meditative practices. Renewal programs support a spiritual ecology, relating Jewish practices to both political as well as ecological action.

The 40 or 50 Jewish Renewal congregations and *chavurot* (friendship groups) around the world (mostly in America) vary widely in their observance of traditional liturgy and ritual. In fact, the group defines itself as "transdenominational," inviting Jews from all aspects of the greater Jewish community to reconnect, learn, and celebrate together.

Humanistic Judaism

What do you do if you feel Jewish — you like the Jewish holidays, food, music, sense of ethics and social involvement, humor, and so on — but you're not into the idea of God? You're certainly not alone. The Humanistic Jewish movement, also called Secular Humanistic Judaism, was established in 1963 by Rabbi Sherwin Wine and is based on Humanist ideals of rational, critical thinking, as well as developing the depths and dimensions of both individuals and communities.

MESSIANIC JEWS

CONTROVERSY

Despite the historical fact that almost all early Christians, like Jesus himself, were Jews, today Judaism is completely incompatible with a belief in Jesus as Messiah (see Chapter 29). However, a tiny minority of Jews and non-Jews who observe Jewish traditions — like wearing yarmulkes and prayer shawls, reciting the Sh'ma, and celebrating the Jewish holidays — do believe that Jesus is the Jewish *Mashiach* (Messiah).

People who believe in both Jewish observance and that Jesus brings redemption are called Messianic Jews. (Some folks call them "Jews for Jesus," but that's just the name of their biggest outreach organization, not the denomination itself.) Some of them go to Messianic synagogues, others go to church, most call Jesus "Y'shua," and, like other Christians, they're all waiting for Jesus to return.

Jewish groups and rabbis almost universally condemn Messianic Judaism (sometimes called *Nazarene Judaism*) as a Christian movement or even a cult, and they insist that the movement is an abomination and a threat to Judaism. Many Christians also find Messianic Judaism confusing and un-Christian, and so the group's beliefs place it between a rock and a hard place.

Humanistic Jews focus on Jewish culture and civilization, celebrating Jewish heritage as a way to find meaning in life, and minimizing the role of God or any cosmic forces. In fact, Humanistic Jews define a Jew as pretty much anyone who identifies with the history and culture of the Jewish people. They completely remove any theistic language from their liturgy.

The approximately 80 Humanistic congregations around North America celebrate the Jewish holidays, Bar and Bat Mitzvahs, and other Jewish traditions, although they ascribe nonreligious interpretations to everything. These Jews tend to be very involved with social action, and it's probably no coincidence that the first ordained Humanistic rabbi was a woman.

Guess Who Else Is Jewish

Many Jewish people love finding out who else is Jewish, especially Jews who are famous (or infamous), and — best of all — people who you'd never guess were Jewish. Here is a list of some lesser-known celebrities and their accomplishments that you can use to test your friends and family:

» Louis Brandeis became a member of the United States Supreme Court in 1916

» Levi Strauss popularized jeans; Ralph Lauren (born Ralph Lifshitz), Calvin Klein, Donna Karan, and Isaac Mizrahi changed the way we dress

» Joe Siegel and Jerry Shuster invented Superman; Stan Lee invented Spiderman, and with Jack Kirby, invented The Hulk and The X-Men; Bob Kane invented Batman, and William Gaines founded *Mad Magazine*

» Musicians Paula Abdul, Neil Diamond, Bob Dylan (born Robert Zimmerman), George Gershwin, Mickey Hart (drummer for the Grateful Dead), Billy Joel, Carole King, Geddy Lee (lead singer for Rush), Barry Manilow (born Barry Pincus), Bette Midler, David Lee Roth (of Van Halen fame), Neil Sedaka, Gene Simmons (bass player for Kiss, born Chaim Witz), Amy Winehouse, and both Paul Simon and Art Garfunkel

» Gangsters Meyer Lansky and Bugsy Siegel, and Lee Harvey Oswald's killer Jack Ruby

» Authors Al Franken, Franz Kafka, Harold Pinter, Ayn Rand (born Alissa Rosenbaum), Harold Robbins, and Marianne Williamson (who some call the "priestess" of New Age spirituality)

» Mark Zuckerberg (founder of Facebook), Larry Ellison (founder of Oracle), and Sergey Brin (founder of Google); Steve Ballmer (currently the CEO of Microsoft)

» Herb Lubalin designed many famous typefaces we use today; architect Frank Gehry (used to be Goldberg) designed many of the most unique buildings in the world

» Actors Sarah Jessica Parker, Natalie Portman, Alyson Hannigan, Winona Ryder, Gwyneth Paltrow, Scarlett Johannson, *Star Trek*'s William Shatner (Captain Kirk), Leonard Nimoy (Spock), and Walter Koenig (Chekov), as well as Rod Serling from *The Twilight Zone* and Goldie Hawn, John Garfield, Tony Curtis (born Bernie Shwartz), and Kirk Douglas (born Issur Danielovitch)

» Famous mime Marcel Marceau, escape artist Harry Houdini (born Erich Weiss), communist Leo Trotsky, and cosmologist Carl Sagan

Chapter **2**

It's All One: Judaism and God

God makes people flinch. Well, the topic of God does, at least.

Would you be disappointed and put the book down if we said that Judaism couldn't care less what you think about God? Or would you be outraged if we insisted that Judaism absolutely requires you to believe in God? In many ways, both of these statements are true: Judaism essentially believes that there is a God — and only One God — but not only leaves *what* God is completely up in the air, but allows for Jews who don't believe in God at all.

Most people are surprised to find out that some practicing Jews are agnostics, insisting that you simply can't know whether or not there's a God. Some Jews are atheists, not believing in God at all. However, when people say, "I don't believe in God," they're usually saying, "I don't believe that God is an old guy sitting on a throne, looking down on us and making decisions about our lives." These same folks can wander out into nature, take a deep breath, and experience a profound sense of wonder about the mystery of life, the unknowable depths of this incredible universe, and the majesty of everything — from a blade of grass to the vastness of a supernova. If you ask us, these people believe in God, they just interpret the word *God* differently.

Fortunately, as we show you in this chapter, Judaism not only allows for all kinds of interpretations of God, but encourages people to wrestle with this issue personally. Do you disagree with somebody (even us) about the nature of God? If so, good: You're getting the hang of Jewish theology!

Pondering Jewish Beliefs about God

Judaism was the first tradition to teach *monotheism*, the belief that there's only one God. As Judaism evolved, the idea of God evolved, too, focusing on One unknowable, universal, image-less Being, Who, because the universe is framed in Love, requires justice of human beings.

A religion of deed, not creed

Judaism tends to focus more on the way that you practice your faith through living in the world than it does on analyzing the nature of God. In fact, biblical monotheism is usually called "ethical monotheism" because of the very strong linkage of right acts to the belief in one God.

REMEMBER

Although some religious traditions consider belief alone to be adequate, Judaism isn't one of them; to Jews, belief is only really significant in light of the actions motivated by that belief.

Arguing with God

What is unique, perhaps, to Judaism is the notion of arguing with God. For example, in the Bible, Abraham argued with God for the sake of the righteous citizens in Sodom and Gomorrah. He didn't just say "Whatever you say, God" — he bargained! You could say that the whole stage was set for a particular kind of exchange with the Divine. Jews are even called the "Children of Israel" because of the Biblical story of Jacob, who wrestled with an angel and got his name changed to Israel, which means "one who wrestles with God."

REMEMBER

Although the idea of a complete surrender to faith, a surrender to God, is harmonious with many Christian and Muslim beliefs, it's much less comfortable for most Jews, who are traditionally taught to question in order to learn more deeply. Judaism tends to encourage individuals to explore their own personal relationship with God. For people who are comfortable with the idea of surrender, God-wrestling isn't an easy concept.

WORDS OF WISDOM

DENYING THE EXISTENCE OF GOD

Jewish tradition allows that there can even be some purpose for not believing in God. Here are the words of a Rabbi Moshe Leib, a great Hasidic teacher:

To what end can the denial of God have been created? If someone comes to you and asks your help, you shall not send him off with pious words, saying: "Have faith and take your troubles to God!" You shall act as if there were no God, as if there were only one person in all the world who could help this man — only yourself.

Where God is

Some Jews see God as an external force, a Being outside of the universe Who listens to prayers, controls lives, creates miracles, and judges. But that doesn't mean that when the Bible talks about "the outstretched arm of God," they think that God literally has an arm. In fact, Jewish thought is very clear on this: Any reference to God being like a human should be taken as poetic metaphor — as though it were followed by the phrase, "so to speak."

Some Jews say that God contains the Universe, but is infinitely greater. Other Jews say that God is the universe, and the universe is God. Some folks say that all these ideas are true. The one thing that Jews won't argue about, period, is that God — whatever you imagine God to be — is ultimately unknowable and therefore can't be captured by any name.

Calling One God Many Names

In the ancient world, naming something meant that you had power over it. Even today, naming implies both understanding and control. What, then, do people do about naming a God Who is beyond full understanding, certainly beyond control, and generally perceived to be far more powerful than puny humans?

A longstanding Jewish tradition states that each name of God (like *Ha-Rakhaman*, "the Merciful One") refers to an aspect or quality of the Divine. The name defines the ways humans experience God rather than limiting God's Unity.

REMEMBER

Most traditional Jews won't even write out the English word "God," so many Jewish books and periodicals print it "G-d." Just as the four-letter name of God isn't supposed to be pronounced (we talk about that in a moment), some Jews extend this restriction to writing names of God. Also, the restriction ensures that a name of God won't be defaced or erased if the paper is ripped up, soiled, or thrown away.

What's in a name?

In much the same way as the Inuit/Eskimo people have a number of different words to describe the various types of snow, the Jewish tradition demonstrates the importance and subtle nuances of the experience of God with many names. Perhaps Jews use so many names because no name can fully capture God's essence, yet people strive to understand more of what can never be fully grasped.

You might say that God has all names, so the simplest name of God in Jewish tradition is *Ha-Shem* (literally "The Name"). Many traditional Jews say *Ha-Shem* instead of any other name of God, except in the context of worship or group study. In the Jewish mystical tradition, God is often referred to as *Ain Sof* ("Without End"), though sometimes this is shortened simply to *Ayin* ("Not" or "No-Thing") to indicate how far beyond words the Reality of God is.

The four-letter Name of God

The *Shem Ha-M'forash* ("The Ineffable Name") is the *Tetragrammaton*, the four-letter name of God comprised of the Hebrew letters *yod-hay-vav-hay* (YHVH), and it's never pronounced as written. Instead, the Jewish tradition teaches that anytime YHVH appears, it should be read *Adonai* (ah-doh-*nai*; another word entirely that actually means "Lord, or "my Lord"). However, it's important to remember that the Name *Adonai* replaces doesn't mean "Lord."

More importantly, no one knows for sure how this word is actually supposed to be pronounced. Historically, YHVH was misread as "Jehovah," and many scholars now think it may be read "Yahweh," but even if it were, we think there is something sad about not honoring the intention of the tradition. This was to be the Name beyond pronouncing, to remind people that God is beyond the limitations implied in being named. The four-letter Name is a form of the Hebrew verb "to be" that signifies Unlimited Being. That's why we translate it in this book as "the Eternal" or "Eternal One."

The Singular Being hidden in the plural

The two most frequently used names for God are the unspeakable YHVH (pronounced "Adonai" and commonly translated "Lord") and the word *Elohim* (usually translated "God"). What makes *Elohim* remarkable is that grammatically it's the plural form of the noun. The singular *Eloah* is also translated "God," but while you'd expect *Elohim* to be translated "gods," it never is when referring to the One. (You can find a few places in the Bible where *Elohim* refers to the gods of other peoples.) Plus, *Elohim* almost always takes verbs and adjectives meant for a singular noun. What is going on here?

One tradition (see Chapter 5) teaches that *Elohim* is the One manifesting as the many — so it's a plural expression of that which is still a Unity. In this sense, YHVH refers to the Totality (the transcendent, which contains everything), and *Elohim* refers to the Immanent, the Spark of Divinity that awakens within each and every expression of the One Being. The name is another way of reminding people that what they see as lots of individual forms (people, animals, plants, rocks, and so on) is, behind the scenes, all part of the One.

God's Own name

REMEMBER

One of the problems in translating Hebrew to English is that every Hebrew noun has a masculine or feminine gender — there is no neuter, like "it," as there is in English — even if no gender is implied. So a table and chair are "feminine," a house and a room are "masculine." Everything is, essentially, either a "he" or a "she." So when we speak of God, we have no way in Hebrew of avoiding calling God either "He" or "She," even though we don't mean that God is either a man or a woman, male or female. Although we try in this book to refrain from translations that suggest a masculine or feminine identity for God, sometimes the limitations of language make it necessary to speak of God as "He" or "She." This is especially true when telling stories.

When God confronted Moses with the burning bush (in the Book of Exodus), Moses experienced the Call to return to Egypt and argue for the freedom of the Hebrews. While Moses was impressed with the pyrotechnics, he wanted something more tangible, so he asked, "When I go to the people and tell them, 'The God of your fathers has sent me to you,' they shall say to me: 'What is His name?' What shall I tell them?" So God replied, "*Eheyeh Asher Eheyeh* . . . Thus shall you say to the children of Israel: '*Eheyeh* has sent me to you.'" This is the only time in the Bible that anyone asks God "His" name.

Eheyeh comes from the same Hebrew root as YHVH, and means "I Am." But this "I Am" is unlimited with respect to both time and place. It's like God saying, "I am here, and I am there, and I am everywhere," as well as, "I was, I am, and I ever shall be." Furthermore, this "I Am" is simply defined as itself: *Eheyeh Asher Eheyeh* literally means, "I Am as I Am." (You may remember the old Popeye cartoon character saying, "I yam what I yam.") With reference to God, this "I-am-ness" is prior to any predication, prior to any limitation. Indeed, in terms of pronoun, the only pronoun that can reflect true Oneness is first-person singular. All other pronouns imply a duality: A *he* implies a *she*, a *we* implies a *they*, and so on. God is the Ultimate and Universal First-Person Singular. In this sense, God is the identity of all that is.

No end to the names of God

Of course, many other Hebrew names of God are sprinkled throughout the Bible and prayer books. Here's a list of just a few:

>> *Yah*: These are the first two letters of the four-letter name of God, and you can find it in the word, "Halleluyah," (praise be to *Yah*).

>> *Shaddai* or *El Shaddai* ("Almighty" or "God Almighty"): You often see the name *Shaddai* — or just the first letter, *shin* — on the outside of the mezuzah attached to the doorpost of a Jewish home (see Chapter 4).

>> *Ribono Shel Olam* ("Ruling Presence of the Universe"): Often used in prayer, this name affirms a sense of God's caring.

>> *Ha-Kadosh Baruch Hu* ("The Holy One Blessed is He"): This is often seen as the masculine aspect of God corresponding to the feminine *Shekhinah*.

>> *Shekhinah* (the "indwelling presence"): This is the feminine aspect of Oneness. Some rabbis teach that the Shekhinah is the part of God that is in exile along with the Jewish people, and some say that the Shekhinah permeates the world in the same way that the soul permeates the body; just as the soul sustains the body, the Shekhinah sustains the world. In some traditions, *Shekhinah* is another name for *Elohim* (the One manifesting as the many).

Looking behind the Name

Naming an Ultimate Reality is one thing; determining the nature of that Reality is another. In many ways, the names themselves speak the nature of the Being and the kinds of relationships experienced between human and Divine.

Jewish tradition holds that any attempt to know God is bound to fail. Perhaps any view of God says more about the person doing the viewing than about the Ultimate Reality. But that hasn't stopped millennia of philosophers and theologians from trying!

The God of the philosophers, of course, tends to be somewhat different from the God of the worshipers. Maimonides, the greatest Jewish theologian of the Middle Ages (see Chapter 28), understood God as the Prime Mover, the "Uncaused Cause," different not only in degree but in essence from humankind. Maimonides' God was the God of reason, the God of the intellect, appreciated according to the scientific axioms of his time. Humans could really not say anything about the nature of this God, because adjectives simply can't apply to God in the same way they apply to people. Since God is unlimited and all-powerful, God can't "want" or "need" anything from humanity.

The God of the mystics, on the other hand, has a very complementary relationship with humankind (see Chapter 5). For the mystic, there is a profound interrelationship between God and person — one in which each party affects the other. God's Presence (*Shekhinah*) actually participates in the experience of exile with the Children of Israel. Similarly, each person's actions make a cosmic difference. The mystics see the actions of humans (especially those relating to performing the *mitzvot*, "commandments") impacting the nature of God's Being because God and people are one.

And the God of the believer — the God of those many generations of Jews who contributed to the continuity and to the expansion of Judaism — is the One Who Creates, the One Who Reveals, and the One Who Redeems. We use capital letters for these terms to remind us that God's actions may be vastly different from the human actions described by these same words.

God creates

Some Jews say that God started the Big Bang and then walked away from the universe, letting it unfold like a scientist watching a magnificent experiment from a distance. Other Jews insist that God is a more involved Creator. The Midrash (see Chapter 3) describes a remarkable image: When God decided to create the world, He opened the Torah scroll and read the beginning of Bereisheet (Genesis) as though the Torah were an instruction manual or set of blueprints. You'll get your brain tied in knots if you try to work this out literally or logically; remember that this stuff is meant to be poetic.

Of course, just as scientists try to figure out how the universe began in order to understand better where mankind is today, Judaism focuses on Creation not just as a historical event, but as an ever-blossoming act. To many thinkers, God is the Creator and the constant source and resource of creation. God is more like a Natural Force behind all life, expressing Itself as that life, and sustaining the rhythms and the order of the universe.

God reveals

ANECDOTE

David likes to tell the old joke, based on a Talmudic story, of two rabbis arguing over a detail in the Torah. The debate almost came to physical blows when, suddenly, there was thunder and lightning. As the rabbis looked on, amazed, a giant hand came down from the Heavens and pointed to one of them. "He's right," said the massive Voice of God. After a moment, the other rabbi shrugged his shoulders and said, "Okay, fine, so it's two against one. Let's ask somebody else."

THE PROBLEM OF EVIL

Everyone asks the question sooner or later: If God is good, why is there so much evil in the world? Couldn't God have created a universe in which there simply is no pain, no grief, no violence? After the Holocaust, with over six million Jews murdered, some people noted that man simply can't understand God or God's "decisions," and there were some who gave up on God entirely, proclaiming, "God is dead!"

For many others, however, it wasn't a matter of God's dying as much as a time to adjust the human, childlike understanding about the nature of God. Maybe God doesn't have "all" the power after all, since human beings are quite literally given the power to create for good or for ill. The Talmudic rabbis noted that the *yetzer tov* ("inclination toward good") and the *yetzer ha-ra* ("inclination toward evil") live within each human being. While "ra" means "evil," this refers to acts that are solely self-serving, like greed. It is crucial that we learn to balance our instincts toward self-satisfaction with our yearnings to be of service to others and to our world.

While some faiths imagine an evil being, a "Satan," with whom God contends, this idea never really developed within Judaism. A character named "Ha-Satan" (pronounced "ha-sah-*tahn*") appears in the Book of Job, but this Satan is literally "the adversary" or "the accuser," and functions as God's prosecuting attorney and not the demonic archangel in which some people believe. In some respects, you could say that Ha-Satan is actually part of God, too — the aspect of God that tests humans to see what they do with their free will.

Some say this story demonstrates how each Jew is ultimately responsible for his or her own interpretations, even if it means arguing with God. Other people see it as a lesson that it's more important to interpret — and reinterpret — the words of the Torah (the oral, as well as the written Torah; see Chapter 3), rather than appeal to new heavenly voices. Either way, there's an underlying message that God Reveals.

Revelation is the channel through which a human being "hears" the Divine word. The Bible is full of revelations, of course, from the first communication to Adam, to Moses and the giving of the Torah at Sinai (see Chapter 25), to the profound messages of the great Prophets. The big question, however, is did God once speak "openly" to human beings, and then decide not to any longer? Or perhaps people could "hear" differently back then. The scholar Julian Jaynes postulated that in biblical times, the human brain itself was in the process of evolving, so that what people now know as intuitive insights might have been experienced as an outer "Voice of God."

The kabbalistic tradition (see Chapter 5) has long taught that God speaks the same today as God always did, but that humans both hear and interpret what they hear differently. They imagine that revelation is always happening, like a "revelation channel" that's always broadcasting, waiting for humans to become sensitive enough to receive and understand its message. Once received, the messages are filtered through the language, culture, and belief of that time in order to make them understandable.

Of course, for some Jews, God doesn't communicate through words, but through relationship. In the experience of love, compassion, and creativity, realizations of God unfold. And for still others, revelation is contained in the beauty of the natural world, so that by relating to that greater world, people can realize the communication.

God redeems

The phrase "God Redeems" doesn't imply that the Universal Being clips coupons or brings glass bottles into a recycling center. Unfortunately, while the idea of redemption is a core concept of Judaism, what, exactly, that means is subject to interpretation. Most Jews agree that redemption is different from the Christian idea of salvation from sin, especially because Christians tend to see it as a result of right belief rather than acts.

The key redemptive event in Jewish history, the event that in many ways created the Jewish people, was the exodus from Egypt (see Chapter 11). Traditional Judaism teaches that God redeemed the Children of Israel from the great hardships of enslavement, and celebrates this event each year during Passover (see Chapter 25). In that redemptive moment lies the beginning of the essential journey of a People in quest of their God. And yet, Jewish tradition also holds that God didn't simply free the slaves; God created a set of options, and each person had to make a choice from free will: Moses, the Pharaoh, and even the Hebrews. For example, biblical commentators note that the majority of Hebrew slaves chose not to leave Egypt!

Throughout biblical history, this theme continues and is deepened through the developing relationship between the Jews and God. It becomes clear that the people have responsibility for following divinely inspired paths and living in accord with principles of justice and compassion, in service to the One God. When they fail in this responsibility, there is punishment, including exile. But even from the midst of such exile, redemption awaits if they reform.

Visions of redemption

Some Jews see this as a metaphor for personal redemption from exile, such as making choices to live in ways that release them from slavery (whether that's addictive behavior, bad habits, anger, fear, or whatever). Redemption is a process of becoming more human and more able to freely experience the world and act more consciously. In this way, perhaps redemption is another word for self-actualization, enlightenment, or God-consciousness.

Others insist that redemption cannot be achieved by the individual alone, but will come all at once to the entire People of Israel, or the entire world. In this traditional interpretation, God guides history through an ever-unfolding path, and the final act will be the redemption of humankind, brought about by a Jewish king called the *Mashiach* (Messiah). At that time, all Jews will return to the ways of Torah (even the "wicked" ones), and be led out of exile to return to the land of Israel. For traditional Judaism, this promise of redemption translates to a future Messianic Age, including the resurrection of the dead.

The paths of redemption

The future promise of redemption provides the idea that history is purposeful, that there is direction and intention involved, rather than simply being chaotic and purposeless. The primary paths toward redemption — whether personal or communal — involve following the mitzvot (see Chapter 4), and performing acts of *tikkun olam*, the healing of the world through a life-long series of socially responsible actions and intentional blessings.

Embarking on a Quest for Ultimate Reality

The spiritual experience, in which a person or a group opens to a Greater Presence, seems a natural part of human consciousness. Throughout the ages, men and women have been touched by this ineffable Presence, and often had the directions of their lives altered forever. This is certainly the experience recounted time and time again through the literature of the Bible and many texts of the Jewish tradition.

Although Judaism doesn't lack for those inquiring into the specific nature of that Divine Being, it tends to focus more on discovering ways to connect that Holiness to ordinary life. God is experienced through fulfillment of the mitzvot (see Chapter 4) as well as through awakening to the wonders of relationship to others and to the natural world. Life is made holy by realizing the ever-present connection to a Greater One.

IN THIS CHAPTER

» Discovering the essence of a faith:
The Five Books of Moses

» Looking at the Hebrew Bible

» Uncovering Judaism's oral tradition:
The Talmud

» Telling stories: The literature of
midrash

Chapter 3

A Never-Ending Torah: The Unfolding of a Tradition

Judaism has survived for almost 4,000 years, including 2,000 years without a homeland, without the Temple in Jerusalem, without any common geographical location, and without support from the outside. Judaism and Jews survived because of Torah. No matter where they lived, no matter what historical horrors or joys they experienced, the heart of their faith was carried and communicated through the way, the path, and the teachings of Torah.

Torah: The Light That Never Dims

The word *Torah* ("teaching") refers to the first five books of the Hebrew Bible, which are written on a scroll and wound around two wooden poles (see Figure 3-1). Hand-lettered on parchment, the text has been carefully copied by scribes for more than 2,500 years. On one level, the five books narrate a story from the creation of the world to the death of Moses, around 1200 BCE On a deeper level, the Torah is the central text that guides the Way called Judaism.

FIGURE 3-1:
Ashkenazi Jews cover the scrolls with a richly decorated cloth.

Rob Melnychuk/Getty Images

The five books of Moses

TIP

The five books are commonly named Genesis, Exodus, Leviticus, Numbers, and Deuteronomy, following the naming in the early Greek translation of the Bible. Ted's wife, Ruth, learned to remember the names with the mnemonic: "General Electric Lightbulbs Never Dim." Note that the Hebrew names for the books are very different (they're taken from the first unique word that appears in each book):

>> **Genesis (*Bereisheet*, "In the beginning"):** Deals with the creation of the world, the patriarchs and matriarchs (including Abraham, Sarah, and Jacob), and concludes with the story of Jacob, Joseph, and the eventual settlement of the Hebrew people in Egypt (see Chapter 11).

>> **Exodus (*Sh'mot*, "Names"):** Tells of the struggle to leave Egypt, the revelation of Torah on Mount Sinai (including the Ten Commandments), and the beginning of the journey in the wilderness.

>> **Leviticus (*Vayikra*, "And He called"):** Largely deals with levitical, or priestly, matters concerning the running of the Sanctuary, although this book includes some incredible ethical teachings, as well.

» **Numbers (*BaMidbar*, "In the wilderness"):** Begins with taking a census of the tribes and continues with the people's journey through the wilderness.

» **Deuteronomy (*D'varim*, "Words"):** Consists of speeches by Moses recapitulating the entire journey. Deuteronomy concludes with the death of Moses and the people's entrance into the Promised Land.

When these five books are printed in book form (rather than on the scroll), they're usually called the *Chumash* (from *chamesh*, "five"; remember that this "ch" is that guttural "kh" sound), or the *Pentateuch* (this is Greek for "five pieces" and not Hebrew, so here the "ch" is a "k" sound, like "touk"). Because tradition teaches that Moses wrote the books based on Divine revelation, basically taking dictation from God, the books are also called the Five Books of Moses.

If you had your latté this morning, you may have noticed that the Torah is said to have been dictated to Moses, even though it includes the story of his own death and burial. Traditional Jews (see Chapter 1) don't have any problem with this contradiction because to a traditional Jew, the words are those of God, not Moses.

The weekly readings

The *Sefer Torah* (Torah book, or scroll) is the most important item in a synagogue, and it "lives" in the *Aron Kodesh* (the "Holy Ark" or cabinet, which is sometimes covered with fancy curtains and decorations). A portion of the Torah is read in every traditional synagogue each week, on Mondays, Thursdays, Shabbat (see Chapter 18), and on holidays (see Figure 3-2).

The five books are divided into 54 portions called *parshiot* (each one is a *parashah*), also called *sidrot* (each one is a *sidra*). At least one parashah is read each week of the year; some weeks have two parshiot to make it fit the Jewish year correctly. Some synagogues divide the Torah portions differently so that it takes three years, instead of one, to read all five books.

During a synagogue service on Shabbat morning, the Torah reading is followed by the *Haftarah* (see the section later in this chapter). Traditionally, the person who reads the Haftarah also repeats the concluding verses of the parashah called the *maftir*.

REMEMBER

Chapters and verses in the Hebrew Bible were a much later invention, when the Latin "Vulgate" translation was created (405 CE). Instead, each parashah of the Torah has its own name, like "Parashat Noakh," which corresponds to Genesis 6:9–11:32.

Eric Delmar/Getty Images

FIGURE 3-2:
The Torah scroll is always read with a pointer so that fingers won't touch the type.

THE MAKING OF A SEFER TORAH

Anyone who's been in the book business knows that a few typos always get by the proofreaders, no matter how carefully they, er, chck. The Torah business is different. The text of each and every Torah is identical because it's copied letter by letter from an original by a *sofer* ("scribe") on to sections of parchment. Even the tiny decorative flourishes on some letters are copied exactly. If the *sofer* makes a mistake, he (traditional *sofrim* are invariably men, though now at least one Torah has been scribed by a woman) has to scratch the ink off the parchment, and if he can't correct the mistake completely, the whole page must be destroyed. In this way, the written Torah has been lovingly preserved for over 2,500 years. It takes about a year to complete a scroll, and the final product can cost $20,000 to over $50,000. (You can usually pick up a used Torah for between $7,500 and $20,000. What a deal!) If a scroll gets damaged or, after perhaps 100 or 200 years, if it wears out beyond repair, it's not thrown away — it's buried in a Jewish cemetery, along with other holy books.

The TaNaKH: The Hebrew Bible

The five books of the Torah appear as the first of three sections of the Hebrew Bible, which contains 39 books reflecting texts that were gathered over almost 2,000 years. Another name for the Hebrew Bible is the *Tanakh*, which is actually an acronym made up of the first letters of the names of each of the three sections: "T" is for *Torah*, "N" is for *Nevi'im* ("Prophets"), and "KH" is for *Ketuvim* ("Writings").

TIP

If you want to sound like a *mayven* (expert), don't call the Hebrew Bible the "Old Testament." The Old Testament is a Christian term based on the idea that there is a *New* Testament that supersedes the Hebrew Bible. Jews prefer to call their Bible either the Hebrew Bible, or simply the Holy Scriptures. What Christians call the New Testament is usually referred to in Jewish settings as the Christian Bible.

Nevi'im ("Prophets")

Nevi'im (neh-vee-*eem*) contains a record of most of the important history for the roughly 700 years after Moses (see Chapters 12 and 13). The history is told in the Books of Joshua, Judges, Samuel, and Kings. *Nevi'im* also includes the words of the great sixth-century BCE prophets like Isaiah, Jeremiah, and Ezekiel. The last 12 books in *Nevi'im* — from Hosea to Malachi — are much shorter, and they're often grouped together as "The 12 Prophets."

Ketuvim ("Writings")

Ketuvim (keh-too-*veem*) is a collection of books, but the books don't necessarily relate to one another. Some (Ezra, Nehemiah, and Chronicles) relate history; some (like Proverbs) relate, well, proverbs. The Books of Ecclesiastes and Lamentations express some of the bleaker reflections on life.

The Book of Psalms, the longest book of the Bible, contains 150 poems of praise, yearning, and celebration that form the basis of many prayers and hymns both in Jewish and Christian traditions. The Books of Job, Ruth, Esther, and Daniel record epic moral and religious quests. The Song of Songs is a beautiful love poem that many people read as a metaphor for the relationship between God and the Jewish people.

After being passed down orally for centuries, most of the individual books of the Tanakh were written down by the third century BCE. However, Jewish scholars didn't determine the official canon — the list of books that "made it" into the Bible — until 90 CE, in the city of Yavneh (also called Jamnia). The scholars of Yavneh left out several books that came to be included in the *Septuagint* (the Greek translation of the Bible), including the *Apocrypha* ("hidden books"), like the four books of Maccabees. However, Roman Catholic and Greek Orthodox Bibles include these books because they're based on the Septuagint.

The Haftarah

Each of the 54 parshiot is associated with a section from *Nevi'im* (historical and prophetic books of the Hebrew Bible). Those 54 sections of the Nevi-im are called *Haftarah* (the name "Haftarah" means "taking leave," representing an additional reading following the Torah portion). Most historians think that during a particularly repressive period, perhaps as early as the second century BCE when public reading of the Torah became a capital offense, scholars instead read non-Torah texts that would remind them either by theme or characters of the weekly Torah portion. In this way, people could remember what Torah portion should have been read. Later, when the ban was lifted, this extra reading was retained, so even today, Jews typically read both the Torah and the Haftarah texts on Shabbat and festivals.

Interpreting the Bible

Jewish "fundamentalism" doesn't focus on the "literal truth" of the Bible like some other forms of religious fundamentalism do. Although many traditional Jews believe that the Tanakh expresses the Word of God, very few Jews would argue that the literal meaning of the words is the right one. An important rabbinic teaching says that there are 70 interpretations for every word in Torah — and they're all correct! Jewish tradition talks of four dimensions of meaning: the literal, the allegorical, the metaphorical, and the mystical.

WORDS OF WISDOM

For example: When Abraham hears *Lekh l'kha may-artz'kha . . .* ("Get you out of your land . . ."), God seems simply to be telling him to move on. But a deeper interpretation encourages the reader to consider the nature of such journeys in a personal context: What is it like to really "leave" a place? Then an even deeper interpretation is addressed to people on a spiritual quest in which they are asked to leave the place of comfort in old ideas and identities and strike out into the unknown. Finally, the first two words (which are usually translated, "Get you out") can also literally be translated, "Go to yourself." On a more mystical level, the call directs us toward an inner journey.

Studying different interpretations is called *hermeneutics,* and it's an important part of the Jewish understanding of Torah. Hermeneutics is why five different rabbis can make five different sermons on the same text. More fundamentalist Jewish groups don't focus on an exclusive interpretation of the Torah text as much as on a very strict application of ritual practice.

A Hidden Revolution: The Oral Torah

The written Torah may be the central text of the Jewish people, but if that's all we Jews had, we'd be in trouble. For example, the Torah doesn't explain how to perform a religious marriage, what "an eye for an eye" really means, or even how to honor Shabbat and the other holidays (especially ever since the Temple was destroyed and Jews could no longer make animal sacrifices). Think of the Torah as the musical score to an amazing symphony; the written music contains the notes but doesn't say how to play them. Jews need more than the Torah scrolls to know how to "play" Judaism.

The "musical direction" is provided by the "Oral Torah," a set of teachings, interpretations, and insights that complement the written Torah. One of Ted's professors in seminary, Dr. Ellis Rivkin, spoke of the development of Oral Torah as one of the most profound religious revolutions of all time. Without it, he taught, Judaism could hardly have survived for as long as it has.

Traditional, Orthodox Jews believe that Moses not only received what became the Written Torah (*Torah sheh-bikh-tav*) at Sinai, but also the Oral Torah (*Torah sheh-b'al peh*). The oral tradition itself states: "Moses received the [Written and Oral] Torah from Sinai and handed it down to Joshua, and Joshua to the elders, the elders to the prophets, and the prophets handed it down to the men of the Great Assembly . . ." So Jews not only see the Written Torah as the word of God, but the Oral Torah, as well.

This oral tradition would, centuries later, itself be written down in the form of the Mishnah, the Talmud, and the midrash — only to be further interpreted by countless more rabbis and students, developing into the Judaism of today. Each time the oral tradition is written, it gives rise to the next step of the process.

CONTROVERSY

More liberal Jews tend to discount the transmission of the Oral Torah at Sinai; instead, they believe that the Oral Torah slowly evolved over time. These folks appreciate that pieces of Mishnah, Talmud, and midrash still hold eternal truths, but they also believe that some passages tied to ancient cultural environments are no longer relevant.

The law of the land: The Mishnah

The early scholars and teachers (roughly between 100 BCE and 100 CE) developed guidelines for a continuing Way of Life, called *halakhah*. Whether or not halakhah (which is usually translated "legal material" or "law," but literally means "the walk" — as in "walking the talk") was originally divinely given, it provided the structure for the community's practice of Judaism. For more than two hundred years this body of material developed orally, and because it was considered an oral tradition, Jews were prohibited from writing it down.

GETTING HIT OVER THE HEAD WITH WISDOM

Two of the most influential rabbis in the developing Oral Tradition were Hillel (70 BCE to 10 CE) and Shammai (50 BCE to 30 CE). Perhaps the most famous story about these two rabbis concerns a non-Jew seeking to discover the essence of Judaism.

First, the man went to Shammai, who was in the midst of working (all the rabbis back then had day jobs, too, and Shammai was a house builder). The man asked Shammai, "Tell me the meaning of Judaism while standing on one foot." Shammai stared at the guy and then whacked him on the head with his measuring rod.

Not particularly satisfied, the man then visited the sage Hillel with the same request: "Tell me the meaning of Judaism while standing on one foot." Hillel looked at him for a moment and then said, "What is hateful to you do not do to others. That is the whole of Torah, all the rest is commentary — go now and learn."

Although this is a wonderful story about Hillel, we think that Shammai's teaching has long been unappreciated. You may be aware of the Zen Buddhist tradition in which a teacher may strike a student in order to startle him into a radically new way of seeing things. Perhaps Shammai knew that understanding the essence of Judaism isn't so much a matter of a gentle principle but rather a matter of deep inner transformation.

But, as you may guess, Hillel's gentle, compassionate, and practical answers, as well as his legal decisions, were virtually always followed. But there are many who suspect that Shammai's teachings were actually more spiritually-based, and tradition has it that while Hillel's decisions are fit for this world, Shammai's will be followed in the World to Come.

However, after hundreds of thousands of Jews were killed by the Romans in the early years of the first millennia (see Chapter 14), and halakhah continued to become more complex, Jews realized the importance of codifying the expanding traditions in writing. Although some of the earlier rabbis had collected material before him, Judah Ha-Nasi ("Judah the Prince," who is also simply called "Rabbi") finally codified the laws, creating the *Mishnah* between 200 and 220 CE.

The Mishnah (the name derives from "a teaching that is repeated," indicating its origin as an oral tradition) includes lessons and quotations by sages from Hillel and Shammai (first-century rabbis) through Judah Ha-Nasi (who lived in the third century). The Mishnah contains a collection of legal rulings and practices upon which Jewish tradition still depends. The Mishnah is organized like a law book (as opposed to the narrative of the Torah), splitting up the Jewish Way into six basic *sedarim* ("orders"):

>> **Zera-im ("Seeds"):** Blessings and prayers, agricultural laws

>> **Mo-ed ("Set Feasts"):** Laws of Sabbath and the holidays

>> **Nashim ("Women"):** Marriage, divorce, and other vows

>> **Nezikin ("Damages"):** Civil laws, idolatry, and *Pirke Avot* ("Ethics of the Fathers," which is a collection of ethical quotes and proverbs by the rabbis)

>> **Kodashim ("Hallowed Things"):** Temple sacrifices, ritual slaughter, and dietary laws

>> **Tohorot ("Purities"):** Ritual cleanliness and uncleanliness

The teachings explained: The Talmud

The ancient sages feared that once the Mishnah was written down it wouldn't meet the demands of changing times, and they were right. Academies of Jewish learning grew in Palestine and Babylonia (modern Iraq) to discuss new issues raised by their consideration of the Mishnah. Most of the rabbis had other jobs, but their true love was meeting in the academies to discuss, argue, and debate concerns arising from the text of the Mishnah, new legal issues, the Torah, stories of supernatural events, and a host of other matters.

Their dialogues were the beginning of another part of the Oral Torah, the *Gemara* ("completion"). The Gemara is basically a commentary on the various teachings of the Mishnah. Where the Mishnah dealt mainly with matters of halakhah, the Gemara contained both halakhah and *aggadah* ("discourse," stories, legends, and pieces of sermons; the tales and the teachings that "read between the lines" of Tanakh and Talmud). The Mishnah with the Gemara became known as the *Talmud* ("teaching").

In size, the Tanakh is dwarfed by the massive Talmud, which often appears in as many as 30 volumes (with translations and commentary). Note that most traditional Jews don't focus on "Bible study"; they focus on the study of the Talmud. However, the Bible does tend to be the focus for more liberal Jews.

Reading the Bible is hard, especially without helpful commentary, but reading the Talmud is orders of magnitude more difficult (take a look at Figure 3-3 to see how much information is crammed on to just one page). Discussions frequently contain several radically different opinions, offered by rabbis who appear to be in the same room but actually lived in different centuries. The arguments often appear nonlinear, like a free-association or like surfing on a cosmic Internet. Some people say that you don't read the Talmud, you swim in it. But behind the complexities of the text, the Talmudic scholars find profound insights and deep meaning.

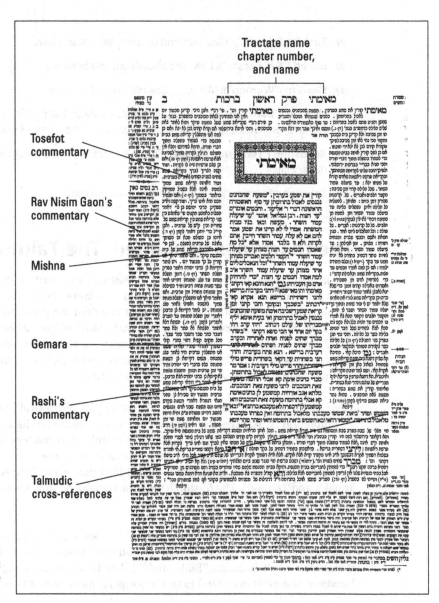

Tractate name chapter number, and name

Tosefot commentary

Rav Nisim Gaon's commentary

Mishna

Gemara

Rashi's commentary

Talmudic cross-references

FIGURE 3-3:
A sample page from the Talmud.

So, with the completion of the Talmud, was the oral tradition finished? Of course not. Commentaries, codifications, questions, and answers continue to unfold through books, articles, and rabbinic discussions. This ongoing, unending discussion is also considered part of the Oral Torah.

A SAMPLE OF TALMUDIC DIALOGUE

Even though few people other than scholars and religious Jews ever read the Talmud, the discussions offer a fascinating window into the essence of the Oral tradition. Here's one small example, focusing on a central Jewish prayer, the Amidah ("Standing"), also known as the Shemoneh Esrey ("The 18").

Mishnah: Raban Gamiliel says that everyone should pray the "Eighteen [Blessings]" daily. Rabbi Yehoshua says that one should only pray an extract of the 18 Blessings. Rabbi Akiba says that if one knows them clearly one should say all 18, otherwise one should pray the extract. Rabbi Eliezer says that whoever prays "on automatic" isn't really praying at all.

Here, three rabbis from the first and second centuries discuss how to recite the central prayer in a Jewish service. Remember that at that time there were no printed prayer books, so people had to know prayers by heart. Then, generations later in the Gemara, rabbis reading this Mishnah wondered why there should be 18 blessings in the first place.

Gemara: On what are these "Eighteen Blessings" based? Rabbi Hillel, the son of Rabbi Shmuel Bar Nachmani, says that they're indicated by the 18 times the name of God is mentioned in Psalm 29. Rav Yosef bases it on the 18 times God's name is mentioned in the Sh'ma. Rabbi Tanchum said in the name of Rabbi Yehoshua Ben Levy that the 18 blessings correspond to the 18 major vertebrae in the human spine.

It looks like Rabbi Hillel is in dialogue with Rav Yosef, even though they lived a century apart (in the third and fourth centuries, respectively). Then Rabbi Tanchum (from the early fourth century) says that his teacher, Rabbi Yehoshua Ben Levy, brought the discussion into the "real world" by relating the number 18 to the central vertebrae of the spine (as understood in medieval anatomy). This is interesting because the spine connects the body's lower and higher functions, and so symbolizes the link between the physical and the spiritual realms. So now the prayer under discussion, because it has 18 sections, acts as a daily reminder of the Jew's role as a bridge between worlds.

Telling stories: The midrash

Perhaps the most fascinating parts of Oral Torah (at least to lay readers) is the large body of *midrash* (from *d'rash*, an "exposition," or "sermon") that contains both halakhic and aggadic materials. Most people focus on the aggadah — those tales and the teachings that "read between the lines" of Tanakh and Talmud. The most well-known collections of midrash span the years between the fourth and sixth centuries, although the midrashic form continued in collections through the 13th century, and midrash even exists today in the form of contemporary sermons, stories, and homilies.

ABRAHAM AND THE IDOLS

One of the most famous midrashic tales concerns the Patriarch Abraham when he was still a boy. As the story goes, Abraham's father was an idol salesman, with a shop full of stone statues of various gods. One day, his father entrusted the care of the shop to Abraham while he went out. Abraham, looking around the room of idols, took a stick and proceeded to smash all the idols except the largest one, into whose hands he then put the stick.

When his father returned, he looked aghast at the destruction in his shop and exclaimed "What happened?" Abraham calmly replied, "That idol smashed all the others." His father said, "Idols can't do that." And Abraham replied, "That's right, father, idols are powerless."

This story, which beautifully brings aspects of the biblical story to life, is so well known that many people grew up thinking that it was actually written in Genesis. Ted only found out in seminary that it was midrash!

It is in midrash that the great creative and imaginative genius of the Jews blossomed, and you often find psychological, emotional, and spiritual insights in it. A kind of play is possible in aggadah that was usually inhibited in Talmudic legal discussions, and tradition has it that God smiles when people write and discuss aggadah.

For example, one famous midrash explains an apparent inconsistency in the Book of Genesis, in which both man and woman are created in the first chapter, but then the man is suddenly alone in the second chapter. A midrash says the first woman was named Lilith, but Adam couldn't get along with her. He complained bitterly to God: "We can't agree on anything. She never listens to me!" So, according to that midrash, God banished Lilith and replaced her with Eve, with whom Adam could better relate. A very long time later, the Jewish feminist movement embraced Lilith because she was created equal to Adam. Remember, this is midrash — just a story.

The Expanding Torah

The word *Torah* has a third and even larger meaning beyond the written and oral law, too. Torah is the Jewish Way. Torah is the whole thing. Torah is 3,800 years and counting. Torah is the expanding, evolving quest of a people exploring the nature of Ultimate Reality and the responsibilities of Human Being.

Chapter **4**

A Path of Blessing: Judaism as a Daily Practice

O ur wives have tried to get us to take yoga classes. We've read the brochures and heard the testimonies, and we know that it would be good for us. But, oy, it's uncomfortable flopping around like a beached porpoise as more experienced classmates (not to mention the instructor) bend, twist, stretch, and generally look amazing.

How did those people get so good? The answer is obvious, but frustrating: practice. They showed up day after day, week after week, and slowly got better, looked better, and felt better. And, to those of us who grew up focusing on getting the job done and reaching the finish line, there's an even more annoying aspect of these activities: There is no finish line. That's why they call yoga — or martial arts, or meditation, or whatever — a _practice:_ You're always practicing, getting better, and going deeper.

Judaism, a religion that focuses far more on deeds than on beliefs, involves practices. When you're new to the practice, it may feel strange. That's okay. Keep practicing anyway. You may be surprised to find yourself opening to deeper meaning in your life — but it probably won't help with your yoga postures.

Connecting With God and Community through Practice: The Mitzvot

You may have heard people say that Judaism is a way of life. Referring to Judaism in this way is apt because the religion is a set of practices. These practices, particularly when they're vehicles through which an individual connects more consciously to God, are called *mitzvot* (mitz-*vote*; it's the plural of *mitzvah*), meaning commandments or religious acts.

How does one discover the mitzvot? Through the *halakhah* — walking the talk of Jewish tradition (head over to Chapter 3 for more information on halakhah). Mitzvot make up the steps on the path of halakhah, along which a Jew discovers his or her connection to God as well as connections to the past, present, and future of the Jewish community.

Mitzvot consist of ritual as well as ethical acts, and they follow from the principles expressed in the Torah (see Chapter 3). Some practices, such as wearing a head covering (*kippah* or *yarmulke*; see "Dressing for God: Jewish Garments and Clothing Customs" later in this chapter), were developed more recently and fall under the category of *minhag* (custom); however, after so many years of practice these customs have become virtual mitzvot.

Undoubtedly the most famous mitzvot are the Ten Commandments. In Hebrew, these ten items are called either *Aseret Ha-Dibrot* (The Ten Statements) or *Aseret Ha-D'varim* (The Ten Principles). The Bible never refers to the practices specifically as *commandments*, perhaps because they were so basic and fundamental to the community. Here are the Ten Principles, numbered according to Jewish tradition (the Christian divisions tend to differ slightly):

1. I am the Eternal your God, who brought you out of the land of Egypt.

2. You shall have no other gods before Me. You shall not make a graven image.

3. You shall not use the name of the Eternal in vain (literally, for nothing).

4. Remember (and Observe) the Sabbath day to keep it holy.

5. Honor your father and your mother.

6. You shall not murder.

7. You shall not commit adultery.

8. You shall not steal.

9. You shall not bear false witness.

10. You shall not covet.

REMEMBER

THE SEVEN UNIVERSAL MITZVOT

When Noah's ark came to rest after the devastation of the flood, tradition teaches that humankind received seven basic laws, called the Noahide Laws. These basic pillars of human civilization were to be observed by all people, not only by the Jews:

- Do not murder.

- Do not steal.

- Do not worship false gods.

- Do not be sexually immoral.

- Do not eat the limb of an animal before it is killed.

- Do not curse God.

- Set up courts and bring offenders to justice.

These are the central principles (mitzvot) that serve as the foundation for all the other mitzvot of Jewish living. According to Jewish tradition, there are 603 more.

613 habits of highly effective people

In the third century, Rabbi Simlai taught that God gave 613 commandments (also called the *taryag mitzvot*) in the Torah. He further divided them into 248 positive commandments (thou shalt's) and 365 negative commandments (thou shalt not's). The number 248 was believed to correspond to the number of organs and sinews in the human body; the number 365 corresponds to the number of days in a solar year.

Examples of positive mitzvot include

Believe in God

Love God

Study and teach Torah

Build a sanctuary for God

Participate at synagogue services

Say the blessing after meals

Spiritually cleanse in a ritual bath (mikvah)

Leave gleanings for the poor

Tithe to the poor

Rest on Shabbat

Eat matzah on Passover

Fast on Yom Kippur

Give charity

Here are some negative mitzvot:

Don't believe in any other god

Don't worship idols

Don't get tattoos (or decorative scars)

Don't enter the sanctuary intoxicated

Don't delay payment of vows

Don't eat an unclean animal

Don't eat blood

Don't eat leavened products on Passover

Don't fail to give charity

Don't convict someone on the testimony of a single witness.

Of the 613 commandments, over 200 of them can no longer be observed because they require the ancient Temple that was destroyed in 70 CE. Additionally, some say 26 of the commandments require living in Israel (like the mitzvah to leave a portion of a field unharvested so there's some left for the poor).

Mitzvot are scattered all over the Bible, so different rabbis include slightly different mitzvot in their lists and order them differently. For example, Maimonides' twelfth-century *Sefer Ha-Mitzvot* (Book of the Commandments) and the Chafetz Chayim's twentieth-century *Sefer Ha-Mitzvot Ha-Kitzur* (The Concise Book of the Commandments) number the commandments differently. The mitzvot are also codified in the sixteenth-century *Shulchan Aruch* (The Arranged Table) by Joseph Caro, which still serves as the basic authority in matters of traditional practice.

Women and mitzvot

All the negative commandments pertain to both men and women, but women are exempted from the positive, time-specific mitzvot because of the demands of child-rearing and taking care of the home. For instance, women aren't required to wear the *tallit* (prayer shawl) or attend daily synagogue worship. Although no specific injunction forbids women from doing these mitzvot, more traditional communities tend to discourage women from doing them; these same communities are troubled by some women's interest in exploring these practices. In less traditional communities, where women are treated with far greater equality, don't be surprised to see a woman wearing a tallit at worship.

The reasons for mitzvot

For traditionalists, the answer to the question "Why perform mitzvot?" is easy. They say that the commandments of the Torah represent the will of God and the covenant between the Jewish people and God. However, even traditionalists make exceptions; in a crisis, you're actually required to violate the mitzvot if it means you can save a life. The exceptions to *that* exception are the mitzvot prohibiting idolatry, murder, and adultery or incest, which aren't allowed under any conditions.

SWEET CHARITY'S JUSTICE

One of the most basic themes of the mitzvot has to do with providing for those unable to provide for themselves, whether financially, physically, emotionally, or mentally. The Hebrew term for this kind of giving is *tzedakah*, and although it's usually translated "charity," the word literally means "justice." In Jewish tradition, such charitable actions aren't simply a matter of a kind heart. Instead, Jews see them as right actions in the world that are just as important as any other mitzvah. For example, Jewish tradition institutes a tithe for those in need (called *ma'aser kesafim*) as a primary social obligation.

Here are Maimonides' (see Chapter 28) famous eight degrees of *tzedakah*, beginning with the lowest level:

- Give only grudgingly.

- Give willingly, but less than is appropriate.

- Give only after being asked.

- Give before being asked.

- Give so that the donor doesn't know who the recipient is.

- Give so that the recipient doesn't know who the donor is.

- Give so that neither donor nor recipient knows the identity of the other.

- Help the poor to rehabilitate themselves by lending them money, taking them into partnership, employing them, or giving them work, for in this way the end is achieved without any loss of self-respect at all.

Many (perhaps most) non-traditional Jews actually have little or no inclination to perform mitzvot or to follow halakhah (see Chapter 3) and consider themselves Jewish because of birth or cultural identity (see Chapter 1). Others observe only those mitzvot that are most meaningful to them and choose not to follow the rest.

Rabbi Arnold Jacob Wolf compares the mitzvot to precious jewels that appear on the Jewish path: Some of them — like lighting Chanukkah candles, eating matzah on Passover, and lighting a memorial candle for a deceased parent — are easy to pick up and carry. Others — such as observing Shabbat more fully and eating according to the Jewish dietary laws of *kashrut* — require special persistence, but they may well be wonderful jewels to carry.

REMEMBER

The Jewish Way is defined by studying and embracing the jewels — the mitzvot — along the path. Those jewels can deeply illuminate your life and connect you more meaningfully to God and to the Jewish people.

Connecting With God and Community through Blessings and Prayers

If you live along the coast in New York, and your friend lives near the bay in San Francisco, and you both step into the ocean, you might appreciate that you're actually connecting to one another. Anytime you enter the ocean, you're in touch with others all over the planet. That's how it is with prayer: When you enter into the depths of prayer, you're connected with all others in that space, including those who inhabited that space in the past. Prayer helps you connect with a shared Being, a Universal Presence through Whom all people are connected.

In Jewish tradition, the holy space of prayer is always available. You can access the holy space through daily communal prayer services and through private prayers and blessings that hallow even the most ordinary moments of daily life. Such regular prayers (*t'fillot*) and blessings (*b'rakhot*) keep you conscious of the bigger context in which you live. Unfortunately, one problem with praying so regularly is the very human tendency to go on automatic — observing the outer form while forgetting the inner content. This is why *kavvanah* is so crucial.

Kavvanah is the intentionality with which the prayers and blessings, and even your acts and your words, are to flow. Tradition often teaches how important kavvanah is with respect to the observance of all mitzvot, including the mitzvot of blessings and prayers.

Sometimes you see Jews rhythmically rock and sway in deep concentration (it's called *shuckling*) while they pray (called *davening*). This is a way of entering prayer with the whole body (see Figure 4-1). Similarly, during worship service you may see Jews participate in a subtle choreography, in which they bend their knees and bow, or take several steps forward and several steps back. These actions help Jews pray with kavvanah.

TIP

These movements are all customs, not commandments, but if you feel comfortable doing them, you can easily learn them by watching other folks.

Photo courtesy David Blatner

FIGURE 4-1:
A traditional Jew performs his morning prayers at the Western Wall in Jerusalem. Stuffed in the wall are small pieces of paper on which prayers are written.

Private worship

Although Jews are encouraged to pray in a community, nothing stops them from praying on their own. Judaism recognizes a number of different kinds of prayer — including praising God, petitioning for help, giving thanks, and even just wrestling with the often-difficult issues in our lives.

REMEMBER

Prayers are almost always directed to God, but Jews disagree on what that God is. The important thing is that you find an interpretation that feels right to you (see Chapter 2).

In addition to the many blessings traditionally recited during group worship, many blessings are meant to be recited alone. For example, many Jews say blessings at the beginning and the end of the day (see Appendix B). Also, although silence isn't part of the traditional communal worship, Jews treat silent meditation as an important part of private worship.

The community worship service

By the time of the Mishnah (completed around 200 CE; see Chapter 3 for details), the synagogue worship services that Jews practice were, for the most part, set. On most days, traditional Jews can attend any of the following three services:

>> **Arvit** or **Ma'ariv:** Evening service (remember that the Jewish day begins at sundown)

>> **Shakharit:** Morning service

>> **Minkhah:** Afternoon service

On Shabbat and festival days, Jews celebrate an additional service:

>> **Musaf:** An additional service, which takes place after the morning service.

The first-century rabbis noted that the Sh'ma was to be recited twice daily (as it had been even in the days of the Second Temple; see Appendix B), with specific blessings before and after. And the daily Amidah (see the following section) was also already pretty much set by 100 CE. The opening formula for a *berakhah*, a blessing (*Baruch Atah Adonai* . . ., "Blessed are You, Eternal One . . ."), became popular following the destruction of the Second Temple and enabled series of blessings to be developed for the service. In addition to public prayer, individuals added their own private prayers, often reciting Psalms.

Traditional services are conducted entirely in Hebrew, although most prayerbooks in North America include English translations, too.

REMEMBER

Jewish law insists that people understand what they're praying, so the law allows for people to pray in whatever language they know (except for the Sh'ma). Nevertheless, most congregations (even Reform) tend to use Hebrew these days.

Traditionally, you need a *minyan* (min-*yahn*, meaning "quorum") of ten men to pray as a community, but non-Orthodox communities now count women as well. Once you've got a minyan, a service usually begins with a few psalms, poems, and readings that are appropriate for the particular service. Several other elements are always included (and which we discuss in the following sections), including the recitation of the Sh'ma, the Amidah, the Aleinu, the Kaddish, and sometimes a reading from the Torah and other books of the Bible.

Sh'ma and its blessings

Jews recite the *Kriyat Sh'ma* (Declaration of the Sh'ma; see Appendix B) during the morning and the evening services. The Kriyat Sh'ma contains three sections from the Torah:

» **Deuteronomy 6:4–9:** The first passage declares the Oneness of God and promotes love as the way of remembering, teaching, and acting in the world.

» **Deuteronomy 11:13–21:** The second section again stresses the love of God and reminds us that human actions make a difference in the world.

» **Numbers 15:37–41:** The final passage encourages worshippers to remember God's redemption by wearing fringes, called *tzitzit,* on the corners of their garments (see "Dressing for God: Jewish Garments and Clothing Customs" later in this chapter).

Additionally, Jews always include in the Sh'ma blessings that are appropriate to the morning or the evening, as well as blessings for Torah, for redemption, and for protection.

The Amidah

The *Amidah* (literally, the "standing," because worshippers always stand while reciting it) is the central prayer of the worship service. It's often also called the *Tefillah* ("the Prayer") or *Shemonah Esray* ("the 18," referring to the 18 original benedictions it originally contained, even though a nineteenth was added long ago). First you read it silently (move your lips while reciting just loudly enough for you to hear), and then the service leader repeats it aloud.

The 19 blessings of the Amidah consist of three sections that reflect the three basic modes of Jewish worship:

» **Shevakh:** The first three blessings express praise for the Jewish patriarchs, the wonders of God, and God's holiness.

» **Bakashah:** The middle 13 blessings speak petitions, broken up as follows:

  • A set of petitions for knowledge, repentance, forgiveness, redemption, healing, and prosperity.

- Seven petitions relating to the restoration of Jerusalem, justice, heretics (this is more of a curse, actually), converts, the righteous, God's Presence in Israel, and restoration of the Davidic line of kings.

- A final petition that God hear all prayers.

>> **Hoda'ah:** Three blessings of thanksgiving concerning acceptance of the worship, expressions of gratitude, and blessings of peace.

REMEMBER

On Shabbat or other holidays Jews replace the middle section, Bakashah, with a single blessing focusing on the holiness of that particular day. They do this because these petitionary prayers are contrary to the spirit of Shabbat — a spirit that imagines the day already to be Eden-like.

Following the Amidah, congregants usually have time for silent worship or personal prayers.

Reading the Torah

During the morning service on Mondays and Thursdays, and on Shabbat afternoons, a rabbi, cantor, or a learned congregant reads sections of the weekly Torah portion. The entire weekly portion is read on Shabbat morning, followed by the *Haftarah*, which are complementary readings from the Prophets. The Torah is also read on festival mornings, along with a number of prayers of praise (*hallel*).

Aleinu

Toward the end of each traditional service comes the *Aleinu,* in which worshippers affirm God's Oneness and pray that God's Oneness might one day truly connect all people.

Kaddish

We discuss the *Kaddish* in more depth in Chapter 10, but basically it's a prayer, written mostly in Aramaic, expressing praise of God and the yearning for the establishment of God's Kingdom on earth. Jews recite the *Chatzi Kaddish* (a shorter version of the prayer) to separate the major sections of the worship, so you hear it more than once during a service.

Finally, at the end of the service, worshippers recite the last Kaddish, called the *Mourner's Kaddish.* Traditionally, only those who are mourning the loss of a close relative rise and recite this Kaddish, but today in many communities, everyone rises. The prayer became associated with memorializing the dead because it came at the very end of the service — when by custom the names of those recently deceased were read. Interestingly, the Mourner's Kaddish makes no mention of death; instead, it focuses on praise of God.

Going to Synagogue

We grew up hearing people talk about going to temple to pray or worship. It wasn't until much later that we found out that most Jews don't call the house of worship a temple, preferring instead to reserve that word for *The Temple* in Jerusalem (the one that was destroyed by the Babylonians in 586 BCE, was rebuilt, and was then destroyed by the Romans in 70 CE). Some Reform congregations still use "temple," but it's becoming more rare.

Today, English-speaking Jews tend to call the Jewish place of worship a "synagogue" (which actually comes from Greek meaning "gathering" or "assembly"). The Hebrew language has a number of different words for *synagogue*, including *Beit Midrash* (House of Learning), *Beit Tefillah* (House of Prayer), and *Beit Knesset* (House of Assembly). These names reflect the various activities that take place at synagogue: education, prayer, and community gatherings. Many people also use the Yiddish word *shul* (from the German word for "school") to refer to synagogue.

TIP

If you want to attend or join a congregation, we strongly urge you to look around (provided that there is more than one where you live). Synagogues can vary significantly not only in their physical appearance but also in the type of congregation that attends them. Physically, some synagogues rival cathedrals, while others are housed in apartment buildings; some congregations even share space with a church. The type of congregation can range from traditional groups that follow halakhah to far less traditional communities that espouse vegetarian, New Age, and feminist values. Take the time to look into your options to find a congregation that best meshes with your own values.

No matter how many differences exist among synagogues, they do share a few commonalities, which we outline in the following section.

Four things you'll find in every synagogue

In every synagogue you usually find the following items:

>> **The Aron Kodesh:** The ark that holds the Torah scrolls. By convention, in Western countries, it's always on the east wall (so when facing it, the congregation is facing Jerusalem). The ark may have doors and is often covered with a curtain (called a *parochet*), which may be ornately decorated.

>> **The Ner Tamid:** The eternal light, which often burns above the ark. The light — these days, usually an electric light or oil lamp — symbolizes the *menorah* (which we talk about later in this chapter) from the ancient Temple

and reflects the Eternal Presence experienced through prayer and study in the synagogue.

>> **The bimah:** The location where the Torah is read and the service is led. It's usually a raised platform, either in the center of the synagogue (this is the Sephardic style) or along the east wall, in front of the Aron Kodesh.

>> **Seating area:** All synagogues have a seating area for the congregations. Non-orthodox synagogues (see Chapter 1) seat men and women in a shared space. Orthodox synagogues have separate seating areas for men and women, separated by a divider called a *mechitzah* (meh-*kheet*-sa). Often the mechitzah is a low curtain or a partial wall, high enough so that men and women can't see each other during the service. We're not going to get into the volatile political issues surrounding the mechitzah; suffice it to say that while in some synagogues the separation clearly de-emphasizes the role of women, in many other Orthodox synagogues, it's designed so that everyone feels separate-but-equal.

Synagogues, for the most part, reflect the sanctuary style of the dominant culture. Many synagogues in the Middle East resemble mosques, while those in England tend to look more like churches. However, synagogues rarely feature statues of animals or people, in adherence with the commandment prohibiting graven images. (One notable exception is the often-seen "Lion of Judah," the insignia of the ancient Kingdom of Judea; see Chapter 12.)

Who's who at shul

A lot of people are involved in running worship services, but the focus is almost always on two people: the rabbi and the cantor.

The rabbi

Although a congregation can conduct religious services without a rabbi, most congregations employ one. The rabbi also serves as an educator and a counselor and officiates at life-cycle events like baby-namings, Bar or Bat Mitzvah ceremonies, weddings, and funerals (see Part II for more information on these events).

Rabbinical students typically do five years of post-graduate work before they're ordained as rabbis. Orthodox *yeshivot* (seminaries) tend to have a less formal course of study, but the study is far more extensive in matters of Jewish law. The ordination (as well as the accompanying diploma) is called a *s'mikhah*, literally referring to the laying on of hands through which ordination is traditionally conferred.

TIP

A FIRST-TIMERS' GUIDE TO SYNAGOGUE

Going to any synagogue for the first time can be overwhelming and confusing. If you're familiar with one synagogue, you're sure to wonder why others do the service so differently (adding prayers, leaving prayers out, and so on). If you're unfamiliar with the worship service in general, then our best advice is to just hang on, keep your eyes and ears open, and plan on going a few times before you catch on. Don't be afraid to ask questions, but ask only when people aren't in the midst of prayer. Here are a few other things to think about:

- Wear modest clothing as a sign of respect. If you're male, wear a *kippah* (a head covering; the plural is *kippot*) in the sanctuary; some women in more liberal congregations wear kippot, too. Most synagogues keep extra kippot in the lobby for visitors to borrow. If you're a woman, you might wear a scarf. Men often wear a white or light blue shirt, women often wear a dress or skirt. You don't need a prayer shawl; you probably shouldn't wear one unless you're Jewish, anyway. We discuss Jewish clothing customs in detail in "Dressing for God: Jewish Garments and Clothing Customs" later in this chapter.

- If you don't have a *siddur* (prayer book), ask for one that has an English translation if you don't speak Hebrew. Even better, ask if there's one that has both a translation and a transliteration, so that you can see how the Hebrew should be pronounced.

- In Orthodox synagogues, men and women always sit separately. This is uncomfortable for some couples, but that's the way it is. In other synagogues, men and women are almost always mixed.

- The whole thing may look really disorganized, especially in some Orthodox shuls. Some people may be standing while others are sitting, then suddenly everyone comes together for a song or prayer, and then people are off on their own again. Remember that Jews are often praying at their own pace, but in the company of other people.

- Try to arrive on time (or early), but if you arrive late, don't walk in while the congregation is standing or during the rabbi's sermon. You may notice other people arriving late (sometimes very late). Instead of just joining in, they often start from the beginning of the prayer service. Sometimes people just leave when they're done, too.

- A collection plate won't be passed around (especially not on Shabbat; see Chapter 18). However, you may find a box for charitable donations in the lobby.

- Stand up (with everyone else) as a sign of respect when the ark is open. Other times, though, you may see people standing or bowing; you don't have to do this if you don't want to.

- Typically, before the Torah reading, the Torah is marched around the synagogue (an act called a *hakafah*), and people reach out, touch it with their fingers (or prayer shawl), and then kiss their fingers (or shawl). You don't have to do this; it's just a way to make contact with the central symbol of Jewish tradition. After the Torah reading, the Torah is usually lifted up and shown to the congregation (called *hagbah*).

In the past a rabbi was always a "he," but since 1972, non-Orthodox rabbis may be either "he" or "she." Although most rabbis are simply called *rabbi* (a Hebrew term conveying honor, similar to "reverend"), some Jews within the Hasidic and Renewal communities refer to their rabbis as *reb* or *rebbe*. Some people also use the Hebrew word for rabbi, which is simply *rav*.

The cantor

In a traditional synagogue, the cantor (*chazan* in Hebrew) actually leads worship services. In most other synagogues, the cantor performs solo musical prayer selections and leads community singing. The cantor leads the traditional chants for reading the Torah, as well as different musical motifs for daily, Shabbat, festival, and High Holiday worship. Cantors bring great musical and liturgical depth to the community. Many rabbinical schools offer training programs for cantors.

Although traditionally cantors, like rabbis, were all men, today women occupy cantorial positions at many synagogues.

Following Jewish Dietary Laws: A Brief Guide to Kosher Food

If we were to pick the one question about Judaism that we're asked more than anything else, it would have to be, "What's with the kosher thing?" The word *kosher* is so well known that it's become part of the common English language, meaning something that's allowed, legal, or proper. However, in Judaism, kosher almost exclusively relates to food: what Jews are and are not allowed to eat.

The Jewish dietary laws are called *kashrut*, and they're so complex that whole volumes have been written on them. However, they more or less boil down to these rules:

>> Animals with cloven hooves that chew their cud are kosher, including cattle, sheep, goats, and deer. Other mammals, like pigs, camels, and hares, aren't kosher (called *trayf*, from the Hebrew word *terayfa*, meaning "torn"). Not only are they not to be eaten, but no products which derive from them are kosher.

>> Certain procedures must be followed to ensure a humane slaughter. For example, the animal's throat must be cut by a trained ritual slaughterer (called a *shochet*), using a single slice of an extremely sharp knife that has no nicks.

» Certain parts of animals aren't kosher, such as the sciatic nerve in the hindquarters. Unfortunately, not only are these parts difficult to remove, they also include some of the choicest cuts, which is why it's rare to find kosher filet mignon, rump and sirloin steaks, leg of lamb, or London broil.

» Animals that are diseased or have physically flawed organs are trayf. When the lungs of animals are examined for irregularities, and none are found, the animal is considered *glatt* ("smooth"). If there is any question about the quality of the meat, even if it proves to be just fine (kosher), it isn't considered glatt kosher.

» Seafood is kosher as long as it has fins and scales. Shellfish like lobsters, oysters, shrimp, octopus, clams, and crabs are forbidden. Some fish, like swordfish and sturgeon, have scales that are questionable, so they're usually considered trayf.

» Domesticated fowl — chicken, turkey, quail, Cornish hens, doves, geese, duck, and pheasant — are kosher, but birds of prey (like eagles and hawks) are trayf.

» All reptiles, insects, and amphibians are trayf. Note that some food additives and colorings are made from insects, so those items are prohibited, too. (Jews make some exceptions: Shellac, which comes from the lac bug and is used to make many foods shiny, is kosher because it's considered more like a rock than a food.)

» The blood of any animal is trayf, so kosher meat (except for fish) has to be *kashered* (made kosher) by draining the blood and washing and salting the meat. ("Kosher salt" doesn't mean it's okay to eat — salt is a mineral, so all salt is kosher — ather, it's called that because it's coarse and good for kashering.) Kosher meat is always cooked well done so that no pink is left.

» The kashrut laws expand the biblical prohibition against cooking an animal in its mother's milk to eating any dairy and meat together. Jews can't put dairy foods and meat on the same plate, or even eat them during the same meal (even a tiny amount of one or the other). So, cheeseburgers — or even a regular burger with a milkshake — are out. Generally, Jews wait several hours after a meat meal (called *fleishig*) before eating dairy (called *milchig*), and vice versa. Fowl, like chicken, was once exempted from this law (because they don't give milk), but long ago, rabbis decided that you can't mix fowl and dairy either. Fish is completely exempt from this rule.

» Food that isn't meat or dairy — including every fruit, vegetable, herb, grain, fungus, nut, root, soy product, or whatever — is *pareve* (parv or *par*-ev) and is neutral. That is, you can eat it with either meat or dairy. Eggs are also pareve (though if an egg has a blood spot in it, it's considered trayf).

» Products made from grapes (juice or wine) must be monitored and authorized as kosher by a rabbi.

>> The kosher status of food can be transferred to utensils or dishes (except for glass). So traditional Jews have at least two sets of dishes — one for milk, and one for meat — as well as two or more sets of utensils, ovens, and washing bins. Because additional kosher laws apply during Passover, some families own a third (or fourth) set of dishes (or they just use paper plates that week; see Chapter 25). Fortunately, there are various ways to kasher (make kosher) metal utensils and pots.

Kashrut laws extend to any item that Jews eat, or that touches the food that Jews eat, so you might even hear about kosher aluminum foil or plastic bags that ensure that the manufacturer only used kosher organic oils in the process of pressing the foil or making the bags. Similarly, most hard cheeses contain rennet, which is often obtained from the stomach linings of non-kosher animals, making the whole cheese non-kosher.

The reasons behind kosher

Everyone loves to conjecture why or how these laws came about. For example, some people say the rules were created for health reasons — because under-cooked pork can carry disease. Ultimately, though, although traditional Jews are encouraged to ask questions in their studies, when it comes to the mitzvot (like keeping kosher), the underlying reasons are much less important than the rules themselves.

But for those of you who like reasons, here are a few possibilities to chew on. First of all, maintaining specific dietary regulations strengthens and defines the integrity of a group. A community that shares requirements for eating tends to stay together. Similarly, eating practices help identify the line between one tribe and another. For example, some scholars believe the prohibition against eating pork resulted from the desire to be different from the neighboring tribes.

Kashrut also forces Jews to be forever thoughtful of what they put into their bodies. Many meditative traditions encourage mindful eating, but Judaism turns it into a law. In this way, Jews show that humans can make choices from free will rather than catering to every desire. Kashrut is a discipline, a practice, that many Jews believe elevates eating to a religious ritual.

Jewish tradition recognizes that all life is holy, and no animal should be killed carelessly or painfully. The Torah even goes so far as to say you should never eat both a bird and her eggs (or chicks), implying that this would be too cruel. Some folks say that kashrut actually encourages Jews to become vegetarians; tradition has it that in the Messianic age — a term that means different things to different Jews — no animal or human will kill or eat another animal.

For some environmentally concerned Jews, the idea of kosher extends beyond the traditional laws, and includes a greater sense of ethical, health-conscious, and earth-friendly behavior. Such Jews ask if it's okay to eat foods with chemical additives, or food in non-recyclable packaging, or meat from animals raised in cages.

OU means OK for most

Keeping kosher is pretty easy if you're a strict vegetarian, you always eat at home, or you were brought up with these rules. Many liberal Jews don't even try to keep kosher, believing that kashrut is among the laws that are outdated in modern times. Some Jews take a middle ground, where they keep a kosher home, but have no trouble eating trayf — like cheeseburgers — in restaurants. As humorist David Bader once noted, to many Jews, "The less a piece of pork actually looks like a pig, the less you need to worry about eating it." Just witness the number of Jews who enjoy the sweet and sour pork in their Chinese takeout.

Many less traditional Jews try to keep kosher by reading ingredients printed on packaging and avoiding ingredients that would not be kosher. However, most Orthodox Jews insist that a trained rabbi, called a *mashgiakh*, supervise and certify that food is kosher. This "seal of approval" is called a *hekhsher* and typically appears as a symbol on the food's packaging. The most famous hekhsher symbols are OU or OK (an "O" with either a little "U" or "K" inside), but dozens of different symbols exist. For example, in Seattle, the local hekhsher has a little logo based on the famous Space Needle. Note that the letter "K" by itself usually means that the company itself certifies the product is kosher, but a rabbi may not have supervised.

Purifying the Spirit: Rites and Rituals

Nothing brings on transformation like a good, hard rainstorm. After the clouds pass and the sun appears, both air and land seem cleansed, and the earth is nourished once again. Water is the transformer and the giver of life, and for millennia people have used water to purify their bodies and possessions — literally, figuratively, and spiritually.

Judaism has a long tradition of caring about ritual and spiritual purity, called *taharah*, stemming from the Biblical instructions regarding priests and sacrifices (a priest had to be ritually pure to participate in the Temple service). Because everyday observance of mitzvot and worship now replace the ancient sacrifices, you need to be ritually pure to participate properly. For example, Jewish law states that being in a room with (or touching) a dead person or animal makes you ritually impure. When people become impure (*tamay*) for one reason or another, they can use a water ritual to become pure (*tahor*) once again. So, Jews often pour water from a pitcher over their hands before coming into the house of mourning after attending a burial (see Chapter 10).

Similarly, traditional Judaism states that while women are menstruating, and for seven days after they finish bleeding, they are tamay (so men and women don't touch each other during this time). When this period is finished, the women immerse themselves in a mikvah, a ritual bath composed at least in part of fresh water (tap water doesn't count as fresh). Most Jewish communities have a "public" mikvah that people can go to, but any natural spring, river, lake, or ocean will do, too.

REMEMBER

The mikvah (or the hand-washing ceremony prior to eating) isn't meant to cleanse physically; participants must be physically clean beforehand. The mikvah is meant to provide a *spiritual* cleansing. Many observant Jews, both men and women, visit a mikvah each week, before Shabbat. Jews traditionally visit the mikvah just before getting married, too.

CONTROVERSY

Many less-traditional women and men view the mikvah with suspicion because this ritual cleansing can be interpreted as "women are dirty and untouchable" after menstruation. We believe that taharah has more to do with the affirmation of life, and the mikvah is a process of being born again and re-focusing on creation. Not surprisingly, the mikvah is called for just before the woman is ovulating, and couples are reunited when the chance of pregnancy is highest. Use of the mikveh by Reform and Reconstructionist Jews is on the rise, particularly before conversions, wedding ceremonies, and even some holidays. Some liberal Jewish communities have also explored use of the mikveh for psychological healing — to help one recover from a trauma, such as rape, for example.

Dressing for God: Jewish Garments and Clothing Customs

Just as Jewish tradition involves special care respecting what you eat, tradition also provides for specific regulations regarding what you wear.

REMEMBER

Most of these rules are based on custom (*minhag*) rather than law. No Jewish law says, "Dress with a big black hat and long black coat," though some Orthodox Jews choose to do so (see Chapter 1). Some of those black hat Jews (primarily the Hasidim) also wear a *gartel* (cloth belt), especially when praying, as a reminder of the distinction between the upper and lower halves of the body, as well as the metaphorical distinction between the spiritual and physical self. Law? No. It's custom, tradition, and choice.

Similarly, some Jews like wearing a Star of David, the word *chai* ("life"), or a *mezuzah* (see the following section) on a chain as either good luck or as a reminder of their faith.

Jews are always encouraged to dress modestly in public. In Orthodox communities, this means covering the arms and legs, and in very traditional areas, women don't wear slacks.

The yarmulka

The music director of Ted's congregation, Stephen Merritt, calls the head covering he wears during worship a "kehpee cover" (*kehpee* is a Yiddish word for "head"). However, the small, flexible, round hat that Jewish men (and, increasingly, Jewish women) wear is actually called a *yarmulka* (usually sounds like *yahmuhka*) or — more common these days — *kippah* (the plural is *kippot*). The kippah (see Figure 4-2) is probably the most recognized Jewish symbol after the six-pointed Star of David.

Many traditional Jewish men keep their heads covered at all times. Less traditional Jews might cover their heads during prayer only; some liberal Jews don't use the head covering at all. However, this is one of those cases where a custom has become as important, if not even more so, than a law.

No Jewish law says that you need to wear a kippah. It probably came from an old Middle Eastern custom of covering one's head in the presence of royalty. Because God is seen as the King of Kings, the Always Present Holy One, Jews began to wear head covering at all times. You can also see wearing a *yarmulka* as one more action that draws a distinction between the spiritual, ceremonial world and the everyday world.

Today, you can find hundreds of different types of kippot, including custom knitted, leather, satin, cotton, flat, boxy, and even ones imprinted with logos or names of sports teams. Some teenage boys collect them like trading cards, and some Orthodox sects wear certain styles to show their affiliation.

REMEMBER

Wearing a kippah is a sign of respect, not faith, so there's no reason that a non-Jew can't wear one. In fact, you see non-Jewish candidates for public office wearing them every election season when they visit synagogues or Jewish community centers.

ANECDOTE

Wearing a kippah in public can be a fascinating and troublesome experience. On one recent foray while wearing a kippah, David (who almost never wears one in public) realized that it was the most blatant symbol of his religious identity that he's ever worn, and years of reading about antisemitism made him constantly wary. On the other hand, when he wandered into a Starbucks for a coffee, he ended up getting special treatment from a complete stranger behind the counter, who quietly said, "Look, you're Jewish, I'm Jewish, I'll do you a favor this once." Talk about "member of the tribe!"

Orthodox women don't wear a kippah, but they almost always cover their heads with *shaytl* (a wig) or a scarf. Some women cover their heads when in synagogue, and others do it anytime they're in public. This is very common in Middle Eastern cultures, where a woman showing her hair to anyone other than her family or husband is considered immodest. Some traditional women go so far as to shave their heads, or cut their hair very short, and wear a shaytl at all times.

FIGURE 4-2: Each morning, traditional Jewish men wear a *kippah*, a *tallit*, and *tefillin* while praying.

Fringes and shawls

The biblical Book of Numbers states that Jews must wear *tzitzit* (fringes) at the corners of their garments to help them remember God and the commandments. This biblical imperative is the basis of the Jewish prayer shawl, called a *tallit* (see

Figure 4-2), which almost all Jewish men wear at the morning shakharit service. (In more liberal congregations, women may also wear it.) Some tallit are only six or seven inches wide, like scarves, and some are wider, like small blankets, but they always have specially knotted fringes hanging from their corners.

The only time traditional Jews wear a tallit at night is Yom Kippur (see Chapter 20). Jews in more liberal congregations (especially Reform), might wear a tallit at the Friday night Shabbat service, as it's the main religious event of the week, and the leaders of the worship often wear a tallit at all services. Most Orthodox men also wear a *tallit katan* (small *tallit*) at all times under their clothes — it looks like a mix between an undershirt and a poncho with the fringes on the four corners. Many Orthodox men tuck the tzitzit into their trousers, but some men leave them hanging out at the waist so that they are visible. Rabbi Hayim Donin once wrote that wearing the tzitzit is like wearing an army uniform; when you wear one, you're very aware of your allegiances.

Jews say a special blessing when putting on a tallit (see Appendix B). You often see people wrap themselves and cover their heads with the tallit after putting it on, or at certain times of the prayer service. This is usually to deepen concentration, and some Jews say that it feels like being wrapped in the wings of God.

You shall bind them as a sign: Laying tefillin

Tefillin are two small leather boxes with compartments that contain passages from the Torah. The boxes are attached to the head and arm by leather straps (see Figure 4-2). Traditional men wear tefillin each morning, except on Shabbat, while worshiping at home or at synagogue.

Laying tefillin (putting them on) is based on a biblical law:

> And you shall love the Eternal your God with all your heart, and with all your soul, and with all your might.
>
> And these words, which I command you this day, shall be in your heart. And you shall teach them diligently to your children, and shall talk of them when you sit in your house, and when you walk by the way, and when you lie down, and when you rise up. *And you shall bind them for a sign upon your hand, and they shall be as frontlets between your eyes.* And you shall write them upon the posts of your house, and on your gates. (Deuteronomy 6:5–9; emphasis added)

Many people over the centuries have insisted that the last few instructions in this passage are figurative, like "Keep your eye on the ball (God), and make sure you follow through with your swing (your practice)." However, the ancient rabbis ruled that these words were to be taken literally. Besides, even if they weren't, wearing tefillin (also called *phylacteries*) is a very powerful physical symbol of faith and devotion. As Joseph Caro (see Chapter 28) taught, the tefillin are placed near the heart, on the head, and on the arm to symbolize that one's heart, mind, and body are all in service to God."

Jews have intricate rules for making kosher tefillin, and a set often costs hundreds of dollars. When laying tefillin, you must follow very specific procedures. If you're right-handed, you should wear it on the bicep of your left arm; if you're left-handed, it goes on the right arm. The two head straps just hang down over your shoulders with a loop loosely holding one box on your forehead, and the arm strap is carefully wrapped seven times around the arm, and then six times around your fingers in a particular pattern. Any traditional rabbi can show you how to do this.

Although it's not contrary to Jewish law, women have been traditionally discouraged (or even banned) from wearing tefillin, even though evidence suggests that some noted women have done so over the centuries. Jews are slowly becoming open to the idea of women wearing tefillin, even if it does ruffle the feathers of traditionalists.

The Jewish Home

Jewish homes are typically similar to other homes in the same neighborhood, inside and out. However, if you keep your eyes open, you may notice a few items that commonly appear in Jewish households. For example, sometimes a piece of art with the Hebrew word *mizrakh* (east) hangs on the home's east wall (facing Jerusalem), and some Jews display their seder plate in a cabinet. The Hebrew word *chai* (life) is a popular symbol in artwork, as is the *hamsa*, an inverted hand, often with an eye in the middle of the palm. The hamsa is shared with other Middle Eastern cultures and isn't exclusively Jewish.

The two most common Jewish items that you may find in a Jewish home are the *mezuzah* and the *menorah*, which we describe in the following sections.

On every doorpost: The mezuzah

A literal reading of Deuteronomy 6 (see the preceding section) says that Jews should post the words of the Sh'ma on their doorposts of their home (for details on Sh'ma, see "Sh'ma and its blessings" earlier in this chapter). A *mezuzah* is a small container that holds a piece of parchment, on which is written the Sh'ma and two other paragraphs from the books of Deuteronomy and Numbers. When you buy a mezuzah, you usually have to buy the little parchment separately (a kosher parchment must be written by hand by a trained scribe, so it can cost even more than the mezuzah).

Most folks just put a mezuzah by the entries to the front and back doors of their homes, though traditional Jews place one at about eye level in every doorway in the house, except for the bathrooms and closets. It's also the custom to place the mezuzah at an angle, inclined inward, on the right side of the doorpost as you enter. (As the story goes, the rabbis couldn't decide whether it should be vertical or horizontal, so they decided it should be at an angle to show that compromise is valued in the home.)

Jews say a special blessing when affixing a mezuzah (see Appendix B). Once it's up, they typically touch it with their fingertips, and then kiss their fingertips, each time they enter the house as a sign of reverence and remembrance.

The candelabra extraordinaire: The menorah

One of the oldest symbols of the Jewish faith, the *menorah,* was originally the candelabra (well before the invention of candles, of course) in the ancient Temple in Jerusalem. It held seven oil dishes for seven lights, three on each side of one central flame. Although this is still the basic shape of the traditional menorah, the term is often also used for candelabras that hold fewer lights.

Some Jews light a menorah on Shabbat evening; others just use it for a symbol in the house and light the more usual two candles before the Shabbat begins. Often the *Chanukkiah,* the special eight-lights-plus-a-helper-light-candelabra, is referred to as a *Chanukkah menorah* (see Chapter 22).

So Go Now and Live

While antisemites have long used the verb *to Jew* as an insult, we think that the word *Jew* can be verbed in a different way, reflecting a Jewish way of living. Traditional practice is certainly a major part of such "Jew-ing," but it doesn't end there. All Jewish practice is aimed at affirming the One Being Who connects all life with Blessing, Compassion, Justice, and Love. The ultimate goal of Judaism is to awaken to a greater awareness of that One Being.

Chapter 5
Jewish Mysticism

M any Jews — even those who have learned the basic rules and regulations of Judaism, along with matters of ritual, practice, and history — still feel that something is missing, something that has to do with the deeper spirit that may seem totally invisible behind such outer teachings.

Many Jews have gotten so frustrated with this missing sense of spirit that they have given up practicing Judaism, often looking to other faiths, such as Buddhism with its meditative practices. Some Jews find the deeper spirit after years of deep, intellectual study of Torah and Talmud. Others awaken to the spirit of Judaism through social action and a life based on Jewish morality and ethics. For us, the key that unlocked the door is Jewish mysticism. We don't think that this path is for everyone, but for those who seek a deeper feeling of connectedness with God, Jewish mysticism lies at the very heart of Jewish spirituality and what it means to be Jewish.

Delving Into Jewish Mysticism

Mysticism focuses on the immediate personal encounter with a Greater Reality, a Reality beyond that which can be talked about or understood rationally. Some folks talk about this shift in awareness as "seeing God," "touching God," or "attaining God-consciousness." In the Jewish mystical tradition, this realization is generally called *devakut* (deh-vay-*koot*), which means "joining or unifying with

God." Some mystics are more interested in attempting to understand this Greater Reality, and some are drawn to finding fuller ways to experience It.

Does this sound like some bad stereotype of a flaky San Francisco hippie scene to you? Well, Jewish mysticism isn't from the 1960s. The practice is at least 2,000 years old, and you can find mystical traditions not just in Judaism, but in Christianity, Islam, and most other world religions. Some say that mysticism links the deeper truths of all the major religions.

What mystics tend to believe

For the mystic, there is always more. The universe, the mystics say, has many levels, and people typically experience only the surface. Like the layers of an onion, each level of reality, although real in itself, has a deeper level within it. Or, you can turn the onion model inside out: If the center of the onion is everyday reality, then going higher means transcending from one level to the next, each one surrounding and containing the last. The mystic meets more profound levels of reality than that which people usually experience. What appears real to our limited senses is simply a façade behind which mysteries of greater and greater significance are waiting to be met.

Mystics through the ages seem to share a common vision: that at the deepest, most inclusive level there is only one One, and we are all part of that One. The Jewish mystic's goal is to know that One, to better understand the words of the Sh'ma (see Appendix B) when it proclaims, "God is One." Mystics also tend to capitalize many of the words they use!

The Kabbalah

Jewish mystics experience and express the Universal Awareness through Jewish identity, culture, language, and symbols. The general term for the tradition at the heart of Jewish mysticism is *kabbalah*, which literally means "that which is received."

For well over 1,500 years the kabbalah was transmitted through teachers meeting with small groups of students. Because the ideas of the kabbalah represented a threat to established religious thought, the study groups often met secretly.

Despite the fact that kabbalistic teachings had been, until recently, reserved for the few, the extent of their influence on the whole of Jewish belief is remarkable. Modern-day Orthodox prayer books contain many passages written by teachers of Jewish mysticism.

GIVE ME A K, GIVE ME A Q . . .

The word "kabbalah" is Hebrew, and it is variously written in English as Kabbalah, Qabbalah, Cabbalah, or Cabala. Although the various spellings illustrate some of the basic difficulties in translating from Hebrew to English, these particular differences hold more meaning. When written "Kabbalah," the reference is almost always to the Jewish mystical tradition and to Jewish writings. When written "Qabbalah," or "Qabalah," the reference is usually to a Christian or other non-Jewish use of some of the basic teachings of the Jewish mystics. When written "Cabbalah," or "Cabalah," the reference can be either Jewish or Christian ("Cabala" is actually the required spelling at the Library of Congress). Some people are surprised that many Christians have an interest in the Jewish mystical tradition, too. In fact, during the Middle Ages, some of those who most awaited the publication of kabbalistic texts were leaders in the Catholic Church.

The kabbalah represents an approach to the study of text, to the performance of ritual, to the practice of acts in the world, and to the experience of worship. The kabbalist reads the same basic Jewish texts and practices the same basic Jewish rituals, but in a very different way. Kabbalistic literature focuses on interpreting traditional Jewish texts, revealing the deeper teachings they contain.

Kabbalists have long explored a host of ideas and practices that most people are surprised to hear in a Jewish context: meditation, reincarnation, belief in angels and demons, praying alone in nature, and, of course, devakut (God-realization). In fact, you can discern a number of differences between traditional, organized Judaism and a more mystical approach, including the following:

>> **No separation between person and God:** The majority of Jews tend to see God as a separate entity, outside the physical universe, or as the Life force within the universe. For them, Judaism is primarily a moral framework, describing God as the king or parent and people as the subjects or children. However, for the Jewish mystic, God is not only the Ultimate Transcendent Being but also the Ultimate Immanent Being. Jewish mystics see no separation between person and God. Jews with a more mystical inclination tend to say that there is nothing but God: Everything is God.

>> **Our actions affect God:** For the traditional, rational Jew, God affects humankind, but is beyond being affected by persons. For the mystic, the relationship between God and human is far more intimate. The relationship is a transaction in which both are always affected. Everything is connected, say the mystics, and every action, thought, or word resonates throughout the universe. The Jewish mystic feels a deep responsibility for creation itself.

>> **Fulfilling the mitzvot perpetuates Creation**: In traditional Judaism, the mitzvot, or commandments (see Chapter 4), are to be fulfilled because they

express the Will of God. For the Jewish mystic, the significance of the mitzvot is radically different: the mitzvot provide precious avenues through which Jews participate in a cosmic process of continuing and completing Creation itself. The commandments are what men and women can do (and not do) in order to ensure the perpetuation of the Universe.

>> **Spirituality comes from within:** Traditionally, Judaism tends to see Spirit coming from outside people and teaches that a person called the Messiah will come to redeem humanity. Mysticism tends to see spirituality and redemption awakening from the inside out and perceives the Messianic Consciousness awakening within each person.

Taking a Magical Mystical Tour

During the nineteenth and early 20th century, Jewish mysticism was little more than a footnote in the midst of a deluge of rational thought. However, as people began to explore and celebrate their own mystical experiences, scholars started translating mystical texts, funding research into mysticism's history, and finding that — lo and behold — Jewish mysticism has a long, deep tradition. Scholars have found documented, authentic mystical traditions within Judaism going back 2,000 years. Among the people who have brought these texts to the surface are Aryeh Kaplan (an Orthodox rabbi who began translating some of the ancient mystical texts in the mid-1980s), Rav Kook (see Chapter 28), and Adin Steinsaltz (considered one of the greatest Talmudic scholars alive today).

Early mystical texts

No one really knows how kabbalah began or who wrote the early books that defined kabbalistic philosophy. Although you can find a few references to mysticism and mystical experiences in the Hebrew Bible, the first known text that is clearly based on Jewish mysticism appeared in the early centuries of the Common Era (CE, what is called AD by the Christian world).

The earliest mystical movements of the first century BCE and the first two centuries CE were broadly known as the *Maaseh Merkavah* ("The Workings of the Chariot") and *Maaseh Bereshit* ("The Workings of Creation"). Bereshit mysticism primarily explored the images from the book of Genesis. Merkavah mysticism focused largely on the prophet Ezekiel's image of the chariot (Ezekiel 1:1–3:27) and was characterized by meditative visualization of a chariot drawn by four mythical beings, each with four faces and four wings, glowing and surrounded by fire and lightning.

Imagine focusing on that fearsome image for an extended time in meditation! If you do, you may see why such practices proved unpopular with a large number of people.

Hechalot (Palace) mysticism, which focuses on images of various chambers of a heavenly palace, also encouraged visualization meditations as avenues to the transcendence of ordinary states of consciousness.

Those early forms of Jewish mystical exploration laid the groundwork for the three most important books in the development of Jewish mysticism, the *Sefer Yetzirah*, the *Sefer Ha-Bahir*, and, most importantly, the *Zohar*.

Sefer Yetzirah

Although the author of the *Sefer Yetzirah* ("Book of Formation") is unknown, the book probably originated sometime between the second and sixth centuries. This very short book focuses on the mystical energies of the 22 letters of the Hebrew alphabet and the ten *sefirot* (levels of awareness or levels of reality; pronounced seh-fee-*roat*; see the "Following Maps to Understanding: The Images and Symbols" section later in this chapter). Together, the ten sefirot and the 22 letters form the 32 "paths of holiness." In this mostly enigmatic book, these paths are related to physical and emotional states as well as to astrology.

The *Sefer Yetzirah* is in many ways the backbone of kabbalah. Many commentaries written on the *Sefer Yetzirah* see it as a meditative manual, providing instruction on ways to use the letters and the sefirot in meditation.

Sefer Ha-Bahir

The *Sefer Ha-Bahir* ("Book of Illumination") appeared in the 12th century in France. *Sefer Ha-Bahir* further advances the basic teachings of the ten sefirot, explores some of the letters of the Hebrew alphabet, and looks into the mysteries of the soul.

The authorship of this text is uncertain, but the work has been attributed to Rabbi Nehunia ben HaKana, a mystical teacher in the first century. Although longer than the *Sefer Yetzirah*, the *Sefer Ha-Bahir* is also a relatively short book of about 12,000 words. The text identifies itself with the *Maaseh Merkavah* tradition. The *Sefer Ha-Bahir* became the basic kabbalistic text until the appearance of the *Zohar*.

Zohar

Without a doubt, the most important book to Jewish mystics is the *Zohar* ("Brilliance" or "Splendor"), which first appeared in Spain during the 13th century. This multivolume work consists mainly of mystical commentaries on the Torah, although it also includes a number of other narratives.

The Jewish mystic relies on the same texts that Jews have always seen as central to their faith. However, the mystic finds hidden layers and deeper levels of meaning in those texts. The mystical commentaries of the *Zohar* probe mystical teachings through the ancient words of Torah (see Chapter 3).

Rabbi Shimon bar Yochai, a great second-century sage, appears as the major character throughout the *Zohar*, almost like the mythical Don Juan in the popular Carlos Castaneda books. For Shimon bar Yochai, the stories and narratives of the Torah are seen as the outer layer of meaning, like the clothes a person wears. And just as the soul is within or behind the visible body, so, too, the Soul of the Torah resides behind both the surface stories and the deeper content. The Torah is seen as a document of many levels to be discovered and appreciated.

The *Zohar*'s allegorical and metaphorical approach to Torah leads to more fanciful descriptions of the ten sefirot and their relationship to traditional motifs. The *Zohar* sets the stage for the further evolution of the Jewish mystical tradition.

Isaac Luria, Safed's sage

The *Zohar* emerged as the central text of Jewish mysticism in the 13th century. A few centuries later the central personality of Jewish mysticism appeared.

Few people can express such an explosion of energy and insight that they draw others toward them. When Rabbi Isaac Luria became a teacher in Safed in 1571, he had that kind of impact on the people around him.

At the time, Safed, a small town in Galilee in northern Israel, was already a center for kabbalistic studies as well as brilliant traditional rabbinic pursuits. When Luria became part of Safed's rich intellectual and spiritual climate, his students gave him the name *Elohi Rabbi Yitzchak* ("The Godly Rabbi Isaac"). The name was then shortened to the initials ARI, which forms the Hebrew word meaning "lion." Rabbi Isaac Luria became known as The Holy Ari, the Holy Lion of the Kabbalah.

The Ari used metaphors to explain his often extremely complex visions of God and the universe.

Tsimtsum

One of the Ari's central images has to do with a process he called *tsimtsum*, the "contraction" of God that allows room for the universe to exist. Imagine this: At the beginning, the Holy Presence is all there is, and there's no room for anything else to be. So after allowing the universe to exist, God must contract into God's Self in order to create a space. Now, God can't totally be absent from such a space, so the *reshimu* ("residue") of God persists even in the "empty" space.

Luria's teaching responds to some of the most long-standing religious questions: If there is a God, how can the world of human experience persist? If there is a God, how can evil exist? Why is there pain, suffering, violence, and hatred? The captivating image of God's withdrawal, by definition, makes room for both evil and good.

Sparks and shells

The second brilliant image Luria introduced was that of sparks and shells. In this metaphor, God attempted to make a perfect universe as though God were an artist pouring liquid gold into molds that had been prepared to receive it. But the gold was primordial Divine Light and proved too powerful for the vessels, most of which shattered, showering the unformed universe with sparks. This is the *shevirat ha-kelim*, the "breaking of the vessels," which Luria said was the primary "accident" at the heart of creation itself.

The sparks (*netzutzot*) became encased in *k'lipot* ("shells" or "husks") of the material world. In this way, God's Divine Light became hidden in the everyday world. Luria taught that the mitzvot (see Chapter 4) liberate and reunite the sparks with their Source. Suddenly, the observance of the ancient principles of Jewish life — matters not only of ritual but of compassionate action — were raised to the status of healing Creation itself. (This is called *tikkun olam* — the healing of the world.)

Kavvanah

The Holy Ari introduced an elaborate set of *kavvanot* ("intentions") that he said should precede ritual acts like putting on the *tallit* ("prayer shawl;" see Chapter 4) and the recitation of prayers. Saying or thinking a kavvanah is meant to inspire one-pointedness of attention, so that both the act and word become a type of meditation. Setting a kavvanah, Luria explained, makes possible the piercing of the husks to liberate the Sparks of Divinity.

Some of the Ari's kavvanot are preserved in traditional prayer books even today. In the blessings for putting on a tallit in the morning, some prayer books include the kavvanah affirming that this act be done with such focus, with such concentration, and with such fullness, that it is as though you had actually fulfilled every one of the 613 commandments (see Chapter 4).

Luria changed kabbalah almost to the degree that the publication of the *Zohar* changed kabbalah. But in the complex and difficult times following his death, his teachings took a strange turn for some followers. Jewish communities in 17th-century Eastern Europe suffered a series of terrible attacks in which over 100,000 Jews were murdered and countless more were terrorized and maimed (see Chapter 15 for more information). These attacks and others that followed sowed the seeds for the rise of two other fascinating personalities in the history of Judaism: Shabbetai Tzvi and Rabbi Israel ben Eliezer, otherwise known as the Ba'al Shem Tov.

FOR THE SAKE OF UNIFICATION

The Holy Ari taught that the intentions with which you perform any act, particularly any ritual act, are of great consequence. What might be called Luria's Great Kavvanah, the Great Intention, dedicates the act about to be performed to the service of unification of that which has become separated, affirming that all Being is One, all people are One, that the Inner Presence (*Shekhinah*) and the Transcendent (*HaKadosh Baruch Hu*) are One. Living with kavvanah is intentional living, dedicating our acts to support a greater healing.

You can experiment with the power of a kavvanah, intentionality, by consciously dedicating your day to the realization of a goal that is important to you. In the morning, take time to identify that goal, imagine how it would feel, and dedicate your day to honoring that intention.

The promise of living with kavvanah is the realization of the holiness of all beings, which is another way of talking about liberating the Sparks of the Divine that are contained, and sometimes deeply hidden, within all things and people.

Israel ben Eliezer, the good master

The humble 18th century teacher Rabbi Israel ben Eliezer (1700–1760) was so loved, and had such an ability to help people heal, that he quickly became known as the *Ba'al Shem Tov* ("Good Master of the Name" or "Master of the Good Name," also called by the acronym *Besht*; see Chapter 28).

Rabbi Israel taught a Way of deep joy, encouraging forms of worship that included music and dance. Even more radically, the Ba'al Shem Tov believed that this spiritual rejoicing was available to every Jew, even if he wasn't highly educated. He opened the doors of the kabbalah to the masses and created both followers (the *Hasidim*) and resisters (the *Mitnagdim*, or "the Opponents").

The Mitnagdim weren't necessarily anti-mystical (their leader, the Vilna Gaon, wrote more on the subject of kabbalah than almost anyone). Like the Establishment's fury against the hippies in the 1960s, the Mitnagdim staunchly opposed Besht's anti-intellectual message and perhaps, remembering the betrayals of the Shabbetai Tzvi drama, feared this healer who drew people around him with similarly intense fervor. The antagonism between these groups grew so fierce that authorities of the Midnagid community tried to have teachers within the Hasidic community arrested.

While the kabbalah had previously been entrusted to relatively small enclaves, the Ba'al Shem Tov and his followers made these teachings available for the entire community, leading the way for a true rebirth of the kabbalah. Even today, his influence is felt in most aspects of Judaism, from Orthodoxy all the way to Reform (see Chapter 1). The Hasidic teaching focused on devakut, a state of being in which an individual is released from the confines of the ego identity, usually through ecstatic worship, and is able to experience "God-consciousness." The Ba'al Shem emphasized the involvement of the heart in prayer, rather than simply the intellect, and encouraged living with kavvanah, with a joyful holy intentionality.

The Ba'al Shem Tov also taught that the Divine Presence (*Shekhinah*) was to be found everywhere and in everything. Even in evil there exists a Divine spark that can be liberated, a topic that continues to be controversial. But for Rabbi Israel, the teaching meant that God's Presence couldn't be denied, and that all of life had the potential to be elevated to its essential holiness.

While every Jew could practice and experience *devakut*, the Besht also taught that holy teachers are required to fully complete *tikkun olam*, liberating the sparks of Divinity which have gone astray in this world. Those special teachers took the form of the *tzaddik* ("righteous one") and the *rebbe* (the Hasidic word for "rabbi"). If you're familiar with Eastern philosophy, you can think of the tzaddik as a "guru" — a person whose connection to Divinity is strong enough to help others along the way. A Hasidic rebbe emphasizes personal connection, a healing presence, and a joyful energy, as opposed to the Mitnagid image of the rabbi as an interpreter of Jewish texts.

Going Above and Beyond: Jewish Meditation

Mysticism in general, and kabbalah in particular, are among the most difficult aspects of Judaism to talk about. They just can't be truly understood through written or spoken words alone. For thousands of years, the primary path to achieving a true understanding has been meditation.

Meditation — sitting alone or in a group, relaxing, quietly breathing — is the exact opposite of most Jewish study, which is typically community-based, loud, and even argumentative. Many people are surprised to discover that Judaism, just like every other major religious tradition, has a long (but often hidden) history of meditation.

The Hebrew word for meditation is *hitbodedut*, which literally means "being alone with oneself" and is almost a definition in itself of the meditative process. In meditation, an altered state of consciousness is encouraged to slow down the rambling meanderings of the mind and to move beyond the boundaries of ordinary perception. This process enables the individual to embrace a more inclusive identity, realizing a connectedness to all life.

DO TRY THIS AT HOME

Rabbi Nachman of Bratslav (1772–1811) encouraged all Jews to create a space dedicated to meditative practice in their homes. A separate room is best, he said, but a corner of a room can suffice. If nothing else, Nachman counseled that you can create a private space by wrapping yourself in a tallit (prayer shawl). Once you have a private, quiet space, try these two simple meditations (one at a time, of course).

The first is based on a *mantra*, a word or phrase that you say out loud or in your head repeatedly in an attempt to free your mind. Jewish mantras use Jewish words or phrases. You can pick a verse from the Bible (like Psalms 16:8, *Shiviti Adonai l'neg'di tamid* — "I set the Eternal before me always"), or — best for beginners — just a word, such as *Shalom* ("Peace") or *Ahavah* ("Love").

Before you start the mantra, be quiet for a few minutes, focusing on your breath. Even though your mind may zoom all over the place, just keep nudging yourself back to your breath. Then, each time you breath in or out, mentally say the mantra, drawing out the word to fill the length of the breath. No matter what thoughts pop into your head, just keep going back to the mantra. Your period of meditation might take five minutes, or it might take a half-hour or more. At the end, release your focus on the mantra, return to the breath, and take a moment simply to be aware. As you open your eyes, you might notice you are calmer and more "present" than before your meditation.

The second meditation encourages you to focus on something visual, which could be a candle flame, a written word, or any of the Hebrew letters. In Jewish mysticism, each Hebrew letter is seen as a unique vehicle through which a universal energy flows toward the earth, and each carries its particular resonance or vibration. After getting quiet and watching your breath, open your eyes and look at the object you have chosen. Study it carefully until you can close your eyes and see it in your mind's eye, and then hold it there, breathing, *being* with the symbol. Focus on the object behind closed eyes for between 5 and 20 minutes. See it fill with light. When you are done, slowly open your eyes and conclude the meditation.

Of course, how you get to that place varies. Pretty much every meditative practice involves your breath — either focusing on it or altering it — but Jewish meditation goes further, using Jewish symbols, imagery, or Hebrew text in the meditation, too.

For example, one practice is to concentrate on one of the names of God (see the "Following Maps to Understanding: The Images and Symbols" section later in this chapter), visualizing the Hebrew letters that make up the name. We include two more basic Jewish meditations that you can explore in the sidebar "Do try this at home."

Ultimately, your success with meditation is based on a willingness to transcend ordinary perceptions of yourself and the world and risk a more holistic relationship with the universe.

Here are a few things to think about when starting to meditate and focus on Jewish mystical practices:

>> If you're not used to thinking in a non-linear, intuitive fashion, it may feel really weird to you at first. Remember that mysticism is a lot like poetry: You can find meaning behind everything, even when at first it seems totally obscure. Like appreciating poetry, you need to learn enough to understand the context, and you need an expansive mind that allows ideas to float in and out freely.

>> Try a fun mystical game called "That's God" to heighten your spiritual awareness. Each day, look carefully at each person you see on the street (or each animal, or thing on your desk, or whatever) and say to yourself, "Hey, that's part of God, too." When you recognize that every person and thing around you is a different facet of One Being, and you can keep that in your heart, then you're winning the game.

Following Maps to Understanding: The Images and Symbols

When you travel to somewhere you've never been before, you consult a map to figure out how to get from Point A to Point B. Maps use symbols to plant an image of a path in the mind. Kabbalah uses maps, too, to indicate the nature of consciousness and the nature of reality. Maps are necessary tools, but, as one of Ted's teachers, Alfred Korzybsky, wisely wrote, it is crucial to remember that "The map is not the territory."

Jewish mysticism uses three basic "maps": The Tree of Life, the Four Worlds, and the Five Levels of Soul. These maps use symbols and ideas that are extremely difficult to pin down, and teachers often disagree on their meanings. It's as if one person says, "The blue line on this map indicates a river you can float down," and someone else says, "No, that blue line indicates a crevasse that you might fall into." The amazing thing about mystical maps is that both answers may be correct.

The Tree of Life

The most famous kabbalistic symbol, the *Eitz Chayim* ("Tree of Life") represents the spectrum of reality between everyday ho-hum reality and the all-embracing

Reality of Absolute Oneness (see Figure 5-1). This idea isn't unique to Judaism; every spiritual tradition maps out such a spectrum, which philosopher Ken Wilber identifies as "the Great Chain of Being" reflected in teachings from all the world's great religions. But the Tree of Life is a central way that Jewish mystics try to understand these levels of being.

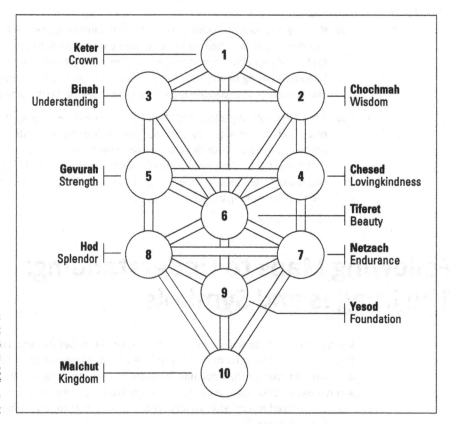

FIGURE 5-1:
The kabbalistic Tree of Life helps mystics explain the underlying dimensions of the universe and spirit

Although it's called the Tree of Life, the diagram really doesn't look much like a tree at all. The Tree of Life is made up of ten circles to indicate the sefirot (levels of awareness or levels of reality) to illustrate this chain of Being (see the following section). The ten circles (each one is called a *sefirah*, pronounced seh-fee-*rah*) are arranged in three columns, or pillars; three *sefirot* are represented in each outer column and four in the center column.

Sefirah literally means "a counting," and comes from around the third century CE when the layers of reality were represented by the numbers from one to ten. Later on, the sefirot were represented as circles within circles, representing the nested nature of the levels of reality. And still later (around the 11th century), the sefirot took on the form called the Tree of Life.

The pillar on the right represents the energies of force, expansion, and expression. Some call this the Pillar of Mercy, describing the constant gift of energy. The pillar on the left contains the sefirot that give form to and actualize the energy received from the right side. The left side is called the Pillar of Severity and represents limitation, constriction, and strength. The four central sefirot comprise the Pillar of Balance between the left and right sides, and they represent the levels of identity, from the most expansive at the top to the most contracted at the bottom.

The right pillar is like a person who can't stop working, but never really completes anything; the left pillar is like the person who holds onto a completed project and won't let it go, so nothing else is possible. Obviously, neither of those pillars (or persons) alone can manage; they need the balance provided by the central pillar in order to complete each other. Through the central pillar, the energy can flow from project to project productively.

Paradoxically, the roots of the Tree are at the top of the diagram, and the flowering is at the bottom. The roots connect the Tree to the all-encompassing Reality Beyond Being, and the Tree portrays the flow of Life that finally manifests as everyday world reality.

The Tree of Life describes stages along a path to awareness. Each step on the path to understanding is whole and true, but each has far fuller meaning when seen from a higher perspective. To illustrate this point, think about focusing on each letter in this book. The letters are gibberish until you take a step back and see that they clump together to form words, sentences, paragraphs, chapters, and so on.

Similarly, the Tree of Life maps out a path of energy and awareness. The path from the top sefirah down to the bottom — sometimes called the Path of Creation — describes the process of moving from "nothing" to "something." We like to think of the sefirot on this path as a series of electrical transformers: Just as our homes couldn't receive the flow of electricity directly from a massive power generator, each sefirah limits the flow that it receives from the prior sefirah to render that energy bearable for the next. The energy flows downward in a zigzag path called the "lightning flash," moving through the sefirot according to how they are numbered, from one to ten.

The path from the bottom up is sometimes called the Path of Awakening, describing the spiritual journey beginning with immersion in the physical world and journeying upward (or inward) toward greater inclusiveness and less separation. Think of the Path of Awakening this way: at each step up the Tree you let go of the limiting forms of the body, of the mind, and of a separate sense of self.

The Tree describes the *path* to God, but doesn't describe God. As we explore in the following section, the uppermost sefirah reaches toward the Unknowable Eternal.

We like to think of it as though the Tree offers a path through multiple levels of reality, each of which is simply a reflection of something far greater and more inclusive.

But the Tree doesn't merely explain a giant cosmic process. One of the most important kabbalistic principles points to the absolute interconnectedness and unity of all that is. In the kabbalah, the Tree describes every aspect of the universe, so it's sometimes applied as a map of the cosmos, sometimes as a map of consciousness, and at other times as a map of the nature of a human being.

The ten sefirot

The sefirot are seen as "emanations," or perhaps "stages" in the unfolding of Creation. Each sefirah reflects a characteristic quality or facet of the One Energy. Besides the general characteristics of each sefirah, teachers of the kabbalah have traditionally attributed a name of God, one of the major biblical characters, and even a part of the body to each sefirah.

The name of God associated with each sefirah serves as a focus for meditation (one can meditate on each of the names) as well as a way to understand that God is reflected on all possible levels of manifestation (see Chapter 2). Associating a biblical character with each sefirah allows the kabbalists to see the stories of the Bible as teachings about the hidden dimensions of reality.

And imagining the sefirot connected with parts of the human body provides a way to understand the biblical statement that people are created "in the image of God." The connection between the sefirot and the body reflects the kabbalistic teaching that each person connects heaven and earth — people walk on the earth but their heads (consciousness) reach to the Infinite.

Here's a short description of each sefirah:

» **Keter:** The highest of the sefirot is called Keter ("crown," pronounced *keh*-tair). Keter is the link between the Absolutely Infinite and the finite, and marks the transition between non-being and being. Keter is imagined at the crown of the head with the name of God being *Eheyeh Asher Eheyeh* ("I Am as I Am").

» **Chokhmah:** The second *sefirah* is *Chokhmah* ("wisdom," pronounced khokh-*mah*). This is the first *sefirah* on the right side of the Tree, the side representing force (in contrast to the form-giving nature of the left side of the Tree). *Chokhmah* represents the emergence of mental energy before it is contained within any idea, thought, or plan. *Chokhmah* is placed at the right hemisphere of the brain. The name of God associated with *Chokhmah* is "Yah" (as in *Halleluyah*, "praise be to the Eternal").

>> **Binah:** Binah ("understanding," pronounced *bee*-nah) is the third sefirah, the first on the left side of the Tree of Life. Binah is the sefirah where specific ideas and thoughts take form, containing the energy received from Chokhmah. Binah is placed at the left hemisphere of the brain. The name of God here is pronounced *Elohim* but spelled with the Hebrew letters of the Tetragrammaton (the four-letter Name of God, YHVH; see Chapter 2).

>> **Chesed:** The fourth *sefirah, Chesed* ("lovingkindness," pronounced *kheh*-sed), signifies unconditional giving, the unlimited outpouring of an energy which might be called "emotion" before it is made specific as a particular feeling. Here, this energy simply flows freely without reservation, an ongoing gift of grace, so the *sefirah* represents Mercy. *Chesed* is imagined at the right shoulder (or right arm). The name of God here is *El* ("God"). Beginning with *Chesed*, each *sefirah* is seen as a representation of a biblical character; *Chesed* is identified with Abraham.

>> **Gevurah:** Gevurah ("strength," pronounced geh-voo-*rah*), sometimes called *Din* ("judgment"), is the fifth sefirah; it provides the forms that restrain and restrict the flow received from *Chesed*. If *Chesed* represents emotion, *Gevurah* provides the forms called "feelings" which contain and limit the undefined emotional energy offered by *Chesed*. This sefirah represents judgment. Gevurah is associated with the left shoulder or left arm, and the name of God here is *Elohim* ("God"). Gevurah is associated with Abraham's son, Isaac.

>> **Tiferet:** Tiferet ("beauty," pronounced tee-*fair*-reht) is the sixth *sefirah*, representing the balance required between the energies of *Chesed* and *Gevurah*. If *Chesed* were to flow unrestricted, there could be no order or meaning in the universe. If Gevurah were to simply limit, the expansion of the universe would cease. So Tiferet's role as the harmonizer between justice and mercy is essential to the ongoing cosmic process of creation. Tiferet represents our Higher Self, a greater identity through which we are able to love unconditionally. Tiferet is seen in the center of the chest (at the level of the heart), and the name of God is "YHVH" ("Eternal," pronounced ah-doh-*nai*). Jacob is the biblical character associated with Tiferet.

>> **Netzakh:** The seventh sefirah, Netzakh ("victory" or "endurance," pronounced *neh*-tzakh), sits on the right side of the Tree, the side of force, and represents the energy that fills each sensation. Netzakh is understood as the force behind physical expression. It's associated with the right side of your solar plexus (some say the right leg) and is symbolized by the divine name *Adonai Tzeva-ot* ("Eternal One of Hosts," pronounced ah-doh-*nai* tzeh-vah-*ot*). Netzakh is related to the prophet Moses.

>> **Hod:** Hod ("splendor" or "glory"), the eighth sefirah, represents the forms of physical experience, the forms of sensation — the images, touches, sounds, tastes, and smells that people perceive. Each sensory perception can be understood as a container in which to experience the greater formless

energies of Netzakh. Hod is seen at the left side of your solar plexus (or the left leg), and the name of God is *Elohim Tzeva-ot* ("God of Hosts," pronounced eh-lo-*heem* tzeh-vah-ot). Aaron is the biblical character associated with Hod.

>> **Yesod:** Yesod ("foundation"), the ninth sefirah, balances the energies of Netzakh and Hod and provides the channel through which all the energies from higher levels of the Tree flow into the final sefirah. Yesod represents the level of individual identity called the personality, or the ego. At Yesod, you discover the "I" in the storm, the "I" that struggles to find security and safety, and also the identity with which you can most effectively act in the world. Yesod is imagined just above or at the genitals. The name of God is *Shaddai* ("God Almighty") or *El Chai,* ("Living God") and the biblical character is Joseph.

>> **Malkhut:** The tenth and final sefirah receives the flow of energy from all of the other nine and is called Malkhut ("kingdom" or "sovereignty"). Malkhut is the everyday world. This sefirah is imagined either at the base of the spine or at the feet. The name of God here is spelled and pronounced *Adonai,* ("Lord"), and David is the biblical character associated with Malkhut.

Beyond the highest sefirah on the Tree of Life is *Ayn Sof* ("Without End") — the fullness of God beyond any manifestation whatsoever. This is the Source of all that is, absolutely without image, name, or quality.

In some descriptions of the Tree, you'll find a quasi-sefirah added beneath Chokhmah and Binah called *Da'at* ("knowledge"). Those who map the Tree on to the human form locate da'at directly at the "third eye" in the middle of the forehead. Note that the name of the international Jewish group Chabad is actually an acronym of the words chokhma, binah, and da'at.

The literature of the kabbalah offers a second way to understand the sefirot. In this alternative view, the lower seven sefirot are called *midot* ("qualities"), and are representative of the qualities of being that people experience and that must be understood and balanced in life. The upper three sefirot are referred to as *mochin* ("brain") and relate to mental processes rather than qualities (that's why they don't have corresponding Biblical characters in the earlier descriptions).

The top three sefirot — Keter, Chokhmah, and Binah — relate to the mental processes of initial creative impulse, intuition, and idea. The lower seven sefirot represent qualities, so there are both positive as well as negative aspects. Chesed represents generosity, and its negative side is "smother love." Gevurah is associated with the quality of strength, and its other side is tyranny. Tiferet stands for compassion, and too much compassion is indulgence. Netzakh is endurance, which carries the negative possibility of not knowing when to stop. Hod relates to truthfulness, and too much truthfulness can become hurtful bluntness. Yesod relates to interdependence, which sometimes slips into codependence, and Malkhut is associated with leadership, which can become too controlling.

WORDS, LETTERS, NUMBERS, AND CODES

Mysticism explores the esoteric and the mysterious. Kabbalists have long looked for hidden meanings behind the holy words and letters that make up the Torah. Because numbers in Hebrew can be represented by letters of the alphabet, you can convert letters into numbers (a practice called *gematria*). If you convert all the letters of a word into numbers, and then add the numbers together, you get another number, which kabbalists have traditionally looked to for deeper meaning.

For example, the gematria of the words *Ahavah* ("love") and *Echad* ("one") both equal 13, indicating a special relationship between them. Then if you add 13 and 13, you get 26, which is the gematria for the Tetragrammaton (the four-letter Name of God, YHVH; see Chapter 2). While some would say these are just coincidences, the kabbalist tends to take them very seriously and ponder their significance. Similarly, because the word for ladder (*sullam*) and the word *Sinai* both equal 130, some rabbis say that the Torah that was given at Sinai is like Jacob's ladder connecting earth and heaven.

The problem is that some folks tend to go overboard, insisting that hidden messages and codes in the Torah prove conclusively that only God could have put them there. After the author of a popular book expounding on this topic challenged skeptical scientists to come up with similar prophetic messages in any other text, several mathematicians fed the complete text of Melville's *Moby Dick* into a computer and spit out virtually identical prophecies and codes. We're not saying that there aren't hidden messages within scriptural texts; we're just suggesting that a dose of skepticism is probably healthy.

Looked at this way, the Tree becomes a model for human actions, teaching how people can remain balanced and productive. Whether used as a model for the spiritual adventure or for the way of living a balanced life on earth, the Tree offers deep insights to support growth.

After the ten sefirot were symbolized in the pattern known as the Tree of Life, 22 paths connecting them were identified (see Figure 5-1), corresponding to the number of letters in the Hebrew alphabet. This allowed an even deeper consideration of the various nuances of energy transmitted among the sefirot.

The Four Worlds

The second major "map" in Jewish mysticism describes the Four Worlds, another way of understanding the spectrum of consciousness or spirit, from the everyday physical realm to the unknowable *Ain Sof* ("Without End"). Each of the four worlds represents a stage, or quality, on this spectrum.

Although the Tree of Life and the Four Worlds are related, different teachers interpret this relationship differently. While most kabbalists identify each world with a part of the single Tree of Life, Isaac Luria (see the section "Isaac Luria, Safed's sage" earlier in this chapter) envisioned an entire Tree of Life in each of the Four Worlds. Here is a description of the four worlds as part of a single Tree of Life:

>> **Atzilut:** The first World is called Atzilut ("emanation," pronounced ah-tzee-*lut*) and is closest to the Infinite. This World can't be known directly. Atzilut is represented on the Tree by the first two sefirot, Keter and Chokhmah, and is often associated with mental processes like inspiration or "ideas in the mind of God"

>> **Beriah:** Beriah ("creation," pronounced b'ree-*ah*) is the second World, which is knowable only through visionary experiences from the most profound levels of meditation. Beriah is associated with the third sefirah, Binah and, therefore, can be identified with the mental forms or images of creation. Some folks see Beriah as a nourishing World where ideas begin to take shape.

>> **Yetzirah:** The World of Yetzirah ("formation," yeh-tzee-*rah*) contains the next six sefirot, from Chesed through Yesod, and represents the formation of the reality that manifests in the fourth and final World.

>> **Assiyah:** Assiyah ("action" or "doing," ah-see-*yah*) represents the physical universe of space and time, of energy and matter, of all that is available to experience. This world represents ordinary reality. On the Tree of Life, Assiyah is represented by the final sefirah, Malkhut. Assiyah is the actual completed project, the manifest reality (flaws and all) in which people usually bumble about.

One way to think about the Four Worlds is that each World is part of, but a pale reflection of, the previous World. It's like the light of the full moon, which only reflects the light from the hidden sun, and then the reflection of the light of the moon on a body of water, and, finally, the visual perception of that light.

The five levels of soul

From a human perspective, awareness of the world depends not only upon the nature of the world "out there," but upon the nature of the world "in here." The "out there" appears differently depending upon your inner mood, thoughts, beliefs, and expectations.

The kabbalah provides a mapping of inner space as well as outer space, and the focus on inner space has to do with the experience of identity. The "who" that you are varies a good deal. Sometimes you're shut down, identified solely with your own personal conflicts and issues. Other times you're more open to an awareness of connection with others and with the world. In the kabbalah, the various major experiences of identity are expressed in terms of the levels of the soul through which consciousness awakens in any given moment. The kabbalah identifies five levels of soul:

>> **Nefesh:** The nefesh ("soul"), represented on the Tree at Yesod, represents the consciousness called ego that is responsible for the safety and the survival of the body. The ego is required for acting effectively in the world, but it sometimes tries to take on more importance than it can actually handle. People mistakenly think of the nefesh as their only identity, but it is only the first level of soul.

>> **Ruakh:** Ruakh ("spirit," "wind," or "breath") is the next level of soul and is centered in the heart space. On the Tree of Life it is represented by the sefirah at the center of the Tree called Tiferet. If nefesh represents separate individual identity, then ruakh represents a more inclusive and interconnected identity. The awareness that awakens at this level of soul experiences its connection to people and planet. At ruakh, people naturally act with greater compassion, because they are aware of a greater Spirit shared by everyone.

>> **Neshamah:** The third Level of Soul is called neshamah ("soul" or "breath," pronounced neh-shah-mah) and relates to the "additional soul" which tradition says is available on the Sabbath (see Chapter 18). Only with this soul can you truly know the inclusive vision of wholeness that marks Shabbat. The neshamah is an "I" that is even more inclusive than ruakh — more like a "shared soul." The neshamah is associated with the world of Beriah ("creation") and is the part of "us" that many mystics imagine survives death.

>> **Khiyah:** Khiyah ("life force" pronounced *khee*-yah) is called the Soul of the Soul, and is associated with the world of Atzilut. Here the inclusivity of the identity opens as a single Life Force, shared by all beings. This is the One "I" at the root of all souls.

>> **Yekhidah:** Finally, Yekhidah ("oneness") represents the ultimate level of soul. In the Lurianic Kabbalah (see "Isaac Luria, Safed's sage" earlier in this chapter), between the Infinite Ayn Sof and the emanations of the sefirot and the four worlds is a Being called *Adam Kadmon* (the "primordial human"). Yekhidah is the level of soul associated with Adam Kadmon and is beyond that which can be imagined.

The five levels of soul help answer the question "Who am I?" by changing the question to "Who am I now?" At this moment, are you defined by your job? Your gender? Your relationship? Your species? People tend to get caught up focusing on the nefesh, without opening toward a greater sense of Self. Ultimately, Jewish mysticism says that your essential being is God. You're part of the Whole just as a drop of water is part of the ocean.

MYSTICS HAVE ALWAYS TOLD STORIES

The mystical impulse in Judaism flows through popular stories to encourage individuals to awaken to their greater Self. Here is one such story from the Hasidic tradition.

A Dream of Treasure

A poor Jew named Yitzchak lived in a village near Krakow, and three nights in a row he had the same dream: He saw a treasure buried behind a gate in the city of Prague. The dream seemed so real that Yitzchak decided to go and look for this hidden treasure. He walked three days to Prague and saw the gate of his dreams. But the gate was heavily guarded, because it surrounded the house of a nobleman. Before he could reach the treasure, he was stopped by a guard. What, the guard wanted to know, was Yitzchak doing by the gate of the nobleman? When Yitzchak told him of his dream, the guard laughed heartily. "If I were to follow my dreams," he said, "I would go to the little house of a Jewish peasant named Yitzchak near Krakow and find the treasure buried beneath his stove!" Yitzchak was stunned by the guard's words, and he hurried back to his home. He looked beneath the stove, where he found a board loose. Beneath it was hidden a great treasure! Yitzchak used the money not only for his own good, but also for the good of his community. He built a *shul* (synagogue) that is still called the Shul of Reb Yitzchak to this very day.

Chapter 6

Ethical Challenges

I n addition to what Judaism has to teach us about Jewish law (*halakhah*), practices (including customs and the mitzvot), and beliefs about God, the Jewish faith also instructs us in one other area: ethics — that is, how we act in the world, in relationships with other people, with our environment, and with God. Ethics is where the tire meets the road, and Jews can apply the lessons Judaism teaches to real world, everyday experiences.

The subject of ethics seems relatively simple and even fun when discussing simple situations. Should two siblings share a toy or should the one with the strongest fist get first rights? If a branch of your neighbor's fruit tree extends over your property, is it okay to pick the fruit? But as the stakes get bigger — as more people are involved, people's lives are at risk, or a sense of scarcity creates tight fists and hardened hearts — the question of ethics becomes simultaneously more crucial to explore and harder to discuss.

Ironically, ethics also teaches one of the hardest lessons to accept: That there is no single right answer. Judaism reflects this idea in several ways. First, remember that Jews have no ultimate moral authority, such as a Pope, to turn to. Each Jew is expected to think for him or herself, through self-education, understanding of the written and oral traditions, and working with the knowledgeable and wise.

Second, remember that the word "Israel" means "wrestling with God," which is a way of saying that Jews value the mental and emotional components of wrestling over the issues as much as the issues themselves. Again, ethics isn't just about arguing with each other —it's also about facing ourselves: our own contradictions, biases, and demons.

Some of the topics in this chapter, including abortion and homosexuality, are controversial and may be upsetting. And yet, no discussion of Judaism would be practical or realistic if it didn't address complex issues that confront our society.

Getting to the Heart of the Matter

We can't distill four thousand years of teachings and tradition into a few paragraphs, but we can tell you about the four fundamental ethical teachings that lay at the heart of Judaism.

The Golden Rule

When the great first-century Rabbi Hillel was asked to explain all of Torah "while standing on one foot" he answered: "Do not do to others that which you would not wish them to do to you." You may recognize this as the Golden Rule," which has been reflected in many other traditions, including Confucianism and Christianity, often stated as "Do unto others as you would have them do unto you."

However you say it, the Golden Rule emerges from the same underlying philosophy: the recognition of the interconnectedness of all being, which we describe as God's Oneness. And it's not a rule; it's a reality! Whether or not you believe in God, it's clear that there is only one "everything," and science clearly demonstrates that we are all connected. Therefore, whatever I do to you I am also doing to myself. The anguish and the suffering of someone else cannot help but be echoed in our own hearts. When we serve others, we are serving all of us; when we punish others, we are punishing all of us.

Expressions of God

A basic belief of Judaism stems from Genesis 1:27, "So God created humankind in God's own image." Many Jews interpret this as statement not just of origin, but as the philosophy of "as above, so below" — that the spirit and nature of the One is reflected in each and every human.

Later, in Leviticus 19, we learn:

> The Eternal said to Moses, "Speak to the entire assembly of Israel and say to them: 'Be holy because I, the Eternal your God, am holy . . .'"

The idea that each person is holy and an expression of the Universal One has extraordinary ramifications, because every human must then be treated with equal dignity and respect, no matter their crime, nationality, or appearance. Then, following up in the same chapter, we learn ethical rules based on the idea that we are, each of us, a reflection of God:

> You shall not steal; neither shall you deal falsely, nor lie to one another . . . You shall not oppress your neighbor, nor rob him . . . You shall not curse the deaf, nor put a stumbling-block before the blind . . . you shall not be partial to the poor, nor defer to the mighty; but in righteousness you shall judge your neighbor.

WORDS OF WISDOM

As the animal rights activist Richard H. Schwartz once wrote, "While Judaism has many beautiful symbols, such as the mezuzah, menorah, and sukkah, there is only one symbol that represents God, and that is each person. As Rabbi Abraham Joshua Heschel taught, more important than to have a symbol is to *be* a symbol. And every person can consider himself or herself a symbol of God."

Tikkun olam

A third basic foundation of Jewish ethical practice is called *tikkun olam*, "repairing the world." Beginning in the early rabbinic period (20 BCE–220 CE), tikkun olam became a rationale for evolving biblical commandments to meet the demands of the current culture. In the 16th-century Jewish mystical communities (see Chapter 5), tikkun olam took on a more expansive spiritual meaning: Acts of righteousness and the fulfillment of mitzvot, according to Lurianic Kabbalah (see Chapter 5), actually help to heal all of Creation, for those actions on earth affect the whole universe.

Today, when so many people around the world feel disempowered, as though nothing they can do will make any difference, tikkun olam reminds us that even the smallest mitzvah or act of loving kindness, or the smallest protest, contributes to the healing of the world. Therefore, modern Jews often apply this concept to the pursuit of social justice and earth care.

Charged to act

All religions have answers regarding what to do when things go wrong. When it comes to righting those wrongs, the ethical teachings of Torah, the prophets, and the unfolding Jewish tradition focus on healing the wounds of the individual, the community, and the world. The words of ancient Jewish prophets still form the foundation for much of the social action and activism that exists today.

Here's how the prophet Micah, in the eighth century BCE, summed up the thrust of ethical teachings flowing from God's Oneness: "It has been told you, human-kind, what is good, and what the Eternal One asks of you: Only to act justly, to love kindness, and to walk with integrity with your God." (6:8)

REMEMBER

Micah's lesson is clear: Jews are charged to act with compassion and righteous-ness in our world. And, furthermore, we may not turn a blind eye. As the Talmud notes, "Anyone who is able to protest against the transgressions of one's house-hold and does not, is punished for the actions of the members of the household. Anyone who is able to protest against the transgressions of one's community and does not, is punished for the transgressions of the community." (Shabbat 54b)

Whether an act is private or public is irrelevant: "Whatever may not properly be done in public is forbidden even in the most secret chamber." (Shabbat 64b)

In the rest of this chapter, we take a look at Jewish responses to several of the most important issues today, in light of the basic three-part injunction provided by Micah. Some things have not changed very much in 2,900 years. We are still struggling to be kinder to one another.

Meeting at the Intersection of Righteousness and Charity

Everyone likes to think that there will come a time when hunger and poverty will no longer be a problem; when all people have enough to eat, have adequate shel-ter, and sufficient means for their survival. The Torah takes a more realistic view when it states, "There will always be poor people in the land. Therefore, I com-mand you to be openhanded toward your brothers and toward the poor and the needy in your land." (Deut. 15:11)

REMEMBER

However, keep in mind that the Hebrew word *tzedakah* — which is often translated as "charity" — actually means "justice." Responding to the needs of the less fortunate is seen in Judaism as a matter of justice and acting righteously. As the Torah com-mands, "Justice, Justice you shall pursue!" (*tzedek, tzedek, tirdof;* Deuteronomy 16:20)

Think of it this way: Judaism places the fortunate and unfortunate on each side of a scale and understands that one side must help the other in order to find some sense of balance. This connection between justice or righteousness and charity is core to the Jewish ethical system.

And yet, finding balance doesn't necessarily mean one should simply give to the other. The great Jewish scholar and ethicist Maimonides pointed out that it's far better to lend someone money to start their own business than it is to give alms. This is in line with the old saying, "Teach a man to fish, and you feed him for a lifetime." This is reflected in the last line of Deuteronomy 15:7–8:

> If there is among you a needy person, one of your brethren, in any of your towns in your land which the Lord your God gives you, you shall not harden your heart, nor close your hand from your poor brother, but you shall freely open your hand to him, and shall generously lend him sufficient for his need in whatever he lacks.

We are not only commanded to provide when there is need but to respect the dignity of those we help. You can see this clearly in Leviticus 19:9–10:

> When you reap the harvest of your land, you shall not reap your field to its very border, neither shall you gather the gleanings after your harvest. And you shall not strip your vineyard bare, neither shall you gather the fallen grapes of your vineyard; you shall leave them for the poor and for the stranger: I am the Eternal your God.

The corners of the field are left for those who are able to harvest for themselves; the fallen grain and fruit for those unable to harvest but still able to pick up from the ground. No matter the ability, no matter the nationality or race, we must offer a dignified opportunity to all.

WORDS OF WISDOM

QUOTATIONS ON TZEDAKAH

The Torah and Talmud are full of instructions on how to live rightly in the face of poverty. Here are a few examples.

"One who is gracious to a poor man lends to the Lord, and God will repay him for his good deed." (Proverbs 19:17)

"To do righteousness and justice is preferred by God more than sacrifice." (Proverbs 21:3)

"Whosoever hath not pity upon his fellow man is no child of Abraham." (Bezah, 32b)

Even a poor person who receives charity is obliged to give charity to others. (Shulkhan Aruch 248:1)

"Whoever sustains and saves a single life it is as if he or she has sustained a whole world." (Mishnah Sanhedrin 4:5).

"Let justice well up as waters, and righteousness as a mighty stream!" (Amos 5:24)

This was one of the key ideas behind the Musar ("morality") movement, started by Rabbi Israel Salanter (1810–1883), which promoted the idea that Talmud study had to be accompanied by ethical good works and great humility in the everyday real world. As Salanter once wrote, "Normally, we worry about our own material well-being and our neighbor's souls; let us rather worry about our neighbor's material well-being and our own souls."

By the way, one of the most effective international agencies providing food for those in need is Mazon: A Jewish Response to Hunger. The word *mazon* is Hebrew for "food" or "sustenance," and the group helps prevent and alleviate hunger among people of all faiths and backgrounds.

Unraveling the Problem of the Other

People often find it tempting to look at individuals with differently colored skin and label them "other." Or perhaps they have a different accent, nationality, style of dress, or behavior that makes them stand out as "different than us" and there-fore somehow suspect. This is not a Jewish issue, of course, but a very natural human one. But Judaism has long taught that we all must find a way to look beyond these differences, to respect everyone as equals.

The Talmud explains: "One person (Adam) was created as the common ancestor of all people, for the sake of the peace of the human race, so that one should not be able to say to a neighbor, 'My ancestor was better than yours' " (Mishnah San-hedrin 4:5). That same discussion goes on to point out how crucial it is that we treat each other with care: "For one who destroys a single life is considered by scripture to have destroyed an entire world, and one who saves a single life is con-sidered by scripture to have saved an entire world."

In fact, Judaism puts extraordinary stress on how we must treat the "other" in our community: You can find the commandment to treat them with kindness and goodwill in one form or another 36 times in the Torah — more than any other mitzvah! For example, "You shall love the stranger; for you were strangers in the land of Egypt" (Deut. 10:19, Exodus 22:21, and Leviticus 19:33–34).

Of course, various Jewish communities have exhibited unfortunate examples of racism and xenophobia, and we've even heard arguments that Judaism is itself inherently racist. But keep in mind that Jews come in every size, color, and race, including Scandinavian Jews, African Jews, Asian Jews, and Jews who look like Arabs. As we explained in Chapter 1, Judaism is far more like a tribe than a race, focusing on ethics and actions more than belief or nationality.

Because of Judaism's strong ethical foundations, and because Jews tend to identify with other disadvantaged people, they have long been on the forefront of civil and human rights. For instance, in 1964, at the height of the civil rights movement in America, 16 rabbis were arrested for participating in a peaceful sit-in in racially divided St. Augustine, Florida. While in jail, they wrote: "We came to St. Augustine mainly because we could not stay away. We could not say no to Martin Luther King, whom we always respected and admired and whose loyal friends we hope we shall be in the days to come. We could not pass by the opportunity to achieve a moral goal by a moral means — a rare modern privilege — which has been the glory of the non-violent struggle for civil rights . . . We came because we could not stand silently by our brother's blood."

Intra- and Interfaith Challenges

We must apply that same dictate to treat others with respect when confronting people with beliefs or religions different than our own. If we truly believe that there is One God, then we have to assume that the God of the Muslims, the Hindus, and the Christians (to name a few) is the same One. And we must respect that the expression of their belief is as much a reflection of that Oneness as our own.

For these reasons, we strongly advocate interfaith dialogue (and intrafaith dialogue, for example, between Orthodox and Secular Humanist Jews). We aren't talking about a yearly Thanksgiving pulpit exchange, but instead consistent conversations among individuals and communities that allow us to get to know each other as human beings. Only then can we transcend our polarized viewpoints, celebrate our shared humanity, and begin to work together on effective responses to the issues of our time. The Jewish community lacks universal agreement on the importance of interfaith and intrafaith relationships. Especially as rates of intermarriage rise, many fear the diminishing of the Jewish population. But nevertheless we believe that there are substantial reasons for supporting interfaith dialogue.

It might sound banal, but getting to know one another behind the slogans and the jargon of our stated points of view can also help us confront practical political issues, as well. Because we don't know each other well enough, we find it often tragically tempting to demonize the other. Discounting the basic humanity of those who differ from us always takes us away from the greater peace we seek.

When inter- and intrafaith groups come together, they can share life experiences, share what is most important to them, and remember that they are all part of one Life; that it's *us* here, not "us and them."

Embracing Our Sexuality

Judaism promotes study, prayer, and practicing mitzvot to have a closer, "right" relationship with the Universal. But there is another method: sex. Some religious traditions consider sex to be shameful or a distraction from spiritual work, but not Judaism. Instead, Judaism emphasizes that sex is a deeply holy act to be performed regularly, and insists that it be pleasurable for both members of a married couple. That said, Judaism does outline a number of strict rules involving physical intimacy — rules that, in fairness, are embraced wholeheartedly by some and rejected by others.

Jewish sexual ethics and practices are rooted in two basic concepts: That all human life is holy (see "Expressions of God," earlier in this chapter), and that people can be in a state of ritual purity or impurity. These lead to the following laws:

» **Menstruation:** Traditionally, sexual relations are not permitted when a woman is menstruating or for seven days after the last sign of blood (see "Purifying the Spirit: Rites and Rituals," in Chapter 4). This is part of the highly intricate laws of purity that, like the kosher laws, reflect a range of meanings. One practical effect is that it encourages couples to resume intercourse when a man's semen count is high and a woman is ovulating — thereby maximizing the chance of conception. It also emphasizes that a marriage must be based on much more than sexuality, as the couple is required to partner together without physical contact virtually half of each month. On the other hand, many liberal Jews consider this an archaic set of rules written by men, based on superstition and a lack of understanding of women's bodies. Therefore, the majority of Jewish women don't participate in the monthly mikvah, or ritual bath that concludes the menstrual cycle, nor do they refrain from physical contact with their husbands.

» **Spilling of seed:** Jewish tradition is focused — you might even say "obsessed" at times — with procreation. This focus makes sense: In the Bible, God's very first instruction is "Be fruitful and multiply" (Genesis 1:28). Plus, historically, the Jews have always been a minority, and building up their community presence was a crucial task. But Orthodox Jews also see each sperm and egg as sacred — a potential life. The result is that they condemn any activity that "spills seed" — ejaculation outside the vagina. Many Jews now disregard this interpretation, tending to appreciate masturbation and other acts as a natural part of human sexuality.

» **Avoiding enticement:** Jews understand that they must maintain a balance between the natural *yetzer hara* (the inclination toward evil or base actions) and the *yetzer hatov* (the inclination toward good). To achieve this balance, they believe that lust must be paired with love, just as the desire to work must be offset by the peace of Shabbat. One of the ways traditional Jews attempt to maintain balance is to avoid lascivious thoughts outside the intimacy of a married partner. Thus, Orthodox men and women dress and act modestly, and are physically separated, especially during religious services. Once again, most liberal Jews attempt to find their own balance without these restrictions.

Additionally, Jews don't traditionally condone premarital sex. Once again, more liberal groups within the Jewish community may look toward religious insights when determining their own behavior, but they are not ruled by it (as the Reconstructionists say, "history has a vote, not a veto").

REMEMBER

Even though Jews have many laws regarding sex, Judaism sees sexuality not just as a method of procreation, but as a pleasure and a joyful responsibility in marriage. Jews have clear laws outlining a man's requirement to marry and a husband's obligation to satisfy his wife.

Mystical visions of sexual union

The mystical Jewish tradition takes sexuality one step farther: that the sexual union between two people is the reflection of God's own nature — reflecting the union of the masculine and the feminine aspects of God, and facilitating the flow of *shefa* (divine abundance, grace, or effluence) in the universe. As author Jay Michaelson notes, "the Zohar says that we are meant to imitate God — who creates, manifests into separation, and unites the separate back into One. For the Zohar and other texts, sexual union re-enacts the union of the high priest into the holy of holies; the union of heaven and earth."

From this perspective, healthy, mindful, and intimate sexuality helps the process of universal Creation — giving a whole different meaning to pro-creation!

Birth control and abortion

Traditionally, Jews consider birth control acceptable as long as it doesn't inhibit the laws regarding procreation (two child minimum, at least one male), but except for disease control, condoms are not an approved birth control method because of the prohibition against the "spilling of seed" (the pill is the approved method). More liberal Jews consider choices about sexuality to be theirs to make, and don't follow a traditional religious authority on such matters, including abortion.

One of the hardest and most important decisions a woman must make is whether to bring a child into the world. Although Judaism clearly honors all human life, the vast majority of Jews believe in a woman's right to choose an abortion. Because neither the Torah nor Talmud says anything specific about abortions, rabbis have long had to make up their own interpretations and rulings on this issue. Some traditions say that the child only becomes human when its head passes the birth canal; others say even the life of a fetus is a life worth saving.

We know rabbis who are pro-choice and those who are pro-life, but the ubiquitous Jewish tradition of *pikuakh nefesh,* the saving of a life, clearly states that abortion should be allowed if the mother's life is danger. In fact, the Central Conference of American Rabbis (Reform) has issued a statement that abortion should be permitted "if there is serious danger to the health of the mother or child. . . [though] we do not encourage abortion, nor favor it for trivial reasons."

Homosexuality

The Torah says very little about homosexuality, but one verse has been used to justify the condemnation of a man's primary relationship with another man: "You shall not lie with a man as with a woman" (Lev. 18:22). Note that the verse calls this behavior *toh-ei-vah,* which is often translated as "abomination" but "taboo" or "foreign" is more accurate — the same word applies to eating unkosher food, feeling unwholesome pride, or using false scales when weighing things.

Nevertheless, the injunction against "spilling seed" effectively means that Orthodox Jews typically restrict themselves from any homosexual acts. Interestingly, there is no condemnation of lesbian relationships in the Bible, but most Orthodox rabbis argue against homosexual behavior by both men and women.

On the other hand, men can't actually "lie with a man as with a woman" because the anatomy is different. So some people in the Jewish community don't take this verse literally, but see it as a product of a different time and culture.

Whatever the case, attitudes toward homosexuals have changed radically in the last 40 years, and Jewish groups have begun to welcome members of the lesbian, gay, bisexual, and transgender (LGBT) community. Furthermore, openly gay rabbis and cantors now serve in all branches of Judaism except the Orthodox. And most liberal (and even some Conservative) rabbis have been performing same-sex marriage or commitment ceremonies for decades.

We are still in a period of change, and those who are more accepting of relationships defined by love rather than by gender certainly support this change.

Prohibited relationships

The principle of *pikuakh nefesh* clearly states that almost every commandment must be transgressed in order to save life. For example, although driving is traditionally forbidden on Shabbat, one must drive a seriously ill person to the hospital for treatment.

REMEMBER

However, Judaism allows no exceptions for the commandments against adultery and incest. They are clearly at odds with the prime directives of Jewish ethical teachings about the value of family and relationships. (Two other commandments that must never be violated are prohibitions against murder and idolatry.)

Finding a Way to Peace

War has been with us from the beginning of recorded history, like a plague always appearing somewhere on the planet. However, Judaism affirms the primary importance of peace, and the Talmudic rabbis pointed out that "All that is written in the Torah was written for the sake of peace" (Tanhuma Shoftim 18).

The rabbis also remind us that war is most often caused by scarcity of resources (such as food and water) and — often hand in hand — scarcity of righteous behavior, as in this statement from Pirke Avot, the Ethics of the Fathers: "The sword comes into the world because of justice delayed and justice denied." Our early history is full of war and violence, but Judaism ultimately celebrates the peacemakers and reminds us that all humans are expressions of God and that we must treat our neighbors (even our enemies) as ourselves.

So while Jewish law condones war in self-defense, it prohibits a wide range of tactics, including poisoning livestock, destroying fruit trees, or laying waste to food or water sources. Similarly, Deuteronomy 20:10 points out that we must always seek a peaceful solution before waging any battle, and Proverbs 25:21 notes: "If your enemy is hungry, give him bread to eat. And if he is thirsty, give him water to drink." Remember the classic comic strip character Pogo, who said, "We have met the enemy, and he is us?" Perhaps that's why Proverbs 24:17 insists: "Do not gloat when your enemy falls; when he stumbles, do not let your heart rejoice."

Breaking the cycle

Numerous teachings support the crucial importance of peace, and yet Jews and Judaism have so often been caught up in violence and war. So how are we to break the cycle?

We remember an old camp song that says, "You can't get to heaven, in . . .," then listing all the conveyances that will fail to deliver us to that goal. Well, it's clear that we can't get to peace in the ways that we have been trying. Namely, we can't ever get to peace through war. No war has ever brought the peace it promised, because war creates winners and losers. The winners too often begin to replicate the very power structures they fought against; and the losers soon begin planning their revenge.

That's why Proverbs 20:22 warns us, "Do not say, 'I'll pay you back for this wrong!'" and in the ninth-century *Avot De Rabbi Natan* we read, "Who is a hero among heroes? One who turns an enemy into a friend." The rabbis of the Talmud go so far as to declare that if two people need help and one of them is your enemy, help your enemy first — the reason being that it's always better to overcome your own inclination toward evil (*yetzer hara*) and convert an enemy to a friend.

The few times in recent history when war was followed by peace stem from substantial support from the winning side for those who had lost. In other words, it was peaceful action that brought true peace — not violence. If we seek peace, the means of our seeking must be peaceful; if we seek love, we must seek it lovingly. When the Torah says, "Justice, justice shall you pursue" (Deuteronomy 16:20), the doubled word "justice" reminds us that justice can only be pursued with just means. This is still one of the most difficult lessons for humans to learn.

Here are two more Jewish ethical teachings regarding violence:

» **Murder:** Although capital punishment is allowed, one may not murder an innocent person. Genesis 9:6 says: "Whoever sheds the blood of man, by man shall his blood be shed; for in the image of God has God made man." This prohibition is true even if killing will save your own life. The Talmud states: "The governor of my town has ordered me, 'Go and kill so and so; if not, I will slay thee.' [The rabbi] answered him, 'Let him rather slay you than that you should commit murder; who knows that your blood is redder? Perhaps his blood is redder'" (Sanhedrin 74a).

» **Capital punishment:** The Bible clearly mandates capital punishment but is very careful about requiring at least two witnesses to support that judgment. Ultimately, however, rabbinic traditions made it so difficult to bring the death penalty that it was practically impossible ever to carry it out. Many Jewish groups are today on record against capital punishment.

In all Jewish prayer services there are prayers for peace. At the very end of worship, the Mourner's Kaddish (see Chapter 4) concludes, "May the One who makes peace in the high places make peace for us." Remember that the Hebrew word Shalom, meaning peace, comes from the word "wholeness" or "complete." Perhaps the real task is to begin within ourselves, finding the inner peace that can contribute best to the tikkun olam of world peace.

WORDS OF WISDOM

PEACE BE WITH YOU

You can find a wealth of quotations in Jewish literature on the importance and ultimate goal of peace in our hearts, relationships, and communities. Here are a few of our favorites:

"Better a patient man than a warrior, a man who controls his temper than one who takes a city." (Proverbs 16:32)

"Be among the disciples of Aaron, loving peace and pursuing peace . . ." (Pirke Avot 1:12)

"Not by might nor by power, but by my Spirit,' says the Lord Almighty." (Zechariah 4:6)

"The fruit of righteousness will be peace; the effect of righteousness will be quietness and confidence forever." (Isaiah 32:17)

"The only reason that the Holy One, blessed be He, created the world was so that there would be peace among humankind." (Bamidbar Rabbah 12A)

"The wolf will live with the lamb, the leopard will lie down with the goat, the calf and the lion and the yearling together . . .. They will neither harm nor destroy on all my holy mountain, for the earth will be full of the knowledge of the Lord as the waters cover the sea." (Isaiah 11:6-9)

"And they shall beat their swords into plowshares, and their spears into pruning hooks; nation shall not lift up sword against nation, neither shall they learn war anymore." (Isaiah 2:4 and Micah 4:3)

Respecting Animals and the Environment

When you take a walk along a pristine beach or through a quiet mountain forest, you can see how everyone — from secular atheist to Orthodox Jew — can appreciate the wonder and awe of the natural world around us. Ecclesiastes Rabbah 7:13 marvelously describes this awesome beauty:

WORDS OF WISDOM

When God created Adam, He took him and led him round all the trees of the Garden of Eden, and said to him, "See My works, how beautiful and praise-worthy they are! Now all that I have created, I created for your benefit. Be careful that you do not ruin and destroy My world; for if you destroy it there is no one to repair it after you.

This deep reverence for nature is deeply rooted in Judaism and forms the basis for two important issues in Jewish ethics: *bal tashkhit* and *tza'ar ba'alei khayim*.

Bal Tashkhit: Do not destroy

We've known for centuries that our survival depends upon a healthy environment where the food we require can be produced, yet we continue to ravage our planet. The ancient code of *bal tashkhit*, literally "do not destroy," prohibits wasteful or senseless destruction of resources and the environment. Instead, Jewish tradition encourages caring for the land, and, by extension, for our entire world. The Torah states that even farmland should observe a 12-month "Shabbat" of rest every seven years. Today, Jewish groups, basing their actions on religious principles, are among those most active in working for a healthier environment (see Chapter 23).

TIP

The great first-century teacher Rabbi Yokhanan ben Zakkai expressed a gentle love of the earth and the cycles of nature when he taught, "If you are planting a new tree, and someone should say to you that the Messiah has come, stay and complete the planting."

Bal tashkhit tells us to behave responsibly: Drive energy efficient cars when possible, turn off the lights when we leave a room, and avoid squandering food, money, or useable things.

Tza'ar ba'alei khayim: Treat living creatures with dignity

Although Judaism places the role of humans above that of animals, the traditional principle of *tza'ar ba'alei khayim*, avoiding "the suffering of any living creatures," insists that we must respect and honor animals in our care. For instance, the Talmud states, "A person is prohibited to eat until he first feeds his animals" (Berachot 40a), and Exodus 20:10 notes that on Shabbat (see Chapter 18) our animals should rest alongside us.

This underlying law has a number of consequences, including the condemnation of hunting and animal fighting for sport, and the rule that animals must be slaughtered as quickly and painlessly as possible. Many Jews today expand this law to avoid any product that came from ill-treated animals.

ANECDOTE

Note that some people use the rule of *tza'ar ba'alei khayim* as one basis for vegetarianism. David, who was a vegetarian for over a decade, was fascinated to learn that Genesis 1:29 clearly states that in an ideal world, we would eat only fruits and vegetables. Ted, on the other hand, was quick to point out that after the story of the Flood, God says, "Everything that lives and moves will be food for you. Just as I gave you the green plants, I now give you everything" (Genesis 9:3).

When we remember that we share one environment, and that our actions in one place impact the water and air everywhere, we realize that we can only successfully protect our environment when we act together. Jewish tradition affirms the essential wholeness and holiness of our natural world. A Hasidic teaching enjoins us to take off our shoes, just as Moses was asked to take off his shoes when approaching the Burning Bush, because the ground we are standing on is holy. We are always standing on holy ground.

Striving for tikkun olam

We're only human. Sometimes we rise to the occasion, reflecting the highest ideals of our culture and ethics; sometimes we sink, heavy with fear or anger. You can find obvious examples of prominent Jews who have made poor ethical choices. Even the state of Israel, which is often held to a higher moral standard than other countries, has made some questionable ethical decisions in the past 60 years. But Judaism understands that we're not expected to get it right all the time; it does expect us to keep trying, though, and learn from our mistakes.

The Talmud records Rabbi Tarfon's words: "It is not incumbent upon you to complete the work, but neither are you free to desist from it altogether" (Pirke Avot 2:21). We prefer a slightly different reading of this text: You don't have to complete the work, but you're not truly free *when* you totally desist from the work.

Crucial issues of our time are a direct invitation to remember our oneness, and to take responsibility for what we are doing. And Judaism asks us to do so with kindness and compassion, in the service of tikkun olam.

2

From Womb to Tomb: The Life Cycle

We lay out every major lifecycle ritual in detail, from birth to death. Did you know that Jews generally have both English names and Hebrew names? That every Jew over age 13 is Bar or Bat Mitzvah, even if they didn't have a ceremony? That Jewish men are traditionally buried in the same white robe in which they were married? Life is precious and short; it's important to mark sacred events with intention and ritual.

Chapter **7**

In the Beginning: Birth and Bris

Nothing is more amazing than having a child — no other event is fraught with as much fear and joy and expectation and hope and shock. Maybe it's genetically built in to our psyches to be blown away by a birth, even if it's not our own child, so that we as a communal species rally together and help out, encourage, and celebrate this extraordinary time and event. Also, many Jews note that the first *mitzvah* ("commandment") in the Bible is "Be fruitful and multiply," and they feel that having children is literally a religious commandment and a spiritual event.

Accordingly, Judaism has a number of important rituals that surround the birth of a child. After a child is born, he or she is greeted by parents, family, and community, and is given a name. Often, a rabbi says special blessings for the child in synagogue, too. For boys, this process is combined with a short ceremony called a *brit milah* (many American Jews call it by its Ashkenazi pronunciation, "bris;" we use both interchangeably). We also discuss the girls' ceremony in this chapter.

Some Jews have also revived an ancient Israeli tradition in which the parents plant a cedar sapling for each newborn boy and a cypress or pine sapling for each girl. By the time the child is married, the tree will be large enough to contribute a branch or two to the chuppah (see Chapter 9).

Making the Cut: Ritual Circumcision

Brit milah means "covenant of circumcision," which describes exactly what happens to the baby boy during this ritual. Circumcision — where the foreskin is removed from the penis — is one of the oldest surgical procedures (it goes back to prehistoric times, though we're at a loss to explain how historians know this), and has long been practiced by some African tribes, most Muslims, and, of course, Jews.

The Bible (Genesis 17:10) says that Abraham made a deal with God: Abraham's wife, Sarah, will bear a child (Isaac), and their descendents will possess the Promised Land. In exchange, God wanted Abraham and every male child to be circumcised. Given that Abraham was 99 years old at the time, it's impressive that he agreed to this deal. But agree he did, and ever since then Jewish parents have continued the covenant.

Traditional Jewish families tend to consider the brit milah as a joyous and positive event. Less traditional folks have a wide variety of responses to circumcision, and a few Jews have even considered not circumcising their sons. (We discuss some of these issues later in this section.) So, even though a non-circumcised Jew is officially still a Jew, most rabbis (and probably most other Jews) won't recognize his Jewishness.

REMEMBER

It's important to note that male circumcision is radically different than what some people call "female circumcision." Jews only remove the foreskin of the penis, which has little or no long-term effects. People who perform female circumcision (which is illegal in most parts of the world) actually mutilate the vagina so that the woman can't experience sexual pleasure; it's really awful.

Some people assume that because the brit milah draws a little blood, it's like a sacrifice. Fortunately, Judaism doesn't allow for any sort of human sacrifice to God. The bris is a rite of passage, unconsciously for the child (who is obviously in no position to make a covenant), and deliberately by the parents of the child.

Part of the process of converting to Judaism includes (if you're a man) being circumcised. If you're already circumcised, you still have to go through a symbolic circumcision, in which a drop of blood is taken from the penis (called *hatafat dam*).

Knowing who's involved

Although rabbis are almost always involved during major transitions (Bar/Bat Mitzvahs, weddings, and funerals, for example), it's completely optional to have a rabbi at a bris, although many of those who traditionally perform circumcisions are specially trained rabbis. Jewish tradition says that if the father of the boy knows how to perform a circumcision, he is duty-bound to do it. However, very few fathers know how, so the task is handed to a proxy, called a *mohel* (in Yiddish it's pronounced "moyl;" in Hebrew it's pronounced "mo-hel").

The mohel is usually a rabbi or a physician; in less traditional settings, the mohel may even be a woman. In fact, because most mohels are specially trained, they have significantly more experience and skill performing circumcisions than do regular doctors. The mohel generally conducts the entire ceremony, though if a family rabbi is present, he or she may help, too.

TIP

Choose a mohel whom you trust and feel completely comfortable with; ask your friends for personal recommendations, and interview more than one mohel if you have several to choose from.

The *sandek* (godparent) is the most honored participant at the brit milah, and is traditionally the grandfather or great-grandfather (though it could be a grand-mother or someone else). The sandek holds the child throughout the ritual — usually with the boy on a pillow or a special brit milah tray during the short circumcision procedure.

REMEMBER

Although we use the translation "godparent" for the word *sandek*, Judaism doesn't really have a tradition of godparents the way Christianity does. If the child becomes an orphan, it's incumbent on the whole Jewish community, not just the godpar-ents, to take care of him or her.

Adhering to the rituals and ceremonies

A brit milah is normally scheduled for the eighth day after a boy is born, even if that day falls on Shabbat (see Chapter 18) or some other holiday, which means that if a child is born on a Wednesday, the bris falls on the following Wednesday. How-ever, if the baby is born on a Wednesday night, then the bris would occur on the following Thursday morning because Jewish days begin at sundown, and the bris is traditionally performed during the day. (Note that the Talmud (see Chapter 3) states if the baby's health is in question, then the bris must be postponed.)

A number of different reasons exist for waiting a week before the ceremony. Some rabbis teach that every baby must experience all seven days of creation before the bris. Others say the baby should first know the sweetness of the Shabbat. Still oth-ers point to medical research, which seems to indicate that this is the optimal time to perform the bris.

Other than a few standard ritual words and items, the ceremony of a brit milah allows for a lot of flexibility. Either way, the actual circumcision only lasts a few minutes (one mohel we know of insists he takes less than 60 seconds). Typically, candles are lit, the child is brought into the room (often handed from one family member to another), and handed to the sandek, whose chair is usually designated as "Elijah's chair." Tradition has it that the prophet Elijah will announce the next messiah, and Elijah is also seen as the "angel of the covenant" and protector of the child.

After the mohel recites some blessings, he or she performs the circumcision, during which one or two drops of blood must be drawn. The foreskin is saved and normally buried after the ceremony. If a tree has been planted to honor the birth, as described at the beginning of this chapter, the foreskin is buried beneath that tree. Then, the baby is officially named and blessed. Traditionally the mohel recites, "Just as this child has been brought into the Covenant, so may he be brought to a life of Torah, to a marriage worthy of blessing, and to a life filled with good deeds," and says a blessing over wine. After this blessing, the parents drink, and some wine is given to the baby on a piece of cloth.

Finally, the child is returned to his parent to rest, and it's time for the *seudat mitz-vah*, the ritual celebratory meal.

TIP

The whole ceremony (not including the meal) is often no more than ten minutes long. Although any additions should be kept brief to ensure the comfort of the baby, here are a few ideas that you may consider when planning a bris:

>> You might read a poem or other short piece before the circumcision.

>> Sephardic communities often use incense during the ceremony.

>> Some people like a rabbi to give a short teaching during the ceremony.

>> Ask each person present to offer a personal blessing for the baby. Even better, have people write their blessings down or ask them to record them on an audio or video recorder, perhaps during the meal.

Making the choice

Most Jews never question whether to perform a circumcision — it's simply part of being Jewish. In fact, for an increasing number of Jews, it's one of the most spiritual and joyful community events. However, for some Jews (like David) who have not been brought up connected to their tradition, circumcision becomes a question rather than a certainty. Here are a few ideas to think about when considering circumcision:

EASING THE PAIN ON BRIS DAY

TIP

Keeping the baby comfortable during the ceremony can make the experience much more pleasant for everyone. While some parents prefer to perform the bris in a hospital or at a synagogue, the baby (and parents) will almost certainly feel more comfortable at home. Keep the number of attendees at the bris to a minimum and invite more people to the reception afterward. In our experience, much of the baby's discomfort comes from having a lot of nervous people standing around him.

Traditionally, the boy is given some gauze soaked with wine to suck on before and during the procedure. This eases the pain and helps him sleep. Medical research does, in fact, suggest that the sugar in a really sweet wine (like Manichevitz red wine) does appear to help. However, some mohels also prescribe some baby Tylenol before and after the bris, too. Less-traditional mohels also use some sort of mild anesthetic, either an injected local anesthetic or a topical cream.

>> In the 1960s, about 98 percent of all boys born in the United States were circumcised because of research that said circumcised boys have fewer medical problems, such as a slightly lower rate of urinary tract infections and a lower chance of contracting sexually transmitted diseases. However, many of these health risks can be avoided by careful daily cleaning, and by 2009, fewer than 40 percent of all boys were being circumcised (though almost all Jews still were).

>> In 2007, the World Health Organization endorsed circumcision of boys, calling it, "an important intervention to reduce the risk of heterosexually acquired H.I.V." Researchers also have strong evidence to suggest that circumcision protects against penile cancer and sexually transmitted diseases, and helps reduce the risk of cervical cancer for female partners.

>> Complications from this procedure are extremely rare and, when they happen, are usually mild.

>> Any pain the boy experiences almost certainly goes away relatively quickly. The child may cry at this event, but it appears that much of this unhappiness comes from being restrained and being surrounded by a bunch of nervous relatives.

>> No parents want their child to suffer, but honestly, there is no way to raise a child without pain — you wouldn't avoid your child getting an injection just because it is going to hurt. You can argue that the baby has no choice in the matter of being circumcised, but sometimes babies don't get choices — parents must choose the right course for their children, not necessarily the least painful one. We make all kinds of decisions for our children when they are young that they probably wouldn't choose for themselves.

TIP

>> If you're considering not having your boy circumcised, think about this: Suppose that your son happens to grow up to really identify as being Jewish and happens to fall in love with a Jewish woman. Very few rabbis will perform a Bar Mitzvah or a Jewish wedding unless the male is circumcised. We can guarantee you that your son will wish you gave him five minutes of pain as an infant instead of 5 or 10 days of major pain later in life.

REMEMBER

Some rabbis teach that the bris is a symbol of taking control over our animal nature — an obvious reminder that men can control sexual urges and lustful appetites. But ultimately, it's important to remember that the brit milah connects a boy to hundreds of generations of men before him, each of whom had a bris on the eighth day of his life.

Thanking God for Little Girls

Although blessings are often said welcoming both girls and boys in the synagogue, the lack of a more intimate celebration and naming ceremony for girls has historically meant that the birth of a girl has appeared less notable. The Reform movement (see Chapter 1) introduced a home naming ceremony for girls, too, and more recently this ceremony has become common practice in Conservative and even some Orthodox communities.

The naming ceremony for girls has a number of different names, including *brit bat* (covenant for a daughter), *simchat bat* (joy of the daughter), and *brit Sarah* (covenant of Sarah). The Sephardic tradition has also long had a custom of *seder zeved habat* (celebration for the gift of a daughter).

The brit bat — often presided over by a rabbi — can be performed at home or in a synagogue, whichever is more comfortable for the parents and baby. Some folks like doing it eight days after the birth (like the brit milah) and others wait for the Shabbat Havdalah ceremony (see Chapter 18) to symbolize the separation of the child from the mother's body. On the other hand, some parents wait until when the mother is fully recovered and when out-of-town family members can arrive, perhaps even as late as 30 days after the birth.

The ceremony can include the child being passed from one family member to another, blessings over wine and the baby girl, the naming, and often a symbolic ritual that takes the place of the circumcision. For example, the parents may wash the baby's hands and feet, or immerse her body (not head) in water.

Playing the Name Game

Judaism has several traditions surrounding the naming of a baby. The Ashkenazi tradition is to name the child after a relative who has died. The Sephardic tradition says to name the child after a living relative. Both traditions suggest that the child should be named after someone you respect and admire, a model for your child to follow (though both traditions rule that a child shouldn't have the same name as his or her parent). Perhaps more importantly, the name should bring up joyful memories and feelings, so you wouldn't name a child after your Uncle Shlomo, who embezzled from the family business.

ANECDOTE

David's parents just liked the name David, but they gave him his grandfather's name (Avram) as a middle name. Ted was named for Theodore Herzl (the "founding father of Israel"), and his middle name, Gary, was in memory of his great grandmother, Gittel, who had recently died.

Note that Jews outside of Israel usually have two given names: one in Hebrew and one in the language of their birthplace. The latter name usually appears on the child's birth certificate, but the Hebrew name is what he or she would be called in religious circles and functions. The Hebrew name is almost always either Biblical in origin (out of 2,800 personal names in the Bible, fewer than 140 are actually used today) or a Hebrew word such as *Tovah* ("goodness") or *Baruch* ("blessed"). In Israel, of course, people just go by their Hebrew names, such as Yoram, Avital, Tamar, and Asher.

While the correlation between someone's common name and Hebrew name is occasionally obvious (like Gabriel and Gavriel), more often you have to really stretch to see the connection. Generally, people choose a Hebrew name and common name that are associated using one of the following criteria:

>> **The common name is a derivative of the Hebrew name.** For example, Sam comes from Samuel, which comes from Shmuel, a famous biblical character.

>> **The names share the same meaning.** Helen comes from the Greek word meaning "light," so you may use the Hebrew name "Orah," which also means "light."

>> **The names sound alike.** The name Lauren comes from the Latin word for the laurel (a symbol of victory). So Lauren may have the Hebrew name Dafna, which also means "laurel," or she may be called Leah simply because they share the "L" sound. Similarly, a boy may be called Max by his schoolmates and Moshe on his Jewish name certificate.

>> **The names have no connection at all.** For example, the parents, wanting to honor the child's great-grandfather Mayer, give their son this Hebrew name.

However, perhaps they can't think of any good corresponding English name (we can't either), so the birth certificate reads "Lawrence." Later in life, when people ask him about the connection between Lawrence and Mayer, he'll get good at making up answers on the fly.

Table 7-1 lists examples of other common Hebrew/English name combinations. Note that Jewish names typically include the name of the child's father, and sometimes both the father and mother. For example, "Shaul ben Noach" ("Saul, son of Noah") or "Orah bat Adam v'Yehudit" ("Orah, daughter of Adam and Judith").

TABLE 7-1

Hebrew and English Names

English name	Hebrew name	Translation
Brett	Baruch	Blessed
Caroline	Kinneret	Harp/Strong
David	Dah-vid	Beloved
Daniel	Dan	Judge
Deborah	Dvorah	A bee or to speak kind words
Esther	Hadassah	Myrtle
Gabriel	Gavriel	God is my Strength
Justin	Yitzchak	Laughter
Max	Moshe	Drawn out
Michael	Mi-cha-el	One Who is like God
Paul	Pinchas	Dark complexion
Ruth	Rut	Friend
Susan	Shoshanna	Rose or Lily
Theodore	Tovya	Good Lord

Traditional Jews don't use a child's name until he or she has been formally announced to the community. For boys, this happens on the eighth day, during the brit milah, when the mohel, rabbi, or father says, "and let him be known in the house of Israel as (his Hebrew name)." Girls are announced at synagogue or in a more private ritual by saying, "and let her be known in the house of Israel as (her Hebrew name)." Most English-speaking parents outside of Israel also announce and explain their child's English name.

A FIRST-TIMERS' GUIDE TO ATTENDING A BRIS

TIP

To be invited to a brit milah (a "bris") is an honor, though the event is almost always fraught with tension from the moment people arrive until the actual circumcision is complete. Fortunately, the trauma is usually milder than people expect, and the release makes the subsequent celebration all the more joyful. Whether the ceremony is for a boy or girl (a girl's ceremony, the brit bat, doesn't include the circumcision, of course), be sure to arrive on time, and you may want to bring a small baby gift for the parents, although it's usually not required. If the event is held at the parents' home, offer to bring some food for the meal that follows the ritual.

We find it very moving when parents take the time to explain why they chose a particular name, especially if they named the child after a deceased family member. You can explain your child's name during the bris or naming ceremony, or even at the festive meal after the ceremony.

Buying Back the First Born

The biblical Book of Numbers (8:17) says "For all the firstborn of the people of Israel are mine, both man and beast," indicating that God has a special relationship with the firstborn. This verse may have been the origin of the ancient Jewish tradition that each family's firstborn son was dedicated to the Temple to work with the priests. However, before you ship your kid off to live at a synagogue, note that Judaism instituted a convenient loophole: You can buy the child back.

Thus, traditional Jews practice the ritual of *Pidyon Haben* ("the redemption of the son") on the thirtieth day after birth. This is a very brief ceremony in which the father "buys" his son back by symbolically or actually giving money to a *Kohein* (a descendent of the priestly class). Nontraditional Jews might instead make a special donation to charity to honor this tradition.

Chapter **8**

Coming of Age: The Bar/Bat Mitzvah

We all live, grow, learn, and die. Judaism has developed rituals to mark and honor each major step in life, so that every child is born into a community with joy, and every person dies within their community with solemn dignity. Sadly, few people outside of traditional communities mark transitions with rituals anymore. Sure, a fortieth birthday party is considered a big event, but compare that to someone stepping through a door like puberty — they're truly never the same afterward.

In this chapter, we take a look at two important steps: coming of age and the confirmation of faith. Jewish tradition says that when girls turn 12 and boys turn 13, they take on new responsibilities in the community. In traditional congregations, this is the point at which boys are expected to start donning tefillin and performing daily prayers in a minyan (see Chapter 4) and girls are expected to learn the ways of keeping a home. Even though in today's day and age no one expects these teenagers to suddenly become adults after the ceremony, Jews honor this change with ritual.

REMEMBER

In Judaism, every boy is automatically Bar Mitzvah at age 13 and a day, and every girl is Bat Mitzvah at age 12 and a day. No lengthy study or an appearance in the synagogue is required. The fancy ceremony is nice, but technically unnecessary.

Bar or Bat Mitzvah is a state of being, not a verb. You can't be "bar mitzvahed," even though you hear the term used in that way. *Bar Mitzvah* means "son of the commandment," and *Bat Mitzvah* means "daughter of the commandment" (some folks still say "bas mitzvah," which is the Ashkenazi pronunciation). The phrases "Bar Mitzvah" and "Bat Mitzvah" may also refer to the boy or girl, as in "The Bat Mitzvah is practicing for her big day."

Preparing for the Big Day

The traditional Bar/Bat Mitzvah ceremony is no easy task, and it requires study and discipline on the part of the boy or girl. They must learn enough Hebrew to read from the Torah (and often Haftarah, too — the section from the Prophets associated with each Torah portion; see Chapter 3 for more information) and master enough Jewish history and law to understand the context of what they're reading. To prepare, kids take classes and often work one-on-one with their rabbi, cantor, or teacher, focusing on their portion of the Torah and/or Haftarah (see the sidebar "Reading your birth parashah").

The Bar/Bat Mitzvah ceremony is almost always scheduled at a synagogue on the Saturday morning Torah reading that follows the child's twelfth (for a girl) or thirteenth (for a boy) birthday, though this can vary widely. Because of scheduling conflicts at synagogues, some Bar/Bat Mitzvahs (the more proper Hebrew plurals are *B'nai Mitzvah* and *B'not Mitzvah*) are set for weeks or even months after the birthday.

HISTORICALLY SPEAKING

Sometime around the 14th century, it became popular to have a ceremony that celebrated the shift from childhood to adulthood and the onset of puberty. Of course, at that time, boys and girls were often getting married in their early teens, so this celebration really was a significant rite of passage.

Of course, because the Bar Mitzvah ceremony generally included reading from the Torah, girls weren't allowed to participate (see Chapter 3). Fortunately, Rabbi Mordecai Kaplan, the founder of the Reconstructionist movement, changed all that in 1922, when he encouraged his eldest daughter, Judith, to have a Bat Mitzvah ceremony. The Bat Mitzvah ceremony didn't become popular until the 1950s, and today the ritual is common in all congregations except the Ultra-Orthodox (see Chapter 1).

The event can be held anywhere, even at home, and it doesn't require a rabbi to be present. Some families even travel to Jerusalem to perform this rite. Also, the ceremony doesn't have to be held on Shabbat; it can be any morning that the Torah is read during services (Monday, Thursday, and Shabbat). Some families like to schedule the ceremony on Saturday afternoon so that the festivities can conclude with Havdalah (see Chapter 18).

Celebrating the Bar/Bat Mitzvah

On the day of the big event, almost everyone is tense and nervous. Often family and friends have traveled long distances to be present, and the Bar Mitzvah boy or Bat Mitzvah girl stresses about the upcoming performance in front of a crowd of people.

Traditionally, the father is called to the Torah for an *aliyah* ("going up," since Torah is read from a raised portion of the synagogue) before the congregation and says a blessing that thanks God for relieving him of legal responsibility for any future negative actions of his child, although this blessing is almost always omitted in more liberal congregations. Instead, the parents may take the opportunity to address the child publicly, saying how proud they are of him or her.

The Bar/Bat Mitzvah is called up, usually to read the final lines of the Torah portion, called the *maftir*, followed by the Haftarah reading. They follow that with a *d'var Torah*, a short talk usually relating the readings to his or her life. Following the service, a celebration commences, and the pressure of the day is happily past. Some congregations follow the Sephardic custom of tossing sweet candies after the Bar/Bat Mitzvah chants the Torah or Haftarah.

Reading from the Good Book

In some less-traditional congregations, the child's grandparents may take the Torah out of the ark and pass it to the child's parents, who then pass it to the boy or girl. We like this ritual because it offers a chance for the whole family to be involved in this rite of passage and symbolizes how Torah is handed down from generation to generation. Then, the Bar/Bat Mitzvah recites the traditional blessings before the reading.

In many cases, especially when the boy or girl doesn't know Hebrew very well, it's sufficient to recite the blessing before and after the Torah reading, (this probably reflects the original ritual of Bar Mitzvah). Remember that reading the Torah is difficult: The text has no written vowels, and so both the pronunciation of words and their melody must be memorized. In some cases, the Bar/Bat Mitzvah just chants the Haftarah portion for the week, and sometimes members of the family are brought up to share in the Torah reading.

Books can tell you what portion of the Torah was being read on the week of your birth, but the Web makes locating the appropriate passage even easier. We provide links to helpful sites such as this at our website, www.joyofjewish.com.

Speech! Speech!

After the Torah reading, the boy or girl usually presents a short speech. Traditionally, the speech focuses on the Torah portion just read (called a *d'rash* or a *d'var Torah*), allowing the child to demonstrate mastery of the passage. However, today, this speech is just as often a time to thank parents and teachers, or an opportunity for the Bar/Bat Mitzvah to make a statement about who he is or what she believes in.

Often the parents present a short speech to their son or daughter after the child's *d'var Torah*, and then the rabbi may give a short sermon and bless the Bar or Bat Mitzvah before the worship service continues.

TIP

READING YOUR BIRTH PARASHAH

Traditionally, the Torah and/or Haftarah portion read during a Bar/Bat Mitzvah is whatever passage would normally be read that week (see Chapter 3). However, Ted recommends a slightly different custom: He believes that no matter when the ceremony is during the year, the portion of the Torah to be read should be the child's birth *parashah* — that is, the Torah passage that was being read on the week that the child was born.

Although other cultures tend to focus on the position of the stars or other historical events that occur at the time of a birth, Jews with a more mystical bent (like Ted) tend to think that the birth portion may provide a profound appreciation and understanding of one's own life. It's kind of like knowing that you were born on the day Pearl Harbor was bombed or the day humans landed on the moon. Because the Torah passage read at a Bar/Bat Mitzvah may be the only part of the Torah that the child ever fully learns to chant, the birth parashah is the perfect reading to focus on.

A night to celebrate

The most controversial aspect of Bar/Bat Mitzvah ceremonies these days is the party that follows them. Jewish tradition states that some sort of *seudat mitzvah* ("festive meal") is required. However, in recent decades this little party has too often grown into a time of social one-upmanship; these are the nights when folks remember the "Bar" more than the "Mitzvah."

You've probably heard stories of families spending a small fortune on an outrageous Bar/Bat Mitzvah celebration simply because it has to be "the best Bar/Bat Mitzvah party ever." And although we know that both children and their parents have social pressures, we believe that it's much more important to focus on the meaning of the day rather than how much you can spend on a party.

TIP

Here are a few ways that you can make the Bar/Bat Mitzvah celebration special without going overboard:

» Choose a reasonable allowance for the celebration and then sit down with your son or daughter and work on the budget together. This is an excellent time for you to work with your child on being responsible with money, by helping him choose where and how to spend it.

» Some congregations now insist that the boy or girl complete some sort of volunteer community service before the big day, as a *mitzvah* project, demonstrating their acceptance of new responsibilities for their community and their world.

» Many people commit 3 percent of the total cost of the celebration to Mazon: A Jewish Response to Hunger, a non-profit organization that funds soup kitchens and other food programs for those in need. See their website at www.mazon.org for more information.

» Sit down with your child in advance to plan what he or she will do with any monetary gifts. She may decide to allot a percentage of the money to charity (you can even ask your child to research and pick the charities). This helps teach the child that being Bar/Bat Mitzvah is not just being responsible for oneself, but also for the rest of the world.

» Shop for a tallit (prayer shawl) with your child, or help your child make a bag to carry the tallit in.

» Study for the ceremony with your child so that the event becomes a family affair. Let your son or daughter pick out books about Judaism and then read them together in preparation.

>> Add special readings, poems, prayers, or music to the service to personalize it.

>> Find ways to give additional rights and responsibilities to your child. Perhaps raise your child's allowance and allow a later bedtime, but also ask him to perform more chores around the house.

REMEMBER

Ultimately, the Bar/Bat Mitzvah ceremony and celebration offers an opportunity for the child to learn that he or she can work hard, complete a big task, and gain a better sense of self in the process. The party should honor that work and that person, not just be a flash in the pan. And when the community truly welcomes the Bar or Bat Mitzvah with added respect as well as with deeper expectations, he or she can experience a true deepening of personal identity and responsibility.

A FIRST-TIMERS' GUIDE TO A BAR/BAT MITVAH CEREMONY

TIP

Just about everyone — Jew and non-Jew — gets invited to a Bar or Bat Mitzvah ceremony sooner or later, making it one of the most visible Jewish rituals. Nonetheless, some folks turn down the invitation because they're not sure what is expected of them. Here's all you need to know:

- Attendees are rarely expected to do anything at a Bar/Bat Mitzvah ceremony except look proud of and impressed by the boy or girl.

- Men should wear a *yarmulke* (*kippah*) during the service, as is proper in most Jewish worship services. If you don't have one, you can usually borrow one as you enter the synagogue. See Chapter 4 for more information.

- Gifts are almost universally expected (unfortunately, for some kids this is the main reason to have the ceremony). One particular gift became so traditional that for many years people joked that on the big day, a kid could stand up and say, "Today I am a fountain pen." However, the gift doesn't have to be big, and often family members and friends just give the boy or girl money; traditionally, a monetary gift is given in multiples of 18. (In Hebrew numerology, the numerical value of the Hebrew letters that make up the word *chai*, or "life," is 18.) If the service is held on Shabbat, you probably should send the gift directly to the home rather than bring it to the ceremony, particularly if the family is more traditional and refrains from carrying things on Shabbat.

- When the ceremony is over, congratulate the Bar Mitzvah boy or Bat Mitzvah girl by saying "Mazel Tov!"

- At the reception, you may want to wait to eat or drink until you know whether a blessing will be given first.

Celebrating as a grown up

Few aspects of the Bar/Bat Mitzvah are set in stone; most are just firmly entrenched customs. That said, you don't have to have a Bar/Bat Mitzvah ceremony when you turn 12 or 13 (remember that being Bar or Bat Mitzvah doesn't require a ceremony at all). In the past 25 years, many adults have celebrated their newfound interest and study of Judaism with a Bar/Bat Mitzvah ceremony, especially if they didn't have one as a teenager.

An adult Bar/Bat Mitzvah celebration usually takes the same format as a regular ceremony (see the previous section). However, learning about Judaism and honoring a Jewish identity as an adult can be significantly more fulfilling and meaningful than for most 12- or 13-year-olds.

Many older adults also choose to have a second Bar/Bat Mitzvah when they're 83. Some folks say that when you turn 70 years old, life begins again, so 13 years later (when you're 83) you can have another ceremony. In fact, Judith Kaplan Eisenstein, the first-ever Bat Mitzvah girl (see the sidebar "Historically speaking" earlier in this chapter), celebrated her second Bat Mitzvah at age 83 in 1992.

Confirming Your Beliefs

We mean no offense to anyone who is 12 or 13 years old, but we just don't think most early teens are in a position to make a deep commitment to Judaism. In fact, a significant number of boys and girls end their studies of Judaism after their Bar/Bat Mitzvah, long before they may appreciate its deeper teachings. This isn't a new problem; in fact, almost 200 years ago the early German Reform Jews recognized that the Bar Mitzvah ceremony was becoming less meaningful. Their solution was to abolish the Bar Mitzvah ceremony altogether and institute a new celebration: the Jewish confirmation, held when the child is between 15 and 17, at the beginning of summer, on Shavuot (see Chapter 26), the day that the Israelites confirmed their faith at Sinai.

CONTROVERSY

Traditional Jews scoffed at the confirmation as a blatant attempt at assimilation (Christian rituals of confirmation were already a common practice), but the 19th-century reformers' intentions were simply to make Judaism more relevant and meaningful. Seeing that 13-year-olds were, on the whole, not yet mature enough, they postponed the coming-of-age ceremony for a few years and changed the name to confirmation. Needless to say, abolishing the Bar Mitzvah ceremony didn't last long, and today most Jews in Reform, Conservative, and Reconstructionist congregations perform both a Bar/Bat Mitzvah ceremony and a confirmation ceremony. Few, if any, Orthodox Jews celebrate confirmation.

As preparation for confirmation, teenagers usually study for two or three more years after their Bar/Bat Mitzvah, and make a conscious choice to become members of the Jewish community. Confirmation ceremonies usually involve the whole confirmation class conducting a service, often adding dramatic readings and creative elements to express their commitment.

IN THIS CHAPTER

» Looking back on the origins of Jewish weddings

» Discovering the *chuppah*, the ring, and the *ketubah*

» Honoring divorce, Jewish style

Chapter 9

Get Me to the Chuppah On Time: Weddings

I n Judaism, weddings are profoundly holy acts, as important as living and dying. In fact, the marriage ceremony is so sacred that it's called *kiddushin* ("sanctification"), and the *Zohar* (see Chapter 5) teaches that marriages are God's way of continuing to create worlds.

Judaism is full of wedding imagery: Each Friday night, Shabbat is welcomed in as a beautiful bride (see Chapter 18), and the relationship between God and the Jewish people has long been described as that of lovers consummating their pledge to each other. In every wedding, the bridegroom and bride play the roles of Adam and Eve in the genesis of a new family.

Looking at the Origins of Jewish Marriage

Marriage may be holy, but it's also a legal institution, and Jewish law details the rules and regulations for a wedding. For example, over 3 millennia ago Jews laid down the law regarding who men couldn't marry, including a mother, grandmother, granddaughter, sister, half-sister, aunt, niece, mother-in-law, step mother, daughter-in-law, and any married woman not granted a religious divorce (more on that later in this chapter).

Unlike many traditional cultures that treat women as property that gets transferred from father to husband, Jewish law is very clear that men and women have full and equal rights when choosing a spouse. Even in marriages arranged by a *shadchan* ("matchmaker") — a practice that was the norm for centuries and is common in Ultra-Orthodox communities — the bride-to-be had the right to veto a prospective groom. Similarly, in a Jewish wedding today, the bride and groom aren't married *by* an officiant. Instead, they marry each other, with the help of a rabbi or cantor (note the subtle but important difference).

Traditionally, a couple could get married in one of three ways:

>> A man could give a woman some item of value and recite a vow of marriage before two male witnesses who weren't relatives or interested parties.

>> A man and woman could sign a wedding document (*ketubah*) with two disinterested legal witnesses.

>> Two witnesses could see a man and woman go into a private room with the intention to consummate their marriage through the sexual act. The witnesses didn't have to see them have sex, of course.

Over time, all three methods coalesced into the modern wedding. In addition, customs grew around these core rituals, especially as Jews picked up other cultures' conventions in the countries in which they settled. Today, while some people would like to insist that there is one Jewish way to get married, there are actually many. Nonetheless, most Jewish weddings include a few particular symbols and rituals, which we take a look at later in this chapter.

Preparing for the Ceremony

The week before a wedding is always filled with last-minute preparations, but here are several additional customs many Jews include at that time (note that these are all customs, not laws; we believe people should do what feels most meaningful for them):

>> At the Shabbat service before the wedding (or, in the Sephardic tradition, after the wedding), the groom (and the bride, too, in more liberal congregations) is called up to the Torah, blessed, and then pelted with nuts or candy by everyone in attendance (called an *aufruf*, from the German meaning "calling

up"). The ritual can be compared to wishing the couple a "sweet" and delightful future together, although sometimes the candy throwing gets a little too energetic for our comfort.

ANECDOTE

>> Women (and some men) traditionally visit a *mikvah* (ritual bath; see Chapter 4) the day before the wedding. A mikveh can be almost any fresh body of water, such as a lake or a river. David decided on an informal 6 a.m. mikveh in the waters of the Puget Sound surrounded by friends — perhaps colder than necessary, though he insists it was a great experience.

>> Some traditionalists insist that the bride and groom shouldn't see each other the entire week before the wedding (or at least the day of). This is one of the first conventions that more liberal-minded Jews throw out.

REMEMBER

Picking a date for the wedding isn't entirely without complication, either. (Or, as one wit quipped: It's really a bad idea to bring a date to your wedding.) An old Jewish custom called *ein m'arvin simcha b'simcha* states that you shouldn't mix a *simcha* ("happiness" or "joyful event") with another *simcha*. This prohibition means a Shabbat wedding is out, as well as a wedding on pretty much any other Jewish holiday. Of course, you also don't want to have a wedding on a day of fasting or mourning (though the catering bills would be lower), and traditional Jews also time the wedding so that it won't fall during a woman's menstrual cycle (otherwise the couple couldn't consummate the marriage on their wedding night; see Chapter 4).

Enjoying the Wedding

When the chosen day comes, the parents of both the *kallah* ("bride") and *khatan* (or *khos'n*, meaning "bridegroom") typically walk their child down the aisle. (In Jewish weddings, the bride stands on the right side of the groom.) In a very traditional setting, the khatan wears a white robe called a *kittel*, which he wears only at his wedding, Pesach Seders (see Chapter 25), Yom Kippur services (see Chapter 20), and his own funeral (see Chapter 10).

The relationship between the parents of the groom and the parents of the bride is considered so important there's a Yiddish word to describe it: *makhatunim* — as in "My son-in-law's parents are my makhatunim."

Most Jewish weddings continue with eight basic symbols and rituals: the *bedeken* (the veiling before the ceremony), the marriage canopy (or *chuppah*), the wine, the rings, the seven blessings, the breaking of a glass, the marriage contract (*ketubah*), and the *yichud* (when the newly-married couple spends a few minutes alone after the ceremony).

Raising the chuppah

Although many people like the idea of being married in a "House of God," Jewish teachers have long insisted that God can be found in any house and, in fact, anywhere at all. The trick isn't looking for a holy place to get married, but rather to create a holy space. Perhaps this is one reason that Jewish weddings are performed under a chuppah, a canopy held over the heads of the bride and groom. The chuppah can be anywhere. In fact, an old Ashkenazi custom holds that you should perform the wedding outside if possible.

The chuppah — a symbol of the new home being created, and, some say, a symbol of the tents used by the ancient Hebrews — can be as simple or as elaborate as you'd like. Many people use a swath of cloth (often a tallit, or prayer shawl), held aloft with four poles by friends of the couple (it makes things easier if the poles reach to the ground). Others decorate the chuppah with flowers or embroidery, or use a self-standing awning.

TIP

One relatively recent custom is to have someone coordinate the construction of the chuppah from squares of material given out to some friends of the couple. After those friends add their own decorations, words, drawings, and colors to the squares, they are then made into a quilt. Following the ceremony, the quilt can become a wall hanging in the couple's home to remind them of their wedding ceremony and the loving support of their community.

One of the stranger traditions at a Jewish wedding (in our humble opinion) is the bride circling the groom either three or seven times (seven is more traditional) as soon as they're under the chuppah. (As we said, it's a custom, not a law, so the practice varies). This tradition may be a holdover from earlier, more superstitious times, when people believed that circling would create a magic shield against evil spirits. Or perhaps it was simply a symbol of binding the two people together. Today, many Jews think it makes the woman look subservient to the man, so they leave the practice out entirely. Others have the groom do it, too, or have the bride and groom circle each other.

Drinking the fruit of the vine

Almost every Jewish celebration includes a blessing with wine. Until the 11th century, Jewish weddings were held as two events — the *erusin* ("betrothal"), also called *kiddushin* ("sanctification"), and the *nissuin* ("taking," or "nuptials") — often celebrated as much as a year apart. Today, the two events have become one, together called *kiddushin*, but traditional Jewish weddings still include blessing and drinking twice from one or two cups of wine under the chuppah.

TIP

We suggest that people choose a special cup for drinking wine, one from which both bride and bridegroom drink (one after the other, of course). Later, the couple can keep this cup in a special place in their home and use it on Shabbat and at special family celebrations.

Exchanging the rings

Everywhere Jews lived, they picked up cultural customs and wove them into the fabric of their lives. Nowhere is this more evident than in weddings. For example, a traditional Jewish wedding has no vows, such as "to have and to hold . . . for better or for worse . . ." and so on. Rather, historically, the groom simply gave the bride some token of marriage (usually a ring), and repeated the following statement:

Ha-rei aht mekudeshet li, be-tahba'at zoh, k'dat Mosheh v'Yisrael.

"With this ring, you are consecrated to me, [as my wife,] according to the tradition of Moses and Israel."

Today, however, many Jews include vows, promises, and a host of other statements along with the ring-giving ceremony. In more liberal Jewish weddings, the bride also gives the groom a ring, along with a statement of consecration.

The ring itself has changed over time, too. Traditional Jews stick with the custom that a wedding ring should be a simple, smooth round band, without stones or carving, perhaps as a reminder that all Jews are equal, no matter their wealth or status. The ring also symbolizes a smooth and happy wedded life, and, of course, the circle is a symbol of perfection and the unbroken circle of the relationship. However, the hands of Jews today display a wide variety of ring styles. We think it's the thought that counts.

Sharing the seven blessings

Special blessings, called the *sheva b'rakhot* ("seven blessings"), mark the moment of a Jewish marriage. The blessings begin by affirming that God's Presence is reflected in everything that exists, and that God is the creator of human beings; they continue with a declaration that the whole community celebrates this union.

The final blessing, which we quote here, concludes by pointing out that this Divine Presence is celebrated in the commitment of love:

> Blessed are You, Eternal One Our God, Universal Ruling Presence [literally: King of the Universe], who created joy and gladness, bridegroom and bride, mirth, song, delight and rejoicing, love and harmony, peace and friendship. Soon may there be heard in the cities of Judah and in the streets of Jerusalem, the voice of joy and gladness, the voice of the bridegroom and the voice of the bride, the sound of rejoicing from bridegrooms at their weddings, and young people at their feasts of song. Blessed are you, Eternal One, who makes the bridegroom rejoice with the bride.

The rabbi or cantor usually read or chant the sheva b'rakhot, though some people like to split the blessings up among friends and family for them to recite. Also, it's a long-standing tradition that a *minyan* (see Chapter 4) of the couple's friends hold dinner parties for the couple every night for a week after the wedding, reciting the sheva b'rakhot each night, which is why these parties are often called *sheva b'rakhot parties.*

CONTROVERSY

INTRAFAITH AND INTERFAITH MARRIAGES

When it comes to the topic of Jews marrying non-Jews, some might cluck their tongues sadly, and others rant about how interfaith marriages will be the end of Judaism. Even today, some Orthodox Jewish families mourn the loss of their child when he or she marries a non-Jew, as though the child has died.

In the past 50 years, the percentage of American Jews who intermarry has skyrocketed from under 10 percent to about 50 percent. However, in many of these cases, the non-Jewish partner either converts to Judaism or the couple raises their children with at least some Jewish education.

All rabbinical groups discourage interfaith marriages, and many rabbis (even Reform rabbis) will not perform interfaith marriages. Even fewer will perform co-officiated weddings with other clergy.

Most rabbis — as well as the greater percentage of affiliated Jewish communities — worry that marriages outside the faith will diminish the Jewish community. On the other hand, those rabbis (including Ted) who participate in interfaith ceremonies feel that the couple is going to get married anyway, and without rabbinic participation, the likelihood that they'll leave Judaism is higher. Perhaps it's better to give the couple a positive Jewish experience as they approach their marriage rather than turn them away. We include several resources for interfaith couples on our website at www.joyofjewish.com.

Breaking the glass

Probably the most well-known Jewish ritual is the custom of stomping on a glass at the conclusion of a Jewish wedding. In case you're wondering, it's not the same cup from which the couple drinks at the wedding).

WORDS OF WISDOM

You can interpret this ritual in many ways. Traditionalists say that the shattered glass refers to the destruction of the Temple in Jerusalem. We believe that breaking the glass is a reminder that even at a time of great joy, shattering and loss, too, are important parts of human experience. Perhaps that which is shattered represents old structures or limitations that must be released in order to create space for new possibilities. Some people say the noise is supposed to drive away evil spirits, or even that the act represents the intensity and release of sexual union. Of course, as comic David Bader points out, it may simply be a reminder that the couple has registered for new wine glasses.

Whatever the case, as soon as the glass is broken, everyone in attendance joyously shouts "Mazel tov!" (see Appendix A), and the wedding ends in raucous singing and celebrating.

TIP

While most folks use an empty wine glass, some people use a light bulb. The important thing is to wrap the object up in cloth (a napkin is usually not big enough) so that no one gets hurt. David and Ted still have the wrapped-up remnants of the glass used at their weddings as special mementos.

Putting it in writing

Judaism has a long history of ensuring the rights of women. Case in point: the *ketubah*, or marriage contract between bride and groom. The terms of the ketubah (the plural is *ketubot*) are negotiated long before the wedding — much like today's prenuptial agreements. The agreement is signed with witnesses just before the ceremony, and then it's usually read aloud during the ritual. The earliest known ketubah is over 2,000 years old, and its wording and contents are virtually identical to that of a modern-day traditional Orthodox ketubah (which is in Aramaic, the language Jews spoke around the beginning of the first millennium).

While in recent years more liberal Jews have taken to writing their own ketubot – usually focusing more on the spiritual and interpersonal aspects of their relationship — the traditional ketubah long used by Orthodox Jews is clearly an unromantic legal document that spells out the financial obligations of each partner. It doesn't even once mention God! And there's no doubt that it's designed to protect the rights of the woman.

For example, the ketubah provides for a lump sum to be paid to the woman in case of death or divorce (typically enough to live for a year, plus the value of any property she brought to the marriage), and it ensures that the man will support her through the life of their marriage. It even notes that a man must provide for his wife sexually. In the days when polygamy was allowed, perhaps this provision protected older or less-desirable women from being neglected.

About 1,000 years ago, people began to commission illustrated ketubot. The art almost died out, but since the 1960s more couples have started using illuminated ketubot, and today you can buy a relatively inexpensive print of a beautiful ketubah from any Judaica shop. (We have links to these resources on our website at www.joyofjewish.com.) Similarly, you can have one custom-made for you.

TIP

Better yet, the Ba'al Shem Tov (see Chapter 28) taught that whenever a couple gets into a bad argument, they should read their ketubah out loud to each other. We all need reminders sooner or later.

Enjoying sacred moments, before and after

So many things happen on the day of a wedding — including coordinating the flowers, the food, and the music, not to mention the family — that it's easy to get distracted and end up with only a photograph or video of a ceremony from which you were mentally absent. The struggle, then, is to find sacred moments to refocus and remember what the wedding is really about.

Jewish custom offers several special moments during a wedding that we find intriguing and useful. For example, just before the ceremony, the *kallah* and *chatan* (bride and groom) meet face-to-face in a short ceremony called a *bedeken* ("covering"), in which the couple has a moment together to affirm their intentions just before entering the ceremony. Originally, this was when the groom made sure he was marrying the right woman before he pulled down her veil, which hid her face from view.

Similarly, Jewish couples traditionally retreat for a few minutes alone in a quiet room immediately after the wedding, a period called a *yichud*. Because the bride and groom customarily fast on their wedding day, the yichud is time for them to share their first meal together (perhaps a snack of fruit and cheese) while they mull over what they've just done. In the old days, this was the time when the marriage was consummated, though fortunately couples no longer have to perform under that kind of pressure.

TIP

ATTENTING A JEWISH WEDDING

The majority of Jewish weddings these days aren't that much different from their Christian counterparts. Besides the obvious differences — like the blessings in Hebrew and breaking a glass at the end of the ceremony — most Jewish weddings take on the flavor of the surrounding dominant culture. Nevertheless, here are just a few things to think about when attending a Jewish wedding:

- At the end of the ceremony (which is usually just after the groom stomps on the glass), yell "Mazel tov!" This really means "good luck," (see Appendix A) but is used in place of "Congratulations" or "Hooray!"

- Expect to dance, especially group dances such as the *hora*, in which everyone holds hands and dances in a long line or a large circle — often around the bride and groom, who are held aloft in chairs. Don't worry if you don't know the steps; you can pick it up quickly enough.

- At more Orthodox weddings, the men and women sit separately during the ceremony and then celebrate separately afterward. Also, you may want to wait until after prayers are said before digging in to the food at the reception.

A word of warning: If the wedding is very traditional, men and women aren't allowed to touch unless they're closely related. When being introduced to a traditional rabbi (if you are a woman) or to his wife (if you are a man), be prepared not to shake hands. The custom is a matter of modesty and propriety and not something to be taken as an insult.

Finally, the celebration after the wedding is a good time to schmooze with relatives, eat, drink, and dance until your *kishkes* (see Appendix A) hurt. However, Jewish sages have long taught that this is really a holy and sacred party, and that everyone in attendance must help make the day joyous for the bride and groom. That explains why the newly married bride and groom are so often hoisted up in chairs and danced around like royalty by their friends and family, each holding one end of a handkerchief.

Getting a Get: Divorce

Divorce has become so commonplace that people joke that officiants should ask at weddings, "Do you take this man to be your *first* husband?" Of course, divorce is nothing new. Over 2,000 years ago the prevailing laws in most places let men divorce their wives simply by expelling them from the house. Judaism made it harder — not much harder, but hard enough to send a message: Try to stay together if possible, but if the relationship becomes deeply painful and destructive, then it's better to divorce.

The Bible states that a divorce is accomplished when a husband gives a document called a *get* to his wife. The get is a complex legal document written by a rabbi, and it acts as a religious divorce, apart from any civil divorce the couple might pursue. (Of course, when the get was established, religious and civil law were both the province of the Jewish community.)

To a traditional Jew, a religious divorce is as important — if not more important — than a divorce granted by the state, because a Conservative or Orthodox rabbi will not remarry someone who has not given or received a *get*.

Compared to many modern-day laws on divorce, Jewish law makes it relatively easy to begin divorce proceedings. You don't have to prove how bad the marriage is. In fact, you need no more compelling reason than "she or he spoiled my dinner." While this may seem frivolous, it helps a couple focus not on what is wrong, but hopefully on what is right, and perhaps save the marriage. Preparing the divorce document and bringing together a rabbinic committee to oversee the ritual is complicated and time-consuming, perhaps providing time for the couple to reconsider their decision.

Walking through a divorce

If the couple can't be reconciled, and both parties agree, the divorce ritual is relatively simple: The get is prepared in the presence of a *bet din*, a three-person rabbinic court, and then given to the man. He hands his wife the get, she places it under her arm (a symbol of receiving it), and then the document is cut or ripped so that it can never be used again. Each person keeps a hand-written copy of the get, and the woman must wait 90 days until she can marry again (just in case she doesn't realize she's pregnant at the time of the divorce). The *bet din* also ensures that the man fulfills his financial obligations under the terms of their ketubah (see "Putting it in writing" earlier in this chapter).

Of course, Orthodox rabbis only recognize a get from an Orthodox bet din. On the other hand, Reform rabbis take the position that all you need is a civil divorce. However, in recent years, non-Orthodox rabbis, often with help from the couple, have created ceremonies of separation that attempt to address the spiritual issues in a divorce and to encourage a deeper understanding that can enhance the chances for better relationships for each partner in the future. For example, this ceremony can include the release of the wedding symbols, including the ring, the wine goblet, the ketubah, and so on.

Encountering rare troubles

If both parties agree on the divorce, the procedure is pretty smooth. However, if a woman wants a divorce and her husband either won't grant it or can't grant it (because he's not present), the woman becomes what's known as an *agunah* ("an anchored woman"), and can't remarry.

You can find terrible stories about unethical or spiteful men who extorted thousands of dollars from their wives in exchange for a get, or, perhaps worse, men who simply won't agree to a get on any terms, even after years of bitter separation. The bet din has the authority to compel the husband to divorce his wife, especially in cases of abuse or neglect, but there are few ways to enforce this, and so unfortunately too many traditional Jewish women still suffer.

If the husband can't be found — for example, if he died but his body wasn't found, and there were no witnesses to his death — the traditional divorce can't take place, and the wife becomes an agunah. Conservative Jews typically include a provision in their ketubot saying that the bet din can be called by either the man or the woman, and a divorce can be granted if either partner is absent and presumed dead.

CONTROVERSY

SAME-SEX CEREMONIES

Judaism can recognize marriages that the legal system doesn't. So, while Orthodox and some Conservative rabbis tend to consider same-sex marriages contrary to Jewish law, an increasing number of Reform, Reconstructionist, and Renewal rabbis now officiate at same-sex unions (some call these commitment ceremonies rather than marriages).

The Reconstructionist movement formally welcomed gays and lesbians in 1985, and in 1992 the movement published a paper stating that "Lesbians and gay men should be welcomed to full participation in every aspect of Jewish community life as individuals, couples, and families." The Reform movement passed a resolution in 2000 permitting same-sex unions, but they also stated that rabbis had the choice whether or not to perform such ceremonies.

As legal systems are more actively debating the validity of same-sex marriages, individuals belonging to liberal religious groups are increasingly supportive of sanctifying loving and committed relationships among their children, friends, parents, or siblings who are gay and want a life-long, monogamous relationship.

IN THIS CHAPTER

» Preparing for death with an ethical will

» Understanding the importance of the local Jewish burial society

» Knowing the do's and don'ts for attending a Jewish funeral

» Saying *kaddish* and other mourning rituals

Chapter **10**

Stepping Through the Valley: The Shadow of Death

J ews' attitudes toward death are different from many other Westerners. For Jews, the opposite of living isn't dying — rather, dying is part of living, and we're all literally in the process of dying right now. As many have noted, "Life itself is a terminal disease with a sad ending." Look, we're not trying to be morbid or weepy here. Instead, we simply want to make the point that if Judaism says anything about death, it's that people must recognize it, honor it, and live with it.

Contrast this embrace of death with the usual response (at least in America and most Western countries), in which people tend to shirk even the mention of death, preferring instead to say that people "pass away" or "are no longer with us." Have you ever noticed how many people at a funeral chatter about sports, or television, or almost anything other than the important event that just occurred? Today's Jews are just as susceptible to this denial as anyone, and yet Judaism itself teaches a different lesson. As one friend, who recently lost her mother, said: "Judaism really 'does death' right."

While Judaism recognizes the intensely personal nature of dying and mourning, it also supports the dying process as a community event. When a Jew has a death in his or her family, he should always call a rabbi or local congregation; even if the Jew isn't a member of a synagogue, the rabbi will know the proper community services that can help.

Judaism has developed customs and traditions with the understanding that people need clarity when they get close to death — either their own or that of a friend or family member. Some customs find their roots in Biblical times — for example, the Book of Genesis says that when Jacob buried his wife Rachel by the side of the road, he "set a pillar upon her grave" (which people interpret as a pillar of stones) — thus the tradition of tombstones and also of leaving a small stone at a grave site. Later tradition of burial beneath a mound of stones reinforced this custom. Other customs stem from a long history of Jewish superstition — such as some people's custom of opening a window after someone dies so that the soul can escape, or immediately lighting a candle at the person's head to symbolize the light of his or her soul.

This chapter focuses on what Jews can do before they die, what happens immediately after a death, and the mourning process. One thing is clear: Jewish tradition strives to accept death as a profoundly important step of the life cycle. To deny death is to deny life itself.

Planning for Death

Judaism, as a moral and ethical system of beliefs, places a great emphasis on people being kind both to themselves and others. In keeping with the call to kindness, Jews are encouraged to prepare for death as much as possible. After all, the more you plan for your death and communicate about it in advance, the easier you make things for your family and friends after you die. You can take several steps to prepare for death properly, including writing an ethical will and making plans for your burial.

Writing an ethical will

If you were to leave a message for your family or friends, to be opened after you die, what would it say? What would you want to tell your children, or your grandchildren (even if they haven't been born yet)?

The idea of writing a will describing what to do with your assets is widely accepted. However, Jewish tradition has long urged writing an ethical will as well, communicating your values and lessons, perhaps in the form of a letter or essay to be read after you die. People have published some wonderful and moving collections of ethical wills, including those written by great Jewish figures such as Maimonides, Nachmanides, and the Vilna Gaon. In modern times, people often create a video of themselves describing their ethical wills, to be shared with their survivors upon their deaths.

Many people include their ethical will as an unofficial "preamble" to their legal wills, although even if you have few or no assets at all, you can still write an ethical will. Many people have reported that this document has become a treasured family heirloom after a parent's or sibling's death.

TIP

Don't worry about sounding official or poetic when writing an ethical will. Here are a few things you may think about including in your ethical will:

>> Your personal and spiritual values

>> Your feelings about Judaism and your Jewish identity

>> How you would like people in your family to treat each other after you die

>> What accomplishments you feel good about and what mistakes you want others to avoid

Some people also include a note in their ethical will forgiving or asking forgiveness, but Jewish tradition also encourages people to ask for or give forgiveness in person whenever possible.

Making final confessions

The Jewish custom of making a "confession" just before death involves asking for a blanket forgiveness for all misdeeds.

REMEMBER

A Jewish "confession" is very different than those of other traditions. For Jews, confession doesn't require a rabbi, although often someone acts as a witness. Similarly, because Judaism holds that each person's confession is between him or her and God, the act of confession doesn't involve being absolved by anyone.

Reciting parting words

If possible, a person who is approaching death may want to recite the central affirmation of Judaism, called the Sh'ma (see Appendix B), which proclaims the absolute oneness of God. This recitation is meant to inspire calmness at a moment of transition, urging us to remember that everything is contained in God and that, in God, nothing can ever be lost.

Often, if the dying person is unable to recite the Sh'ma, family and friends can say it for him or her. At the moment of death, all of us need the reminder that we are always connected to the Source of all being.

CONTROVERSY

ENDING A LIFE

Judaism sees life as a gift from God — maybe not the gift you were hoping for, but a gift nonetheless. Therefore, Jews are generally opposed to anyone taking life, whether it's someone else's or their own. Suicide is considered disrespectful not only of a living being, but also of God, so Judaism has harsh rules against honoring someone who has willingly committed suicide: They can't be buried in a Jewish cemetery, mourning (including saying mourning prayers) isn't traditionally allowed, and sometimes family members feel shame in the community. That said, many rabbis, today and over the centuries, have gone to great lengths to show that suicide victims were mentally disturbed at the time of that act, so almost all Jewish suicides are buried in Jewish cemeteries.

Similarly, Jewish organizations are uniformly against physician-assisted suicide, arguing that no one has the right to choose death. On the other hand, many Jews recognize a gray area: If someone is terminally ill and in great discomfort, Judaism generally allows that they can refuse additional "unnecessary" medical treatment. That is, if someone is clearly going to die anyway, and treatment would simply prolong an unpleasant life for a short time, then the treatment isn't considered "healing." Along these same lines, most Jewish authorities allow do not resuscitate (DNR) instructions. Terminal illness poses an obviously a tricky situation, and one that is probably best discussed with a rabbi.

We encourage you to prepare a living will, or an advance directive, which stipulates what should be done in case you're in a coma and probably couldn't survive without life support. This can supplement any of the legal documents that you may wish to prepare to serve as guidelines for those who may have to make very difficult decisions. Communicating your wishes to your friends and family is a great kindness and is seen as a *mitzvah* (a path that brings people closer to God).

Arranging the Funeral

Judaism is very clear on what you do immediately after someone dies. First, upon witnessing or hearing about a death, Jews traditionally recite a blessing:

Barukh ata Adonai, Eloheynu melekh ha-olam Dayan ha-emet.

Blessed are You, Eternal One our God, Universal Ruler, the True Judge.

You may also hear people use a shorter version: *Barukh Dayan ha-emet* ("Blessed is the one true Judge"). Then, everything done between death and the funeral focuses on respecting and honoring the person who has just died, as well as preparing for the funeral and burial.

Jews believe that the funeral should happen as quickly after death as possible — preferably the same or next day, though the funeral is often postponed a day or two if family must travel from out of town. Also, funerals aren't held on Shabbat or other holidays.

Traditionally, the body isn't left alone, and people take turns being a *shomer* ("guard"), reciting Psalms next to the deceased until the funeral. A family sometimes pays someone to serve as shomer.

Similarly, out of respect for the dead, the body isn't traditionally displayed in an open casket, although if close family members want to see the body one last time before the funeral service, they can arrange to do so with the funeral home.

Returning to the earth

Much of the focus in Jewish tradition regarding death revolves around returning the body to the earth in a consecrated Jewish cemetery as quickly and naturally as possible — again, a respectful appreciation that death is a natural part of life. That's why the first thing that a Jewish community traditionally does when establishing itself in a new community is to consecrate land as a Jewish cemetery.

Embalming the body — which slows the decomposition process — is out. Being buried above ground is out, although many rabbis agree that crypts and mausoleums are okay. Also, Jews don't use make-up to make the deceased look more lifelike.

Cremation is definitely out for traditional Jews, who tend to consider it as terrible as committing suicide (many rabbis won't even officiate at a funeral if the body was cremated). We personally don't object to cremation, since it just speeds up a process that occurs naturally, anyway. However, perhaps early Jews were simply trying to draw a clear distinction between Judaism and pagan religions that customarily cremated their dead. And many Jews are sensitive about cremation because it draws up images of the Holocaust. Whatever the case, many more liberal Jews choose cremation, though some also request that their ashes be buried so that a tombstone can be erected, allowing friends and relatives to later return to mourn.

CONTROVERSY

Jewish tradition is less clear on the topics of autopsies and organ donations. On the one hand, Jews have long held that maiming a body (even a dead one) is a desecration. (In fact, if a traditional Jew requires a limb to be amputated, he or she will often have it buried and then request that it be reburied with the body after death.) On the other hand, Jewish law clearly states that saving another life takes precedence over just about every other principle. So, most rabbis would agree that donating an organ to save someone else's life is a mitzvah (see Chapter 4). On the third hand, many rabbis argue that Jews should avoid autopsies unless they're vitally important. Ultimately, we believe that all these decisions are private and should be discussed with a rabbi on a case-by-case basis.

Preparing the body

Given that the casket will be closed, you'd think a Jewish funeral home wouldn't care about the state of the body. Far from it! Jewish tradition holds that the body must be carefully washed, dressed in a plain white shroud (it's the same for both men and women), and blessed with special prayers in a process called *taharah* ("purification"). In many ways, this is like the dressing of the high priests in the biblical Temple days, as they prepared to enter the Holy of Holies (see Chapter 13). Perhaps taharah is meant to remind people that the process of death isn't just an exit from this world, but also an entrance into a higher, holier world.

One of the greatest *mitzvot* (commandments) is to do an act of charity for the dead, because they can never repay you. And performing taharah is certainly a great act of charity. In the 16th century, the idea of the *chevra kadisha* (the burial society, though literally the "holy society") first appeared in Prague. Today, every community with enough Jews has a chevra kadisha made up of volunteers who are trained in the proper rites to prepare bodies for burial. Men work on men, women work on women; they wash the body in a reverent silence, speaking only when necessary. Always respecting the dead, they uncover a small part of the body at a time to clean it, and they walk around the body rather than reaching across it.

Finally, the chevra kadisha places the corpse in a casket, sometimes wrapped in a *tallit* (prayer shawl) with its *tzitzit* ("fringes") cut off to signify that the tallit can no longer be used for prayer, and sometimes with a pillow of straw and some dirt from Israel poured over the eyes and heart. (Some Orthodox Jews believe that those who are buried in the dirt of Israel will rise first at the resurrection.)

By the way, if you've ever dealt with the funeral industry, you know that they love to sell expensive caskets. They're beautiful, but it's like burying money. It has long been the Jewish tradition for the casket to be as simple as possible — preferably just a pine box with handles. In fact, outside of America, many Jews are buried without a casket at all. If you want to cut through the salesperson's banter, just ask for the least expensive kosher casket.

Attending a funeral and burial

The funeral and burial are set up both to honor the dead and begin the mourning process for those still living. Jewish funerals usually take place in a synagogue, a funeral chapel, or at a cemetery, and while by tradition they're simple (symbolizing the belief that people are all equal in death), they vary widely and have no set liturgy.

Just before the funeral, close relatives (traditionally, siblings, spouse, parents, or children of the deceased) observe the rite of *k'riah*, making a small rip — in a tie, a coat, a blouse, or perhaps the sleeve of a dress — as a symbol of grief. Many Jews pin a black ribbon to their jacket and then tear that. Generally, those mourning the loss of a parent rip the left side of their garment (or place the ribbon on the left), and rip the right side for other relatives. The point is that Judaism doesn't want you to just show up; it wants you to really show your grief, without regard to vanity or decorum, and the k'riah is like ripping open a bag of grief to allow the tears and strong emotions to fall out.

Similarly, the eulogy (called a *hesped*) given by a rabbi, friend, or family member, honors the deceased and helps the mourners feel the depth of the loss. The Hebrew word for funeral is *levayah*, which means "to accompany," and you may see Jews walking behind the hearse to the graveside, often stopping to recite psalms, and then finally reciting the Mourner's Kaddish (see "Saying Kaddish" later in this chapter).

At the end of the funeral, when the casket is lowered into the ground, the closest family or friends throw the first dirt over it, often using a shovel or even their hands. By encouraging the mourners to actively participate in the burial, to hear the earth landing on the casket, Jewish tradition ensures that people recognize the reality of death and helps them begin the process of letting go. The traditional practice is for each family member to add three shovels of dirt to the grave using the back or rounded part of the shovel rather than the scoop to symbolically say how reluctant one is to lose this loved one. Perhaps it's just superstitious, but it's also the custom for each person to return the shovel to the mound of dirt because passing it directly to the next person in line is like handing them sorrow.

A FIRST-TIMERS' GUIDE TO ATTENDING A JEWISH FUNERAL

TIP

Jewish funerals rarely offer surprises to anyone who has been to a Christian funeral. The rites are similar, though the words and prayers are often different. There are, however, a few things you should keep in mind when attending a Jewish funeral or visiting the mourners afterward:

- Even though the casket is always closed, some mourners pass by it before or immediately following the funeral service to pay their last respects.

- Men should wear a dark *yarmulke* (*kippah*) in the synagogue and at the gravesite. One is usually provided if you don't have one.

- Because idle conversation is generally discouraged during a funeral, it's probably best to remain silent or only participate in the prayers during the service.

- Anyone (male, female, Jew, or non-Jew) can be a pallbearer, and it's a great blessing and a mitzvah (see Chapter 4) to do so.

- At the end of the burial, rabbis often ask that friends and more distant relatives stand in two lines so that the immediate mourners can walk between them, a symbol that they aren't alone and that others support their grief. Those assembled say, *"Ha-Makom y'nachem etchem b'toch sh'ar av'lay Tzion Veerushalayim."* ("May God comfort you together with all the mourners of Zion and Jerusalem.")

- After the funeral, the family usually holds a reception. Come in quietly, sit near the mourner(s) and take your cues from them: Don't speak until spoken to, talk about what they want to talk about rather than impose your own thoughts, and don't try to cheer them up. The reception sometimes turns into a time for socializing and catching up — if that happens, make sure it happens someplace else, away from the mourners. These courtesies also apply when visiting someone during the week following the funeral. Remember that you're providing consolation simply by being there.

- Sending flowers to a funeral or a mourner's home is *strongly* discouraged in Judaism. Not only will they wither and die in a few days (reminding everyone of the painful loss), but Jews think of flowers as "prettying up" or hiding a stark reality. Instead, simply offer your presence. It is customary to give charity in memory of the one who died (either to a charity of your choice or to one important to the deceased).

- Ask the individuals organizing the reception and care of the family during the week of mourning what you can do to help: bring food, do a few hours of babysitting, make a trip to the grocery or the airport. The idea is that the mourners shouldn't have to do anything themselves, and small acts make a big difference at this time.

You may attend a Jewish funeral and find a traditional Jew remaining outside the funeral parlor or cemetery, even if he is a close friend or relative of the deceased. Men who are descendants of the priestly class, called *Kohanim* (and who often have last names like Cohen or Kahn) are forbidden by Jewish law to come close to a corpse. Except for very close relatives, Kohanim don't enter the actual cemetery area. Sometimes their relatives are buried near the outer perimeter of the lot so that they can approach as closely as possible. In fact, all traditional Jews consider being near a dead person an act that makes them ritually impure (see Chapter 4), so they typically wash their hands either before leaving the cemetery or before entering the house of mourning. Often, a pitcher of water is made available outside the house of mourning for all to rinse their hands in symbolic purification.

Observing the Mourning Period

At the reception held immediately after the funeral (called a *seudat havra'ah*, "meal of consolation") friends and family traditionally eat eggs and other nonmeat, round foods (lentils, chickpeas, bagels, and so on) as a symbol of cycles and the constant renewal of life. Note that the mourners should never have to prepare this food themselves; that's a job for more distant relatives, friends, and neighbors.

Jews also traditionally cover the mirrors in the house where the mourning is taking place, often where the deceased lived. Perhaps this is a reminder that people shouldn't be concerned with vanity at a time of mourning, and should instead be a mirror to themselves, focusing inside rather than out. We also like the more mystical belief that when a body dies, the *nefesh* (the level of soul most identified with the body; see Chapter 5) may be confused and return home for a short time before dissipating — so we cover the mirrors so that the nefesh won't become even more upset when it sees no reflection of itself.

Everything is topsy-turvy during the week following a family member's death. To symbolize upheaval, as well as the sense that the mourners are struck low with grief, immediate family members customarily sit on low chairs or benches during the reception and during the first week after the funeral. Note that other guests — friends, neighbors, distant family members — aren't expected to do this.

The first week following a funeral

The first week after a funeral is an important time for reflection and healing, and it's traditional for Jews to "sit *shiva*" during this time. *Shiva* literally means "seven," referring to the week-long lamentation, when, in traditional households, immediate family members (the parents, children, siblings, and spouse) refrain from working, cutting their hair (or shaving), having sex, listening to music, doing anything joyous, or even doing laundry. Traditional Jews also refrain from wearing leather shoes (because in ancient times they were considered too comfortable), reading Torah (except for the depressing parts, like the Book of Job), swimming, and taking luxurious baths (though basic bathing is, of course, permitted).

For the first week, most Orthodox mourners don't leave home, and their synagogue makes sure that a *minyan* (a quorum of at least ten men) shows up for a daily service at the house. If there is no minyan, the mourners may attend a daily service at the synagogue in order to say *Kaddish*, the special memorial prayer. Other, less traditional Jews, may also have an evening home service that is more creative in nature. A nice tradition is to keep a candle burning for the entire seven days as a constant reminder of the soul who has left (you can buy "seven-day candles," although they don't always last a full seven days).

REMEMBER

The point of shiva is to stay focused on the death that has just occurred — taking the time to cry, grieve, feel the loss as well as the anger and other emotions — rather than getting distracted by other, less important tasks or diversions. Amazingly, psychologists have found that people who let themselves grieve using these age-old customs tend to heal faster and better. We wouldn't dare tell a mourner what he or she *should* do; rather, the key is to stay present as long as necessary. Many Jews today only sit shiva for three days, and they seem to feel this works for them.

Whatever the case, almost all the mourning practices are halted for Shabbat, when Jews attend services at the synagogue (though they still don't have sex or become too joyous). Although you don't observe the customs of mourning on Shabbat, that day does count as one of the traditional seven. Then, finally, in the morning of the last day, the formal shiva ends and the mourners enter back into the world. Often, friends or the rabbi may show up to take the mourners out for a post-shiva walk around the neighborhood.

The first month and year

Of course, no one gets over the death of a loved one in a week. The next three weeks (until the thirtieth day after the funeral) is called *shloshim* ("thirty"), when mourners begin to rebuild their lives, but traditional Jews still refrain from cutting their hair or shaving (unless it's necessary for their livelihood), or going to parties or entertainment (like movies and the theater). After this time, all mourners except the children of the deceased are expected to let go and cease their official mourning.

Because the loss of a parent is especially difficult, the children are obligated under Jewish tradition to mourn for a full year (based on the Hebrew calendar), avoiding parties and celebrations (unless it's something like your own wedding), and saying kaddish daily until the end of the eleventh month. (Some traditional Jews believe that a child's actions and prayers can help the soul of his or her parent in the first year after death. However, because only the most wicked need help for a full year — see the sidebar "What happens next" later in this chapter — the tradition is only to say kaddish for 11 months.)

Sometime during the first year after a family member's death, usually between six months and the first *yahrtzeit* (the anniversary of the death), it's traditional to have a short unveiling ceremony for a tombstone or a metal plaque at the gravesite. However, this is based entirely on local custom, so it varies widely.

Saying Kaddish

The Mourner's Kaddish is a prayer written mostly in Aramaic (which is similar to Hebrew). Jews recite it at the end of most synagogue services and at funerals. Here's the first paragraph:

> *Yitgadal v'yitkadash sh'may raba, b'alma dee v'ra khe-rutay v'yamlikh mal'khutay b'kha-yaykhon uv'yo-maykhon uv'kha-yay d'khol bayt Yisrael, b'agala uviz'man kariv v'imru: Amen.*

> Glorified and sanctified be God's great name throughout the Universe created from Eternal Will. May the Kingdom be established in your lifetime and during your days, and within the lifetime of the entire House of Israel, speedily and soon, and let us say: Amen.

Although Jews often think that the kaddish prayer is a prayer for the dead, the prayer doesn't even mention death or dying. The name *kaddish* is related to *kadosh* ("holy"), and the prayer glorifies the holiness of God, praising the Eternal One for the gift of life. After all, Judaism focuses on the idea that "it's all One" (see Chapter 2), and you can't have life without death.

Jewish tradition (probably originating around the 13th century) holds that the eldest son must say kaddish for his deceased parent every day for eleven months. (In fact, in Yiddish, this son is actually called "the kaddish," and in the old days people who only had daughters agonized over this because there would be no "kaddish" to say the kaddish for them.) More recently, however, all the children in a family may say kaddish during this mourning period, including women.

WORDS OF WISDOM

The Kaddish means to me that the survivor publicly and markedly manifests his wish and intention to assume the relation to the Jewish community which his parents had ... so the chain of tradition remains unbroken from generation to generation, each adding its own link.
— HENRIETTA SZOLD (ON WHY SHE CHOSE
TO RECITE KADDISH HERSELF RATHER
THAN HAVE A MALE FRIEND DO IT)

REMEMBER

In many communities, if a stranger suddenly starts showing up for the early morning services, everyone there simply assumes that he or she is in mourning.

Remembering the Dead

Many people find it baffling that so many Jews remember when people died, but not when they were born. In America, especially, people celebrate births — of friends, family, presidents, and famous figures. Jewish tradition tends to focus more on the day someone died, called his or her *yahrtzeit* (from the German for "anniversary"; pronounced *yar*-tsite). Israeli citizens even celebrate the yahrtzeit of past leaders, much the way Americans honor Washington and Lincoln's birthdays.

The yahrtzeit of a famous person (based on the Hebrew calendar, not the Western one) is often a quiet-but-joyous occasion, but that of a family member is seen as a time for solemn contemplation, remembering the deceased with prayers and by lighting a 24-hour candle (called a "yahrtzeit candle," in part symbolizing Proverbs 20:27 — "the spirit of humankind is the light of the Eternal"). Most Jews avoid celebrating or going to parties on a parent's yahrtzeit, and some even fast all day, study Torah, and go to services. On the first yahrtzeit, many Jews buy a memorial plaque, which is placed on their synagogue's wall.

Similarly, Jews remember their deceased friends and family at a special prayer service — called *Yizkor* — on four other holidays throughout the year: Yom Kippur (see Chapter 20), Sh'mini Atzeret (the last day of Sukkot; see Chapter 21), the last day of Passover (see Chapter 25), and the final day of Shavuot (see Chapter 26). The service contains a special series of prayers beginning with *Yizkor Elohim*, which means "May God remember."

You may hear Jews add a short Hebrew phrase after saying the name of someone who has died, usually *alav ha-shalom* or *aleha ha-shalom* ("peace be with him or her"). Or, if they're talking about a particularly righteous person, they may instead say *zai-cher tzaddik livrakhah* ("may the memory of the righteous be for a blessing") or *zikhrono livrakhah* ("may his memory be for a blessing," often written *z'l* after someone's name).

WHAT HAPPENS NEXT?

One of the biggest surprises in Judaism is that the Bible, the foundation of the faith that led to both Christianity and Islam, has nothing to say about what happens after you die. Heaven, hell, purgatory, reincarnation . . . these are all concepts foreign to the Torah, though not necessarily foreign to Judaism. The Bible itself (at least on the surface; traditionalists may argue that there are hidden meanings) is concerned specifically with how to live in this world, and the idea of an afterlife hasn't been central to Jewish belief.

Ultimately, Judaism throws up its hands and offers many options for what may happen after we've "shuffled off this mortal coil," as Shakespeare's Hamlet poetically described death. Here are just a few beliefs about the time after death:

- Many Jewish teachers suggest that basically nothing happens after death but that our souls and bodies will be resurrected when God decides it's time. Some believe a Jerusalem of Gold will manifest in that messianic time. No one seems to know what'll happen then.

- Jewish mystical tradition suggests that after you die, you travel deep into the cave of the patriarchs where you encounter Adam, who appears as a being of light. After reviewing your life, you spend up to a year in *gehenna* ("purgatory") — perhaps during those eleven months when your relatives are reciting the daily kaddish — and then you either move up to a higher level of paradise or you return to Earth in a process called *gilgul* (the Jewish notion of reincarnation) to complete more mitzvot.

- Some Jews imagine that after death, everyone listens to Moses teach Torah. For the righteous, this is heaven; for the wicked, it's hell.

- A famous folktale says that in both heaven and hell human beings sit at tables filled with wonderful foods, but they can't bend their elbows. In hell the people are perpetually starved, since they can't bring the food to their mouths; in heaven each person feeds his or her neighbor.

The fact is that in Judaism the life well lived is its own reward, while a wicked life is its own punishment. That's why in two of the stories quoted above, Heaven and Hell are described as identical places. The difference between them stems from us, reflecting the quality of our souls and the way we engage life; it really has nothing to do with divine Judgment after death. Even in its discussion of death, Judaism is concerned first and foremost with celebrating life, and with teaching us how to live well.

3

An Overview of Jewish History

You get to see the big picture, all 4,000 years of Jewish history from Abraham (the Patriarch) to Abe (you know, that guy who lives down the street from you). Jewish history is unquestionably full of pain and sadness, but it's also chock-full of triumph and joy. Judaism teaches that you can't have one without the other, so we delve into it all.

IN THIS CHAPTER

» The mything truth of the Bible

» The origin of the Jewish people

» How to make a fortune by interpreting dreams

» From Egypt to the Promised Land

Chapter **11**

Let My People Go: From Abraham to Exodus

Many modern Jews enjoy reading other people's myths — Native American legends, Hindu fables, Buddhist allegories — they all seem fascinating. Of course, if you ask, "Well, what about the stories of the Jews?" those same Jews may look at you funny and say, "You mean the Bible? Oh, that stuff is so tired!" (Or "passé" or "limp" or whatever the current slang is.) However, the nearly 4,000-year-old story of the Jews is anything but tired. In fact, if you look closely enough, you'll find that Jewish history is just as wild as anything else you might find — it's filled with mystery, sexual exploits, psychedelic imagery, and even car chases (well, chariot chases).

You can't tell the story of human civilization — in the East or the West — without exploring the history of the Jews. That's pretty strange if you think about it, because the Jews have never embodied any more than a tiny percentage of the population on any continent.

In this chapter, we dive in to the oldest part of Jewish history: the myths and legends so old that their only recorded evidence appears in the Bible. The earliest history of the Jews is told in the biblical books of Genesis and Exodus (called *Bereshit* and *Sh'mot* in Hebrew). The story lays out a series of beginnings: the beginning of civilization, the beginning of a monotheistic faith tradition, the beginning of codified law, and the beginning of the Jewish people. In fact, the word "genesis" means the origin or the roots, and by looking at the roots of Judaism, you can find out a lot about who Jews are today.

REMEMBER

Memorizing an endless series of historical dates and events isn't the important thing; instead, strive to understand how those beginnings unfolded to place you (yes, you) where you are right now.

These "creation myths" have been told and retold by Jews for at least 2,600 years (probably much longer), by Christians for some 2,000 years, and by Muslims for well over a millennium. Each event recounted holds deeper meaning: Sometimes it's a foreshadowing of events to come, sometimes it's a lesson to apply to daily life. While many Jews take the stories of the Bible as actual history, many more read them as myths — fictional tales carrying deep and timeless truths. The mythic dimension of these stories yields new meanings both personal and communal in every generation that reads them.

THE HISTORY BEFORE HISTORY

Are the stories in the Bible true? Did Noah really live until he was 950 years old? Did Abraham actually argue with God over the fate of the cities of Sodom and Gomorrah? Some people believe every story in the Bible happened just the way it's written. Others just as fervently believe that these stories have kernels of deep and profound truths, but that it's unlikely that the versions we have today are absolutely historically accurate.

Skeptics note that surprisingly little archeological evidence exists supporting the early biblical stories. In fact, the idea of historicity ("historical truth") wasn't even invented until much later by the ancient Greeks. However, a hundred years of archeology hasn't uncovered anything that necessarily contradicts the Bible, and the basic outlines of history and geography are almost certainly accurate. You can tour Israel today and recognize the cities, lakes, and other geographic features mentioned in the Bible.

One reason that many people think the Bible is accurate is that it says so many negative things about great Jewish leaders (like King David) and some positive things about people who later became enemies of the Jews (like the Midianites).

Judaism teaches that every verse in the Torah can be interpreted 70 different ways, indicating that at its essence Judaism believes in "truths" but not "the truth."

Ultimately, the Bible is a religious document rather than a historical document. Although many traditionalists say that the Torah is the end-all and be-all of human knowledge, it's probably safe to say that God won't strike you dead for maintaining a healthy skepticism about the historical accuracy of this admittedly extraordinary work.

The Genesis of a People

The shadowy origins of human beings first take form in the early chapters of Genesis, soon after the world is created. Hard-core traditionalists place this event around 3800 BCE. Curiously, this is just about the time that civilization first sprang up in Mesopotamia (in the area of present-day Iraq). Perhaps Adam and Eve weren't the first humans, but rather symbolic representations of the first civilized man and woman. Some say the Garden of Eden was watered by the Tigris and Euphrates rivers, which encompass that land and can still be visited today (with the proper visas, of course).

REMEMBER

Rabbis use the symbolism of Adam and Eve to present an important idea: If all humans are descended from the same couple, then no person can insist that he or she is of better lineage. This lesson appears a number of times throughout the Bible and later rabbinic literature and is a cornerstone in the idea of equality of all humans (see Chapter 6).

Beginnings of a Way

Of course, the Hebrews weren't around back then to keep Adam and Eve company. The story of the Hebrews unfolds later in Genesis and Exodus almost like a soap opera, telling the trials and tribulations of one family over many generations.

The story starts with a guy named Abram (or *Avram*, in Hebrew), who, around 1800 BCE, lives in a city called Ur with his wife, Sarai, and his father, Terah. Then, after some years, they all move to a town called Haran (see Figure 11-1).

Most people of that era believe in many gods, not just one; they worship gods of cities, gods of mountains, and so on. Abram, however, believes in a single God, who speaks to him, telling him to take Sarai south to the land of Canaan (which is today called Israel). God tells Abram and Sarai that their family will become a great nation and a blessing for all humankind, which is no small promise, given that Sarai can't have children, and Abram is 75 years old.

This one step — agreeing to follow the voice of his One God and travel to Canaan — establishes Abram as the patriarch of monotheism and the originator of the clan that was to become the Jewish People. On a more symbolic level, Abram leaves everything that is familiar to him and trusts something deeper. He lets go of his old way of life in order to see the Land, a new way of doing things.

After traveling to Canaan, God gives Abram and Sarai new names: Abraham and Sarah. Names in Judaism are linked with identity; the change in their names reflects a change in who they are, and "Abraham" in Hebrew means "father of a multitude." "Sarah" means "princess," or a woman of high rank.

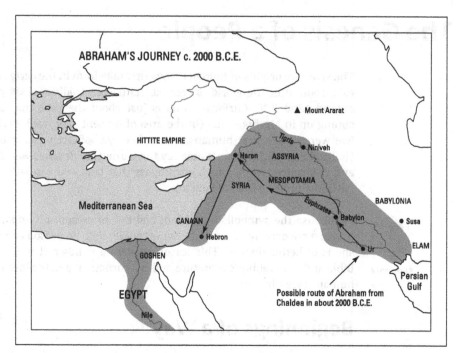

FIGURE 11-1:
Abraham's
journey from Ur
to Canaan begins
the Jewish story.

The next generation

Sarah is frustrated that she can't have children (they are both in their 80s); she suggests that Abraham sleep with her Egyptian maidservant, Hagar. This works for Abraham, and soon after, Hagar gives birth to a son, Ishmael. God blesses Ishmael, and both Jewish and Islamic traditions hold that Ishmael later becomes the father of the Arab tribes (thus making Jews and Arabs cousins).

Finally, when Abraham is 99 years old, God comes once again to make a deal: God will grant him a child with Sarah, and the child will be the ancestor of a great nation — but first Abraham must seal a covenant with God by circumcising himself, his male servants, his 13-year old son Ishmael, and agree that all his male descendants must be circumcised. The choice couldn't have been an easy one, but Abraham agrees, and Sarah soon after conceives, giving birth to a son, whom they circumcise and name Isaac. ("Isaac" stems from the word "laughter.")

Problems have been brewing for years between Sarah and Hagar, and now Sarah insists that Abraham send Hagar and Ishmael away, a task he doesn't relish. But God tells him to do what Sarah says, so he sends them off.

Now the Bible launches into a baffling story in which God seems to test Abraham's faith. Abraham hears God calling to him, "Abraham," and Abraham responds *"Hineini"* ("Here I am.") Then, God tells Abraham to sacrifice his beloved son Isaac.

Can you imagine choosing to do this to your own son, especially one for whom you've waited a hundred years? This is a powerful and complex story of faith, and one that Jews reread and re-examine each year at Rosh Hashanah (see Chapter 19). However, remember that every story in Genesis is a teaching story, and this hair-raising tale is an important aspect of the commitments of the Jewish people.

Abraham takes Isaac to Mount Moriah (the future site of the great Temples, in the center of modern-day Jerusalem) and binds him for the sacrifice. (That's why this story is commonly known as the *Akeda* or "the binding.") However, just as he raises his knife, Abraham hears an angel say, "Do not hurt the boy . . . Now I know that you truly fear God, for you have not withheld even your son from God." Abraham releases Isaac and instead sacrifices a ram that he finds caught in a nearby thicket.

The *Akeda* story illustrates the prohibition against child-sacrifice, which had been a part of previous cultures in that area. Jews also believe that it speaks to a deep question of healthy and unhealthy ways in which to demonstrate faith.

Who gets blessed?

Isaac, too, is considered one of the great patriarchs of Judaism, but the Bible doesn't say he did much other than marry Rebecca, grow to be prosperous, and father two boys: Esau and Jacob (more on them in a moment).

REMEMBER

Even though this story is usually called the Story of the Patriarchs, women are extremely powerful players in this drama. For example, Sarah provides strength for Abraham's journey, and some even infer that because God tells Abraham to listen to Sarah, she is actually the greater of the two. Similarly, Rebecca engineers the basic events that allow the family tradition to follow Jacob rather than Esau.

Jacob and Esau are twins, and they fight incessantly even while in Rebecca's womb. Esau is born first, and Jacob follows, clutching Esau's heel, a sign that he would be a "usurper." (The Hebrew name for Jacob stems from the Hebrew word "heel" and has the sense of "one who seizes the power of another.") The two boys represent the conflict between the hunter Esau and the gentle man (who later becomes the prototype for the scholar) Jacob.

Isaac clearly favors Esau's virile strength over the more gentle and quiet energies of Jacob. However, when Isaac grows old and blind and it comes time for him to bless Esau with his birthright, Rebecca tricks him into giving the blessing to Jacob instead. (In case you need to try this at home, she dresses Jacob in goat skins so that he smells like and feels as hairy as Esau.) Esau returns from the hunt, is understandably upset, and vows to kill Jacob as soon as his father dies.

Jacob takes the hint and gets out of town. Fast. But on his sojourn, he begins to mature into his own spiritual wholeness. The first night out, he dreams of a ladder that connects heaven and earth. He experiences himself accompanied by the Divine Presence, watching angels ascending and descending that ladder. He awakens with newfound awareness: "Surely the Eternal is in this place, and I did not know it"

He begins walking his own path and goes to live with his mother's brother Laban (or *Lavan*) in Haran. There, he falls in love with Laban's daughter Rachel and agrees to work for Laban for seven years in order to marry her. Seven years pass, and Jacob and Rachel marry. But the next morning Jacob finds out that he actually married and slept with Rachel's sister Leah. (What, did she wear a veil the whole night?) Laban confesses to the trick, but says that Jacob will have to work another seven years to get Rachel, too. (Remember that it wasn't uncommon at the time — around 1650 BCE — to have more than one wife.)

REMEMBER

The years working for Laban strengthen Jacob so that he is ready to return home to make peace with his brother. Perhaps he needed these extra years to grow physically, emotionally, and spiritually.

Wrestling with God

While Jacob lives and works in Haran, he and Leah have seven kids: Reuben, Simeon, Levi, Judah, Issachar, Zebulun, and Dinah (his only daughter). He also fathers four sons — Gad, Asher, Dan, and Naphtali — with Leah and Rachel's maidservants. And finally, he and Rachel have a son: Joseph. (Jacob and Rachel later have one more son, Benjamin; sadly, she dies while birthing him.) So by the time Jacob is ready to return to Canaan, he's got quite a lot of family and resources.

On the way south to Canaan, Jacob decides to spend the last night alone before his reunion with his estranged twin, Esau, so he sends everyone else ahead. In a very sparse biblical narrative, "a man" comes and wrestles with Jacob all that night. When daylight is about to break, the man asks Jacob to let go of him. Even though Jacob is wounded in his thigh, he doesn't release him, and says, "I will not release you until you bless me."

Jewish tradition holds that the "man" was, in fact, an angel of God. The angel's blessing comes in the form of a significant change of name: The angel says, "Your name is no longer Jacob, but rather Israel (*Yisrael*), for you have contended with God and with men and you have prevailed." Of course, this makes no sense what-soever unless you know that the name *Yisrael* can mean "one who wrestles with God" (some translate it "one who persists for God," or "prince of God").

Jacob's descendants, then, become the "children of Israel," and every one of Jacob's sons (except Joseph and Levi) later grows up to become the leader of a major tribe: the Tribes of Israel. Joseph's two sons grow up to lead their own tribes, and the Levites become teachers and priests for the other tribes.

WORDS OF WISDOM

After this episode Jacob is sometimes called "Israel" and sometimes "Jacob." Perhaps "Israel" reflects a deeper spiritual identity, and "Jacob" ("the usurper"), the everyday self. This patriarch, just like all humans, sometimes remembers and sometimes forgets his deeper self.

The Son Also Rises

Many tales help define the people who will later become the Jews, and they all begin with the story of Joseph. Because of Jacob's deep love for Rachel, the woman for whom he served Laban so many years, her firstborn son Joseph was clearly his favorite child. Joseph's brothers, not surprisingly, were jealous, and as Joseph grew older, he seemed to play into that jealousy rather than try to downplay it.

Joseph seems to be an obnoxious sibling. He rats out his older brothers when they do less-than-honorable acts, and he tells everyone about his dreams in which, symbolically, his brothers, and even his parents, bow down to him. His brothers finally plot against him, and, when they have the chance, capture him and fling him into a pit. However, instead of killing him, they sell him as a slave to a group of traveling traders and return home with his famous many-colored coat (the symbol of his special status with his father) soaked in the blood of a goat. Jacob believes that Joseph has been killed by a wild animal and grieves for his lost son.

Meanwhile, Joseph begins an unexpected journey to greatness. He's nothing if not resourceful, and instead of meeting the fate common to slaves at the time (an early death from overwork), Joseph proves himself to be a master manager. After he's brought to Egypt, he ends up in the home of Potiphar, an influential member of the Pharaoh's court, and Joseph is soon given authority over the entire household.

Joseph happens to be very handsome, and he attracts the interest of Potiphar's wife, who makes more than one pass at him. When Joseph continually refuses her advances, she finally becomes enraged, grabs his shirt as evidence, and screams that he has molested her against her wishes. Joseph is thrown into the dungeon. But even then he doesn't bemoan his fate. Instead, he demonstrates such managerial skills and competence that he is soon running the dungeon.

Interpreting dreams

Dreams hold a special place in the Bible, providing deeper insight into the events of this early, mostly mythical, history. As a child, Joseph's dreams of grandeur got him in trouble with his siblings, but sitting in prison, he finds that, with God's help, he can interpret the dreams of two other inmates, a cupbearer and a baker. He says that their dreams mean that in three days the cupbearer will be released and the baker will be executed — both of which come true. Two years later, the Pharaoh himself has a series of dreams that no one else in the kingdom can interpret. The cupbearer remembers Joseph and recommends him to the Pharaoh, who has him brought up from the dungeon.

The Pharaoh dreamt that seven lean cows consumed seven fat cows, and then that seven withered ears of grain swallowed seven full and ripe ears of grain. Acknowledging God's help, Joseph explains that following seven years of abundance, there will be a seven-year famine in the land of Egypt. He then encourages the Pharaoh to plan for the bad years by storing food during the years of plenty. He further indicates that this planning will enable Egypt to gain power during the bad years, since people from near and far will come to Egypt for food. He also suggests that the Pharaoh appoint someone to organize and manage such an enterprise, and the Pharaoh (of course) chooses Joseph, making him second-in-command over all Egypt.

THE JOSEPH SCHOOL OF SUCCESS

Somehow, Jacob and Rachel's son Joseph always lands on his feet. Even when circumstances seem to go awry, he achieves personal success and, at the same time, supports others. If we didn't know better, we'd think these stories were teaching us lessons in how to succeed in business by being yourself:

- Don't be afraid to dream your dreams, even if they seem far-fetched at the moment.

- No matter what happens, don't fill yourself with anger and resentment. Stay alert, make the best of circumstances, and look for the bigger picture.

- Help those around you, and act honestly on their behalf.

- Honor intuitive insights by sharing them to help others.

- Stand up for your own abilities without putting anyone else down.

- Don't get caught up in your ego; remember that a higher wisdom may be working through you.

- Keep your commitments.

- Don't forget to save up in case of leaner years ahead; your savings add up over time.

- Don't hold grudges. Be willing to support even those who once did you wrong.

A dream comes true

Everything Joseph predicts comes to pass, and after seven years of bounty, during which Joseph organizes the storage of produce, the land is struck with a terrible drought. The people of Egypt and the outlying areas trade their riches and their lands to the Pharaoh (through Joseph) for food. Before long, Joseph's brothers arrive from Canaan, sent by Jacob to buy grain. They don't recognize Joseph, but Joseph certainly recognizes them, and as they bow before him, his childhood dreams come true. However, time has changed Joseph from a spoiled brat to a real mensch (a stand-up guy; see Appendix A for details), and instead of treating his brothers poorly, he acts compassionately.

Joseph tests his brothers' integrity, and finds that they, too, have changed over the years. Of course, when he finally reveals his identity to them, they're terrified that he will seek retribution. But Joseph reassures them, saying it wasn't them who had sold him to slavery, but God, and that God had clearly meant for all this to happen so that he would be able to provide food for his family. (This is one of our favorite passages in the Bible, and especially helpful to remember when everything seems to be going wrong.)

In the final scene of this act, the Pharaoh tells Joseph to bring his family to Egypt and gives them the fertile area called Goshen (which was probably in the Nile delta area) as their home. Coming from a place stricken by famine, Egypt must have seemed like a real promised land for Jacob and his family. And perhaps it was for a time. But then things changed.

The Enslavement and Exodus

Beginning with the book of Exodus, the Bible shifts from telling stories of a family to telling stories of a people. The Children of Israel thrived while in Egypt, but after a couple centuries, "A king arose in Egypt who did not know of Joseph," and because he feared the Hebrews, he enslaved them.

Although archeologists haven't found any direct archeological evidence of the enslavement of the Hebrews, historians can point to an overlap between the Bible and known history. For example, early records tell of a people, called *Apiru* or *Hapiru*, who appeared in Egypt in the fifteenth century BCE. The word "Hapiru" may be the origin of the word "Hebrew," although it seems to have indicated a social class rather than a particular clan or family; some scholars note that the word "Hapiru" may have meant "refugee" or "someone on the fringe of society" in the ancient Canaanite language.

Historians have documented cases of non-Egyptian courtiers (perhaps like Joseph) who rose to significant power in the eighteenth and nineteenth Egyptian dynasties. However, when the Pharaoh Ramses II took the throne (around 1290 BCE), he began a series of massive building projects, and he probably enslaved a number of groups in Egypt, including perhaps the early tribes of Israel. This matches the Biblical description, which says the Children of Israel were enslaved and forced to build cities called Pithom and Ramses. Note that, contrary to common belief, the Hebrews didn't build the pyramids. The pyramids were seen as holy sites for the Egyptians that could not be constructed by a slave class.

A star is born

The real birth of the people Israel takes place during their exodus from enslavement in Egypt and their travels back to Canaan. Leading them out of Egypt is the one man who will hold more influence over the Jews than any other: Moses.

The Bible says that Moses was born after the Pharaoh has decreed that all male Hebrew newborns should be killed; so to save his life, his mother places him in a basket in the river, where he is discovered and rescued by a daughter of the Pharaoh. In this way, Moses is actually raised in the Pharaoh's home as a prince of Egypt.

Moses grows up, kills an Egyptian who was beating a Hebrew slave, flees to the land of Midian, attaches himself to Jethro, a priest of Midian, marries Jethro's daughter, and has kids. Perhaps while living with Jethro Moses undergoes his own spiritual training, and one day, out by himself with the flock, he sees a burning bush and hears his call from God. Like Abraham before him, Moses knew what to say: *Hineini!* ("Here I am!").

God charges Moses with leading the Hebrews out of slavery, and although Moses argues and kvetches, he returns to Egypt to carry out his duty. The experience of God's Presence is enough to influence Moses to take on an incredibly demanding career.

Finally, after confronting the Pharaoh repeatedly and announcing a series of plagues involving locusts, boils, and finally the killing of the first-born of Egypt, Moses finally gets the Pharaoh to release the Hebrews. As they flee, they approach a body of water that the Bible calls *Yam Suf*, the "Sea of Reeds." *Yam Suf* is usually translated as "the Red Sea," but it clearly isn't the same as the body of water known today by that name.

Extraordinary miracles happen throughout the Bible, but this is major: The Bible says that the water of the Sea of Reeds separates so that Moses and the people can cross, but then closes up again over the pursuing chariots of the Pharaoh. For those of you who like more rational explanations, some scholars say that the "sea of reeds" was marsh-like in places, so that the people could walk through it, but the heavy chariots were trapped by the muddy bottom. Whether you accept the miraculous image of the Biblical account or a more mundane possibility, the Hebrews made the crossing safely, and the Egyptians gave up pursuit at that point.

Are we there yet?

The Bible says that 600,000 men over the age of 20 and their families left Egypt. The ancient rabbis figured that the total community, including women and children, could have been 3 million. What a camp out that must have been! Once again, some historians disagree, observing that there probably weren't that many people in all of Egypt. What's more, later rabbinic commentators suggest that not all of the Hebrews were willing to leave Egypt. Rashi, one of the most famous rabbinic commentators (see Chapter 28), suggests that only 20 percent of the total Hebrew population left, reflecting how difficult it is to leave known places and strike out for something new.

No matter how many were actually there, the trip from Egypt to Canaan wasn't a simple one for the Hebrews, and it turned out to be a good deal longer than anyone may have imagined. After the experience at the Reed Sea, Moses led the people to Mount Sinai, in the southern part of the Sinai Peninsula. There, the Bible tells how the people beheld the Presence of God and received God's instructions to them — what people call the Ten Commandments. At this time they were officially consecrated to God's service as a holy people.

The Bible itself allows that the journey to Canaan might have only been an 11-day trip, but because the people lost faith that God would enable them to overcome the Canaanite tribes, the journey stretches to 40 years. Historically, this statistic isn't as outrageous as it sounds. The Hebrews likely chose a route that avoided the most fortified areas, including the Egyptian outposts along the Mediterranean coast and the kingdoms of Edom and Moab (which were in the area we now know as Jordan). Instead, they traveled far east, conquering the Amorite kingdom, and then approached Canaan (and the city of Jericho) from east of the Jordan river.

Moses died at this point, and leadership was given over to Joshua through the first act of *s'micha*, the laying on of hands, which even today is used to convey the ordination of rabbis and special blessing. The Bible states that no one knows where Moses is buried, perhaps to inhibit any kind of worship that such a place might draw.

Ultimately, everyone in the generation of the exodus, except Joshua and Caleb, would die in the desert before entering the Promised Land.

Entering the Promised Land

Traditional Jews today insist that God gave a large patch of land to the Israelites just before Moses died, an area that actually reaches far beyond current-day Israel. More liberal interpreters of the scripture point out that the Israelites were simply one more conquering nation in a land that had already been conquered numerous times in history.

The Bible has two versions of what happened when the tribes entered Canaan. In one story, they conquered Jericho, and then in three triumphant military campaigns took the whole land, dividing it among the 12 tribes of Israel. In another place, the Bible indicates that the battles weren't quite so neatly accomplished, and that there was considerable disarray among the tribes.

Whatever the case, for the next 2 centuries — from the end of the 13th to the end of the 11th century BCE — the Israelites lived in Canaan as separate tribes. During these times, they had no central government, and the tribes operated relatively independently unless they were threatened. They were linked by a covenant with a God they shared, and they all cherished the Ark of the Covenant, a shrine located in Shiloh, in the central hill country. In time, the Israelites changed from being a seminomadic people to an agricultural people, building cities and farming the land.

But the seeds of future conflict were already planted. Groups of Canaanites remained in the area. Archeologists have a wealth of evidence showing that the coastal areas were controlled by groups such as the Philistines (who were known as the "Sea People"). By around 1050 BCE, the Philistines — for whom the land "Palestine" was much later named by the Romans — had become powerful enough to defeat the Israelites at Aphek, destroying Shiloh and capturing the Ark of the Covenant. The defeat prompted the Israelites to create their own monarchy in order to more effectively defend themselves against such enemies.

Chapter **12**

The Kings of Israel: The First Temple

About a bazillion years ago (give or take a few years), single-celled creatures figured out that they could fend off the attacks of other vicious single-celled creatures by huddling together, and thus multicelled life forms (such as people) were born.

Similar scenarios have been replayed countless times throughout history: the American states are stronger as a united country, workers can demand more rights when they band together in a union, and organizations can succeed where individuals fail. The situation was no different around 1100 BCE, when the 12 tribes of Israel were living in Canaan and fending off the attacks of the Philistines and other tribes (see the previous chapter). None of the individual tribes was big enough to fight off the intruders. This was a time of intense chaos. The tribes needed to band together and follow a single leader.

The tale of the joining of the tribes is told in the biblical books of Judges and Samuel, a story so full of war, sex, political machinations, sin, and repentance that many scholars argue that it should be read as literature rather than history. Read either way, it tells of a period of almost constant warfare between the 12 individual tribes and their neighbors, as well as internal conflicts among the tribes themselves.

Because there was no central government, each tribe was ruled by a Judge, Prophet, Prophetess, or Chieftain. It was a bit like having state governors but no president. This period of chaos lasted roughly from 1200 BCE to sometime around 1020 BCE, when the people of Israel became so tired of this loose confederation that they complained to God and demanded a united government with a single king.

Finding the Right Guy to Be King

Can you imagine these 12 tribes, who had such great difficulty coordinating their energies, ever agreeing on a king? No, the King of Israel could hardly be chosen by vote, debate, or even battle. Only a man perceived as chosen directly by God would suffice.

The First Book of Samuel (there are two books of Samuel in the Bible) describes how this Divine choice manifested: first by revelation and then by lots. The first account explains that while a rather shy, confused young man named Saul was wandering near home, unsuccessfully trying to find his father's donkeys, he met the Prophet Samuel. God told Samuel, "This is the guy" (more or less) and instructed Samuel to anoint Saul with oil.

THE POWER OF THE PROPHETS

From the time that the Israelites left Egypt (see Chapter 11) people called prophets (*nevi'im*), with whom God communicated directly, spurred the Israelites, and their rulers, to more ethical action. The true prophet foretold doom during times of too much ease and forgetfulness, and spoke of future hope during times of defeat and despair, keeping the people on track in their quest for the Divine.

Here, for example, is the hopeful vision that the prophet Isaiah addresses to a people caught in great anguish during the exile in Babylonia (see Chapter 13). He looked forward to a time when:

Violence shall no more be heard in your land, wasting nor destruction within your borders; but you shall call your walls Salvation, and your gates Praise.

Your sun shall no more go down; nor shall your moon withdraw itself; for the Eternal shall be your everlasting light, and the days of your mourning shall be ended. (Isaiah 60:18, 20)

Next, because the people of Israel didn't yet know that Saul, clearly someone with no leadership experience, was to be king, they decided to select a king using a kind of divine lottery. The idea was that because God controls everything, whoever won the lottery was obviously the chosen one. First, each tribe chose lots (like choosing numbers, or throwing dice, or picking the long straw) to decide from which tribe the king was to be found. The tribe of Benjamin was picked. Then lots were picked by the Benjaminites, and the family of the Matrites was picked. Finally, lots were thrown yet again, and Saul, the son of Kish, from the tribe of Benjamin, was revealed to be the king.

Whether or not Saul was chosen exactly as described in the biblical text, many scholars suspect that this story provided a way to reduce the strain among the tribes and prevent warfare. It's far more likely that Saul, like King David and the other later kings, was a great warrior and charismatic leader.

Continuing War and Peace

As the first King of the Israelites, Saul had a tough job. Throughout his fifteen-year reign (beginning around 1020 BCE) he was almost constantly at war with the neighboring non-Israelite groups, particularly the Philistines.

Enter David, stage left

During the constant warfare under Saul, a young man named David became a war hero. The Bible says that David first became prominent when he defeated a veritable giant of a man named Goliath in combat by throwing a rock with his slingshot. Perhaps as a reward, or perhaps just to keep his eye on the young warrior, Saul invited David into his home and gave him one of his daughters as a wife. David soon became an essential part of the household, writing songs (psalms) and singing them while playing a harp to alleviate Saul's terrible depressions. In fact, tradition ascribes many or all of the Book of Psalms to David, even though scholars find evidence that suggests otherwise.

Unfortunately for Saul, the Israelites began to think that David could keep the peace better than Saul. Saul, not the most secure person in the world, began to hate David because the people would shout, "Saul kills hundreds of Philistines but David kills thousands." Perhaps Saul's paranoia was justified, perhaps not. David's extremely close relationship with one of Saul's sons, Jonathan, must also have been difficult for Saul to watch. Whatever the reasons, Saul actually attempted to assassinate David on several occasions. David fled from Saul for the next 15 or more years, during which time he continued to fight the Philistines (sometimes after first pretending to be allied with them) as the leader of his own private mercenary army.

Magic and mayhem

Poor Saul. Things just went from bad to worse—until he wound up breaking his own law and seeking answers from the dead. As the story goes, Saul was greatly outnumbered by the Philistine enemies. Saul sought counsel directly from God, but God wouldn't answer him. So he tried to talk to the judge and prophet Samuel. Unfortunately, Samuel had recently died. But this is the king! A little thing like death shouldn't get in his way, so Saul visited the Witch of Endor and begged her to raise Samuel's spirit from the dead. Saul himself, in line with earlier prohibitions, had outlawed witchcraft and necromancy, so the witch of Endor wasn't eager to violate the law. After Saul promised that she wouldn't be punished for practicing her craft, she reluctantly agreed.

Samuel's sprit arose from the dead and spoke to Saul, asking, "Why have you disturbed me? God has turned away from you and appointed another, David." This wasn't the news Saul had been hoping for. Old, tired, and renounced by God, Saul and all but one of his sons died in their next battle against the Philistines.

Living under the Lion of Judah

After Saul's death, his only surviving son ruled for a very short time. David quickly claimed his place as the most loved leader and the undisputed king over the land (see Figure 12-1).

While Saul was a Benjaminite, David's ancestral tribe was Judah (whose tribal symbol was a lion). This new kingdom was called the Kingdom of Judah and later became known as Judea. Sound familiar? If David had never become king, this book might be called *Benjaminism For Dummies*.

Many people think of King David as a beautiful, beloved, and kind ruler who played his harp and sang all day. But David's rule, from around 998 until 967 BCE, was far from easy. He fought many wars with the Philistines and the other neighboring nations, in particular the Jebusites, from whom he acquired the city of Jerusalem, centrally located between the northern and southern halves of his kingdom. This city became the crown jewel in his empire, his political capital, and the new home of the Ark of the Covenant, thus the religious center of his empire.

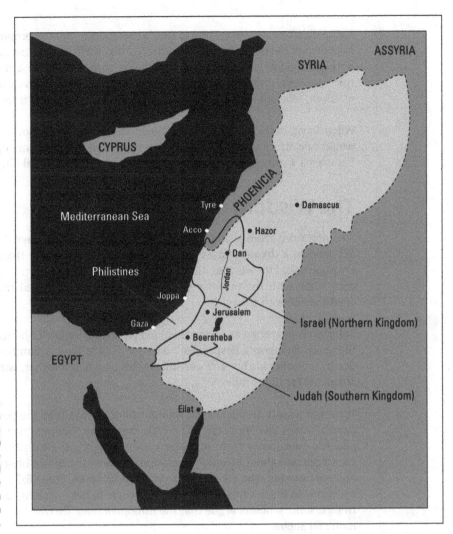

FIGURE 12-1:
Israel's
boundaries (in
the dashed lines)
during the time
of King David
and then the
later Northern
and Southern
Kingdoms.

David didn't just defend the land, he sought to expand it. In fact, he was so successful at conquest that the Israelites had control of more land than ever before — a vast empire that stretched from the Mediterranean Sea to the desert to the east, and from the Sinai desert all the way north toward Tyre and northeast to the Euphrates.

However, after David conquered the land, he spent the remainder of his life struggling to keep it. Not only did he have to fight "foreign" invaders trying to capture and recapture land, but he also got bad press from a sex scandal.

David's weakness was Bathsheba, a married woman whom he greatly desired, and whose husband David sent on a military suicide mission. Needless to say, his action didn't exactly place him in God's best graces, and the prophet Nathan came to confront David with his misdeeds. To his credit, David heeded the message Nathan brought, and he deepened his own commitment to a more appropriate rule. However, that rule wasn't without its special pains. Even his beloved son, Absalom, rebelled against him, and David was forced into civil war.

When David grew old and was unable to rule, the question of which of his sons would rule after him was in doubt. After much plotting and manipulation, it was Bathsheba's son, Solomon, who became the heir and eventual king of Judea.

The Wisdom of Solomon

Solomon ruled from around 967 until 928 BCE. The Bible says that God came to Solomon in a dream and asked him what he wanted more than anything, and Solomon asked for wisdom. God is supposed to have given him special divine wisdom along with the promise that as long as his line obeyed the law, kingship would reside with them.

Solomon is described as a wise ruler, judge, and diplomat. To battle various palace intrigues, Solomon's first "wise" decision was to have a number of men put to death, including his father's general and his own half-brother, with whom he had competed for the throne.

His reign wasn't all bloodshed, though. Solomon could be the poster boy for the slogan "Make love; not war." The Bible states that Solomon had 700 royal wives and 300 concubines from just about every neighboring kingdom. Many stories have been told about Solomon's relationship with the Queen of Sheba, a beautiful and wise woman who visited Jerusalem and Solomon. Some folks believe that she converted to Judaism and converted the people in her own kingdom in Africa, too. In fact, some scholars argue that the Ethiopian Jews are the descendants of Solomon and Sheba.

Building the Temple

Although today Solomon is probably best remembered for his decision to cut a baby in half to settle a dispute between two alleged mothers (the false mother agreed and the real mother screamed), to the Jews, he's known as the man who built the First Temple in Jerusalem. This had been the dream of his father, King David, who wanted to build a giant Temple around the Ark of the Covenant, but God wouldn't let him. The ancient rabbis note that because David was too bloodied by battle, it was fated that he wouldn't build the Temple, but his son would.

About ten years after Solomon became king, and with God's approval, he decided it was time to start building. Where David settled Jerusalem as the center of Israel, Solomon, with the building of the Temple, established the city once and for all as the central location for the worship of God.

Tradition holds Solomon in high regard as the writer of the Book of Proverbs, Song of Songs, and the Book of Ecclesiastes. Other scholars argue that although Solomon may have written some Proverbs and songs, the versions in the Bible were probably compiled if not composed at a later date by someone other than Solomon.

Telling a Tale of Two Kingdoms

Expanding an empire and embarking on massive building projects takes lots of human labor, preferably cheap human labor. In order for King Solomon to carry out his ambitious building projects throughout Judea, he raised taxes and drafted a number of people into enforced labor. Not a popular move, but it seemed to work out for a while.

Unfortunately, when Solomon died (around 928 BCE), his son Rehoboam became king. The Bible recalls that upon Solomon's death, the people went to Rehoboam to ask him to ease the workload Solomon had imposed. The king responded quite rudely, even comparing his own father's private anatomy to his little finger. The answer was clear: longer hours, no pay.

Strangely, Rehoboam was surprised when almost all the tribes rebelled against him — with the exception of the tribes of Benjamin and Judah, the Temple priests, and some of the Levites. The rebelling tribes invited a man named Jeroboam to be their new king, and they declared a separate Israelite kingdom, also called the Northern Kingdom (as opposed to the Southern Kingdom of Judea).

A hundred years of unity were shattered, and from then on, the Israelite Kingdom and the Judean Kingdom were almost constantly at war with each other. Jeroboam built two Temples in the Israelite Kingdom in order to keep his subjects from visiting Jerusalem, which was in Judea. These Temples, however, were considered idolatrous to the people of Judea.

Many different families ruled the Northern Kingdom over the next two centuries with no one family maintaining the kingship for very long. The various Biblical accounts depict most of these kings and their wives as terrible human beings who led the people into idolatry, sin, and mistreatment of the poor and the unfortunate.

WHERE ARE THE LOST TRIBES?

The so-called Lost Tribes of Israel — those dispersed by the Assyrians in 722 BCE — pose an interesting question to history: Where did they go when they got chased out of their homes? Some scholars say that the Lost Tribes became the Native Americans, the Eskimo, the Irish, the Ethiopian Jews, the Japanese, and other peoples all over the planet. However, most historians suggest that the Israelites assimilated into Assyrian culture and lost their Israelite identity. It's also possible that some Israelites maintained their beliefs until they were joined in exile by the Judean kingdom in 586 BCE.

For just over 200 years, the Northern Israelite Kingdom ruled and fought off invaders. They survived in large part by paying a tribute (some might call it "protection money") to the larger and more powerful Assyrians, who lived farther to the North. When, in 722 BCE, the Israelite Kingdom decided to stop paying the tribute, the Assyrians swept down, easily overthrew the Israelite army, and deported the ten tribes of Israel (see the sidebar "Where are the Lost Tribes?").

The Southern Judean Kingdom continued to be ruled by descendants from the house of David (who, by the way, did learn from others' mistakes: They kept paying the Assyrians the protection money). Most of the kings were, according to the Books of Kings and the works of various prophets, bad kings who led the people into idolatry and questionable ethics. Perhaps such temptations come with the job — those with the greatest power too often misuse that power for their personal enjoyment.

A notable exception to this line of poor rulers was King Josiah, a very innovative king who began to rule around 640 BCE. During his rule, a missing book of the Bible (probably the book of Deuteronomy), was "miraculously" recovered, leading to great religious changes. The biggest change was the emphasis on the centrality of Jerusalem. All sacrifice was outlawed except at the Temple in Jerusalem, a decision that was probably quite good for the economy.

The Fall of the First Temple

When the Israelite Kingdom was destroyed and the Judean Kingdom was left standing, several prophets and kings argued that the Judeans were vindicated. Unfortunately for them, Judea was still caught in the land struggles of three much-larger empires: Egypt, Babylonia, and Assyria. The final endgame reads like a New York-style mafia story: Josiah tried to help the Babylonians by holding back the advancing Egyptians. The tactics worked for a time, but then Josiah got killed, Egypt took over the Judean "turf," and Babylonia invaded, pushing out the Egyptians.

At first, the Babylonian King Nebuchadnezzar imposed taxes but left the ruling power intact; however, he became less patient after the Judean King Yehoyakim began a rebellion against Babylonia. It wasn't long before Yehoyakim was killed and Nebuchadnezzar charged in once again. Still somewhat patient, Nebuchadnezzar initially left the Temple standing. He placed Zedekiah, a son of Josiah, on the thrown as a puppet king but left everything else pretty much alone.

Around 587 BCE, Zedekiah, supposed to be a king in name only, rebelled against the Babylonians. After a long siege, Nebuchadnezzar's troops broke through the walls of Jerusalem. They killed Zedekiah's children in front of him, blinded him, burned down the king's palace, and, more importantly, burned down the first Temple. The jig was up, the game was over, and Nebuchadnezzar dragged just about anyone who was anyone off to exile in Babylon.

Chapter 13

Bracketed by Exile: The Second Temple

When we hear someone talking about "the sixth century BCE" it's almost as though they're telling us about some other planet. When reading all this history, it's so easy to forget that people 2,500 years ago weren't all that different than today. They had relationships, paid taxes, and complained about the government, just like people do now. So when we talk about what was happening in the sixth century BCE, remember that this isn't *Tales from Planet 9*, but rather the real-life history of real-life people who were caught up in forces bigger than themselves.

In this chapter, we talk about what happened after the Babylonian exile (see the preceding chapter). The Jewish people and the land of Israel (of course, it wasn't called *Israel* back then) got caught up in a game dominated by four enormous empires: Babylonia, Persia, Greece, and Rome.

The sixth century BCE was a spiritually rich time, when the prophets Isaiah, Jeremiah, and Ezekiel helped lead a Jewish renewal. At the same time, two other major religions were being founded: Zoroastrianism began in Persia, and the Buddha became enlightened in India.

Finding a Home away from Home

Nebuchadnezzer's destruction of the Temple (see the previous chapter) signaled a radical change for the Children of Israel: There were now more Jews in exile than in Judea — mostly in Babylon, though some lived in Egypt and other lands.

The Jews who were taken to live in Babylon, aside from being upset about being torn away from their homes, actually lived fairly well. They were allowed to own land, to farm, and to practice Judaism — although for the first time in Jewish history, the practice no longer included animal sacrifice (because they were separated from the Temple).

The exile from Judea lasted almost 50 years, until 539 BCE, when Cyrus of Persia conquered Babylonia. Under a remarkable policy of ethnic tolerance, Cyrus gave permission for the exiled Jews to return to Judea and rebuild the Temple in Jerusalem. In fact, because of his respect and open-mindedness, Cyrus is today considered one of the most important non-Jews in the Bible.

There's no place like home

Although 50 years in exile doesn't sound that long, it was long enough for the Jews to learn a new language (some even forgetting Hebrew in the process) and become comfortable in the very fertile land of Babylon. So when Cyrus announced that they could leave, only a handful jumped at the chance — mostly priests, a few prophets, and several people who claimed to be descendants of King David (perhaps with political aspirations).

In fact, several prophets, in particular Zechariah and Haggai, were very enthusiastic about creating a new Judean kingdom. The Persian government was tolerant, but not that tolerant, and around this time, anyone who spoke too loudly about being of Davidic descent tended to disappear.

In the meantime, the Jews in exile in Babylon acted much as Jews outside of Israel do today: A few emigrated, but most chose to stay put and send charitable donations to support the home-team effort. The Babylonian Jewish community flourished, laying the intellectual and religious foundations that would flower as the major center of Jewish culture and learning 500 years later (see Chapter 14).

Building and rebuilding

The returning Jews built the Second Temple in Jerusalem, but Judaism seemed to flounder for some 50 years, until the Persian government sent Nehemiah as a new provincial governor. Some years later the king of Persia sent Ezra, a Jewish scribe of priestly descent, to enforce the law of the God of Israel (and probably the Persian law, too).

Both Ezra and Nehemiah rededicated the Temple together in 428 BCE by gathering the community and reading the entire Torah. The reading was translated into Aramaic for those who had forgotten Hebrew while living in exile.

While the "kingdom" was a kind of "Temple State," ruled by the high priests and governors of the Persian empire, the next 100 years were relatively good for the Jewish people. The only real difficulty during this time was a power struggle between those who returned to Judea from exile and those who had never left. It's an interesting issue that in some way continues to this day in a slightly different form: "Who is more Jewish? The people who never left the area or the people from the Diaspora (outside of Israel)?"

It's All Greek to Me

Nothing lasts forever, including the Persian empire, which was conquered by the Greeks (led by Alexander the Great) in 332 BCE. At first, this meant little to the Jews, other than having to learn Greek. However, after Alexander's death, nine years later, the empire was split among four Greek generals, two of whom are important to Jewish history:

>> **Seleucas:** He formed the Seleucid (pronounced "sell-*oo*-sid") empire and had control over what had been the Persian empire.

>> **Ptolemy:** He formed the Ptolemaic (pronounced "p'tall-eh-*may*-ick") empire and had control over Egypt.

The Seleucid and Ptolemaic empires were in almost constant warfare over their boundaries. Unfortunately, Judea sat right in the middle of the two and was passed back and forth many times.

The ptol and short of it

For most of the next century, Jerusalem and the Judean "kingdom" were ruled by the Ptolemaic empire, and life was fairly good. It was so good that many Jews spoke only Greek (especially those who lived in the Egyptian city of Alexandria), and Jews became increasingly "Hellenized" — that is, they assimilated into the Greek culture of philosophy, art, and sport. Above all, the culture focused on physical pleasure and beauty, which may have felt like a relief to many of the Jews who yearned to become part of the new cultural opportunities.

At around 250 BCE the biblical texts were translated for the first time (legend has it that the Ptolemaic emperor wanted the translation for his vast library collection at Alexandria). Of course, any text loses something in translation, and the priests worried that the new Greek version of the Holy Scriptures wouldn't be faithful to the original. There is a wonderful story that 70 scholars, each separated from the others, miraculously translated the texts exactly the same way, proving that this one translation was correct.

This translation, along with texts added later, became known as the *Septuagint* (which means "the seventy"), and it included a number of books that the Jews didn't keep in the Hebrew Bible, such as Tobit, Judith, Maccabees, and Sirach (also called Ecclesiasticus). Today, Roman Catholic and Eastern Orthodox Bibles still include these additions — called the *Apocrypha* — but Protestant and Jewish bibles don't.

The last emperor

This period of relative calm and peace came to an end when Judea fell under control of the Seleucid emperor Antiochus IV, around 176 BCE. Antiochus, apparently more neurotic than his predecessors, insisted that the peoples of his empire assimilate or die (not unlike the Borg in *Star Trek: The Next Generation*). As Antiochus imposed greater taxes and restrictions on acting Jewish, the resentment against his rule grew.

Life for the Jews got worse after Antiochus looted the Temple to fill his wallet, removed the current high priest, and then replaced him with the highest bidder, a scheming guy who probably wasn't even an official priest. The situation was ugly, and the future didn't look good for this little tribe.

A Parting of Ways

When people say that the land of Israel has been a land of strife and combat for thousands of years, they really mean it! After 15 years of increasingly harsh rule under Antiochus, rebellion broke out. It began with a small-town Jewish priest named Mattathias who, with his sons, used guerilla warfare tactics to attack the Seleucid armies and the false high priests, as well as destroy the Greek pagan temples. Mattathias died in battle, but his sons fought on, especially Judah, who soon became known as Judah Maccabee ("Judah the Hammer").

A year later, Jerusalem was recaptured by the religious Jews and the Temple was rededicated, ending about 175 years of Greek rule over the city, a feat that is to this day celebrated on Chanukkah (see Chapter 22). Unfortunately, the fighting didn't stop there. As soon as the Maccabees (the whole family took on the name) were in power, they became as tight-fisted as the Seleucids they had conquered.

After a short time, all but one of the Maccabee brothers had died or been assassinated, and the last Maccabee, Simeon, decided to appoint himself king. For the first time in nearly 400 years Judea was ruled by a Jewish king and so no longer subject to the approval of a non-Jewish power. His dynasty (known as the Hasmonean dynasty) lasted a century, but it was a century of turmoil, not only with neighboring countries but especially between the two major parties that grew up within Judaism: the Pharisees and the Sadducees.

All Roads Lead to Rome

The kings and priests who followed Simeon supported the Sadducees, the priestly Jews who believed fervently and righteously in the sacrificial services of the Temple (also called the Temple Cult). Some Jews, disgusted by what they considered the desecration of the Temple, and the leaders' attraction to Greek practices, split off and became the Essenes, a semimonastic group widely believed to have written the Dead Sea Scrolls.

The other group unhappy with the Hasmonean and Sadducean rule were the Pharisees, who believed in the Oral Torah (an additional teaching they understood was received by Moses along with the contents of the written Torah, and which later became the basis of the Talmud; see Chapter 3). Insisting that each Jew was responsible for his or her own relationship with God, the Pharisees firmly downplayed the primacy of the Temple and its sacrifices. They didn't accept the authority of the priests of the Temple, and they urged Jews to worship in synagogues and to study Torah. In this way, the Pharisees laid the groundwork for an intellectual and theological flexibility that enabled Judaism to survive the destruction of the Second Temple and allowed it to continue to evolve over the ages. At the time, however, this support didn't put them in good stead with the priestly ruling powers.

John Hyrcanus and his son Alexander Jannaeus were two rulers who often resorted to violence to repress the Pharisees and support the Sadducees, killing thousands of Pharisees in order to maintain power. At the same time, these two men also greatly expanded the land of Judea, resulting in the forced conversion of other tribes to Judaism. As we discuss later in this chapter, it's rarely a good idea to convert people against their will.

Alexander's wife, Queen Salome (this is a different Salome than the one, some years later, who wanted John the Baptist dead) became more political after he died, keeping the peace by offering much more power to the Pharisees while still maintaining her son Hyrcanus II as high priest. But trouble brewed under the surface, and after Queen Salome died in 67 BCE, her younger son, backed by the Sadducees, wrested power from his brother and assumed not only the role of King but also of high priest.

With Judea continually involved in a civil war for three years, Hyrcanus II finally decided to invite the Roman Emperor Pompey to settle the dispute between the two brothers. Pompey did what any reasonable Roman general would do: He decided in favor of Rome, stripping both brothers of power and insisting that Judea start paying tribute as a vassal state (though he did leave Hyrcanus II as high priest). Rome was the dominant power across Europe, Egypt, and now Judea.

An Edifice Complex

Hyrcanus II continued ruling as high priest under the greater control of Rome for over 20 years. After Pompey died, Julius Caesar became the uncontested leader of the entire Roman empire, though he was soon murdered and was eventually succeeded by Mark Antony. Antony wanted a governor of Judea whose first loyalty would be Rome, and so he picked a man who, while Jewish "in name," had little connection to the Jews: Herod, whose father had been forcibly converted to Judaism by John Hyrcanus.

Herod was an ambitious, scheming, paranoid man — and those were his good qualities. He didn't favor the Pharisees or the Sadducees, but rather annoyed just about every Jewish faction. For example, one of his early orders of business was to marry the only living Hasmonean female and have the high priest, her brother, assassinated. He then angered many by appointing a new high priest whenever he wanted to. Later, afraid of a possible coup, he had his wife and two children killed. He was that kind of leader.

Herod was clearly a terrible guy, but he is widely remembered for the amazing structures he built or rebuilt, including the desert fortress of Masada and the port city of Caesarea. You can still see the ruins of both today. Most importantly, while Herod wasn't the least bit religious, he vastly built up the Second Temple, creating one of the most amazing architectural wonders in the Empire. The Western Wall in Jerusalem, which some people call the "Wailing Wall," is the remnant of the outer retaining wall that Herod built around the rebuilt Temple.

Not one but many messiahs

It seems that no one, except perhaps Herod himself, was happy under his rule. Each sect — the Sadducees, the Pharisees, and many others — wanted to rebel.

False prophets and false descendants of King David appeared out of the woodwork, spreading unrest among the people. To add to the complexities, the nature of messianism changed during this time period.

In earlier years, the term *mashiach* ("anointed one," or "messiah") simply referred to both high priests and kings, who were anointed with oils as a sign of office. However, during Herod's reign, in the first century BCE, the idea that a messiah would come who could perform miracles began to gain popularity. Later, when Herod died in 4 BCE, the chaos and wild hopes in the land intensified. People were primed for change and for something new in which to believe.

Death and dismemberment

After Herod's death, his sons fought for control over the land. Rome, while not eliminating the Herodian Dynasty, decided to limit its control, so they appointed each of Herod's four sons to a small part of the greater kingdom. Then the Romans brought in "procurators" to act as governors, maintaining Roman law. These men were mostly scoundrels, more concerned with filling their wallets than with keeping the peace or taking care of the people under their control.

Today, the most famous of Herod's sons was Herod Antipas, who had John the Baptist beheaded, possibly for speaking publicly against Antipas's marriage to his own sister-in-law. Similarly, the most famous of the Roman procurators was Pontius Pilate, who ordered the crucifixion of a young Jewish preacher from Galilee named Jesus, along with hundreds, and probably even thousands of other Jews who threatened the political power of the Romans. (For a discussion on whether the Jews killed Jesus, see Chapter 17; for information on why Jews don't believe Jesus was the messiah, see Chapter 29.) A few years later, Pilate was dismissed as governor because he proved too cruel to his subjects.

Sects and Violence

It's tempting to talk about what "the Jews" and "Judaism" were like in the first century CE as if there was only one thing going on. But, then as now, there were many groups within Judaism and many factions of the community.

Judea was a mess politically: The Sadducees fought with the Pharisees over philosophy, religious practice, and control of the Temple compound. Class differences also existed; the Sadducean priests were aristocratic, while the Pharisees were mostly farmers as well as scribes and scholars who would go on to become the rabbis. Most Jews were lower class subsistence farmers working for absentee landlords and were taxed to death by the Temple and Rome.

More than anything, though, none of the Jewish groups liked the Romans. Gangs of Jews, called the Zealots, began to appear, violently attacking Jews who were known to be in collaboration with the Romans or were simply not anti-Roman enough. Ultimately, in 66 CE, this popular uprising evolved into a full-scale war against Rome.

Unlike most wars, this war was incredibly disorganized. Although the various sections of Judean society all agreed in the "freedom of Zion" (a slogan seen on coins dating from this era), they disagreed over who should lead the rebellion. In fact, near the end of the war, when the walls of Jerusalem were about to fall to the Romans, there were three factions in Jerusalem fighting for control of the Temple. They clearly preferred to fight each other rather than the really dangerous enemy.

In the end, Titus, the son of Vespasian, the new Roman Emperor, conquered Judea and Jerusalem in 70 CE on the day of Tisha B'Av (see Chapter 27). The great Temple was destroyed and legions of Jews, along with their religious artifacts, were marched more than 1,500 miles back to Rome as prisoners and slaves.

The war wasn't entirely over, though. Over the next few years, several small Jewish outposts continued to fight the Romans. The last surviving group lived at Masada (the mountain fortress built by Herod that overlooked the Dead Sea). When the Romans finally broke into the fortress, they found that the Jews had killed themselves rather than be captured. Although some scholars debate the truth of this story, it has great meaning in modern Israeli ideology; up until recently, the soldiers of the Israeli Defense Forces were sworn in on top of the mountain, which served as a symbol of Jewish heroism.

THE FIRST JEWISH HISTORY FOR "DUMMIES"

The only contemporary written source for the period of the revolt are the works of a man named Josephus, a Jewish general who was captured in 67 CE and later worked for the Romans. Some scholars suspect that his history is unreliable — not only did he write his account after the war, when Rome had won, but his work was largely self-serving — but there's a good chance that much of what he said was correct. He clearly tried to salvage the reputation of the Jews in Roman eyes. Ultimately, however, he is the first, best, and only historical source that exists for Judean life leading up to the revolt, as well as for information about the revolt itself. And for the understanding of history, a questionable source is better than no source at all. The Talmud (see Chapter 3) also contains historical material from this time, which had been passed down as oral tradition through the generations.

Chapter **14**

The Exiles Continue: The First Millennium

What do you do when everything around you crumbles, when everything of value to you is taken away or turns to dust? In the 1950s, after the Chinese army invaded Tibet, the Dalai Lama and many other Tibetans fled into exile. The Chinese destroyed Buddhist temples, killed many monks and nuns who remained, and generally tried to impose their will over the land.

Years later, in 1990, the Dalai Lama met with a group of rabbis who had flown to India to discuss one particular subject: How can a people and a religion survive while in exile? If anyone had an answer, the Dalai Lama surmised, it was the Jews. The Chinese occupation of Tibet mirrored another occupation, one 1,900 years earlier, when the Romans marched into Judea, destroyed the Second Temple, killed thousands of Jews, and flung an entire people into exile (see the previous chapter). The rabbis had differing answers for the Tibetan leader, but few if any Jews would argue one point: Judaism survived because it could evolve and change.

Beware, the End Is Nigh!

After the Second Temple was destroyed in 70 CE, Rome enslaved most Judean aristocrats and priests and brought them — along with the surviving treasures of the Temple — to Rome. Following the final failed revolt of the Jews in 135 CE, the Romans changed the name of Judea to Palestine and prohibited Jews from living in the area of Jerusalem.

While Jews were allowed to remain Jewish and were allowed to live in most areas of Palestine, they were charged a special tax for the privilege. However, ultimately, the destruction of the Second Temple had much less impact on the remaining Jews (three out of four of whom actually lived outside of Palestine at the time) than it did on Judaism itself. Sacrifices could no longer be offered at the Temple. High priests were no longer available to decide matters of Jewish observance.

This was a major turning point for Judaism. The Pharisees, who believed in the study of the written and oral Torah and downplayed the importance of the priestly sacrifices, were in a position to revitalize Judaism because their practices weren't dependent on the physical location of the Temple. Although the Temple had long been the central focus of worship, a few synagogues had been established around Palestine, where smaller, more prayer-and-study-based groups had met (the word synagogue is from the Greek word "assembly"). The sages of the Pharisees, who tended to be middle-class merchants or scribes, took the title "rabbi" (meaning "honored one," or "teacher"), in order to help other Jews learn to study and practice a new kind of Judaism not dependent on the Temple.

Revolutions and messiahs

Many scholars suggest that the intense Roman oppression led many Jews to remember the apocalyptic teachings of earlier prophets. It became popular to think that the end of the world would be preceded by major disasters, like the destruction of the Temple, as well as the coming of a messiah who would lead the Jews to redemption. Suddenly, messianic movements sprung up everywhere.

One well-known movement was led by the Nazarenes, a group of Jews who were no different than any other Jews of the time — except that they believed that Jesus of Nazareth was the anointed one. Because the Greek word for "messiah" was *christos*, these adherents later became known as Christians. Of course, we don't have the space here to discuss the twists and turns of early Christianity, but suffice it to say that many of the early Christians fought to differentiate themselves from the Judaism of the time, especially later in the first century, when the gospels of the Christian Bible were first written.

THE PHARISEES GOT A BAD REP

Because the Christian Bible was written for a non-Jewish audience by those who were distancing themselves from Judaism, some of the stories conflict with what scholars now know of Jewish history. For example, when Jesus got angry and chased the money-changers and merchants out of the Temple, he wasn't opposing the Pharisees, but rather the Sadducees. The Sadducees were the priestly class committed to the Temple service, believing that the only way to serve God was through the sacrificial system. The Pharisees, forerunners of modern-day Jewish religious scholars and rabbis, believed that Judaism was an evolving tradition, and they interpreted ancient texts in light of a changing world, allowing the tradition to renew itself. Jesus was actually more aligned with the Pharisees in the way he taught traditional texts, particularly those teachings on love of God and of humankind.

A second messianic movement led to war from 132 to 135 CE, and was actually much larger than the one that led to the destruction of the Second Temple in 70 CE (see Chapter 13). This second war was led by a man known as Simon bar Kokhba ("son of a star"), who was also considered a messiah by his followers, including the famous Talmudic scholar Rabbi Akiba. The Bar Kokhba rebellion, as it's now known, may have reflected an outpouring of messianic zeal, as well as a reaction to increased persecution by the Roman Emperor Hadrian, who had forbidden circumcision.

Even though Bar Kokhba's rebellion was much better organized than the earlier revolution, it was quickly squashed by the immense power of the Roman army. Not only were the leaders killed, but Hadrian also deported almost every remaining Jew from the country, selling most of them as slaves. Around the time of the war, Hadrian renamed Jerusalem *Aelia Capitolina* and prohibited any Jew from entering the city.

The raising of the Talmud

Fortunately, many rabbis and their students ended up in the Galilee, north of what was Judea. Without their homeland or the Temple, they focused on studying the Torah — both the written Bible and the inherited oral tradition, which they believed was passed down through the generations from Moses to them.

The first section of the "oral" Torah was finally written down around 200 CE by Yehuda haNasi (Judah the Prince). This work, which came to be known as the *Mishnah* ("that which is taught by repetition"), became the cornerstone of rabbinic thought and came to define the new non-Temple-based Judaism.

However, in the third century, the power of the rabbis' schools in Palestine waned, and Jewish scholarship shifted to the increasingly prosperous schools of Babylonia. Rav, a disciple of Yehuda haNasi, brought the Mishnah to Babylonia, where Jews studied it and commented on it for hundreds of years (see the discussion on the Talmud in Chapter 3).

The creation of the Mishnah and the focus on study certainly helped save Judaism during these dark years. This growing emphasis on study led to a greater predisposition to learning in general and created a portable culture. Ultimately, much of Jewish history over the following 1,500 years had to do with just one thing: How intent the current ruling leader was to impose his religious beliefs over his Jewish subjects.

Running Out of Rome

Although the Romans performed all kinds of great feats, including building roads, creating aqueducts to carry fresh water into cities, and so on, they were terrible when it came to tolerating minorities. In the first few centuries of the Common Era, the Romans persecuted both the Christians and the Jews, but then a really extraordinary thing happened. The fourth-century Roman Emperor Constantine converted to Christianity, bringing much of the Roman Empire with him. This was quite a turn-around, as unlikely as a successor to Hitler suddenly converting all Germans to Judaism.

Unfortunately, while Christianity and Judaism have always basically agreed on morality, monotheism, and so on, Christians have historically been antagonistic to Jews (see Chapter 17). Early Christianity was heavily influenced by Judaism, and many Roman Christians actually seemed to enjoy going to synagogues more than their own churches. Perhaps in an attempt to limit religious ambiguity for the new Christian converts, the Christians in power felt it would be better if Judaism had as little influence as possible.

Jews who had been granted Roman citizenship now found both their religious and civil rights threatened by new anti-Jewish laws — laws instituted to make Christianity more appealing and Judaism less appealing. Jews were no longer allowed to build, rebuild, or repair synagogues. Interfaith marriage was punishable by death.

However, just as Jewish life was becoming really difficult, the Roman Empire pitched deeply into decline. Later in the fourth century, the vast empire split into two parts: the Western world (centered in Rome), and the Eastern world, renamed the Byzantine Empire and centered in Constantinople (what is now called Istanbul). As the two empires fought each other and other invaders, many Jews chose to leave Palestine for better economic waters in Babylonia, Italy, Spain, and even as far away as Germany.

The Jews who stayed in Palestine throughout the fourth and fifth centuries compiled a set of commentaries and discussions based on the Mishnah, which became the Palestinian Talmud (also known as the Jerusalem Talmud). At the same time, the great schools in Babylonia were compiling the Babylonian Talmud (also called the *Bavli*). Both sets of text exist to this day, though the impending Islamic explosion (see the following section) ensured that the Babylonian Talmud would become the larger and the more authoritative of the two versions.

Jews under Islam

When we went to school, we learned that the whole world fell into the Dark Ages after the Visigoths and the Vandals ransacked Rome, and the Western Roman Empire came crashing down. This is kind of like calling the baseball finals the "World Series" even though it's obviously an American event. In other words, yes, Western Europe fell apart, but there was a lot going on elsewhere.

For example, throughout the fifth and sixth centuries, Jewish, Christian, and pagan traders and farmers lived together in relative peace in the area we now call the Middle East. Sometime around 600 CE, an Arab merchant named Muhammad — who probably learned about monotheism from the Jews and Christians around him — had a series of visions. These revelations taught him that even though both the ancient Jewish and the newer Christian beliefs were true, he was to be the new and final prophet of the One God.

Muhammad and his small group of adherents moved from Mecca to Medina, where Islam (literally meaning "a way of peace," or "submission to God") flourished and spread the word of One God. Muhammad's words and teachings were written down, compiled, and became the Quran.

Why is this relevant in a book about Judaism? Because Islam was the big success story of the latter half of the first millennium, and by the eighth century, nine out of ten of the world's Jews were living under Islamic rule. The Arabic-speaking Islamic Empire quickly became larger and more powerful than either the Greek or Roman Empires had ever been, stretching from Persia in the East to Spain and North Africa in the West. Europe's Dark Ages were undoubtedly the golden age of Islam.

Second class is better than no class

In general, Jews tended to be better off in Islamic lands than Christian lands during the Middle Ages. Muslims considered Jews and Christians to be "Peoples of the Book" — worshiping the same God as Muslims and using holy scriptures — and were therefore protected under Islamic law. The Jewish focus on scholarship gained them admiration, and the Jews, who quickly learned to speak Arabic, were allowed to be a part of the robust intellectual life of the Islamic Empire. The Christians, who had been the dominant power for so long, found the Islamic restrictions terrible, but to the Jews, Islamic rule was actually a relief from the humiliating treatment they had gotten from the Christians.

But the relationship wasn't exactly perfect. For example, the Jews were heavily taxed. The land tax especially made it difficult for Jews to own land, causing many of them to turn to nonagricultural professions, such as merchants, tanners, silk workers, and weavers. They also had to wear distinctive clothing and were unable to carry weapons, ride horses, or live in houses larger than their Muslim neighbors. Islam recognized the "truths" of Judaism but was convinced that Muhammad's revelations superseded those of the Jews.

Granted, not all Islamic leaders were the same. While most were tolerant and ensured the security of life and property, every now and again leaders enacted massive forced conversions to Islam, confiscated property, and so on. However, as a whole, these persecutions were shorter in duration and less ferocious than had occurred, and were later to occur, in Christian lands.

The rise of the Gaon

By the eighth century, there was little Jewish activity happening in Palestine. On the other hand, the Jews living north, in Baghdad, were doing great. The major Jewish schools of Babylonia had moved to Baghdad and had become the most important centers of Jewish study and culture. Of course, they preferred "their own" Babylonian Talmud to the one written in Jerusalem (see "The raising of the Talmud" earlier in this chapter), and spread it far and wide throughout the empire.

Even before the conquest of the Islamic Empire, the head of each rabbinic academy was known as a *Gaon* ("genius"). The Gaonim — the most famous of whom was Saadia Gaon, who lived from about 882 to 942 CE — had tremendous religious authority throughout the Persian Empire, and then throughout the Islamic Empire.

Not everyone was happy about this, of course. In the late eighth century, a Jew named Anan ben David tried to overthrow the authority of the Gaon by declaring that the entire rabbinic tradition of Oral Torah was false. His claims — that the Talmud was a fraud and that the Bible was the sole religious authority — proved popular among some Jews, who broke away from mainstream Judaism and became known as *Karaites* ("readers," referring to readers of the Hebrew Bible). The movement was never as successful as rabbinic Judaism, but there are some small Karaite communities even today.

All that glitters is gold

The high point in Jewish-Islamic relations occurred in Spain, beginning when the first Muslims conquered Spain in the eighth century. This period under Ummayad Muslim rule was especially good for the Jews and is referred to as the "Golden Age of Spain." Jews from all areas of the Islamic world as well as from many areas of the previously Roman world flocked to Spain and were able to work in all areas of trade. Many were even able to own land. Jewish scholars interacted with their non-Jewish neighbors, studied the same texts, learned mathematics, philosophy, and science, and created a vast amount of rich commentary and beautiful poetry.

Where Persia had long been considered the center for all things Jewish, a rabbinic academy now opened in Spain around 955 CE and quickly became a major center for Jewish law and culture. Unfortunately, the golden age lost much of its luster once Christians reconquered Spain in 1150 CE, imposing new restrictions and ultimately expelling the Jews entirely (more on that later).

Let My People Stay: Prosperity and Persecution

When the Western Roman Empire fell apart in the middle of the first millennium, it was replaced by many smaller countries ruled by kings, emperors, tzars, and kaisers. Where Jews were second-class citizens in the Muslim world, they weren't even that in the Christian world. They were more like tenants without a lease. The quality of a Jew's life (or anyone else's, for that matter) depended almost entirely upon the whims of the county's ruler or the local nobleman. In general, Jews couldn't own or work the land, they weren't allowed to join guilds, and they were typically restricted in the work they could perform. If you ever wondered why Jews were stereotyped as moneylenders or peddlers, it's simply because there were few other jobs open to them.

On the other hand, the Jews gained a reputation for being good at trade, and some kings, like Charlemagne of France, actually invited Jews to settle in their lands in order to encourage economic growth.

Judaism was extremely decentralized in Western Europe; with few or no great centers of learning or renowned rabbis (as there were in the Islamic world). Each community had its own rabbis who would interpret Jewish law when necessary. Nonetheless, a few renowned Western European rabbis had far-reaching power, including Rabbenu Gershom, who lived around 960 to 1028 CE; he is most famous for several amendments to the Talmudic principles (called *takanot*) which outlawed elaborate funerals, polygamy, and reading other people's mail (not necessarily in that order). Similarly, Rashi — famous for his commentaries on the Tanach and Talmud — was another brilliant French Jewish scholar of the time (see Chapter 28).

Turn the other cheek

Life for the Jews of Western Europe went from bad to worse in 1095, when Pope Urban II promised salvation to any Christian who went to Palestine to fight (or convert) the Muslims and recapture the Holy Land of Palestine for Christendom. This was the first Crusade of many, and during each of them, a number of ignorant and violent Christians decided that charity begins at home: Instead of going all the way to Palestine, they decided to forcibly convert or slaughter the unbelievers in their midst — the Jews.

The Church sometimes tried to save the Jews and stop the mobs they themselves had created, but to little avail. The Jews, too, often tried to fight, but because they were rarely allowed to own weapons, they were only minimally successful. Some Jews decided to kill their families and themselves rather than convert or be attacked. As we discuss in Chapter 17, anti-Semitic zeal reached a highpoint in the early years of the second millennium, and massacres often followed accusations that Jews killed Christian children for their blood, or that Jews poisoned drinking water to cause a plague.

Take the money and run

Of course, anti-Jewish sentiment waxed and waned from country to country. Often, just as one area was persecuting the Jews, another was protecting them (see Figure 14-1). Sometimes, the mood just depended on the area's economic state. The Jews were often invited in to stimulate a country's economy with trade and money lending. (Jews often had family connections in other lands, providing a ready-built international network.) Unfortunately, as soon as the Jews became too affluent and the non-Jewish community became in too much debt, the Jews' property was seized by the ruling powers. If the Jews were lucky, they'd simply be run out of town; if they were unlucky, they were killed.

For example, England's King Henry IV tried to institute a number of pro-Jewish reforms around 1103, but by 1275 King Edward I ruled that all debts due to Jews were forfeit. Fourteen years later he ordered the expulsion of all the Jews in Gascony and the seizure of all their property. This must have proved profitable, because the following year, in 1290, he banished Jews from England entirely.

The pattern of "make it nice" then "make it painful" was repeated time and time again, in France, Spain, Portugal, Germany, Italy, and so on. And, frequently after a number of years had passed or a particular ruler had died, Jews were once again invited back. However, after the Jews were expelled from England in 1290, they weren't allowed to legally re-enter the country until 1730.

FIGURE 14-1: Jews traveled west to North Africa and throughout Europe.

The Reign in Spain

As Christian kings conquered Spain in the twelfth and thirteenth centuries, they turned to its Jewish communities to help run the country. James I of Aragon granted the Jews many of the same rights and privileges they had enjoyed under Islamic rule, and while the Jews weren't allowed to hold government office, they frequently acted as advisors to the royal court. The Jews also translated hundreds of scientific, mathematical, and philosophical works from Arabic and Greek into Western European languages.

In those early years — while many Jews were being slaughtered elsewhere in Europe — Spanish Jewry remained prosperous and secure, though never reaching the glory they had achieved under Islamic rule. All that changed in 1391, when mobs of Spanish Christians, perhaps fueled by resentment over the affluence of some Jews, rioted, seizing property and attacking Jewish communities.

The Jews weren't a small minority in Spain; by some estimates, one out of every ten Spaniards was either Jewish or had some Jewish blood. What would you do if your neighbors suddenly started attacking you because you didn't believe in the same religion? Some Jews took refuge in safer communities in North Africa. However, for many, it seemed a reasonable choice to convert to Christianity and attempt to assimilate into the dominant culture. These new Christians were known politely as *conversos* ("converts") or, less flatteringly, as *marranos* ("pigs").

Some Jews clearly became faithful Christians, but for others, the conversion was only skin deep. They continued practicing Judaism in secret (modern-day historians call these "crypto-Jews"). By 1480, suspicion of conversos was so great that Queen Isabella — a devout Catholic — decided that the allegations of hidden Jewish practices needed to be examined. Fortunately for her, the Catholic Church had long-before instituted a special corps trained to root out heretics, called the *Inquisition.*

No one expects the Spanish Inquisition

The Inquisition acted like a secret police and investigated every aspect of a suspected converso's life to ensure that he or she accepted Christianity completely. If someone became suspicious that a convert (or the descendant of a convert) was secretly practicing Judaism, the suspect's family was broken up, the children given to monasteries and nunneries to be raised, and the adults tortured until they confessed — whether they were guilty or not. The Church could then automatically seize the property and monies of anyone who confessed.

The conversos soon realized that they were caught in a catch-22. They were attacked as Jews, but they also would never be accepted into Spanish society as Christians. Many families tried to escape to the Netherlands or the New World, lands that came to be controlled by Spain but were out of the immediate purview of the Inquisition. The Inquisition — which only targeted Jews who had converted — slowly spread across Europe, and in later centuries even tracked down nonpracticing Christians who had escaped to the Americas.

Christianity or bust

Finally, after a century of anti-Jewish attitudes and policies, Queen Isabella and her husband King Ferdinand, urged by Father Tomás de Torquemada, made a fateful decree in 1492. They ordered that within four months every Jew had to either convert to Christianity or leave the country. Some scholars argue that the government truly believed that most Jews would convert if the penalties were high enough. After all, many of the top government advisors, legal scholars, and financiers were Jewish, and the decree made it clear that the Jews wouldn't be allowed to leave with any property or money.

But the Jews did leave. And so, the same month Christopher Columbus began his fateful expedition that ended in the Americas, over 200,000 Jews embarked upon a trail of tears looking for countries that would allow them entry. Many went to Portugal, which welcomed them with open arms, only to forcibly convert them to Christianity a few years later. Some fled into Western Europe, particularly the Netherlands, and a hundred years later their descendants would join the effort to colonize the New World.

The luckiest of the Jews ended up in Turkey, where they were welcomed by Sultan Bayazid of the Ottoman Empire, who clearly understood the long-term good that would come from embracing a people so well skilled. The expelled "Sephardic" Jews (see Chapter 1) quickly rebuilt communities throughout the vast Ottoman Empire, spreading through Greece, Turkey, Iraq, North Africa, Egypt, and Palestine.

Around this time many brilliant Jewish scholars fled to Safed, in northern Palestine, creating an intense mystical community that generated scholarship, poetry, and prayers that are still used today (see Chapter 5). Many other Sephardic communities flourished in peace and security for over 500 years, until, in the middle of the twentieth century, they were destroyed in the Holocaust.

Chapter **15**

The Greatest Horror, the Greatest Triumph

Most history books (and news reports) are filled with two kinds of stories: "We kicked their collective butt" (military conquests and defeats) and "However bad your life looks right now, it's nothing compared to how bad these folks had it." But each of these stories is only part of a much bigger story of human progress. This is especially true when it comes to Jewish history, which so often focuses on how hard the Jews have had it rather than the periods when life was truly wonderful.

That said, the parts of the Jewish story we are visiting in this chapter aren't exactly full of good laughs. Jewish history in the past 500 years has been a rollercoaster of events, with thrilling highs and catastrophic lows. Although many of the details in this chapter are sad, the essential strength of Judaism and the Jewish people shines through.

When Poland Was a Heartland

Polish and Lithuanian kings, like many other Christian rulers, invited Jews to settle in their lands during the thirteenth and fourteenth centuries. The Jews brought experience with trade and money lending, and they helped boost the heavily agricultural economies of these Eastern European countries.

Perhaps because Poland and Lithuania were far from the major centers of Western Europe and the Catholic Church, the Jews were relatively protected and allowed to participate in a wide array of career options not available elsewhere. Of course, the Jews suffered times of persecution and the occasional riot, but during the period of expulsions from other lands, Poland and Lithuania offered relative peace.

Over time, the Jews were able to rent land and farm, and as their families grew, the Jews spread throughout Eastern Europe. However, they still usually lived separated from their Christian neighbors, in small villages called *shtetls*. It's a measure of how insular their communities were that these Jews spoke a combination of Hebrew, German, Polish, and Russian (which would come to be called *Yiddish*, see Appendix A), more often than Polish or Lithuanian.

Four lands, one people

Over the centuries of relative freedom, the thousands of separate shtetls around Western Russia, Lithuania, and Poland came to form a federation called the Council of the Four Lands. The Council, which acted like a behind-the-scenes, independent Jewish parliament transcending national boundaries, ruled on legal issues concerning the Jewish people. Surprisingly, the Council was heavily secular, though, of course, it included some rabbis. The Four Lands area was like a haven for many Ashkenazi Jews, much like the Ottoman Empire was for the Sephardim (see Chapter 14), and Jewish life remained reasonably good until the middle of the seventeenth century.

The Chmielnicki massacres

Over time, Poland had slowly annexed increasing portions of the Ukraine. However, many of the Greek Orthodox Christians in the Ukraine weren't exactly pleased to be gobbled up by a Catholic country. In 1648, the Ukrainian Cossacks rebelled, led by a man named Bogdan Chmielnicki (khmel-*nyit*-ski). Much like the ethnic cleansing that later occurred in the late 1990s in Serbia and Croatia, the Cossacks tortured and massacred everyone who wasn't of their religious faith, slaughtering Polish nobles, Catholic clergy, and Jews.

Poland allied with Sweden to fight off the rebellion; the Cossacks allied with Russia. The warfare was intense, and both sides slaughtered the Jews. By some accounts, as many as 100,000 Jews died, and the fighting led countless thousands of Jews to flee to Germany and Lithuania. These areas became major centers for Jewish education and culture over the next 300 years, developing such luminaries as the Ba'al Shem Tov (see Chapter 28) and Elijah ben Solomon Zalman, known as the Vilna Gaon.

The Dawning of a New Age

Outside of Poland and the surrounding areas, the sixteenth and seventeenth centuries were less violent, but in many respects more restrictive. For example, in 1555 Pope Paul IV ordered that all Jews had to live separated from non-Jews, in walled neighborhoods. The first of these communities was placed next to a cannon foundry, called a *ghetto* in Italian, leading to the name still used today to describe a section set aside for a particular population. The ghettos quickly became overcrowded and disease-ridden.

Some lands, like Germany and Prussia, made it uncomfortable to be a Jew in other ways. Some cities imposed a head tax imposed on all cattle and Jews that entered town. Throughout Europe, Jews were also at a disadvantage because they weren't permitted to attend secular schools or universities. Wealthy Jews were often given more rights, such as the right to live within city limits and — subject to a difficult permit process — the right to marry.

The Enlightenment

You may remember seeing the opening scene in the movie *2001: A Space Odyssey*. The one where the apes are sitting around and suddenly one realizes that it can use a bone as a tool to break another bone? Every now and then, a shift in consciousness happens on the planet, after which the world will never be the same. That appears to be what happened in the early 1700s, though no single event or person (or even ape) caused the shift.

Philosophers such as Rousseau suddenly started asking questions like, "Why not treat non-Christians the same as Christians? The Jews may have different rituals, customs, and beliefs, but they're human beings, too." For most people today, this idea is as obvious as using a tool, but ideas such as these were outrageous for the day and reflected a revolution of thinking that came to be called the *Enlightenment*.

By the late eighteenth century, a large number of people in the American colonies — people who had built a country with their own hands — felt that they should no longer be beholden to any other government. The American revolution was led in large part by well-read intellectuals like Thomas Jefferson who, upon penning the Declaration of Independence, laid the backbone of the very first government in history that offered the Jews full rights as citizens. Of course, there were only about 2,000 Jews living in the United States at the time, but this freedom would later bring over a million Jews to the American shores.

The question of citizenship

The French revolution of 1789 changed the face of Europe, and the French Declaration of the Rights of Man, which specifically notes that no one should be persecuted for their religion, brought the Enlightenment (or at least many facets of it) to the political arena. However, when a group of Jews soon after asked to be accepted as citizens, the French National Assembly debated the issue for two years before finally agreeing.

Although there were many people in the Assembly who didn't want to see the Jews given any rights, the question of citizenship echoed inside the Jewish community, too: Were the Jews a separate nation or people, or were they French people (or German people or Italian people, or whatever) who were adherents of a Jewish religion? Napoleon Bonaparte raised this issue once again in 1807 by gathering a number of rabbis and Jewish scholars as a new Sanhedrin (ruling legal body) that would decide important Jewish matters.

As it turned out, this Sanhedrin was only a shallow political gesture. Napoleon called it to assembly only once for the express purpose of asking a series of questions about the Jews' loyalty to France. Astonishingly, this was the first time in history that a Jewish court of authority officially agreed that Judaism was a religion and not a separate people. The Jews of France first had loyalty to France, they said, not to the Jewish people.

Napoleon was pleased with the result and spread this particular message of Enlightenment throughout the countries he conquered. Other rulers, too, began to be more tolerant of religious differences during this time. The Jews were often allowed to leave their ghettos and attend schools, though most Jews tended to be wary of mixing too much with the non-Jewish population.

Going Beyond the Pale

Most people believe there are two basic kinds of Jews: Ashkenazi and Sephardic (see Chapter 1). However, throughout the eighteenth and nineteenth centuries, the European Ashkenazi population became increasingly split between those Jews who participated in the Enlightenment (in countries such as Germany and France), and those who didn't (in countries such as Russia, Poland, and Lithuania).

In the 1770s, after years of fighting, Poland was partitioned and absorbed by Lithuania, Austria, and Russia. Russia had little interest in the Enlightenment or emancipating the Jews, or just about anyone else, for that matter. Trying to figure out what to do with the hundreds of thousands (perhaps millions) of Jews it had recently acquired, Russia set aside an area, called the Pale of Settlement, inside which the Jews were allowed to live. The region was enormous, but its segregation from the rest of Russia kept contact and trade with Christian communities to a minimum.

The result was a pressure cooker in which the Hasidic and Mitnaggid movements were born (see Chapter 1), creating the "black hat" Jewish culture that has become a fixture of Jewish life in large communities around the world.

Tsar Nicholas I of Russia, not content simply to segregate the Jews, tried various means to convert them to Christianity. He used all the old tactics, like making life as miserable as possible (throwing them out of cities, and so on). Then he created special Jewish schools to teach the "enlightenment," which to him meant simply eliminating the Talmud. Finally, in 1827, the Tsar instituted a quota of Jewish boys to be conscripted into the Russian army and lowered the minimum age from 18 to 12, sometimes as early as age 8. The term of service was 25 years; many either converted or died due to poor treatment. Such tactics were clearly systematic and cruel attempts to humiliate and punish the Jews into assimilating.

Responses to Enlightenment

Back in enlightened nineteenth century Western Europe, Jews began considering the same issues that many Jews debate to this day: How Jewish can you be and still be part of the modern world? And what does it mean to be Jewish anyway? After all, if Judaism was a religion — rather than a nation or a people — then Jews could *choose* whether or not to be Jewish. Suddenly, many Jews in Germany and France no longer felt they had to conform to a Jewish culture, resulting in the loss of a strong Jewish community.

These Western European Jews reacted to the enlightenment in several ways. Some, finding Western society and culture more exciting than the Judaism they had grown up with, decided to convert to Christianity. Of course, most of these Jews didn't believe in Christian theology any more than a Jewish one. For example, the poet Heinrich Heine, who as a Jew was unable to get a permit to live in Germany's capital, converted, noting "The Baptismal certificate is the ticket of admission to European culture. Berlin is well worth a sermon."

Reform

Instead of converting, some Jews responded by demonstrating that Judaism could conform to what they saw as the advances of modern secular life. Believing that being Jewish wouldn't be so "bad" if it weren't so obviously different, these Jews radically recoiled from traditional Judaism, creating the Reform movement. Here are some highlights of the movement:

>> Early Reform Judaism insisted that there was no such thing as a Jewish people; Judaism was only a religion. They later reversed their position on this.

>> When religious scholarship began to recognize that Judaism had always evolved over time, the reformers felt that all sorts of changes were possible. For example, they replaced references to Jerusalem and the Messiah with prayers for justice and brotherhood for all humanity.

>> They tried to make their observance look like those of their Protestant Christian neighbors. They played organ music on Shabbat (against Jewish tradition, which reserved music for the ancient Temple), they spoke in the dominant language (mostly German) instead of Yiddish, and some congregations even attempted to celebrate Shabbat on Sunday!

>> They instituted Jewish schools that emphasized secular studies over Talmudic studies, and they generally taught that Jewish law (Torah and Talmud) was less important than the ethical teachings of the Prophets.

The Reform movement reacted in large part to what they considered empty ritual and dogma. We can certainly understand the need for more spiritual fulfillment, but in the early years, the Reform movement tended to drop Jewish observances rather than actually reform them. The result was fulfilling for some, and just as empty and disillusioning as strict traditionalism for others. As we discuss in Chapter 1, the Reform movement has slowly been shifting back to increased observance and more attention to spirituality.

To change or not to change

Many Western European Jews rejected the Reform movement's policies; some even tried to get the government to stop them. However, the traditional orthodox world also split into two camps. Some Jews wanted to continue living as they had in the ghetto, speaking Yiddish and having little to do with the modern world. For them, maintaining tradition meant never changing with the times. These are the folks whom today we tend to call "Ultra-Orthodox."

Other rabbis felt the necessity to change with the times but refused to strip away the millennia of Jewish tradition. Rabbi Samson Raphael Hirsch, who laid the foundation for much of Modern Orthodox or Neo-Orthodox Judaism, said, "Judaism is not a religion; the synagogue is not a church; and a rabbi is not a priest. Judaism is not a mere adjunct to life. To be a Jew is the sum total of our task in life."

However, the neo-Orthodox movement agreed that Jews should learn the language of the land and have both religious and secular education. Hirsch led his prayer services in Hebrew but gave his sermon in German (not Yiddish). He argued that while it was important to be a part of the world, *halakhah* (Jewish law) was to be followed even if it meant less acceptance by the non-Jewish world, even including the loss of a job.

Between Reform and Orthodoxy, a number of other movements sprang up in the 1800s. For example, the roots of Conservative Judaism, which would have a major impact in America during the twentieth century, were laid by Zachariah Frankel (1801–1875), who accepted that the Jews were a people but rejected the literal truth of the Torah (see Chapter 3).

The Rise of Nationalism and Racism

The nineteenth century saw the growing zeal of nationalism around Europe, and large nationalist groups in Germany and France became increasingly powerful. All nationalist ideology rests on an "us-versus-them" mentality, whether it's "our country is better than theirs" or "our pure white race makes this country great, and impure racial stock weakens us." In an us-versus-them mentality — no matter how ludicrous or simple-minded — the Jews were slated to be on the losing "them" side. The Jews, especially those who believed that as they assimilated they would be increasingly accepted, had a rude awakening.

The return of anti-Jewish policies

It quickly became clear that many people didn't care whether or not the Jews considered themselves a separate nation, or even whether or not the Jews were fiercely nationalistic French or German citizens. In some countries, such as Austria, politicians began running — and winning — on specifically anti-Jewish platforms.

In England, no Jew could be inducted into Parliament because he would have to take an oath "on the true faith of a Christian." Over an eleven-year period in the mid-1800s, the wealthy and influential Lionel de Rothschild was elected to Parliament six times by his London community; however, he was forced to withdraw each time until the government finally found a way to let him take his oath as a Jew, using the Hebrew Bible.

France, once the bastion of Enlightenment, showed its continuing deep distrust of the Jews in 1894 when a high-ranking official in the French army, Alfred Dreyfus, was framed for treason because he was Jewish. Surprisingly, Dreyfus was extremely assimilated and didn't even show interest in Judaism. Nonetheless, at his public trial mobs repeatedly chanted "Death to the Jews."

Around this time many nationalists began embracing the concepts of "race" and "racism" that were part of the emerging anthropology and theories of evolution. Suddenly, even converting to Christianity was no longer a reasonable alternative for the Jews because they were perceived not as a nation or as a religion, but as a race — and one inferior to the dominant whites. (As we say in Chapter 1, the idea of Judaism being a race is clearly absurd — there are African Jews, Asian Jews, Indian Jews, and so on. Even the racial characteristics of Ashkenazi Jews and Sephardic Jews are different.)

The pogroms

In the 1880s the Russian government began tolerating and even sponsoring *pogroms* (massacres, or literally "riots") directed at the Jews. At the time, over half the world's Jews lived under Russian rule. Over the next few decades, hundreds of thousands of Jews were killed or maimed in these massacres.

In large part, the sadistic pogroms were a policy tool of the government, helping to turn anger away from the nobility toward the "other" in their midst.

REMEMBER

Although the word "pogroms" conjures up visions of "the old country" a long time ago, the pogroms continued into the twentieth century.

Getting Worse and Getting Out

After the assassination of Tsar Alexander II in 1881, the Russian pogroms became significantly worse, and tens of thousands of Russian Jews decided that things wouldn't get better anytime soon. Granted, it wasn't just the violence; poverty and general economic conditions also worsened drastically. Between 1880 and 1920, about two million Jews (about a third of the Jews in Europe) decided enough was enough, and they emigrated.

Some rugged individualists — like those cowboy types who settled the "Wild West" of America — moved to Palestine (which was ruled by the Ottoman Empire until 1917). Others simply moved to other Western European nations. The vast majority, however, moved to the United States of America, where the Constitution defended people's rights, and, it was said, "the streets were paved with gold."

Passage to Palestine

Among the many journalists who attended the trial of Alfred Dreyfus (see "The return of anti-Jewish policies" earlier in this chapter) was a man named Theodore Herzl. Herzl was, like so many other Jews of the time, nonreligious and very assimilated. So when he saw the French crowd almost riot with bloodlust, shouting "Death to the Jews," he was deeply unnerved. Herzl, shocked and horrified that in this modern civilized country such a travesty of justice could take place, became convinced that Jewry was doomed in Europe. The only solution, Herzl decided, was for the Jews to have their own homeland, a country that would always take them in.

Although he was nonreligious, Herzl became obsessed with Zionism (the movement promoting a Jewish state), and today he is known as the father of modern Zionism. After the First Zionist Congress in 1897, Herzl tried to talk the Sultan of the Ottoman Empire into giving up Palestine, to no avail. He discussed the problem with Pope Pius X, who told him, "The Jews have not recognized our Lord, therefore we cannot recognize the Jewish people."

As pogroms became increasingly bad in Eastern Europe, Herzl approached England for assistance. Their offer: Jews could use Uganda as a temporary refuge until Palestine worked out. However, as bad as the violence against the Jews became, the vast majority of the Zionist Congress insisted that only Palestine would do.

Many Jews did sneak into Palestine, where they were able to buy land and build settlements. By 1909, the Jews bought enough empty land on the Mediterranean coast that they founded a new city, the first all-Jewish city in Palestine, called Tel Aviv.

Close, but not quite there

When World War I erupted in 1914, Jews enlisted in every country where they were allowed to serve. Many people don't remember that there were Jews in the French military, American military, and — notably — the German military, where they fought and died wearing German insignia. After the Ottoman Empire entered the war, Britain and France conquered much of the Middle East, and in 1917 England gained control of Palestine.

England almost immediately issued the Balfour Declaration, which advocated a Jewish state. Unfortunately for the Zionists, because of the political realities of the day, it would be another 31 years until the English actually handed over the power of the province to the Jews.

In 1919, Germany, the biggest aggressor of the war, was defeated and forced to sign the Treaty of Versailles. The loss of territory and incredible reparations they had to pay pushed the country into a terrible economic and emotional depression in the early 1920s. Germany seemed to go from super-power to super-shame overnight.

Hitler's rise to power

In the minds of some Germans, the loss of the war was a flaw of emancipation. Rather than blaming the German nation and the German people, they blamed the Jews — seen as an insidious race of foreigners — for sapping the German spirit. By the early 1930s, much of the world had fallen into an economic depression. In Germany, a man who claimed to have the answer for the country's problems rose to power: Adolf Hitler.

Hitler's National Socialist party (which was known by the contraction "Nazi") offered glory, prosperity, purpose, and a solution to Germany's "Jewish problem." Hitler was democratically voted in as Chancellor of Germany in 1932. (He won the most votes, but it wasn't a majority of the populace). A year later, he dismantled the German democracy and became a dictator.

The Jews, Hitler believed, were responsible for Germany losing the war, for the economic depression, for the communist revolution in Russia, and for every other problem imaginable. He turned rationality on its head, arguing that racial purity was the key to success. The Nordic Aryans were the most pure, the Slavic peoples were less pure, black people were near the bottom of the list, and the worst were the Jewish people, a race that he considered genetically criminal and by its very nature eroding to the fabric of society.

Hitler's original plan was simple: Make life so bad for the Jews that they would leave the country. But by 1940, Hitler had changed his tune: The only way to succeed, he felt, was to murder every Jewish person in his expanding empire.

The Holocaust

We can't do justice to the enormity of what is today generally called the "Holocaust" and, by many Jews, the *Shoah* (Devastation). The Shoah is just too big. Here, we attempt to briefly tell what happened and explain how this nightmare became reality.

In the mid-1930s, the Nazi party instituted laws that were meant to make the Jews miserable enough to emigrate. Laws prohibited Jews from work for the government, placed boycotts on their businesses, expelled their children from schools, and so on. The government created concentration camps to hold anyone, Jewish or non-Jewish, considered dangerous: political activists, communists, members of trade unions, Romani (gypsies), homosexuals, Jehovah's Witnesses, and many Jewish journalists, lawyers, and community leaders. These concentration camps were basically prisons and were different than "death camps," which appeared later and were specifically designed to kill people. Some concentration camps also became death camps, but some were simply sources of slave labor for the Germans.

Too little, too late

Finally, in 1935, the Nazis instituted the Nuremberg Laws, which stripped Jews of their citizenship and prohibited mixed marriages. The Jews had no choice of converting; the Nazis considered anyone who had Jewish blood (meaning at least one grandparent was Jewish) to be racially impure.

Many Jews left Germany during this time. Other well-off, assimilated Jews were optimistic enough to believe that their enlightened neighbors would never stand for this kind of behavior for very long. However, many thousands of Jews couldn't leave simply because no other country would take them in. As Chaim Weizmann, who later became the first president of Israel, said in 1936, "The world is divided into places where [the Jews] cannot live and places into which they cannot enter."

For example, England reversed its position on Palestine in the 1930s, issuing the infamous "White Paper," which effectively stopped Jewish immigration to the area. Similarly, when one Canadian official was asked how many Jewish refugees his country could take, he answered, "None is too many." When the ship *S.S. St. Louis* was turned away from Cuba (even though its 937 German Jewish passengers held valid Cuban visas), America not only refused their entry but even fired a warning shot to keep them away from Florida's shores. The ship finally had to return to Europe, where over a quarter of the passengers were later killed in death camps.

The final straw for most German Jews came on November 9, 1938, which will forever be known as *Kristallnacht* ("night of broken glass"). That evening, a nationwide pogrom was unleashed against the Jewish community, smashing windows, burning buildings, killing 91 Jews, and arresting 30,000 others who were taken to concentration camps. To add insult to injury, the German government then imposed a billion mark fine on the Jews, arguing that the pogrom was their own fault.

Immediately, most Jews in Germany tried desperately to escape, selling their homes and businesses for a pittance. But for most of them, it was too late.

The war against the Jews

WORDS OF WISDOM

"Where one burns books, one will, in the end, burn people."
— HEINRICH HEINE, NINETEENTH-CENTURY GERMAN-JEWISH POET

By the end of 1939, emigration out of Germany was nearly impossible for the Jews, and the German government decided it was time to change their policy from terror to murder. Many Jews were routinely tortured and shot both in Germany and Poland (which Germany had annexed), and the Nazis killed more than 250,000 Jews in their communities within a few months. Other Jews were forced to move into ghettos (they were shot if they left the walled neighborhoods), where they were kept in a state of perpetual starvation. The Germans, like the Romans 2,000 years earlier, conscripted thousands of Jews to work as slave labor for the war effort, where they were worked so hard and fed so little that most died within a year.

As World War II broke out, the Nazis instituted the same policies wherever they conquered — Hungary, the Netherlands, Czechoslovakia, Greece, Italy, and so on. The governments and people of some countries (often called "Righteous Gentiles") were clearly opposed to the anti-Jewish persecution and refused to cooperate. For example, the people of Denmark helped transport almost every Danish Jew to Sweden, where they were safe. Years later, when the Jews returned, they found that the Danish people had even saved their property from vandals and promptly returned it to the rightful owners.

On the other hand, the Nazis found that many people in other countries were all too willing to help. Many French citizens enthusiastically rounded up Jews to offer to the Germans. Some French citizens were clearly more compassionate, but try asking any Israeli over age 70 what they think of the French (but get out of the way fast in case they spit).

After Germany invaded the Soviet Union in 1941, the Nazis accomplished even larger-scale murders. Squads of trained killers, typically with the help of the local non-Jewish community (whether Ukrainian, Russian, Latvian, Lithuanian, Romanian, or whatever), rounded up Jews, Romani (gypsies), and communist officials and killed them, typically by machine gun, drowning, or asphyxiation with truck exhaust. In a single September weekend in 1941, on Rosh Hashanah (see Chapter 19), the Germans and Ukrainians murdered over 33,000 Jews in the town of Babi Yar.

The death camps

To most people today, a little over 70 years later, the Nazi machine makes no sense at all. How could Germany, the center of rational thought, suddenly unleash such centuries-old irrational anti-Semitism? But the greatest villains never think of themselves as evil. The Germans seemed to feel that they were being sensible; they seem to have truly believed that the Jews were subhuman parasites that would destroy the world if they weren't wiped out.

In 1942, Hitler met with a group of high-ranking officials to prepare what they considered "the final solution of the Jewish problem." They would now systematically kill them, as efficiently as possible. The goal: The "extermination" of every Jewish person in Europe (and ultimately, the world).

The Nazis had already turned some concentration camps into death camps. For example, at Ravensbrük, an all-women's camp, they began using lethal gas to kill Jewish women who were pregnant or chronically ill. They had also added crematoria to several camps in order to more easily dispose of the large number of people who were dying. Now, they devised methods to murder not just thousands, but millions, of Jews. Typically, a group of 700 or 800 Jews were brought to a facility to be "deloused," and, believing that they were going to get showers, they dutifully undressed and entered a large room. The door was closed behind them and the room was filled with Zyklon-B gas, an extremely toxic insecticide that killed every person after four or five excruciating minutes. The bodies were then buried in giant pits or cremated.

Unbelievably, the Germans actually forced other Jewish prisoners to perform most of this work. Those who refused were killed immediately. Those who did the work were typically killed after a month or two, anyway.

Jews who had escaped Germany to other European countries were captured and killed. Entire communities that had prospered for hundreds of years — like the incredible Sephardic community of Salonika, Greece, with over 65,000 Jews — were wiped out. Thousands of well-educated men and women — lawyers, accountants, housewives, bankers, architects — of Russia, Germany, France, Poland, and other countries not only stood by silently in the face of the death camps but actively rounded up whole communities of Jews, forced them at gunpoint to dig large pits, and then machine-gunned them into their own graves.

Those who survived often became the subjects of insane tortures. Nazi doctors injected Jewish men and women with slow-acting poison or placed them in freezers to test how long it would take for them to die. Some surgeons tried to create conjoined twins by sewing people together.

Jews endured so many other horrors — each one as sad and frightening as the last — that we can't describe them in this short space. If you get a chance to visit Yad Vashem in Jerusalem, the National Holocaust Museum in Washington, D.C., or the Simon Wiesenthal Center in Los Angeles, you'll get a better idea of the scope of this horror. Among the artifacts there are letters from people who knew their fate but were powerless to stop it, and many of them wrote of their greatest fear: that their lives and deaths would simply be forgotten by future generations.

The fall of the Third Reich

The idea of killing the Jews wasn't a secondary objective during the Second World War; the Germans were so obsessed with the Jews that they threw resources at this goal even when it was tactically stupid to do so. For example, trains that should have been used to help German soldiers retreat in the final months of the war were directed instead to transport more Jews to their deaths. Army officials who suggested that they put military aims over anti-Jewish actions were demoted. While the world was at war with Germany, Germany was at war with the Jews.

Many Jews did fight back against the Nazi machine through guerilla action or by working with the resistance movement. One of the most important battles the Jews fought began on April 19, 1943 in the Warsaw ghetto. There, young Jews who had smuggled in a small stash of arms fought off the German army. The Germans burned the ghetto down, and after several weeks, killed all the Jews. But news of the battle spread and was an inspiration to Jews in other communities, even in the concentration camps.

The German army, weakened by the long war and fighting in Russia, finally fell in 1945. Adolf Hitler, still raging against the Jews in his final days, committed suicide as the Allied forces marched on Berlin. The American, English, and Russian soldiers who liberated the concentration and death camps were shocked and sickened at what they found. While rumors had spread for years about what the Germans were doing to the Jews, the "final solution" had largely been kept a secret from most of the world.

In the year following the war, many Jews, perhaps forever optimistic, returned home to their villages in Poland and the Ukraine. Sadly, killing the head of the beast didn't kill the spirit of the people, and many of these Jews were murdered by their old neighbors.

In the end, some 6 million Jews — over a million and a half of whom were children — brought three new words into modern common language. The first word is *genocide*, the extermination of an entire people, which had never been attempted on this scale before. The second word is *Holocaust*, which, two millennia earlier, had been used to describe the ancient sacrificial offering that was completely burned when offered at the Temple. Even later, the tragedy became known by the Hebrew word, *Shoah*, which means "devastation." Today, *Yom Ha-Shoah*, Holocaust Remembrance Day, is marked each year in the spring.

Founding a New Jewish State

Theodore Herzl (see "Passage to Palestine" earlier in this chapter) knew where Europe was headed 35 years before the rise of Nazi Germany when he wrote, in 1896, "The Jews have but one way of saving themselves — a return to their own people and an emigration to their own land." Zionists would spend the next 50 years trying to create just such a country, a Jewish state, a refuge for Jewry around the world, and a foundation on which to rebuild after the Holocaust.

Although Jews had been moving to British-held Palestine for many years, the numbers threatened to explode in the 1930s, as anti-Jewish persecutions intensified in Germany. Thousands of Jews reached Palestine, often with the help of the *Hagganah*, a Jewish military organization that during World War II fought as a British brigade against the Axis powers. The Hagganah — the precursor to the Israeli army — secretly smuggled Jews out of Europe and into Palestine, and it later fought in the battle of Israeli independence.

After the war, the British turned their attention once again to figuring out what to do with Palestine. A second Jewish military group, called the *Irgun*, was fanatically anti-British; the Irgun carried out various violent acts against the Brits, once killing 91 British soldiers when they blew up a wing of the King David Hotel in Jerusalem.

Neither the Arabs nor the Jews wanted the British in Palestine, and in 1946, the British government dropped the decision of what to do in the lap of the United Nations. On November 29, 1947, the United Nations voted for a plan to partition Palestine into two states: a small independent Jewish state of Israel and a larger Arab state (see Figure 15-1). (We say "Arab state" here rather than a "Palestinian state" because at that time the Jews were also called Palestinians. After all, they were citizens of Palestine.) Because of its global importance, the plan called for Jerusalem to be monitored by the United Nations as an "international city."

On May 14, 1948, the British mandate over Palestine ended, and David Ben-Gurion read a Proclamation of Independence over the radio — an announcement most interesting because while it declares an independent Jewish state, it never once mentions the word "God." The State of Israel had become a reality in large part from the work of secular Jews who insisted on a homeland for their people.

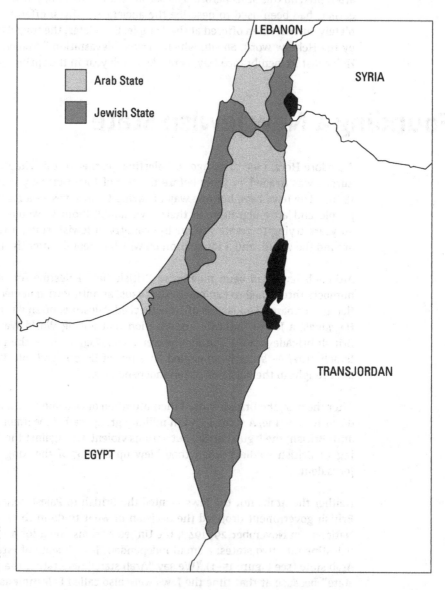

FIGURE 15-1:
The 1947
United Nations
partition plan.

While the United States immediately recognized the new country, Israel's Arab neighbors were less hospitable. The following day, six countries — Lebanon, Syria, Jordan, Egypt, Saudi Arabia, and Iraq — attacked Israel. Very few people expected Israel to survive this onslaught, but within weeks the Jews had actually captured a significant amount of land, and within months, the Arabs — while not defeated — agreed to a cease-fire.

After 1,877 years, the Jews once again ruled over their own country. Figure 15-2 shows the state's boundaries in the year 2012.

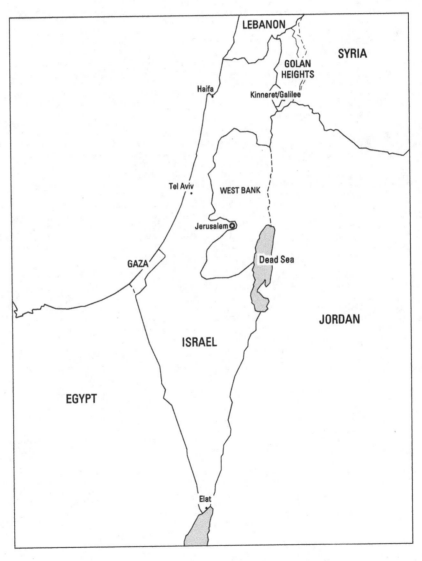

FIGURE 15-2:
Israeli boundaries in 2012 CE.

Chapter **16**

Jewish Buddhists and Other Challenges of the New Age

The last 60 years have brought an overwhelming and often-confusing array of opportunities for Jews and Judaism. What some people considered bliss-ful liberation, others considered an avalanche of options. The ways in which Jews reacted to these choices have forever changed the face of Judaism, resulting in deep challenges for the future.

In the Shadow of the Holocaust

The Holocaust (or *Shoah*, as many Jews prefer to call it; see Chapter 15) destroyed at least a third of the world's Jews. This blow not only affected the future of Juda-ism but also had a deep emotional impact on every surviving Jew, whether or not she or he was directly touched by the destruction. For at least a full generation following World War II, the Holocaust formed one of the firmest foundations of Jewish identity.

The birth of Israel in 1948 also had a profound effect on Jews everywhere. Suddenly, after so many countries had turned them away, there was a haven, a refuge in which Jews would always be welcomed. To this day, Jews on their first visit to Israel remark with astonishment at seeing Jewish soldiers, Jewish bus drivers, Jewish tour guides, and so on. Just knowing Israel existed gave the Jews a sense of strength and reassurance, and Jews around the world (especially in America) made it a point of pride to send money to plant trees, drain swamps, and generally support the developing nation.

The Mixed Blessing of America

Jews had settled in the Americas even before there was a United States, and they fought in the Revolutionary War and on both sides of the Civil War. The United States of America — which tends to value the abilities of individuals over race or belief — has offered an astonishing amount of freedom for Jews at times when they were restricted in most places on the planet. Nonetheless, some anti-Jewish attitudes existed in America. For many years, some universities limited the number of Jews who could enroll, and even today some private social clubs won't accept Jews. But on the whole, America has been a wonderful place to live if you're Jewish.

At the same time, it has also been fertile ground for those who want to assimilate, convert, or ignore their Jewish heritage. The result is a country that offers unparalleled opportunities to celebrate and honor being Jewish while also offering possibilities for losing Jewish identity.

You will be assimilated

Of course, America has long been home to a small group of religious Jews, but on the whole, American Judaism has never been particularly traditional or observant. The largest branch of Judaism in America, the Reform Movement, focused for many years on social justice and social action rather than ritual observance. For example, when Ted was at the Reform rabbinical school, he learned how to apply traditional texts to current social conditions, but wearing a kippah was frowned upon.

From the 1930s through the early 1960s, American culture as a whole encouraged assimilation rather than ethnic diversity, and many Jews whose names hadn't been changed when they (or their ancestors) immigrated changed them then.

ANECDOTE

Ted's father's family was furious when he changed "Falcovich" to "Falcon," though within the next ten years, every cousin had switched to "Falk," "Falkner," or "Falcon." In the entertainment business — the zenith of American culture — Bernie Schwartz, Issur Danielovich Demsky, and Robert Zimmerman became Tony Curtis, Kirk Douglas, and Bob Dylan (respectively).

Jews became Americans first and foremost, often discarding their Jewish heritage, or at least tabling it while they climbed the ladders of success. After all, Jewish composer Irving Berlin not only wrote "White Christmas" but also "God Bless America."

By the 1950s, the senselessness of the Holocaust had caused many people to declare that "God is dead," further removing them from any religious conviction. And the secular bent of the new state of Israel sent a clear message to Jews in America: We're a people, not necessarily a religion.

Through the 1950s and 1960s, many American Jews' connection to Judaism revealed itself primarily in synagogue membership (paying dues even if they didn't attend most of the year) and support of Israel (again, most often with their checkbooks). But the turbulent 1960s announced a change that rippled throughout America, a change that resonated deeply for many Jews.

The choosing people

In America, Judaism increasingly became a matter of choice rather than a matter of necessity; Jews became a "choosing" people rather than simply a chosen people, and many experts felt that American Judaism would simply die out. Certainly the rebellious nature of the 1960s and early 1970s was cause for many younger Jews to reject their parents' attitudes.

But something interesting happened: People started hungering for a deeper spiritual connection. The Human Potential Movement — mixed with newly imported Eastern philosophies (Buddhism, Hinduism, and so on) and the influx of consciousness-expanding drugs — started turning people on to the idea that there was more to this world than met the eye. This awakening emerged in (at least) three ways in the American Jewish community: Some Jews found what they longed for in other spiritual traditions, some grew more excited about their cultural heritage, and many American Jews discovered the deep spiritual aspects of their own roots.

Jews as Spiritual Teachers of Other Traditions

Rabbi Rami Shapiro once told us of a world religions conference that he attended. At one point during the meeting, a curious fact emerged: Every presenter — Hindu, Buddhist, Sufi, and even Christian — was Jewish by birth. Amazingly, a glance through any bookstore confirms that many (perhaps most) of the non-Asian meditation teachers were born Jewish, including Jack Kornfield, Ram Dass, Sylvia Boorstein, Surya Das, Stephen Levine, Sharon Salzberg, Joan Borysenko, and Thubten Chodren.

Many Jews feel a pull toward the esoteric — the hidden, the deeper truths. Some people believe that there is something innate in Jewish consciousness that urges Jews to seek that which is deeper and of greater meaning, even if they have to look outside Judaism to find it.

I didn't know Jews did that!

Astonishingly, when Ted was in seminary, the topic of spirituality never came up. Sure, teachers would say a few words every now and again, but the idea of an inner path toward the One (or however else you want to define spirituality) just didn't seem that important. Conservative, Reconstructionist, and Orthodox teachers also tend to buy into the idea that Judaism is based on what you do — whether it's following the mitzvot (see Chapter 4) or engaging in social action — and that the bigger spiritual picture just isn't that important.

Many years later, and in a deep crisis of faith, Ted discovered (with some relief) that Judaism held a number of secrets — from meditative practices to ecstatic teachings, and above all, a wondrous spirituality. But if even rabbis were largely unaware of Judaism's spiritual component, then what about the rest of the Jewish community?

From the 1950s through the 1980s, Judaism had often become a child-centered religion, watering down its teachings so that people without much understanding of Hebrew or Jewish traditions could understand them. Because most American Jews of the time stopped their Jewish education after their Bar or Bat Mitzvah (see Chapter 8) — or at best after graduating from high school — they never achieved an adult appreciation for some of the greater depths possible in Jewish teaching.

And so generations of Jews grew up with only superficial understandings of their own traditions. In an age when spirituality was blossoming, most Jews saw nothing within their own traditions that responded to the spiritual yearnings they were experiencing. The result? They dropped Jewish practices (if they had been observant at all) and embraced different traditions. Today, according to some reports, over a quarter of non-Asian-American Buddhists were born Jewish. Jewish Buddhists have become so common that they have their own nickname: JuBu (*jew*-boo).

Finding parallels

Many practices and beliefs that people ascribe to Buddhism or Hinduism — like meditation, working with gurus, contemplation in nature, even reincarnation — actually were taught in Judaism for hundreds or thousands of years and only later fell out of favor (see Chapter 5). In the past 40 years, Jews have rediscovered these ideas, and many Jews who previously had no interest in observing their Jewishness, are now returning, seeking out congregations that share their interests (see "The New Jewish Spirituality," later in this chapter).

Of course, many Jews are still turned off by what seems like a dark sense of guilt and suffering associated with Judaism. The idea that "we've got to keep Judaism alive at all costs," along with the stark vision of a benevolent-but-vengeful God, has caused thousands of Jews to retreat to philosophies that don't carry such a heavy burden. On the other hand, we find it ironic that so many Jews became interested in pagan, Hindu, or Buddhist rituals with a sense that the ideas are so much fresher than the "old and stifling" ways of Judaism. (Okay, so Buddhism is only 2,500 years old instead of 4,000. It's still no spring chicken!)

Yes, there is clearly cause for concern in the Jewish community that Jews have been looking for their spiritual nourishment in other practices and faiths. However, many of these people don't see these practices as necessarily incompatible to their own identity as Jews. We suspect that the increased interest in spirituality, even when first discovered within other traditions, has the possibility of reinvigorating modern Judaism.

The New Jewish Spirituality

One of the most unexpected shifts in modern Jewish history (especially in America) has been the increased interest in traditional Jewish practices. Perhaps this shouldn't have come as such a surprise; after all, as some historians have noted, "What the child wants to forget, the grandchild longs to remember." (In this case, it was often the great-grandchildren!)

REMEMBER

A Jew who becomes more observant is called a *ba'al teshuvah* ("master of return"). The term refers to someone who becomes Orthodox (or even Ultra-Orthodox), in a similar way to the Christian idea of being "born again." Of course, taking the Torah to heart and becoming observant is very different than accepting a belief in Jesus as Messiah; see Chapter 3.

While some Jews became very traditional, joining Orthodox or Ultra-Orthodox communities, others embraced more liberal interpretations of Jewish observance. In the 1960s and 1970s, the Chavurah Movement — first outside of and later within organized synagogues — encouraged smaller group meetings (called *chavurot*, "friendship groups") that supported creative spiritual expressions of Judaism that were largely egalitarian, family-based, liberal, and social-action-oriented. Many synagogues in the Reform Movement became more observant and at the same time began to look at the more spiritual aspects of Judaism. The Reconstructionist Movement (see Chapter 1) also mushroomed around this time, bringing its own set of interpretations and practices.

Similarly, in the last 30 years, the Jewish Renewal Movement — under the leadership of Rabbi Zalman Schachter-Shalomi, with spokespersons like Arthur Waskow firmly tying Jewish spirituality to concerns of environment and social justice — has emerged as one of the growing forces in modern Judaism. Jewish Renewal is in many ways transdenominational, and it has tried hard to re-energize and re-enrich other Jewish movements without becoming a separate movement itself; nonetheless, many Renewal congregations have sprung up over the years.

One of the most exciting movements in Judaism today is the recent surge in independent *minyanim* (singular *minyan*) — lay groups unaffiliated with any particular synagogue or denomination, often with a focus on egalitarian roles for men and women. These groups may offer traditional services but are often socially liberal and appeal to many younger Jews.

Jew versus Jew versus Jew

Perhaps you know the joke about the two Jews who were stranded on a deserted island. When they were finally rescued, they invited their rescuers to take a tour of the little village they had built. Their rescuers were amazed at what they had done, but they were also confused by the existence of three different synagogues. "Oh," explained one survivor, "One synagogue is where I go, one is where he goes, and the third is the synagogue neither of us would be caught dead in."

True, the Jewish people have a long history of fighting with each other — the tribes fought among themselves 3,000 years ago, the Pharisees fought the

Sadducees, the Karaites argued with the Talmudists, and so on. But we believe that there's more open fighting between Jewish groups today than there has been in over 2,000 years. We see few signs of it getting better, and there are ample indications that the confrontations will get worse.

Who is a Jew

CONTROVERSY

The biggest issue in Judaism today — bigger than anti-Semitism, or the Palestinian conflict, or even interfaith marriage — is the friction emerging between ultra-observant and less-observant parts of the Jewish community. The disagreements are not new; there have always been stories of the son who became Ultra-Orthodox against the wishes of his family, or a daughter who rebelled against her Orthodox parents and became increasingly secular. But today, the issues are increasingly taking place in the streets and in politics, in America, Europe, and most obviously Israel.

Sadly, some Reform and secular Jews consider the Ultra-Orthodox to be simply crazy, and many of these highly observant Jews consider their accusers to be deeply misguided and dangerous to Judaism as a whole.

ANECDOTE

On a recent trip to Israel, David and his wife hired a tour guide to take them around Jerusalem. The man, a secular Jew who was born and raised in Jerusalem, fought in the Israeli army during the War of Independence, the Six-Day War, and the Yom Kippur War. He was as committed a Jew as you could find, but when he drove near the Ultra-Orthodox community of Mea Shearim, he declared the black-hatted Jews to be "parasites," living off welfare and giving nothing of value back. Our guide made it clear that while the Ultra-Orthodox might be Jews, he didn't consider how they lived to be "Jewish."

Conversely, the Israeli news is filled with stories of the Ultra-Orthodox (also called *Haredi*) Jews becoming increasingly intolerant of Jews who are secular or less religious. Most often their focus is on women and their place in society: Haredi radio stations censor the voices of female politicians; one newspaper actually used Photoshop to remove Hilary Clinton from an important news photograph before printing it; and the Ultra-Orthodox health minister of Israel refused to allow a female pediatrics professor to come on stage to receive an award. Worst of all, Ultra-Orthodox students have been known to spit on or throw rocks at even modestly dressed Jewish girls who walk near their neighborhoods.

REMEMBER

While many people consider Judaism to be a spectrum — the Reform Jews on one side and the Ultra-Orthodox Jews on the other — to an observant ("*frum*") Orthodox Jew, Judaism is more like a light switch: You're either doing it right or you're not. For example, a person in a Conservative or Reconstructionist congregation might be Jewish by birth, but many Orthodox Jews wouldn't consider him or her to be practicing an authentic Judaism. In fact, Ultra-Orthodox rabbis have gone so far as to declare that non-Orthodox "rabbis" are heretics and to prohibit Jews from saying "Amen" after liberal rabbis recite a blessing.

Even becoming a *ba'al teshuvah* doesn't mean that you're fully accepted by the Ultra-Orthodox, who often take people's family background and upbringing into account with friendships and marriages, and make a quiet distinction between "BTs" and "FFBs" (*frum* from birth).

This attitude isn't universal, of course. Most modern Orthodox Jews are significantly more tolerant of differences in beliefs, and many secular and liberal Jews tend to respect the more-observant Orthodox lifestyle — as long as it doesn't get in their way.

Can't we just work it out?

CONTROVERSY

The ultra-observant seek to create their own enclaves, their own communities, in which they can feel supported in their chosen lifestyle. Yet their clannishness, their dress, and their observances make life more difficult for other Jews who don't share their level of observance and don't want their own neighborhoods so radically changed. Each group views the other as an enemy of Jewish continuity.

The differences don't only appear between the two extremes, of course. Topics like interfaith marriage or support for Israel cause rifts among Reform, Secular, Conservative, Renewal, and Reconstructionist Jews, too. But there's a difference: While the rivalries between non-Orthodox groups can still support intergroup communication, the ability of the ultra-observant to share with others is far more limited. In many communities, Orthodox rabbis won't even meet with groups that include non-Orthodox rabbis.

Of course, most Jews tend to downplay these conflicts because it's so much easier to worry about external issues like anti-Semitism or the State of Israel. As always, it's harder to focus on the "we" than the "us and them."

WORDS OF WISDOM

Rabbi David Zeller once remarked on the Jewish tradition that teaches that the Messiah will come when all the Children of Israel around the planet observe a Shabbat, even just once. He taught that the Messiah — which you might think of as the awakening to a shared Universal Consciousness — will come when the Jews who observe Shabbat love those who don't, and those who don't keep Shabbat love those who do.

Considering the Future of Judaism

Whenever we hear someone insist that the Jewish people will disappear any year now, we think of Mark Twain's quip after seeing his own obituary: "The reports of my death are greatly exaggerated." There is a distinct possibility that the Jewish people are, right now, in a process of change perhaps as great as the Talmudic period (see Chapter 14). And no matter how loudly some Jews exclaim that everything is going to hell in a handbasket, the new ideas and observances that are appearing may in fact ensure the survival of Judaism for future millennia.

The trend of the past 30 years is clear: The two fastest-growing religious populations (in the United States, and possibly the world) are the fundamentalists and the universalists, or the Orthodox and the Spiritual Seekers. But because Orthodox Jews strive to have large families (with five or even ten children), while non-Orthodox families often have only one or two; it doesn't take a rocket scientist to see how the two groups may balance out in a few generations.

REMEMBER

Ultimately, the general trend toward greater spirituality is reflected in both traditional and less-traditional Jewish institutions (and, perhaps even more importantly, outside the institutions, in the people themselves). You can find deeply spiritual Jews in the most Orthodox communities and in the most secular; it may sound like a cliché, but it's only through opening to a greater understanding of all people that humanity can really move forward into the new millennium.

Chapter 17

The Problem of Anti-Semitism

ANECDOTE

When Ted was 14, his family moved from a largely Jewish neighborhood to an area where far fewer Jews lived, and he was one of three Jewish kids in his school. It was the first time he got beat up simply because he was Jewish. But what he remembers hurting even more was his best friend, some months into the school year, announcing, "My parents say I can't come to your house anymore because you're Jewish." To this day, Ted can't figure out what his friend's parents were worried about, but these events sensitized him to the common anti-Jewish feelings that often still exist just below the surface.

Many younger Jews who may never have been personally touched by anti-Semitism still sense that dealing with anti-Jewish sentiment is somehow part of being Jewish. Many people are surprised to find out that hate crimes against Jews and Jewish institutions in the United States are still many times more prevalent than attacks on Muslims or any other religious group. In fact, the reality and the threat of hatred against Jews, particularly following the unspeakable horrors of the Holocaust (see Chapter 15), led whole generations to base their Jewish identity on being victims. At the same time, Jews increasingly want to avoid this victim role.

Anti-Semitism has been, and is, a fact of life for many Jews. However, in this chapter, our goal is to discuss the historical truth of anti-Semitism without overemphasizing its importance in the development of Jewish identity.

Recounting the Incomprehensible

No other group of people has suffered as much throughout history (and still survives) as the Jewish people. The centuries of oppression and exile seem so senseless, based on incredible ignorance, suspicion, and fear. As Harry Golden, a great American Jewish humorist, once wrote, "Let's face it — anti-Semitism cannot possibly be explained; it can merely be recounted." Table 17-1 lists a few of the many consequences of anti-Semitism over the past two millennia.

TABLE 17-1   **Selected Acts of Anti-Semitism in the Common Era**

Date (All dates are in the Common Era.)	Event
135	Romans prohibit (upon pain of death) circumcision, reading the Torah, eating unleavened bread during Passover, and other required Jewish rituals
200	The Roman Emperor Severus prohibits conversion to Judaism upon penalty of death
306	Roman law prohibits Jews and Christians from eating together, intermarrying, or having sexual relations
489	Citizens of Antioch slaughter Jews, burn the synagogue, and throw the bodies of Jews into the fire
681	The Synod of Toledo mandates to burn the Talmud and other Jewish texts
855	Louis II expels Jews from Italy
1021	A group of Jews in Rome are arrested, accused of causing an earthquake and hurricane by tormenting a "host" (the wafer used in Mass), and then burned to death after confessing under torture
1099	The First Crusaders arrive in Palestine and slaughter 30,000 Muslims and Jews. Jerusalem's Jews are gathered in the synagogue and burned alive
1180	The King of France, Philip Augustus, seizes all Jewish property and expels Jews from the country
1290	England expels Jews from the country
1306	France expels Jews from the country
1349	Jews throughout Europe are massacred: The entire Jewish community of Basle is burned to death; 6,000 Jews are burned to death in Mainz; 500 Jews are killed in Brussels; Jews in Frankfurt and Vienna commit suicide to avoid torture

Date (All dates are in the Common Era.)	Event
1391	Tens of thousands of Jews are killed in anti-Jewish riots in Spain, tens of thousands more are saved by forced conversion; the Inquisition begins, during which 50,000 Jews are killed
1492	Expulsion of Jews from Spain
1517	The Pope declares all Jews must wear badges of shame and live in ghettos
1543	Martin Luther, founder of the Protestant Reformation, declares that the Jews' "synagogues should be set on fire . . . their houses should likewise be broken down and destroyed . . . their rabbis must be forbidden under threat of death to teach . . ."
1648	The Chmielnicki Pogroms occur: 100,000 to 200,000 Jews are killed in the Ukraine
1862	General Ulysses Grant orders all Jews to be expelled from Tennessee (an order almost immediately rescinded by President Abraham Lincoln)
1894	Alfred Dreyfus, an assimilated Jew, is falsely accused of espionage in France
1900–1920	Thousands of Jews are killed in pogroms across Eastern Europe
1915	Russia forcibly moves 600,000 Jews from the Western border to the interior; over 100,000 die of exposure or starvation
1925	Adolf Hitler publishes *Mein Kampf*, in which he writes, "Today I believe that I am acting in accordance with the will of the Almighty Creator: by defending myself against the Jew, I am fighting for the work of the Lord."
1941 – 1945	The Holocaust. Almost six million Jews (including 1.5 million children) are killed in death camps

Fearing an Unknown Quantity: The Origins of Hate

Historically, Jewish law has led to Jews being misunderstood. Jews couldn't traditionally eat in non-Jewish (nonkosher) homes or intermarry with non-Jews, so there was little social interaction between the communities. Similarly, Jews had to be able to walk to synagogue for Shabbat (see Chapter 18), so they tended to live in small clusters, apart from non-Jews. And, because Jews insisted on practicing their own religion their own way, they were labeled "against the gods" by early pagans — which was later echoed as "against Christ" by the early Christians. Although Judaism posed little or no threat to the non-Jews, Jews were different, and just being different is often seen as a threat in itself.

WHAT IS ANTI-SEMITISM?

The word "anti-Semitism" was coined in the mid-nineteenth century, most likely by a renowned anti-Semite as a less-offensive substitute for the German word *Judenhass* ("Jew-hatred"). The problem is that these people don't hate Semites, they hate Jews. The word "Semite" includes all the descendants of Shem — who was the eldest son of Noah in the Bible — including both Jews and Arabs (and all the other tribes originally from the Middle East). Of course, there now are plenty of Jew-hating Arabs, so the word "anti-Semite" doesn't really make any sense.

Some folks now say "Jew-hater" to be more clear, and others have begun to write "anti-semite" as a single un-hyphenated word in order to downplay the idea of a separate "Semite" population.

Because non-Jews knew little about Jews, it was easy for them to paint the Jews as whatever they most feared. Jews have alternately been described as being radical liberals or tight-fisted capitalists, pushy and butting in where they're not wanted or clannish and reclusive, stingy or excessive and flamboyant. Curiously, however, unlike many persecuted groups, the Jews are almost never seen as stupid, poor, or uneducated (though many Jews have certainly fallen into those categories).

For centuries, Jews were forbidden to own land, barred from trades, and often forced to live in ghettos, effectively cornering them into roles such as lending money or brokering loans (which may have been considered un-Christian because these professions involved handling money). Of course, everyone loves a guy who loans them money . . . until he asks for it to be paid back.

Exploding Dangerous and False Beliefs

Anti-Semites have long justified their terrible beliefs and acts by accusing the objects of their hatred of even worse beliefs and deeds. Here are some of the myths that Jew haters have generated to defend anti-Semitic acts.

Belief #1: The Jews killed Jesus

Probably the most common war cry among anti-Semites in the past 2,000 years has been "the Jews killed Jesus." To get the facts straight: The Jews didn't kill Jesus. The Romans killed Jesus. Jesus's followers and supporters were all

Jewish (as was Jesus, of course). The Sadducee priests, who largely managed the Roman protectorate, were clearly in league with the Roman authorities, and many others in the Jewish community feared punishment if they appeared to support Jesus — or anyone else considered a threat to the status quo. However, the worst you could say is that a tiny fraction of Jews today may be the descendants of those priests or others who were involved.

On the other hand, the Romans had a clear policy: Crucify any Jewish authority figure who rebelled against Roman rule. Some historians say up to 100,000 anti-Roman revolutionaries were crucified, most of whom were likely Jewish. Jesus was clearly Jewish, clearly rabbinic (he prayed and taught in Jewish synagogues), and clearly against the authority of the pagan Romans. Saying that the Jews killed Jesus is like saying the Jews ran the Nazi death camps.

Nevertheless, this didn't stop Christian leaders from declaring the Jews guilty for nearly 2,000 years. St. John Chrysostom (344 to 407) announced that the Jews were ". . . lustful, rapacious, greedy, perfidious bandits . . . inveterate murderers, destroyers, men possessed by the devil . . . they have surpassed the ferocity of wild beasts, for they murder their offspring and immolate them to the devil."

The reformist Martin Luther (1483 to 1546), founder of the Protestant movement, was surprisingly sympathetic in his attitudes toward the Jews — until he found that they didn't want to follow his form of Christianity any more than the Catholicism against which he had revolted. From then on, he advocated burning synagogues and killing Jews.

Somehow the idea that the Jews wouldn't embrace Jesus as the Christ, the Messiah, was so upsetting to Christians that they felt that each rejection itself amounted to a "killing" of Jesus.

Fortunately, the tide appears to be shifting. Incidents of Jews being beaten or urinated on by thugs yelling "Christ-killer" — events that weren't uncommon even 40 or 50 years ago — are relatively rare today. This is partly due to the enlightened views of Pope John XXIII, who, in the shadow of the Holocaust, ordered that the reference to "perfidious Jews" be removed from the Good Friday liturgy in the late 1950s, and later pushed through Church reforms that paved the way for better relationships between Catholics and Jews.

In 1997, Pope John Paul II declared that "In the Christian world . . . the wrong and unjust interpretations of the New Testament relating to the Jewish people and their presumed guilt circulated for too long, contributing to feelings of hostility toward these people." And finally, in the year 2000, on a visit to Jerusalem, he offered a deep and profound apology to the Jews for the long history of persecution.

Belief #2: There's an international Jewish conspiracy

When we were growing up, we thought all the talk about an "international Jewish conspiracy" was just a joke, and we'd each laugh with our friends about it. After all, the Jews couldn't stop the Holocaust — they couldn't even get the Allies to bomb the train tracks leading to the death camps during World War II — much less control the destiny of everyone else. Sure, some Jews who manage big companies, but far more non-Jews hold those kinds of positions. So why do so many people really believe the Jews run the world?

A tract produced in Russia in the nineteenth century called *The Protocols of the Elders of Zion* has played a large role in perpetuating the myth of an international Jewish conspiracy. This short book purports to be the minutes of a committee meeting in which powerful Jewish conspirators discuss how to overthrow Christianity and the world powers. It wouldn't be an understatement to say that thousands (perhaps millions) of Jews have suffered and died because people believed this document to be true.

However, *The Protocols* is clearly a work of fiction. In fact, it's a work of fiction based on another fiction! In 1797, a French Jesuit wrote a political satire in which the French Revolution was blamed on the Order of Freemasons. If you compare *The Protocols* with this satire, it becomes clear what happened: Russian secret police in the late nineteenth century changed the names, characters, and some details, and "leaked" it out to the public as a newly discovered document — and a clear reason to persecute the Jews.

The Protocols traveled widely and quickly and was translated into many languages. In America, Henry Ford (the founder of Ford Motor Company) was deeply influenced by *The Protocols,* and he published a column called The International Jew (discussing ongoing "Jewish conspiracies") in a newspaper he owned. Ford was such a prominent anti-Semite that Adolf Hitler reportedly kept a photo of him on his desk and, in the 1920s, said, "We look to Heinrich Ford as the leader of the growing Fascist movement in America . . . We have had his anti-Jewish articles translated and published. The book is being circulated in millions throughout Germany."

Sadly, this myth continues to live on, as *The Protocols* continues to be distributed in many Muslim countries.

Belief #3: Jews practice ritual murder

Before accusations of international Jewish conspiracies were all the rage, anti-Semites routinely accused Jews of three other crimes:

>> **Mass murder:** Somewhere between a quarter and a half of the entire population of Europe — perhaps as many as 25 million people — died during the Black Death epidemic (1348 to 1350). The cause was clearly a bacteria spread by rats, but no one knew about that sort of thing in the fourteenth century. Rather, rumors spread widely that Jews had poisoned the wells in the afflicted areas, causing enraged mobs to slaughter more than 20,000 Jews.

>> **Blood libel:** You can make almost anyone squirm by talking about the idea of drinking human blood — it's just one of those things that people immediately see as sick and wrong. So when some Christian authorities started accusing Jews of ritually murdering Christians (usually children) in order to drink their blood or use the blood in preparation of Passover *matzah* (unleavened bread) in the twelfth century (such accusations are referred to as "blood libel"), it caused a panic and terrible retributions against Jewish communities.

However, Judaism was the first religion to specifically outlaw human sacrifice and especially to outlaw drinking any blood (even that of animals). It would be easy to laugh off the blood libel as just an old medieval fable, but even as recently as 1970, books were printed in America that included folksongs about Jews drinking blood; and in that same year, King Faisal of Saudi Arabia declared that Jews annually celebrate Passover by drinking the blood of non-Jews. He also enjoyed giving out copies of *The Protocols of the Elders of Zion* to visitors.

>> **Desecration of the host:** Catholics believe in transubstantiation, meaning that the wine and wafer (called a "host") used in a Catholic mass actually transform into the blood and body of Jesus Christ, which are then eaten by the believers. Sometime in the Middle Ages, Christians began to accuse Jews of "desecrating the host" — that is, of breaking into churches, stealing the wafers, and then torturing these wafers by stepping on them or sticking pins in them. The accusers even said that Jews would stick nails in the host and that Jesus's blood would leak out. Fortunately, this insane accusation has died out, for the most part.

Anti-Semitism in literature and art

For those of us who grew up in communities with a lot of Jews, it's hard to understand that most people in the world — and even many people in America — may never have met a Jewish person. Remember that Jews comprise only 2.2 percent of the American population and fewer than a quarter of 1 percent of the world population (almost three times as many people live in California as there are Jews worldwide).

In fact, Ted has been a "first Jew" for a number of people. It's not surprising, perhaps, that many people have no idea what Jews are really like and base their opinions almost entirely on gossip and what they read, hear, or see in the media. Maybe things could have been different if someone way back when had written *Judaism For Dummies*!

If you relied on what great authors such as Shakespeare or Chaucer wrote, you'd think Jews were greedy and sadistic Shylocks (see *The Merchant of Venice*) who drank Christians' blood (see *The Canterbury Tales*). Charles Dickens' most famous Jew was *Oliver Twist*'s Fagin, who Dickens calls the "merry old gentleman," a popular colloquialism for the devil.

Of course, Shakespeare may have never met a Jewish person when he wrote the role of Shylock (the Jews had been expelled from England centuries earlier), and Dickens became surprisingly sympathetic to Jews only near the end of his life after actually getting to know some.

The artist Michelangelo didn't help the cause of the Jews any when he sculpted Moses with two horns on his head. To this day, some people still believe that Jews have horns. Don't laugh! A few years ago a friend of David's had his head felt by someone who had simply grown up to believe this. Why would a luminary like Michelangelo paint such an image? A simple mistranslation of the Bible into Greek, in which "rays of light" was translated as "horns."

Samuel Clemens (better known as Mark Twain) has long been trusted as a "sensible voice of America," but any uneducated reader of his satirical essay *Concerning the Jews* would be swayed to believe a number of anti-Semitic stereotypes found there. He argues that the main reason Jews are hated is that they are too smart and wily at business and Christians can't hope to compete with them.

Because he also noted a number of positive Jewish traits — such as honesty and trustworthiness — he was considered a Jew-lover and a foe to the anti-Semites.

From Religion to Race: Anti-Semitism in Modern Times

Before the nineteenth century, most anti-Jewish feeling was based on religious belief — if a Jew truly converted to Christianity, the persecution would likely end. However, with the rise of nationalism in the nineteenth century (see Chapter 15), anti-Semitic attitudes shifted from the focus on religious beliefs and practices to the theory that the Jews comprise an inferior race. This focus on ethnic Judaism led anti-Semites to use slurs like *kike, yid, hebe,* and *sheeny.* Or, on a more humorous note, the satirical description of a Jew in the Monty Python film *The Life of Brian:* "a Red Sea pedestrian."

In his book *To Life!,* Rabbi Harold Kushner remembers Mordecai Kaplan saying that "expecting the antisemite to like you better because you were a nonobservant Jew was like expecting the bull not to attack you because you were a vegetarian." And social class didn't matter — because of the distribution of Jews throughout every level of society, rich Germans could hate the poor Jews, and poor Germans could hate the rich Jews. The epitome of this hatred, of course, was the Nazi charge not only to remove Jews from their lands but to actually kill every single Jewish person.

Israel and anti-Semitism

The establishment of the State of Israel in 1948 led to the rise of anti-Semitism in Arab communities, where it had been less prevalent. People often forget that Jews and Muslims — members of sibling religions, each tracing their ancestry back to Abraham — lived peacefully together for centuries. In fact, Jews tended to live much better in Muslim countries than Christians lands. However, based on political realities, anti-Semitic feelings began to rise in Arab countries. Following the establishment of the State of Israel, the number of Jews expelled from Muslim countries was approximately the same as the number of Palestinians disenfranchised by the Jewish population.

REMEMBER

Many contemporary attacks on Jews (whether, verbal, written, or physical) have an anti-Zionist basis — that is, the attacker is angry at the country of Israel (its politicians, its actions, or even just its existence). However, the anger is unfairly expressed at Jews as a whole. For example, in 2011, soon after Israel's defense forces stopped a ship from bringing supplies to the blockaded area of Gaza and nine pro-Palestinian activists were killed, anti-Semitic propaganda increased around the world, including swastikas painted on Jewish gravestones and hateful comments written on pro-Islamic online forums.

On the other hand, some attacks are clearly anti-Jewish but are targeted at Israel as a country. Ultimately, untangling the two is usually impossible.

The color of anti-Semitism

Although people of African descent tend to see Jews as simply part of the white majority, from the standpoint of the white racist, Jews are more or less the same category as those with darker skin — a nonwhite inferior "race." Even though they share a minority status, many African-Americans have held anti-Semitic beliefs over the past 40 or 50 years.

For example, some people have claimed that the majority of slave holders were Jewish or that Jews created the slave trade, even though very few Jews were involved in the slave industry. Others claim that Jews have long oppressed the African-Americans in their communities, even though the Jews were often the only "white folks" who would hire their black neighbors for decent jobs at decent wages. Undoubtedly, suspicion and racism existed among many Jews (thus, the Yiddish epithet *shvartze*, which literally means "black," but usually holds negative connotations), and it's easy to point to business practices among some in the Jewish community that were racially unfair. But on the whole, the Jewish community has long been much more accepting than most other people.

Many people today don't remember that Jews (identified as liberals) were among the forefront of those helping African-Americans gain basic civil rights, marching alongside Martin Luther King, Jr., and risking their lives (and losing them, in some cases) in order to help voter registration in the southern states. In fact, the NAACP — America's leading black rights organization — not only had prominent Jews among it founders, but from 1966 to 1975, a Jew — Kivie Kaplan — was the group's last non-Black president.

In the 1960s, as some African-Americans became increasingly interested in Islam, they began to identify more strongly with Arab nations and therefore became more anti-Israel and anti-Jewish. In the past 25 years, groups such as the Nation of Islam have spread significantly more anti-Semitic propaganda, such as Reverend Louis Farrakhan's comments that Jews "are the most organized, rich, and powerful people, not only in America but in the world. . . .. They are plotting against us even as we speak." Other black leaders have announced that Jewish doctors caused AIDS by injecting it into black people and that Jews "undermined the very fabric of the society" in Germany. Somehow, even some Christian African-Americans seem to believe these outrageous claims.

Perhaps black organizations feel they need to build cohesiveness by rallying against a common enemy, and perhaps they feel that the Jew is an easier target than the larger "white power structure." Whatever the case, it's clear that an increasing divide exists between these two groups that were once bound together by similar experiences of oppression.

Twenty-first century anti-Semitism

Anti-Semitism has significantly declined around the world in the past 30 years, but it's far from gone. According to the Anti-Defamation League (ADL), more than 1,200 cases of anti-Semitism (including vandalism, harassment, and assault) were reported in the United States in 2010. Anti-Jewish activity is still widespread throughout the world; here are just a few examples:

- **France:** In 2012, thugs attacked three Jews on their way to synagogue, beating them with hammers and iron bars as they yelled, "Dirty Jews! If we see you again, you're dead!"

- **Poland:** In 2010, fans of a Polish soccer team displayed a giant banner with a caricature of a Jew wearing a kippah, labeled "Death to the Crooked Noses."

- **Spain:** In 2005, a Gallup Organization national survey showed that 69 percent believe that Jews are too powerful, 55 percent attribute "dark intentions" to them, and 72 percent were in favor of deporting Jews to Israel.

- **United States:** The American National Socialist Movement (one of the larger neo-Nazi groups) sells an album called *Jew Slaughter* on its website, while noting in their membership materials that the Holocaust never happened and the world economy is a "Jew-infected system."

CAUTION

The explosion of anti-Jewish material on the Internet, where various groups replay all the old myths of hatred, is certainly cause for concern and ongoing vigilance.

Toward Healing

We believe that there is healing to be done on all sides. Clearly, Jews need to become less focused on past victimizations and more willing to forgive. Non-Jews need to become more educated about the realities of Jews and Judaism in order to dispel old stereotypes and myths. Ultimately, we must all remember that creating any enemy called "them" dehumanizes everyone.

4

Celebrations and Holy Days

IN THIS PART . . .

You'll find the answers to pretty much anything you want to know about Jewish holidays, whether it's the High Holidays of Rosh Hashanah and Yom Kippur or the festive *seder* meal of Passover. You'll find out how to build a *sukkah,* light the candles at Chanukkah, and honor Shabbat (the only holiday that shows up in the Ten Commandments). Jewish holidays are fun and perhaps the best ways to really get to the heart of what Judaism is all about.

Chapter **18**

A Taste of Paradise: Shabbat

I f you're like us, your life has gotten so full of work projects, social engagements, and other obligations that you hardly have time to read this book, much less sit down and figure out where all the time goes each day. Folks like to think of this aptitude for filling time with things to do as a modern-day affliction, but people had this problem even 4,000 years ago. They needed a break then as much as people do today.

The weekly holiday of *Shabbat* (shah-*baht*), the most important Jewish holiday, lets people take a break from the pressures of the workweek. The English translation is usually "Sabbath," and people of Ashkenazi descent often say *Shabbos*, with the emphasis on the "shah" sound. The ancient holiday of Shabbat is the one day each week that observant Jews stop working, traveling, building, and fussing, and they instead ask themselves "Am I a human *doing*, or a human *being*?"

Understanding Shabbat

Shabbat, a peaceful oasis from sunset on Friday until darkness falls on Saturday, is as radical an idea today as it was in ancient times: You take a day off to study, reflect, sing, get quiet, be with family and community, and refresh your body and soul. The sages describe it as a taste of the world to come — a glimpse into the Messianic Time of true peace and lovingkindness. No matter what your station in life, a day of rest — a day to focus on the deeper meaning and values in life — is a religious imperative. In fact, observing Shabbat is one of the Ten Commandments (see Chapter 3).

You can find hundreds of different interpretations of what Shabbat is all about, including the following:

>> **Shabbat stresses the freedom from human masters.** As author and Holocaust survivor Victor Frankl noted, even some prisoners in Nazi concentration camps honored Shabbat as a reminder that while the human body can be broken, each person is ultimately free to choose how to respond to the world.

>> **On Shabbat, humans aren't to do anything with the world or to mess with it in any way.** Instead, people can simply *be* in the world, appreciating its beauty and its rightness.

>> **On Shabbat, each person can connect with his or her higher soul (*neshamah y'tayrah*).** They can experience the world from a more inclusive, spiritual perspective (see "The Five Levels of Soul" in Chapter 5).

>> **On Shabbat, Jews should rest as though every undertaking begun were completed.** The Bible says "Six days shall you labor and do all your work" before Shabbat begins. Jews should enjoy the kind of rest that happens at the end of a project, when one is free to stop and appreciate what has been created.

Shabbat: Restriction or Relief?

Traditional Shabbat observance stems from the biblical injunction that no work shall be done on that day by anyone in a Jewish household — even employees and livestock.

CONTROVERSY

Of course, the Bible didn't actually define exactly what constituted "work," and discussions still continue regarding this issue. Sometimes the definitions create rules that cause many people to feel more restricted than relieved, more frustrated than freshened. Nevertheless, one thing is clear: The intention of Shabbat was to provide relief from everyday demands and to support a gentle environment for study, prayer, conversation, and, quite literally, rest.

Knowing what work to avoid

On Shabbat, the Torah prohibits *melakhah*, which is usually translated "work" but actually has a much more subtle meaning. If Jews couldn't work at all on Shabbat, then rabbis couldn't lead services! Instead, the word *melakhah* seems to refer to work that reflects control or dominion over the world.

The ancient rabbis of the Talmud came up with 39 categories of activity that are considered "work" in terms of Shabbat observance, including cooking, grinding, washing clothes, knitting, sewing, constructing or repairing, writing, cutting, kindling or extinguishing a fire, fishing, and gardening. (These were based on the types of work necessary to build the portable tabernacle while the Hebrews were in the wilderness.) Also, you can't carry or even move an object more than six feet outside of the house or from a private domain into public domain and *vice versa*.

Rabbinical law extends these categories to include activities that Jews may confuse with a forbidden task that may lead to a restricted activity. So in order to avoid breaking a twig off a tree, traditional Jews won't climb trees, and they won't even handle items — like money — that can't be used on Shabbat.

Over time, as new inventions have appeared, rabbis have been called on to make decisions on their use. For example, in modern times, rabbis decided that switching an electrical device on or off should be prohibited because the act completes a circuit, which isn't allowed. Driving a car is prohibited because it involves both moving an object and igniting the fuel in the engine. Obviously, if you observe Shabbat according to traditional definitions, you must live within walking distance of the synagogue. This explains why traditional Jews tend to cluster in neighborhoods that allow them to visit each other's homes and still fulfill the Shabbat requirements.

Discovering what's enough

In the Coen Brothers' film *The Big Lebowski*, a recent convert to Judaism repeatedly refuses to do certain things because he's "*shomer shabbos*," meaning someone who follows the traditional Shabbat rules carefully. While his comments are humorous in the movie, to many Orthodox Jews, avoiding *melakhot* (plural of *melakhah*) is no laughing matter. The sense among these folks is that violating even one regulation debases the whole day.

Keeping Shabbat at this level of observance isn't easy, and nobody bats a thousand. Matters of lifestyle and belief have led most Jews to make choices about the level of traditional observance they keep, and many Jews believe that honoring some aspects of Shabbat is better than nothing at all. Most Conservative Jews feel comfortable driving a car to get to synagogue, so they let go of some restrictions in order to better observe others. Many Reform Jews ignore the overall restrictions entirely, but they try to attend Friday night services (see "Welcoming the Sabbath," later in this chapter) and focus on fun family activities on Saturday.

Redefining the rules

Every law is a boundary, every boundary needs definition, and every definition is subject to redefinition as time goes by.

Traditional Jews, in an honest attempt to follow Jewish law, have defined boundaries that sometimes appear incredibly peculiar to less-observant folks. For example, Orthodox Jews unscrew the light bulbs in their ovens and refrigerators before Shabbat begins, so that opening the door won't turn on a light. Because it's customary to eat some hot food on Shabbat, many people leave their oven or stove on low throughout the day, placing a sheet of aluminum or tin over any burners that they leave on.

Some Jews install timers on their lights so that they turn on and off in a preset pattern without any personal involvement. Also, in days gone by, it was common to find a "Shabbos Goy" in many synagogues — a non-Jew who performed tasks that the Jews couldn't. Orthodox Jews don't consider these practices breaking the spirit of the law. Rather, doing so complies with an underlying Jewish belief, *v'khai ba-hem* ("and you will live with them"), which means you must find a way to make these restrictive laws livable.

For example, many communities have expanded their private domain by surrounding an area (sometimes an entire city) with a boundary, called an *eruv*, made of fences, wires strung from tall poles, and landmarks. They consider it to be okay to carry things (like your kids) on Shabbat inside the eruv. Jews have installed eruvim in many American cities, including Boston, San Antonio, Seattle, and Washington, D.C.

WHEN TO BREAK SHABBAT RULES

All Shabbat rules are suspended in cases where a person's life is in danger. As the Talmud says, "Desecrate one Shabbat, so that one may live to fulfill many Shabbatot" (the plural of Shabbat). In fact, Jewish tradition is clear: You must do everything possible to save a life (except murder or worship idols). So, hypothetically, if you have a terrible, life-threatening disease, and the only cure is to cook (which is prohibited on Shabbat) and eat pork (which is prohibited all the time), then you've got to do it.

Doing what you can on Shabbat

Enough with the restrictions, already! What do Jews actually do on Shabbat? Traditional activities include going to synagogue, reading, studying, taking leisurely strolls, and socializing with neighbors, friends, and family. People play games (like board games), attend lectures, and go to study groups. Many folks use the day to get some extra sleep (sleeping late and napping are considered excellent uses of time).

Many Jewish neighborhoods and synagogues organize activities for both children and adults each Shabbat. In addition, husbands and wives traditionally make love on Shabbat.

REMEMBER

Of course, having children makes Shabbat exponentially more difficult (just try telling a three-year-old to sit quietly and reflect). But having the parents available during that day can actually make it more special, even for children. Shabbat is a day when no one has to say, "I'm too busy to spend time with you."

Welcoming the Sabbath

Shabbat is like a special guest who comes to visit each Friday night and stays until nightfall on Saturday. This guest is so full of grace and light, so loved and so loving, that to have her arrive is a pleasure and to see her leave brings sadness. In the Talmud (see Chapter 3), the rabbis personified Shabbat as a beautiful bride, a partner for the Jewish people, who they would greet with joy each week.

Everything you would do to prepare for a special guest is appropriate for Shabbat (although you don't need to prepare a guest bed for her). For example, before sundown, many Jewish households clean house, set the table with the best dishes, prepare the best meal of the week, bathe, and dress nicely. Somehow, personalizing this day helps people sense the presence of the *Shekhinah* ("Divine Presence," see Chapter 2) during Shabbat.

Shabbat is welcomed in the home with three blessings — over light (candles), wine (or juice), and challah, the special braided egg bread (see Figure 18-1). Because Shabbat is perceived as a time of greater love, the light symbolizes the nourishing love that awakens in the mind, the wine the love that awakens in the heart, and the bread the love that awakens in and through the body.

FIGURE 18-1:
Welcoming Shabbat in the home with candles, wine, and braided loaves of challah.

Lighting the candles

The Jewish tradition encourages the woman of the house to light two or more candles no later than 18 minutes before sundown. (Most Jews just use two candles, but others light a seven-branched menorah, or oil lamps, or one candle for each person in a family.) Hebrew calendars and daily papers often list when sundown comes each Friday. Men, too, can fulfill the candle-lighting ritual.

Although people usually say a blessing before performing an action, lighting the Shabbat candles is slightly different. Lighting the candles after saying the blessing would violate Shabbat, so first you light the candles, and then you cover your eyes with your hands (so that you don't see the light while you recite the blessing), and finally, you uncover your eyes. Jews say the following blessing over the candles:

Barukh atah Adonai, Eloheynu Melekh ha-olam, asher kid'shanu b'mitzvotav v'tzivanu l'hadlik ner shel Shabbat.

Blessed are You, Eternal One our God, Universal Ruling Presence, Who makes us holy with mitzvot [acts that connect us to our Source], and gives us this mitzvah of kindling the Sabbath lights.

TAKING A FIRST STEP TOWARD SHABBAT

TIP

If you haven't celebrated Shabbat before, jumping in and trying to be completely observant can be overwhelming. Instead, at first, try just lighting candles each week. On Friday afternoon, before sunset if possible, take a few moments of silence before lighting your candles. Remember that Shabbat is about to begin, and set your intention for the day to gently deepen your experience of life. Then light the candles (at least two), and cover your eyes. Speak the words of blessing, or just say a silent blessing using whatever words you choose. And then slowly uncover your eyes. Imagine that you are seeing the light of those candles for the very first time. Take a few moments to appreciate that light as a symbol of the very special Light that accompanies you throughout Shabbat.

If you have children, even infants, hold them while you bring this special light into your home. You don't need to explain what you are doing; simply let the quiet elegance of the moment speak to your heart and to theirs. You may find other ways to enhance this day for yourself. For example, you may want to experiment with different synagogue services and with gatherings of your friends.

Curiously, this custom has evolved over time so that some women ritually wave their hands over the candles, as though they were drawing incense over their heads before covering their eyes. This has no actual basis in Jewish law, but that shouldn't stop people from doing so if it's meaningful for them.

Saying the blessings over family, wine, and bread

In traditional Jewish families, the men are typically at synagogue when the women light the candles. When the men return, the whole family converges for four other blessings before the Sabbath meal: blessings over the children (if there are any), the wine, the washing of hands, and the bread. In more liberal households (probably the majority of Jews these days), the candle-lighting and blessings are often performed together as a family.

First, many Jewish families enjoy singing together before the meal (one customary song is *Shalom Aleikhem*, "Peace to You"), which helps set the scene for the lovely togetherness of the holiday. Jews like to take a moment to welcome the Shabbat, the *Shekhinah* (see Chapter 2), each other, and themselves to this moment.

Next, fathers customarily bless their children (though we think it's great when mothers also perform this blessing). Typically, the father places his hands on the head of his child (for multiple children, he just wraps his arms around them all) and says this blessing:

>> **For a son:** *Y'sim'kha Elohim k'Efraim v'khi-M'nasheh* ("May God make you as Ephraim and Menasheh." These are the two sons of Joseph in the Bible.)

>> **For a daughter:** *Y'simaikh Elohim k'Sa-rah, Riv-kah, Ra-khel v'Ley-ah* ("May God make you as Sarah, Rebecca, Rachel, and Leah." These are the four matriarchs of the Bible.)

Then he follows this with the ancient biblical blessing:

The Eternal One blesses you and protects you. The Eternal One shines God's Presence upon you and is gracious to you. The Eternal One lifts up God's Presence to you and grants you Peace.

Traditionally, a husband also honors his wife at this time by reading from Proverbs 31:10–31, which includes high praise beginning, "What a rare find is a capable wife! Her worth is far beyond that of rubies. Her husband puts his confidence in her, and lacks no good thing." Some aspects of the passage are sure to tweak some modern sensibilities, so some people might selectively edit it.

Today, as we become more sensitive to same-sex couples as well as individuals living alone, this poem can help turn the energy of the evening toward the special guest, the Shekhinah, which many people understand as the feminine aspect of God.

Saying blessings over wine: Shabbat Kiddush

Next, the male head of the household (women can also do it, of course) recites the *Shabbat Kiddush* (Sabbath Sanctification), usually while holding a full cup of wine or grape juice:

It was evening and it was morning.

On the sixth day the heavens and the earth and all their hosts were completed. For by the seventh day God had completed the work that God had made, and God rested on the seventh day from all the work that God had made. Then God blessed the seventh day and hallowed it, because on it God rested from all the work that God had created to make.

Barukh Atah Adonai, Eloheynu Melekh ha-olam, boray p'ree ha-gafen.

Barukh Atah Adonai, Eloheynu Melekh ha-olam, asher kid'shanu b'mitzvotav v'ratzah vanu, v'shabbat kod'sho b'ahavah uv'ratzon hinkhi-lanu, zikaron l'ma-asay v'raysheet. Ki hu yom t'khilah l'mik'ra-ay kodesh, zaykher litzi-at Mitzrayim. Ki vanu va-kharta, v'otanu kidashta, mikol ha-amim. V'shabbat kod'sh'cha b'ahavah uv'ratzon hinkhaltanu. Barukh Atah Adonai, m'kadesh ha-shabbat.

Blessed are You, Eternal our God, Universal Ruling Presence, Creator of the fruit of the vine.

Blessed are You, Eternal our God, Universal Ruling Presence, who has sanctified us with commandments and finds favor in us; giving us the holy Sabbath as a heritage in love and favor, a remembrance of the creation, that day being also the first among all the holy occasions, a reminder of the Exodus from Egypt. For You have chosen us and hallowed us above all nations, giving us Your holy Sabbath as a heritage in love and favor. Blessed are You, Eternal One, who sanctifies the Sabbath.

Everyone responds with "Amen" following the Kiddush.

REMEMBER

This blessing doesn't sanctify the wine itself, but rather the whole day of Shabbat. Some people are uncomfortable with the words "You have chosen us . . ." and change or omit this (see Chapter 29 for what it means to be "chosen").

Washing the hands

Traditional Jews follow the Kiddush with a ritual washing of the hands, reflecting the rituals of purity associated with the ancient Temple. Everyone has already washed their hands with soap in preparation for eating; this second washing isn't about cleansing, it's about purifying.

Each person pours a little water over each hand (usually over the right hand first and then the left hand) using a vessel like a glass or pitcher. (You can use the faucet on Shabbat, as long you use only cold water.) Before drying his or her hands on a towel, each person recites a blessing:

> *Barukh Atah Adonai, Eloheynu Melekh ha-olam, asher kid'shanu b'mitzvotav v'tzivanu ahl n'tilat ya-da-yim.*

Blessed are You, Eternal One Our God, Universal Ruling Presence, Who sanctifies us with mitzvot [paths of holiness] and gives us this mitzvah of washing the hands.

TIP

Except for saying the preceding blessing, Jews customarily avoid speaking between washing the hands and saying the next blessing, the *Motzi*.

Saying a blessing over bread: The Motzi

While many less-traditional Jews skip the washing of the hands, almost everyone who observes Shabbat sits or stands around the table for the *Motzi*, the blessing over bread.

On Shabbat, Jews traditionally have two loaves of challah (rich egg-bread, usually braided, representing the very finest of bread) or — in the Sephardic tradition — good quality pita bread, which they cover with a napkin or with a special cover. Some say the two loaves represent the double portion of manna that the Hebrews received prior to Shabbat when they were in the wilderness. Others say they're like the two tablets that Moses brought down, or representations of male and female. If two loaves of challah aren't available, you can say the *Motzi* over whatever bread you have.

Whoever leads this blessing uncovers and picks up the two loaves and then recites the blessing (as long as everyone says "amen" afterward, they don't all have to say the blessing):

> *Barukh Atah Adonai, Eloheynu Melekh ha-olam, ha-motzi lekhem min ha-aretz.*

> Blessed are You, Eternal One our God, Universal Ruling Presence, who brings forth bread from the earth.

Some families cut the challah into slices; in other families, each person pulls a piece off. Either way, Jews customarily sprinkle the piece of bread with salt (or dip it in salt) — the way the ancient sacrifices were — and then eat one or two bites.

Finally, they say (or shout!) greetings of *Shabbat Shalom!* ("Sabbath Peace!") or *Gut Shabbes!* to each other. People usually begin saying this to each other earlier in the day, and they keep saying it until Saturday afternoon.

Eating the meal

Friday night dinner is usually the most festive and tasty of the week, and the mood of the meal is supposed to be one of celebration, even if the week has brought sad news. The meal often includes matzah ball soup, a Jewish holiday staple. *Matzah balls* are dumplings, and they're usually served in a chicken or vegetarian broth (see our favorite basic recipe in this chapter). After the meal, many Jewish families sing more songs (*z'mirot*) and chant the traditional blessing (*birkat ha-mazon*; see Appendix B) with a fullness and energy — sometimes verging on rowdiness — greater than on other nights of the week.

Matzah Balls

PREP TIME: 10 MINUTES	CHILL TIME: 30 MINUTES	COOK TIME: 40 MINUTES	YIELD: ABOUT 16 MATZAH BALLS

INGREDIENTS

2 eggs

¾ teaspoon salt

Dash of white pepper

¼ cup vegetable oil

¼ cup water

¾ cup matzah meal

1 to 2 teaspoons chopped parsley (optional)

Dash of ginger (optional)

DIRECTIONS

1 In a large bowl combine eggs, salt, pepper, oil, and water and beat well with a mixer. Add matzah meal (and parsley and ginger, if using) and mix well. Cover the mixture with wax paper or plastic wrap and chill for about 30 minutes.

2 When you're reading to make the matzah balls, bring a large pot of salted water (at least 2 or 3 quarts of water) to a boil. Alternatively, you can cook the matzah balls in the soup broth (we think this gives the *knaidlakh* a better taste).

3 Wet your hands and form the chilled batter into balls no larger than the size of ping-pong balls. Immediately drop the ball into the boiling water or soup broth. When you drop them in the water, the balls will sink to the bottom; as they cook they'll double in size and float to the top. Cover the pot and cook the balls for 30 minutes or until tender and cooked through. To test for doneness, remove one ball and cut it open. When balls are done, drain them in a colander or a slotted spoon and place them into your soup.

PER SERVING: *Calories 55 (From Fat 38); Fat 4g (Saturated 0g); Cholesterol 23mg; Sodium 117mg; Carbohydrate 3g (Dietary Fiber 0g); Protein 1g.*

VARIATION: You can drop the matzah balls directly into the soup broth instead of into boiling water.

NOTE: Everyone has a favorite secret recipe for the perfect matzah ball. Some cook a long time, some a short time; some add seltzer water, some just swear by the recipe that's on every box of matzah meal. Just remember that no matter how you prepare this dish, your Aunt Pearl will tell you that you're doing it wrong.

A FIRST-TIMERS' GUIDE TO
A SHABBAT MEAL

TIP

Many Jews consider it a *mitzvah* (a holy act; see Chapter 4) to invite friends to share in the Shabbat meal on Friday evening. When you're invited, you know that the mood will be joyous and the meal special. Here are a few other things to think about if you're invited:

- You might ask whether you can bring something, but flowers are generally welcomed (unless there has been a death in the family; see Chapter 10). If you bring something to an observant household, make sure you drop it off before sundown.

- If you want to bring food or wine, ask whether the family observes laws of *kashrut* (keeping kosher; see Chapter 4). If they keep kosher, the meal will contain either meat or dairy, but not both, so make sure you know which if you're going to bring food (even dessert). Vegan dishes (with neither dairy or meat, called *pareve*) are always a good bet.

- You'll impress your guests if you bring a *kippah* (your own ritual head covering; see Chapter 4). This honors the traditions that may be celebrated.

- Many families like to dress nicely for Shabbat dinner and services; men traditionally wear either white or light blue shirts.

- Don't talk between washing your hands and saying the blessing over the bread. And don't stress over saying the blessings; you can always just say "Amen" after hearing a blessing, which is as good as if you had said it yourself.

- You're usually welcome, too, to attend Shabbat services (see the sidebar "A first-timer's guide to synagogue" in Chapter 4). A money offering is rarely made during Shabbat services because Jews traditionally don't carry money during Shabbat. However, some congregations do have a box in the lobby for charity donations, which is especially used for the services during the week.

- Remember the simple greeting of the day: *Shabbat Shalom!* You can say this anytime from Friday afternoon through Saturday afternoon.

- Keep in mind that, due to the wide spectrum of Jewish practice, the home you visit may not maintain the particular traditions that we speak of in this chapter. Ultimately, remember that asking questions is not only acceptable, but usually encouraged.

Attending Shabbat evening services

All synagogues hold services on Friday evening, but ironically, the services at Reform, Conservative, and Reconstructionist synagogues are often longer than those in Orthodox congregations and include a sermon. For Orthodox Jews, the Saturday morning service is the main Shabbat service, and the Friday night service is earlier and relatively short (for them, 45 minutes is short).

The Friday night service is similar to the service on other nights of the week, with the addition of several prayers and blessings, called *Kabbalat Shabbat*, to welcome the Shabbat. Traditionally, the Jews at synagogue sing *L'kha Dodi* ("Come, my beloved," a poem written in the sixteenth-century mystical community of Safed; see Chapter 5) and then read Psalm 92, *Mizmor shir l'yom ha-Shabbat*. While instrumental music is never allowed in Orthodox synagogues during Shabbat, more liberal congregations often have piano, guitar, or even organ music along with singing at various times in the service.

Many congregations follow the Friday night service with an *Oneg Shabbat* ("Delight of the Sabbath"), which is usually a social hour, or a time for educational lectures and the like. When David was a kid, the *Oneg* was the only fun part of the service.

Morning has broken

In traditional Jewish communities, the morning Shabbat service is the longest service of the week. One reason it's longer is the Torah reading (Jews read sections of the *parashah*, or weekly portion, on Monday and Thursday and the entire parashah on Shabbat), along with the corresponding section of the prophetic literature called the *Haftarah*. Before the reading, however, Jews honor the Torah by removing it from the Ark with prayer and song, then marching it around the sanctuary in a *hakafah* ("circuit"). Those present often reach out to touch the Torah cover with a prayer book or with a *tallit* (prayer shawl) and then bring the book or tallit to touch the lips.

Shabbat morning services also include congregational singing, additional prayers, and liturgical selections on the Shabbat. Often, rabbis give sermons (in more liberal synagogues, rabbis usually give the sermon on Friday night). Sometimes the service includes a Bar Mitzvah or Bat Mitzvah celebration, which can significantly lengthen the service (see Chapter 8 for more information).

Each reading from the Torah requires a blessing before and after, often performed from the *bima* (typically an elevated platform in the front of the synagogue) by someone the congregation wants to honor. Reading these blessings is called an *aliyah* ("going up") because reading from the Torah is like going to a higher plane.

THREE SHABBAT MEALS

Back in ancient times, people were lucky to eat even two meals a day. However, centuries ago, it became a tradition to eat three meals on Shabbat. The first meal is the festive Friday night dinner. The second meal usually follows the morning worship, and the third meal is typically a lighter meal in the late afternoon before sundown.

While traditionally you can't actually cook anything on Shabbat, you can start something cooking before Shabbat begins. Many people make a stew called *cholent* (the "ch" here is the English sound, not the Hebrew sound), with beans, potatoes, barley, spices, and often meat, which can cook on a low heat for 12 or 15 hours. In some very traditional communities, slow-cooking electric pots aren't allowed (for technical reasons), and in other communities they are.

Bidding Farewell to Shabbat

Shabbat officially ends at nightfall on Saturday — about 45 minutes after sundown, when at least three stars are visible in the sky — but many communities invite Shabbat to linger a little longer, even after the official nightfall in that area.

Just as Jews have ceremonies dedicated to the welcoming of Shabbat, they have ceremonies associated with the conclusion of this special day. *Havdalah*, which means "separation," is celebrated after nightfall, either in the synagogue after a brief *maariv* (evening) service, or in the home.

The Havdalah service consists of blessings over wine, fragrant spices, the light of a havdalah candle, and then the final blessing of the havdalah itself — the blessing for the separation of holy time from ordinary time.

Wine and candles

To begin Havdalah, Jews fill a small wine cup all the way to the brim. Some Jews overfill the cup — spilling some wine into a small plate under the cup — as a symbol of overflowing blessings for the week. Next, they light the havdalah candle (there's no blessing for lighting the candle), which is a special candle with at least two wicks but usually four or more wicks braided together (see Figure 18-2).

If you don't have an actual havdalah candle, you can just hold two candles with their wicks together.

TIP

In many Jewish families a child holds the candle under close adult supervision (the large flame can be dangerous and the braided candles are notorious for dripping over everything). Next, the leader of the ceremony raises the cup of wine in his or her right hand and recites the blessing over wine:

Barukh Atah Adonai, Eloheynu Melekh ha-olam, borey p'ri ha-gafen.

Blessed are You, Eternal One our God, Universal Ruling Presence, Creator of the fruit of the vine.

But they don't drink the wine yet! This is the one time that the blessing isn't immediately followed with drinking. Instead, the leader puts the cup down until the havdalah blessing later.

Sugar, spice, and everything nice

Fragrant spices lend their aroma to the Havdalah service, creating a sensual experience. Jews traditionally use sweet spices like cloves, and they often put them in ornate spice boxes, although doing so isn't required. The spices are like "Jewish smelling salts" — they bring people back to their "real world" senses, compensate for the fact that Shabbat is leaving, and wake up the "ordinary" soul.

At this point in the ceremony, whoever is saying the blessing raises the spice box and recites the following blessing over the spices before passing the box around so that everyone present can smell it:

Barukh Atah Adonai, Eloheynu Melkch ha-olam, boray minay v'samim.

Blessed are You, Eternal One our God, Universal Ruling Presence, Creator of various kinds of spices.

Next, Jews turn their attention to the havdalah candle (see Figure 18-2). Customarily, as one of the celebrants says the following blessing, everyone loosely curls their fingers and looks at the light of the candle reflected on their fingernails, noting the shadows cast on the palms of their hands. (Some folks say that the purpose of looking at the shadows is so that the candlelight is actually used for something and the blessing won't be said in vain, but we like to think it symbolizes that both light and shadow result from the One Light. On the other hand, some folks insist this action is to show how clean your fingernails are — a clear indication that you didn't do any work during the day!) Here's the blessing:

Barukh Atah Adonai, Eloheynu Melekh ha-olam, borey m'oray ha-aish.

Blessed are You, Eternal One our God, Universal Ruling Presence, Creator of the illumination of the fire.

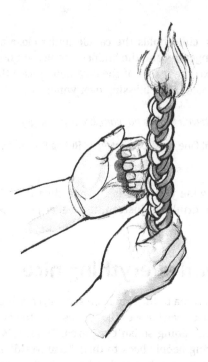

FIGURE 18-2:
Celebrating the
light of the
havdalah candle.

Finally, one person raises the cup of wine and recites the havdalah blessing:

Barukh Atah Adonai, Eloheynu Melekh ha-olam, ha-Mavdil bayn kodesh l'khol, bayn ohr l'khoshech, bayn Yis-ra-el la-amim, bayn yom ha-sh'vi-i l'sheyshet y'may ha-ma-aseh. Barukh Atah Adonai, ha-Mavdil bayn kodesh l'khol.

Blessed are You, Eternal One our God, Universal Ruling Presence, Who makes a distinction between holy and ordinary, between light and darkness, between Israel and the other nations, between the seventh day and the six days of work. Blessed are You, Eternal One, Who makes a distinction between that which is holy and that which is not yet holy.

Everyone present can drink the wine, and then they extinguish the candle either in the remaining wine (in the cup) or in the wine that was spilled into the saucer.

With the separation from Shabbat officially completed, Jews greet each other with *Shavuah tov* ("a good week!") or *Gute voch* (Yiddish for "good week"). For many Jews, though, the celebration isn't over, since people use this as another opportunity for a party, called *melavah malkah* ("escorting the queen").

The Universal Aspects of Shabbat

The word *sabbath* is a rough transliteration of the Hebrew word *Shabbat*. This uniquely Jewish institution has been adapted in both the Christian and the Islamic traditions. In the early centuries of Christianity, observance of the Jewish sabbath was outlawed and replaced with the Sunday celebration of the Lord's Day. But over time, many of the restful aspects of the sabbath have been transferred to that day. Muslims celebrate the Islamic sabbath on Friday. Should there ever come a time (dare we hope?) when these three great Abrahamic traditions can honor each other as authentic paths to a shared Universal Truth, everyone would be enriched with the energies of a *shabbat* that spans three days.

Chapter 19

In with the New: Rosh Hashanah

I f you dissect the average family argument or disagreement between friends, you find a curious fact: The conflict is almost always based on people forgetting their priorities and commitments. In the heat of the moment it's hard to remember what's really important in life. Judaism has a "built-in" system to help get you back on track with your priorities, and it begins with Rosh Hashanah — the autumn festival called the Jewish New Year. Rosh Hashanah is a holiday of remembrance.

REMEMBER

Rosh Hashanah and Yom Kippur (which follows ten days later; see Chapter 20) are together called the "High Holidays," or the "High Holy Days." They are among the most important and holiest days of the Jewish year. For over 2,000 years, the High Holidays have been celebrated as a time for judgment, remembrance, and *teshuvah* (return or repentance). While every other holiday commemorates a transition in nature or a historic event, the High Holidays don't — they focus on people and their relationship with God.

A Day for Making Judgments

In Chapter 25, we explore the spring holiday of Passover and how it encourages people to seek out ways in which they are enslaved by habits, addictions, fears, and so on. Jewish tradition states that each Jew must yearly experience the release from slavery into freedom, just as the early Hebrews were freed from slavery in Egypt. By the time Rosh Hashanah rolls around, some six months after Passover, it's time to start asking, "What have I made of my freedom? Am I still following the path on which I set out?"

New year's celebrations in most cultures are boisterous events, but Rosh Hashanah is a solemn time — solemn, but not sad. In fact, there's great happiness on this day, but this happiness is typically honored in quiet ways because of the focus on judgment. To reflect this solemnity, Rosh Hashanah is also called *Yom Ha-Zikaron* (The Day of Remembrance) and *Yom Ha-Din* (The Day of Judgment).

The Talmud's chief metaphor for this judgment is that God opens three books on Rosh Hashanah. One book is for the names of the thoroughly wicked, who are immediately inscribed in the Book of Death. Another book is for the completely righteous, who are immediately inscribed in the Book of Life. The third book is for those in between — those who are sometimes righteous and sometimes wicked. Final judgment is suspended for these "in-betweeners" until Yom Kippur. Acts of charity, true repentance, and prayer make a positive outcome more possible.

Growing up, this idea of being judged really bugged us. But we now see that the metaphor serves to inspire some serious self-reflection about one's life and soul. Rosh Hashanah is the time to pull out your calendar, review your year, and consider:

>> Were there times that you could have been nicer to someone?

>> Were there people that you hurt, intentionally or unintentionally?

>> Are you fulfilling the dreams and goals that you set out for yourself?

>> Have you been honest with yourself and everyone around you?

>> When you consider your year, what are the things that you are proud of, and what are the things you are sorry about?

>> What are the things you wish you had done that you didn't? And the things that you did do that you wish you hadn't?

REMEMBER

Doing Rosh Hashanah "right" isn't an easy task. Being honest with yourself — acting like a detective, rooting out your less-than-honorable thoughts, words, and deeds — is often painful. At Rosh Hashanah, all Jews undergo this self-exploration together so that no one person feels like he's on his own.

HAPPY NEW YEAR . . . AGAIN

The Jewish calendar is a never-ending source of mystery. For example, if Rosh Hashanah is the Jewish New Year, why is it celebrated on the first day of Tishrei — the seventh month of the year? As it turns out, Jewish tradition holds that there are four new years:

- The Bible states (in Exodus 12:2) that the Jewish calendar should begin in the month of Nisan. Therefore, Nisan is considered the beginning of the religious year, making Passover (15 Nisan) the first festival of the year (see Chapter 25).

- The months may begin in Nisan, but the year number changes on Rosh Hashanah (1 Tishrei). Many Jews say that Adam was created on Rosh Hashanah, so in some ways, this day is a birthday for all humanity. Rosh Hashanah was also the day that the prophet Ezra chose to reintroduce the Torah to the Jews who returned after the Babylonian exile (see Chapter 13).

- Tu B'Shvat (15 Shvat) is the New Year for the Trees (see Chapter 23).

- The "fiscal" year for the ancient tax on cattle began on the first of the month of Elul.

Ultimately, however, when you say "Jewish New Year," almost everyone thinks of Rosh Hashanah.

The Book of Life: Take two

REMEMBER

Remember that the image of the books is just a metaphor. Inscription in the Book of Life doesn't guarantee that you will live the entire year, nor does inscription in the Book of Death mean that you will literally die. In Judaism, people don't die because they've sinned, they die because they're human and dying is a part of life.

Perhaps the story of the books is most helpful as an opportunity to look at how you will live in the coming year. By freeing yourself from past guilts and pains, from past grudges against others, you open yourself to truly living and experiencing the incredible joys of life — hence, you become "inscribed in the Book of Life." If you don't do this work, you remain encased in old angers and in old patterns, and you aren't present for the wonders of the moment. You are therefore "written in the Book of Death."

TIP

We find it useful to remember that God already knows everything you could ever confess to, and — incredibly — is already forgiving and merciful. But you can't appreciate that mercy until you open up, examine your life, and work toward making changes.

Teshuvah: Getting back on track

Perhaps the most important aspect of Rosh Hashanah isn't the judgment, but the teshuvah — the return, renewal, or repentance that each Jew is called to. This isn't just another "I promise to do better in the future" kind of response. Instead, teshuvah is a serious stab at beginning the process of forgiveness and of forgiving others. The process continues through Yom Kippur (see Chapter 20).

REMEMBER

Tradition teaches that there are three primary ways to repent: deep prayer, change of conduct, and gifts to charity. However, as Rabbi Soleveitchik, the founder of Modern Orthodox Judaism noted, the main path of repentance is confession — telling the truth, whether to yourself, to God, or to another person. Of course, Judaism has no mechanism for anyone to grant you absolution; sins against another person must be forgiven by that person, and sins against God . . . well, that's strictly between you and God (see the sidebar "Sinning, Jewish style" in Chapter 20).

Ultimately, the goal of teshuvah is to let go of the past — through self-judgment, making amends, and so on — to make room for what is coming in the new year. Rosh Hashanah arrives like a wake-up call just before winter, offering a chance to renew and refresh your intentions, your priorities, and your sense of spiritual connectedness.

The 40-Day Plan

Judaism recognizes that you can't be expected to undertake this kind of major life review in just one day, so tradition calls for a 40-day plan. Just as the Jewish day always begins at sundown, the year begins at the waning of summer, when winter is approaching (in the Northern Hemisphere, at least). The cycle begins in the last month of the year, Elul (which has 29 days), and then ends 10 days after Rosh Hashanah, on Yom Kippur. Tradition says that after Moses smashed the first set of tablets (when he found the Jews dancing around the golden calf idol) he ascended the mountain for the second time on the first of Elul. That meant that he descended with the second tablets (40 days later) on what would become Yom Kippur.

(Those of you who love math may have noticed that this adds up to only 39 days. However, Jews celebrate the day of *Rosh Chodesh* Elul — the beginning of the month of Elul —one day before the month, making it a total of 40.)

The days of Elul

The month of Elul is dedicated to study and self-examination. Honestly, though, it's hard to keep the focus that long, so relatively few Jews spend the entire month in reflection. Fortunately, the point isn't to be dogmatic about it, but rather to start the process gradually. Some Jews only start seriously thinking about this stuff the last week or so of the month.

Jews customarily blow the *shofar* (ram's horn; see "Blowing your horn," later in this chapter) at the synagogue briefly each morning during Elul (except on Shabbat and on the last day of the month). Blowing the shofar is like a wake-up call to the soul.

During Elul, Jews read Psalm 27 each day. The Psalm begins, "The Eternal is my light and my salvation. Whom shall I fear? The Eternal is the strength of my life. Of whom shall I be afraid?" Rabbis have long taught that the enemy spoken of in the Psalm can be interpreted as the enemy within — the parts of oneself that work from a place of forgetfulness, ignorance, fear, or anger. The reading assures you that you can rely on the strength of the Greater Presence awakening within you.

Preparations: S'lichot

During the entire month of Elul, traditional congregations add a series of prayers to their services called *s'lichot* (pronounced slee-*khot*). The word *s'lichot* means "forgivenesses." (If you bump into someone on the street in Israel, you should say *s'licha*, which means "excuse me" or "forgive me.") The *s'lichot* prayers call out to God asking for forgiveness.

On the Saturday night before Rosh Hashanah, however, congregations hold a special service — often held at midnight, when it is said that the heavens are especially open to prayers — called the *S'lichot* service. (If Rosh Hashanah falls on a Monday or Tuesday, *S'lichot* is held a week earlier.) Even nontraditional Jews are increasingly observing this service because it seems to resonate with an important need: Letting go of the previous year's resolutions and really beginning the process of preparing for forgiveness and repentance.

In many communities, *S'lichot* has become a time for people to search out their neighbors to ask for or to offer forgiveness, like clearing the air and releasing themselves and others of the heavy betrayals and failures that accrued over the year.

Celebrating Rosh Hashanah

Rosh Hashanah is a holiday of several "only's." It is the only Jewish holiday that falls on a new moon, that Jews blow the shofar horn more than once (traditionally for a hundred blasts), and that lasts two days in and outside of Israel. Actually, these days, while Conservative and Orthodox synagogues typically celebrate for two days, most Reform Jews only observe Rosh Hashanah for a single day.

The High Holidays are among the most important celebrations of the year, and for many less-observant Jews, this may be the only time they set foot in a synagogue all year. Surprisingly, there's very little unique ritual involved in either Rosh Hashanah or Yom Kippur. The Bible states that you should blow a ram's horn on Rosh Hashanah. That doesn't take very long, so then what? You pray. And, oy, are there a lot of prayers!

The celebration begins with a lighting of candles at sundown (usually at home) and saying two blessings: the *yom tov* ("holiday") blessing and the *Sheh-heh-khi-yanu* blessing (see Appendix B). Then, everyone heads off for the evening service at the synagogue. Remember that many traditional Jews attend services at the synagogue every night (see Chapter 3), and this service is simply an extension of the "regular" service, with additional prayers and readings (which we discuss in a moment).

At the synagogue, the Torah covers, the curtain of the ark, and the reading table (where the Torah will be placed) are often covered with white as a sign of purity, and many Jews also dress in white at services. Although most Jews dress nicely for services year-round, for some this is one of the great social events of the year, and they may dress in their very best for the evening.

Finally, after the evening service (on both nights), it's customary to eat sweet foods — especially apples dipped in honey — and toast to "a good and sweet year." Similarly, people eat challah (often with raisins or dipped in honey to make it sweeter) that has been baked in round loaves. (Round foods symbolize the cyclical nature of life.)

Some Jews add foods to their table based on puns. For example, if you invite a single friend to dinner, you might offer dates with the wish, "May you have many good dates this year." People also eat *tsimmis* (a sweet casserole that's often made with carrots, sweet potatoes, and dried fruits such as prunes) or kugel (a sweet noodle pudding that acts best as a dessert; see the kugel recipe later in this chapter if you want to make your own). Just thinking about this stuff makes us hungry.

Jews typically go to Rosh Hashanah services both in the evening and the next day (especially the morning service and the additional *Musaf* service that follows it). Then they repeat the whole thing for the second day (with a few minor changes in the readings).

Kugel

PREP TIME: 15 MINUTES   COOK TIME: 60 MINUTES   YIELD: 6-8 SERVINGS

INGREDIENTS

8 ounces of flat egg noodles (medium width is best)

3 eggs, beaten

½ cup sugar

½ cup raisins

1 red apple such as a Braeburn or Macintosh, peeled and diced

½ cup coarsely chopped nuts (generally almonds or walnuts)

1 cup cottage cheese (optional)*

2 ounces butter* or margarine, melted

¼ teaspoon salt

¼ teaspoon cinnamon

DIRECTIONS

1 Preheat the over to 350 degrees.

2 Cook the noodles according to the package directions on the package (usually 8 minutes for store-bought noodles), but don't over-cook them! When the noodles are done, drain them well.

3 In a large bowl, combine the noodles, eggs, sugar, raisins, apple, nuts, salt, and cottage cheese (if using) and mix well with a spoon.

4 Grease a baking pan (about a 9-inch square pan should do it) with the butter or margarine, spread the noodle mixture evenly into the baking pan, and then sprinkle the top with cinnamon. Bake for 50 to 60 minutes, or until the kugel is browned, but not burned, on top.

PER SERVING: *Calories 411 (From Fat 164); Fat 18g (Saturated 7g); Cholesterol 144mg; Sodium 43mg; Carbohydrate 55g (Dietary Fiber 3g); Protein 10g.*

VARIATION: Like many Jewish recipes, kugel is a great opportunity to experiment. You can replace the raisins with dates, add some chopped figs or prunes, spice it up with clove or cardamom — the options are endless.

*NOTE: Kosher dietary laws say you shouldn't mix meat and dairy (see Chapter 4). So, traditionally, if you serve kugel alongside a meat dish, use non-dairy (pareve) margarine and leave out the cheese.

SAVORY OR SWEET?

The wonderful, flexible kugel sits somewhere between a pudding and a casserole, depending on the wide range of ingredients you might choose to use. Sometimes the kugel is sweet, sometimes it's savory. Usually, when we think "kugel," we think of a sweet noodle pudding that acts best as a dessert. However, the noodles are often replaced with matzah, shredded potato, farfel (sort of like little matzah chips), or even corn. We've seen kugel recipes that include broccoli and zucchini, and others that focus on dates and raisins.

The Makhzor: The High Holy Day prayer book

During the High Holidays, the ordinary prayerbook used in synagogue, the *siddur*, is replaced with a special prayerbook called the *makhzor* (cycle). The makhzor varies as widely among congregations or denominations as the siddur (a lot!), but you can generally count on a few similarities.

While the service includes most of the standard prayers, additional prayers and readings focus on three themes (which are also the names of sections in the Rosh Hashanah *Musaf* service, the additional service added after the morning service on Shabbat and holidays):

>> **Malkhiyot** ("Kingship"). More than any other time during the year, the High Holidays are a time to visualize and pray to God as King. Prayers repeat the words *HaMelekh!* ("O King!") and *Avinu Malkenu* ("Our Father, our King") multiple times. The focus is on the Majesty of the Greater Presence in the Universe, the "sovereignty" of God.

>> **Zikhronot** ("Remembrances"). Many of the additional prayers focus on remembering, particularly pleas to God to remember humankind during this time and for humans to remember all that God has done. Again, many people interpret these prayers as calls to wake up from a forgetful sleep, remembering that people are greater than their lowly ego-selves.

>> **Shofarot** ("*Shofar* blasts"). These prayers focus on the Torah and on Zion (the Promised Land), both of which are interpretations of the symbolic *shofar* blasts.

In addition to these prayers, the Rosh Hashanah Musaf service includes other verses from the Bible. A traditional machzor might include three verses from the Torah (the first five books of the Bible), three from Prophets (like the book of

Samuel or Jeremiah), three from the Writings (like the book of Psalms or Proverbs), and then one more from the Torah again. This pattern may repeat for each of the three sections: Malkhiyot, Zikhronot, and Shofarot.

On top of all of this, the Torah scroll is opened and read during each morning service of Rosh Hashanah. Typically, on the first morning the congregation reads the story of Abraham sending Hagar and his son Ishmael away (Genesis 21). The second morning, they read the extraordinary story of Abraham almost sacrificing his other son, Isaac (Genesis 22). Liberal congregations that only celebrate Rosh Hashanah on one day usually just read the second story.

Why these particular stories? Why roll the Torah scroll back to its early chapters just as the year of Torah reading is about to end? The readings stimulate people to think about the meaning of faith at the beginning of the new year. Also, they make people consider how awesome a commitment Abraham had, to place the lives of his only two children in the hands of God.

Blowing your horn

Nothing says "Wake up!" more than hearing a ram's horn blown during the Musaf service on Rosh Hashanah day. And it's not just blown once — it's traditionally blown 100 times in varying ways and times throughout the service. Usually one person is given the honor of blowing the *shofar*, but sometimes more than one person blows at the same time, or they take turns blowing.

In ancient days the shofar was blown quite often (to signal a fast or the beginning of a holiday, and so on), but these days the shofar is usually only blown during Elul (once a day), on Rosh Hashanah (a lot), and on Yom Kippur (once, at the end of the holiday). However, to say that it's just "blown" doesn't do the act justice. Various ways of blowing on the shofar have specific meanings:

>> **Tekiah:** One long note like an alarm

>> **Shevarim:** Three medium blasts

>> **Teruah:** Eight quick staccato notes followed by one slightly longer blast

Each of these "notes" evokes a different sense of crying: sorrowful moaning, grievous wailing, or sharp sobbing. The sounds resonate not only in sad ways, though; for many Jews, the blasts of the shofar are indescribably beautiful and moving.

During the Musaf service, one person quietly calls out the order of the pattern, which is printed in the makhzor (like, "tekiah, teruah-shevarim, tekiah," and so on). The last note of the pattern is always a *tekiah gedolah*, which is a particularly long blow, usually ending with a more forceful blast at the end.

Here are a few things to think about when listening to the shofar:

>> According to the Bible, the sound the ancient Hebrews heard at Mount Sinai was the blast of a shofar.

>> Curiously, the tradition requires Jews to *hear* the sounds of the shofar, not to blow the horn themselves.

>> Abraham sacrificed a ram after God spared Isaac (see Chapter 11). Tradition holds that God blew one of the ram's horns at Sinai and will blow the other horn to announce the coming of the messiah. For those who aren't into the idea of an external, redeeming messiah, the shofar blast is like a taste of what it's like to be really wide awake and aware in a "messianic consciousness," a taste of expanded love and compassion which marks the messianic time.

>> Some folks think of the shofar as an alarm, warning people to wake up and turn their lives around. Others see it as piercing the shell that has hardened around their hearts in the previous year.

>> Focus on the sound, remembering that though words and melodies have changed over centuries, the sound of the shofar remains a constant.

Note that traditional congregations don't blow the shofar when Rosh Hashanah falls on Shabbat.

Tashlikh

One of our favorite Rosh Hashanah customs, called *Tashlikh*, calls for Jews to visit a body of free-flowing water (like a river, lake, or ocean) and empty their pockets and cuffs of crumbs and lint in a symbolic gesture of casting away guilt and letting go of the previous year. Some Jews just throw bread crumbs into the water, feeding ducks and fish while they're at it. Typically, people do this after the afternoon service on the first day of Rosh Hashanah, though if that falls on a Shabbat, Tashlikh is moved to Sunday.

Tashlikh (which literally means "You will cast") stems from a biblical passage in the book of Micah (7:18-19): "And you will cast all their sins into the depths of the sea."

Many rabbis over the centuries were uncomfortable with this custom — thinking that it promoted magical thinking — but Jews continue to embrace the custom, perhaps partly because it's just so good to get outdoors after so many hours praying and socializing in the synagogue. Also, water is universally considered spiritually cleansing and transforming.

Of course, as Rabbi Richard Israel joked, "Taking a few crumbs to Tashlikh from whatever old bread is in the house lacks subtlety, nuance, and religious sensitivity." He then goes on to note that you should bring the right kind of bread for the right kind of guilt. For example:

>> For ordinary sins, use white bread

>> For dark sins, use pumpernickel

>> For auto theft, use caraway

>> For being money-hungry, use raw dough

>> For being holier-than-thou, use bagels

The Ten Days of Awe

The period of *teshuvah* ("return" or "repentance") lasts 40 days, from the day before Elul to Yom Kippur. Most Jews tend to focus on Rosh Hashanah and Yom Kippur, but the days between them are in some ways just as important. These days, along with the High Holidays, are called the *Yamim Nora'im* ("Days of Awe") or *Aseret Y'mai Teshuvah* ("Ten Days of Repentance").

Cleaning your spiritual house

At Passover, Jews cleanse themselves of built-up ego (in the form of *chametz*; see Chapter 25). Similarly, the Days of Awe are a time for spiritual cleansing, awakening to the fact that people tend to become forgetful, and letting go of the past year to make room for the year to come.

CONTROVERSY

Traditionally, this is your last chance to repent and make amends for any wrongs you've committed before the Book of Life is sealed on Yom Kippur. Many Jewish teachers note that this concept is unfair; they stress that teshuvah is available at any time during the year when you seek it.

Nevertheless, at Rosh Hashanah, Jews are clearly directed toward a renewed appreciation of God's transcendence. They perceive God as the Greater Being in Whose Presence people become most aware of their human frailties and shortcomings.

TIP

A FIRST-TIMERS' GUIDE TO ROSH HASHANAH SERVICES

Rosh Hashanah services are among the easiest services of the year to attend. A large percentage of the people who attend are "two-day-a-year Jews" (they only attend services at Rosh Hashanah and Yom Kippur), so the rabbi is perhaps more careful than usual to explain what's going on. However, you might be especially aware of the frame of mind required: This is a time to really be self-reflective and humble — a much harder task than it sounds like.

However you approach Rosh Hashanah, here are a few things you might want to keep in mind:

- Before, during, and after services, people often wish each other *Shanah Tovah* ("Happy New Year") or *L'shanah tovah tikateyvu v'tikhatemu* ("May you be inscribed and sealed for a good year"). Others just use the Yiddish, *Gut Yuntoff* ("Good Holiday") or *Gut Yor!* ("A Good Year"). Jews also traditionally send *Shanah Tovah* cards to friends and relatives.

- Round and sweet foods are most appropriate, if you're asked to bring something to a dinner or party. For example, challah is traditionally baked in round loaves rather than longer braided loaves at this time of year.

- Rosh Hashanah and Yom Kippur are every synagogue's busiest times of the year, and you usually must purchase tickets in advance. It's become an international Jewish pastime to complain about how expensive these tickets are, but believe us, they wouldn't charge so much if it wasn't necessary for the survival of the synagogue. If you really can't afford a ticket, call ahead and ask if it's okay to pay less. Most congregations don't want to turn anyone away.

REMEMBER

At Rosh Hashanah the process of self-examination begins, almost as if you are opening the books, the records, of your life over the past year. During the ten days, you become more familiar with what you find in the books, and hopefully you discover new ways to overcome past failings, so that there can truly be a sense of accomplishment at Yom Kippur.

Kapparot

Every culture and religion has some customs that seem really weird — stuff that really makes you go "huh?!" Judaism certainly has its fair share. *Kapparot,* which some very traditional Jews still perform on the last day before Yom Kippur, is one of these oddities. In this ritual, Jews swing live chickens over their head three times (men swing a rooster, and women swing a hen), announce that the animal serves as a substitute for them, slaughter it, and then donate it to the poor. In lieu of chickens, some wave money that they then donate to the needy. After all, it's easier to swing a bag of money, and these days many needy folks welcome money more than a dead chicken.

Rabbis have long insisted that Judaism really doesn't provide any grounds for this kind of vicarious sacrifice. Nonetheless, many Jews continue to do it, explaining that it's an old tradition based on the giving of *tzedakah* (charity).

Real Beginnings Mean Real Changes

REMEMBER

Rosh Hashanah is the beginning of a crucial process in the Jewish yearly cycle, calling Jews to realize and take responsibility for their thoughts and actions, both good and bad, and urging them to have an elevated consciousness for the year that is beginning.

IN THIS CHAPTER

» **Reaching toward forgiveness**

» **Understanding the Jewish idea of sin**

» **Hearing the melody of the holiest night: Kol Nidre**

» **Fasting on Yom Kippur**

Chapter **20**

Getting Serious: Yom Kippur

Being human (yes, this means you) has certain ramifications. Death and taxes are among these, of course. But so are making mistakes and getting self-righteous. Perhaps most of all, we humans suffer from our limitations: Sometimes it's hard to see the big picture.

For example, have you ever met a child who acts out by yelling, kicking, and generally being obnoxious? We don't know about you, but it's easy for us to get angry at kids who behave like that. Sometimes this anger comes from not seeing the whole picture, from having a limited viewpoint. What if you found out that the child's mother is at home, in bed, dying of cancer? You might not forgive the child entirely, but you would probably soften your feelings if you found out that other factors were involved in the child's behavior.

We all get so caught up in our own perspectives that it's hard to remember that we're all in it together. This forgetting causes us to suffer and to cause pain to others. Fortunately, Jews — and non-Jews, if they want — have an opportunity to see a bigger picture. The Ten Days of Awe, which include the High Holidays (or High Holy Days) of Rosh Hashanah (see Chapter 19) and Yom Kippur, are a time for Jews to reflect on the previous year, let go of grudges, ask forgiveness from people, and broaden their perspectives. Finally, on Yom Kippur, they can look around with confidence that they faced everything and survived, that they let go of what needed letting go, and that they made reparations whenever possible.

Yom Kippur, the tenth of the month Tishrei (often spelled *Tishri*), is perhaps the most cathartic, holy, and emotional day of the Jewish year. The nonstop day of prayer and meditation can rattle and inspire the Jewish soul in a way that no other holiday seems to do.

Yom Kippur Means Always Having to Say You're Sorry

Many non-Jews (as well as Jews who had little connection with their heritage growing up) find Yom Kippur, which literally means "The Day of Atonement," baffling. The holiday has no Christian equivalent. But even though most Jews can't explain why Yom Kippur resonates so deeply for them, they're drawn to Yom Kippur services, even if it's the only time they wander into a synagogue all year.

For many Jews, Yom Kippur services (especially the first night's Kol Nidre service, which we discuss later in this chapter) provide a chance to say, "I'm still Jewish, even if I don't know what that means." For other Jews, Yom Kippur is the high-light of their year, a day that seems sad but is actually uplifting, a day during which "atonement" becomes "at-one-ment." They feel an extraordinary sense of release and spiritual unity that comes with forgiveness.

Seeking forgiveness from God

Aside from being a holiday when people strive to let go of grudges, seek forgive-ness, and unite with each other, Yom Kippur also serves as an important time to seek forgiveness from God. This High Holy Day is called the Shabbat of Shabbats, and is traditionally seen as the day on which God finalizes the judgment of all Jews each year, sealing people's names in the Books of Life or Death (see Chapter 19). Yom Kippur is the last chance to change, to repent, and to atone before this judgment.

REMEMBER

By the time Yom Kippur rolls around, Jews are expected to have asked for forgive-ness for sins against other people. The actual day of Yom Kippur is then reserved for atoning for sins against God. Of course, if you believe that God is One (and includes everything), then all our sins impact everyone on some level.

Repenting

When most people hear the word *repentance*, they think of a system in which some authority figure absolves people of their sins. In Judaism, however, there is no such authority. Jewish tradition clearly states that Yom Kippur offers a blanket forgiveness from God if (and only if) you have both repented and atoned for any wrongs. The Hebrew word for repentance is *teshuvah*, which signifies a psychological or emotional "turning," resulting in a retargeting of your life.

Atonement has more to do with actually making amends, fixing something that you have broken. Just apologizing isn't enough; you have to find a way to make reparation. A rabbi might help you discover a suitable action, but ultimately he or she can't prescribe anything — that's between you and the other person, or between you and God.

REMEMBER

The Talmud states that you can't just go out and sin with the understanding that you'll be forgiven by God on Yom Kippur. You can't circumvent the important work of reconciliation with yourself, your family, your neighbors, and so on. Ultimately, the point of all of this is to change, to grow, and to develop. In fact, the ancient Jewish rabbis taught that you haven't fully repented until you're twice confronted with the opportunity to engage in the same sin, and you refuse.

SINNING, JEWISH STYLE

The word for "sin" in Hebrew is *khet*, an archery term that means "missing the mark." The Hebrew meaning exposes an important difference between the Christian and Jewish concepts of sin. Jews don't believe in original sin, believing instead that each person is born innocent. Judaism also believes that each person is responsible only for his or her own sins or mistakes.

To a Jew, sinning means going astray, not following through, or losing focus. Certainly, lack of honesty or integrity is sinful, as is ignoring or contradicting the Jewish laws. But an unconscious or accidental omission or slight can also be considered sinful. Jewish sin isn't just what you do; it can even be what you don't do. For example, walking by someone in need can be considered a sin because of the missed opportunity to do a good deed. Rabbi Nachman of Bratslav said that the worst sin is despair, perhaps because it so deeply undermines faith.

Jews believe that there are three ways of sinning: sinning against God (making a vow that you don't keep or violating ritual law), sinning against another person (acting illegally, hurtfully, or deceitfully), and sinning against yourself (hiding behind addictive behavior or bringing harm to yourself). Although Yom Kippur stresses the sins against God, the High Holidays as a whole encourage people to focus on all three types of sin, providing an opportunity to actively seek and extend forgiveness, and freeing people to act with greater integrity and truthfulness in the New Year.

HOW TO FORGIVE OTHERS

Jewish tradition identifies three stages in the process of forgiveness, whether you're being forgiven or you're forgiving others. The steps are identified by the words *s'lichot* ("forgiveness"), *m'khilah* ("letting go"), and *kapparah* ("atonement"). Forgiveness begins with the conscious intention to forgive. But if the process ends there, the feelings of guilt or resentment reappear when you least expect them. Letting go means, "I no longer need the past to have been any different than it was." At this stage, you may remember the pain, but you are no longer consumed either with guilt or resentment. With atonement, you can accomplish something positive that otherwise wouldn't have been possible. You still remember, and you still may feel the pain, but the act of atonement transforms the pain into a blessing.

Although Yom Kippur is traditionally the last day to atone, Judaism ultimately says that the doors of repentance are open all the time — it's never too late. But if there wasn't at least a symbolic deadline, would anyone ever really get around to it?

Celebrating Yom Kippur

Most Jewish holidays are distinguished by what you're supposed to do; Yom Kippur, however, is famous for what you're not supposed to do. Tradition states that on this day Jews should refrain from bathing luxuriously (though necessary washing with cold water to remove dirt is okay), anointing themselves with perfume or moisturizers, having sex, wearing leather (the soles of shoes, specifically, though some Jews don't wear any leather), and — probably the most-commonly observed restriction — eating or drinking. Of course, because Jews consider Yom Kippur to be like Shabbat, all the regular Shabbat restrictions apply (see Chapter 18).

Fasting, but not quickly

Rabbis have interpreted the fast — which lasts for 25 hours from sundown to just after sundown — in a number of ways:

>> Some say that fasting afflicts the body (because eating is pleasurable) and thereby atones for every sin committed that hasn't been atoned for in another way.

>> Instead of seeing the fast as a punishment, many rabbis see it as freeing Jews from thinking about ordinary things, which allows them to focus on their prayers and the spiritual energies of the day.

>> The fact that humans can choose to fast symbolizes the freedom of choice that gives humans a greater responsibility in the world than other animals.

>> Yom Kippur is like the prayer before a meal, and the meal is the whole year to come. So just as you wouldn't eat during a blessing, you don't eat during Yom Kippur.

REMEMBER

The Talmud states that you shouldn't fast if you're really sick, pregnant (or recovering from giving birth), or if you're under 13 years old. Some children refrain from eating one or two meals during the day as a way to "warm up" to the fast they'll perform when they get older. And although tradition clearly calls for a fast from both food and fluid, some Jews do drink a little water throughout the day. No, you can't eat at McDonald's, even if they do serve "fast" food.

TIP

Here are a few suggestions to think about if you choose to fast:

>> Most healthy adults can last a month or more without eating. However, you do need water. If you're going to go without fluids on Yom Kippur, make sure you drink a lot in advance. However, avoid alcohol or caffeine, which dry you out.

>> If you're avoiding fluids, don't eat salty foods (pickled or smoked foods, commercial tomato sauce, and so on) the day before. David ate sushi with soy sauce before Yom Kippur a few years ago — big mistake!

>> Doctors report that the nausea and headaches that some people experience when fasting have nothing to do with not eating or drinking. Rather, these symptoms are generally the result of caffeine withdrawal. Laying off caffeine a day or two earlier may help significantly.

>> Some traditional Jews bring fragrant herbs or essential oils with them to synagogue in order to nourish the soul through smell. Others find that smelling such fragrances just makes them hungrier.

>> After the fast, don't pig out (pun intended). It's best to begin your "break-fast" meal with a couple glasses of juice in order to put some sugar into your bloodstream.

Taking a long day's journey

Celebrating Yom Kippur includes five different services:

>> The Kol Nidre (described later in this chapter) begins the standard evening *Ma'ariv* service (though there are additional readings and prayers). Tradition

holds that the evening Yom Kippur service never really ends, and actually blends right into the morning services.

>> The morning *Shakharit* service (see Chapter 4), with additional readings and prayers.

>> The *Musaf* ("additional") service, which is typically added on Shabbat and holidays.

>> The standard afternoon *Minkhah* service, again with additional prayers.

>> The *Neilah* ("closing" or "locking") service, signifying the closing of the gates of heaven. Yom Kippur is the only time during the year that this service is performed.

In each service, Jews read the *Amidah* (the traditional standing prayer), and during the entire Neilah the doors to the Torah Ark remain open, so that the congregation may be standing for as long as an hour. Often, the time between services is brief — people may be praying almost all day.

Preparing for Yom Kippur

TIP

Traditionally, the first evening service (Kol Nidre, described in the following section) begins early on Yom Kippur, while there is still some light in the sky, so an early dinner before the service helps. Many Jews have a regular supper before beginning Yom Kippur, but others have a festive meal like on Shabbat (see Chapter 18). Jews have a special blessing for lighting candles prior to dinner on Yom Kippur eve:

Barukh Atah Adonai Eloheynu Melekh Ha-Olam, asher kid'shanu b'mitzvotav vitzivanu l'hadlik ner shel Yom ha-Kippurim.

Blessed are You, Eternal One Our God, Universal Ruling Presence, Who sanctifies us with mitzvot [paths of holiness] and gives us this mitzvah of kindling the light of Yom Kippur.

In addition to the holiday candles, many Jews also light 24-hour *yartzheit* candles (see Chapter 10) to remember family members who have died.

Many traditional Jews wear white as a sign of purity, and some men may wear a *kittel,* the simple white robe in which they were married and will eventually be buried. Yom Kippur is also the only day in the year that traditional Jews wear a *tallit* (prayer shawl) in the evening and in the afternoon, and not just in the morning.

Considering the Kol Nidre: The evening service

The name of the opening Yom Kippur service — Kol Nidre (pronounced kohl nee-*dray*), considered one of the highlights of an observant Jew's year — is named after a portion of liturgy that is sung during the service. Strangely, its lyrics read more like a legal contract than a prayer. In fact, the Kol Nidre is a legal document. (Jewish law states that legal proceedings must be taken care of during daylight hours, which is why the Kol Nidre service traditionally begins while there's still light in the sky.) Although the words to Kol Nidre are certainly important, the haunting melody makes a stronger impression on many people. Many Jews who know little or no Hebrew (the Kol Nidre is actually in Aramaic) find the melody mysteriously and deeply moving, like a memory from early childhood, a childhood that is hundreds of years in the past.

In some ways, we think Kol Nidre is more powerful if you don't know the words, because the words are kind of confusing. Nevertheless, here's a translation:

> All vows and oaths, all promises and obligations, all renunciations and responses, that we shall make from this Yom Kippur till the next — may it come to us in peace — all of them we retract. May we be absolved of them all, may we be released from them all, may they all be null and void, may they all be of no effect. May these vows not be vows, may these oaths not be oaths, may these responses not be responses.

The words of Kol Nidre at first glance appear to absolve Jews of every promise they make in the next year. Anti-Semites have had a field day with this one, claiming that this proves how untrustworthy Jews are. However, rabbis have always taught that Kol Nidre only speaks to vows that people make with God.

These words may originally refer to the vows made under duress, like during the forced conversions to Christianity. Now, the Kol Nidre recognizes that you can't always keep the promises you make to yourself or to God. For example, you might say "God, I promise to be good if only you make my mom recover from this illness." If your mom heals, are you then held to being a "saint" for the rest of your life? No, Judaism recognizes the realities of human nature.

ANECDOTE

Some people have argued that the text of Kol Nidre has little meaning today and should be removed or changed. However, for the vast majority of Jews, Yom Kippur just wouldn't be the same without it. When Ted was a student rabbi, he was sent to perform High Holiday services in Casper, Wyoming, a "Wild West" city — one of those places that you wonder, "are there really any Jews living there?" As a student, Ted wasn't confident enough in his voice to chant the Kol Nidre, so he instructed the elderly Jewish caretaker to play the music on a record player in the back of the synagogue. On that night, even in this remote corner of the world, Kol Nidre resonated in the hearts of the small crowd. Unfortunately, the man forgot to turn the music off, and the record then proceeded to an upbeat song that had nothing to do with Yom Kippur. Well, no holiday service is perfect.

Every service on Yom Kippur includes a set of *vidui* ("confessional") prayers, primarily made up of the *Ashamnu* ("we have sinned") and the *Al Khet* ("for the sin of"). Both of these prayers are alphabetical poems (called *acrostics*) that list all the sins that humankind has committed, like "We have Abused, Betrayed, been Cruel," and so on.

Of course, few, if any, individual Jews have erred in all of these ways; rather, they read the confessional in the plural "we" so that no one person has to embarrass him- or herself. Also, as Rabbi Isaac Luria once explained, all of the children of Israel are considered a single body, and each person is a limb of that body. Each Jew confesses to the sins of the whole body. As someone else once said, it takes a village.

LIVE LONG AND PROSPER: THE BLESSINGS OF YOM KIPPUR

Anyone who's seen the original *Star Trek* series on television has seen Mr. Spock hold up his hand — spread wide, with his index and middle finger held together, and his pinkie and ring finger held together — in the famous "Vulcan handsign." Few people realize that the actor who plays Spock, Leonard Nimoy, is Jewish, and that this gesture is one half of the ancient Jewish sign of blessing, practiced by the early priesthood during the Temple period (see Chapter 12).

Today, this handsign is still used during the Amidah section of the special Musaf service during holidays. In more traditional congregations, all the men descended from the Kohanim families (associated with the ancient priesthood, typically men with last names like Cohn, Cohen, Kahn, Katz, and so on) are invited up to the bimah (the front of the synagogue) to perform the priestly blessing for the community (called the *Birkat Kohanim*). These men, draped in prayer shawls, hold both their hands in what has become known as the "Vulcan greeting," often with the thumbs outstretched and touching, while saying a benediction over the whole community (called *dukhan-ing*).

In more liberal communities, the blessings are performed in a number of different ways. Usually, the rabbi pronounces the blessing. Encouraging greater participation of all participants, in Ted's congregation, first all the men bless all the women, and then all the women bless all the men (or *vice versa*).

Traditionally, Jews repeatedly beat their chests with their fists while reading the *Ashamnu* and the *Al Khet*. While this presents a rather dramatic scene, some rabbis teach that there has been enough beating over the ages, that the confessions already hurt enough, and that perhaps people should just gently and lovingly touch the area over their hearts instead.

Reading and kneeling

The High Holidays include a number of special customs. For example, when most congregations read the *Aleinu* (the prayer that includes "we bend the knee, bow down, and offer praise") during regular services, each person bends the knees slightly and then bows at the waist, signifying service to the Higher Spirit. However, on Yom Kippur, many Jews actually kneel on the ground at the word *kore'im* ("bend the knee"), and then bring their heads to the floor in prostration at the word *u-mishta-khavim* ("bow down"). Some Jews, when there is enough room in the synagogue, lay completely flat on the ground, with arms and hands stretched forward in an ultimate form of respect and supplication.

For thousands of years Jews have made it a point never to bow or kneel to anyone except God. Some rabbis teach that God brought the Jews out of slavery from the Pharaoh in Egypt (see Chapter 11) in order to become servants to a Higher Ruler, namely God, but we see it a slightly different way: The Aleinu is an opportunity for each Jew to show his or her dedication to being of service — service to God, service to humanity, service to the planet, service to a greater good. As Bob Dylan once sang, "You gotta' serve somebody!"

Other exclusives during the High Holidays are the *Avinu Malkenu* ("Our Father, Our King") prayers, the *Avodah* (a detailed account of the rites performed by the High Priest of the Second Temple on Yom Kippur) and, often, the martyrology, in which the names of ten ancient rabbis who were killed for teaching Torah are listed, often alongside the names of other Jewish martyrs and a special note about the six million Jews killed in the Holocaust. And, on Yom Kippur, most congregations read the Biblical book of Jonah aloud in the afternoon.

Traditionally, between the Torah reading and Neilah, the rabbi leads the memorial Yizkor service, in remembrance of friends and family who have died, particularly parents of those in attendance. (In most Reform congregations the Yizkor service takes place later in the afternoon.) Many Jews consider it bad luck to participate in a Yizkor service while their parents are still alive, so typically all the youngsters leave the room. For those who are less superstitious, the Yizkor service can be a deeply moving and important memorial, whether or not your parents are still living.

A FIRST-TIMERS' GUIDE TO YOM KIPPUR SERVICES

TIP

Yom Kippur services vary radically depending on the observance of the synagogue. A traditional Orthodox service might be wonderfully intense, but deeply indecipherable for the novice. More liberal congregations may have a much simpler *makhzor* (Holy Day prayer book), leaving out some of the readings and prayers in favor of more explanation or a break between services. Here are a few things to keep in mind when you show up for services:

- Like at Rosh Hashanah (see Chapter 19), Yom Kippur services require buying tickets in advance at most synagogues. If money is tight, try calling ahead to see if they offer a sliding scale.

- Remember that many Jews don't wear leather shoes during Yom Kippur, and some wear no leather at all. So while most Jews wear their finest clothes, you may see people in suits or dresses wearing canvas high-tops, sneakers, or other shoes made without leather.

- Most Jews who attend services also fast on Yom Kippur, so if you bring any food or drink, keep it out of sight (and smell).

- Don't expect the best hygiene of your neighbors on this day. Traditional Jews don't brush their teeth or bathe on Yom Kippur.

- Yom Kippur is an ideal time to remember that all human beings make mistakes; the important thing is to continually review your life, learn, and grow. With this in mind, don't worry if you can't pronounce all the words of the prayers, or if you mess something up. By showing up and trying, you fulfill the spirit of the day.

At the very end of the Yom Kippur services, when the Neilah has concluded, a member of the congregation blows one long blast on the *shofar* (ram's horn). Yom Kippur is now over. Believe it or not, many Jews then stick around for the evening service, which follows immediately. Others rush for the doors in search of their break-fast meal. Either way, it's become a tradition that after the meal, Jews go out and hammer two pieces of wood together or plant a stake in the ground to signify that they've begun to build a *sukkah* (a temporary structure) in preparation for Sukkot (see Chapter 21). Some teachers point out that this shifts attention from your own emotional and spiritual rebuilding during the High Holidays to a renewed focus on rebuilding and repairing the world around you.

Honoring the Light of Yom Kippur

On Yom Kippur, Jewish tradition says that the day itself makes the atonement. Something about the day carries the energy of healing and forgiveness and touches on the deeply human need for the release of guilt and resentment.

WORDS OF WISDOM

In the eighteenth century, an Italian kabbalistic scholar named Rabbi Moshe Chaim Luzzatto wrote that, "Any great light that radiated at a certain time, when that time comes around again, the radiance of that light will shine again . . . and be available for whoever is there to receive it."

Yom Kippur, the Day of Atonement, is such a time of radiant light — the radiant light of forgiveness. If the day itself carries such energy, then the task of the participant is to allow herself to be fully present, to allow himself to be available for the healing influences of the moment.

Chapter **21**

The Great Outdoors: Sukkot

Most people associate Judaism with the "great indoors." Jews usually pray inside synagogues or at home, and religious American Jews have the reputation of being indoor types who'd rather face a book than the sun. We hate to disappoint you, but Judaism not only embraces the great outdoors but in many ways is inextricably tied to it. Case in point: the holiday of Sukkot.

Over 3,000 years old (making it among the oldest of Jewish holidays, likely predating Rosh Hashanah and Yom Kippur), Sukkot reflects an earlier festival celebrating the gathering of the autumn crops. Like many Jewish holidays, Sukkot has several names, including *Hag ha-Asif* ("Festival of Ingathering") and *Z'man Simkhateinu* ("Time of our Joy"). Over the millennia, Sukkot gained additional historical and spiritual meaning, but it never lost its connection to agriculture and the land.

A Jewish Thanksgiving

Five days after Yom Kippur (see Chapter 20), exactly half a year away from Passover (see Chapter 25), Sukkot is a weeklong festival that begins on the full moon of the month of Tishrei. The festival actually lasts eight or nine days, though, because Jews tack on Sh'mini Atzeret and Simkhat Torah (we discuss these days later in this chapter).

The Bible notes that King Solomon dedicated the First Temple (see Chapter 12) on Sukkot. Then, during the Temple period, Sukkot was one of three pilgrimage festivals — along with Passover and Shavuot — during which Jews would travel from all over to visit Jerusalem. Sukkot was traditionally the most festive and jubilant of the holidays, a time of feasting, drinking, singing, and ecstatic dancing in the streets and in the Temple. To this day, Sukkot remains one of the most important Jewish holidays.

Giving thanks

Every culture and every major religion has a day or a time of year for giving thanks. You might say that Sukkot is the "Jewish Thanksgiving," during which Jews offer praise and thanks for the abundant harvest. Sukkot falls near the Autumnal Equinox, and the holiday symbolizes the turning point toward winter. On the day after Sukkot, called Sh'mini Atzeret (which we discuss later in this chapter), Jews say prayers for fertile rains to fall throughout the desert land of Israel.

REMEMBER

Most Jews are no longer farmers, but that doesn't mean the harvest metaphor no longer works. During Sukkot, you can think about the emotional and spiritual work completed over Rosh Hashanah and Yom Kippur, like you're harvesting the benefits of repentance and forgiveness.

While Sukkot (which people sometimes call *Ha-Khag*, or "The Festival") has plenty of ritual associated with it, the liturgy itself is quite similar to that of a regular Shabbat service. Sure, congregants say some additional prayers, and the cantor reads aloud the entire book of Ecclesiastes (*Kohelet* in Hebrew) on the Shabbat during Sukkot. However, unlike the High Holidays, no special events require extra attendance at a synagogue, and while some people do perform some of the Sukkot rituals at a synagogue (like waving the *lulav*, which we talk about in a moment), many others honor the entire holiday at home.

Getting outdoorsy: Building a sukkah

The most visible tradition on Sukkot is building a *sukkah* — which is translated as "hut," "booth," or "tabernacle" — somewhere outdoors, usually in a backyard, a park, or outside the synagogue. (The plural of *sukkah* is — surprise! — *sukkot*.) The Bible states that people should live in the *sukkah* for the entire week of Sukkot, but the definition of "live" is complicated, and almost no one actually sleeps in them.

These huts may have originally represented the temporary shelters people lived in during the harvest. However, the Bible explains that Jews build a sukkah to remember the huts that the Hebrews lived in during the 40 years in the wilderness after the exodus from Egypt (see Chapter 11). The temporary dwelling reminds people not to get too attached to physical comforts, and it also renews the attachment people have to the natural cycles of the planet. On a metaphorical level, the sukkah reflects another temporary dwelling: the body, which houses the soul.

How to Sukkot

Unlike the High Holidays of Rosh Hashanah and Yom Kippur, which aren't the most child-friendly days of the Jewish year, Sukkot is a fun-filled family event. Whether it's building the sukkah, waving the *lulav*, or picnicking in the sukkah and hoping the bees don't find you, kids of all ages enjoy taking advantage of all that Sukkot has to offer.

A sukkah born every minute

A sukkah (see Figure 21-1) is a temporary hut that people typically build in their backyard — though people in apartment buildings often build them on the roof or even on a balcony (see "Getting outdoorsy: Building a *sukkah*" for more information). The structure is traditionally assembled before Sukkot begins. Here are the rules for creating a "kosher" sukkah:

» The structure needs four sides, though one or more of them can be the wall of a house (and one side can even be completely open, like a giant door). All the walls must be strong enough to withstand reasonable wind. The sukkah needs some sort of entranceway, of course, and some even have elaborate doorways and even windows.

» The roof must be made of plant material, like branches, bamboo, cut wood, or big leaves, as long as the material is no longer attached to a plant. The roof can't be solid — that is, you have to be able to see the stars through it — but it must provide more shade than sunlight.

» Many Jews decorate the sukkah, so let your kids go nuts hanging fruit (real or dried), ornaments, colored paper cut into funky shapes, pictures they've drawn, and anything else that adds to the fun. Note that some folks have just the opposite custom, leaving the whole thing completely unadorned.

» The sukkah can't be entirely covered by something else, so no fair building it underneath a tree or in your carport. Well, to be precise, you're allowed to build it under something as long as some reasonable amount remains uncovered.

Although the classified ads in any Jewish magazine or newspaper offer commercial sukkot that you can buy and easily assemble just before the holiday, we think it's more fun to design and build our own. Some people build the basic structure with a bunch of two-by-fours, some rope, and some cement cinder blocks. Each year, Ted's congregation builds a community sukkah using 16 inexpensive, rectangular trellises from a nursery held together with plastic ties from a hardware store over a basic foundation made by two-by-fours.

FIGURE 21-1:
Building a sukkah is a fun project for the whole family.

The sukkah should be large enough that you can sit, eat, and sleep in it for the entire week of Sukkot. Jews often entertain guests in the sukkah, study Torah in it, play music, and just basically hang out there. Of course, while this might be reasonable in a very safe neighborhood or in Israel (where it's still relatively warm during Sukkot), those of us in colder climates might find ourselves in a chilly rainstorm, considering burning the sukkah for heat!

Most Jews limit their sukkah activities to saying blessings over the candles, wine, and bread (see Appendix B), as well as the blessing over the sukkah each time they enter it:

Barukh atah Adonai, Eloheynu melekh ha-olam asher kid'shanu b'mitzvotav v'tzivanu leysheyv ba-sukkah.

Blessed are you, Eternal One our God, Universal Ruling Presence, Who makes us holy through Your mitzvot [paths of holiness], and gives us this mitzvah of sitting in the sukkah.

Waving the lulav and etrog

Celebrating Sukkot involves using a couple of special props during the morning services on each day of the holiday (see Figure 21-2):

» **Lulav:** A collection of freshly cut branches — a palm frond, two willow branches, and three myrtle branches — that are secured together.

» **Etrog:** A citrus fruit, also known as *citron,* that looks sort of like a big lemon but smells and tastes different, and has a much thicker rind.

TIP

When selecting an etrog, make sure the stub (*pitom*) at the end of the fruit hasn't been broken off. If you live in a large Jewish neighborhood, it's relatively easy to buy the etrog and lulav; otherwise, you can typically buy the set through mail order or over the Internet.

Rabbis offer a number of different interpretations for why these four plants are used in particular, including the following:

» The palm frond is tall and straight like the human spine, the etrog is shaped like the heart, the willow leaves are like lips, and the myrtle leaves are like eyes. Therefore, using all four species is like involving your whole body in the ritual.

» The etrog has both a pleasant taste and aroma, symbolizing a person who is both learned and who does good deeds. The palm tree has fruit (dates) that taste good but have no aroma, symbolizing a person who is learned but does no good deeds. The myrtle has a pleasant aroma but no taste, so it is like someone who does good deeds but is not learned. Finally, the willow has neither taste nor smell, a symbol of someone who is neither learned nor does good deeds. Some say that all four types of people are important in a community.

FIGURE 21-2:
The lulav and
etrog.

These props are used in a ritual dance that involves shaking the lulav and etrog in various directions. Here's how to perform the dance:

1. **Facing east, hold the lulav in your right hand and the etrog in your left, with both of your hands close together.**

2. **Extend the lulav forward and then pull it back while shaking both the lulav and etrog.**

3. **While still facing east, point the lulav and etrog to the north (to the right) and repeat the extending, pulling back, and shaking, almost as if you're drawing in a fish on a fishing line.**

4. **Repeat the whole dance to the west (behind), the south (to the left), to the heavens (up), and finally down toward the earth.**

Some teachers note that this ritual is a reminder that God is everywhere, and it also honors the unique "energies" that each direction symbolizes:

>> East is the land of the rising sun, and it symbolizes new possibilities, beginnings, and awakenings.

- North is the direction of clarity, rationality, and the coolness of intellect.

- West is the land of the setting sun and journeys completed.

- South is the direction of warmth, emotion, verdant growth, and sensual energy.

- Up is the land of dreams and visions, the land of spirituality.

- Down is the connection to the earth, and recognition of people's environmental responsibilities.

When Sukkot is over, consider saving these plants for other purposes. For example, some Jews use the palm frond as a giant "feather" with which to hunt for chametz just before Passover (see Chapter 25). Or you can save the lulav and burn it with the chametz. Another custom is to press whole cloves into the etrog and then use it as a "spice box" during the Havdalah ceremony after Shabbat (see Chapter 18).

TIP

A FIRST-TIMERS' GUIDE TO SUKKOT

Sukkot is a sweet and lively week in the Jewish calendar, and it's a wonderful opportunity to relax and enjoy hanging out with your family and neighbors. If you see your neighbors building a strange hut just after Yom Kippur, they're probably not remodeling their house! You get extra brownie points for wandering over and saying, "Hey, what a lovely sukkah!"

If you're trimming your trees or shrubs around this time of year, you can add the branches to your own sukkah or offer them to a neighbor who is building one. Similarly, the Parks Department in many cities trims the trees (especially palm trees in cities that have them) and lets people pick up the branches for the roofs of their sukkot.

Remember that people who build sukkot love to have guests, and it's considered a good deed to drop by and sit under the leafy green roof together. (Well, maybe it's a good idea to call ahead.) Better yet, bring a guitar and sing songs, or bring some wine, fruit, nuts, or something sweet to munch on together.

Sh'mini Atzeret

The day after Sukkot, called *Sh'mini Atzeret* ("the eighth day of solemn assembly"), tends to be under-appreciated by many Jews. Sh'mini Atzeret also means "setting a boundary" or "restraining," and there's no doubt that Sh'mini Atzeret acts as a way to move through the revelry and hoopla of the previous week and focus attention on the serious prospect of the coming winter.

Sh'mini Atzeret and Simchat Torah (see the following section), even though they are officially separate holidays, are still considered the final days of the festival season and have the status of a *chag*, a festival on which no work is done.

REMEMBER

In Israel and in Reform communities, Sh'mini Atzeret and Simchat Torah are celebrated on the same day; in Conservative and Orthodox communities outside of Israel, Simchat Torah has its own day.

After a week sitting in the sukkah hoping that it won't rain, on Sh'mini Atzeret Jews recite a prayer called *geshem* ("rain"), wishing for a generous downpour to start the winter off properly and ensure that the land will be fertile, the crops will grow, and the people will eat.

In many traditional communities, the ceremonies actually begin a day earlier, on the seventh day of Sukkot, called *Hoshanah Rabbah*. (*Hoshanah* is the same word as the English "Hosanah," meaning "help, I pray." *Rabbah* means "great.") On Hoshanah Rabbah, Jews circle the *bimah* (the reading stand at the front of the synagogue) seven times as they beat the ground with willow branches. Many see this act as a talisman for making the earth fertile or for casting off old sins.

Simkhat Torah

Sukkot, Chanukkah, and Purim are all joyful, but Simkhat Torah — which traditionally falls the day after Sh'mini Atzeret (see the previous section) — is deeply and expansively joyful. Indeed, *Simkhat Torah* means "Rejoicing in the Torah." On Shavuot, Jews honor the giving of Torah, and on Simkhat Torah, Jews celebrate the Torah itself as they complete the yearly reading cycle and then immediately begin the cycle again (see Chapter 3).

Simkhat Torah, which didn't exist in biblical days, has no formal liturgy or ritual, but customs have certainly evolved for this day over the years:

>> Almost every congregation reads the last section of the Book of Deuteronomy (the end of the five books of Moses) and the first section of the Book of Genesis. (The evening service on Simkhat Torah is the only time in traditional communities when the Torah can be read at night.) Whoever is called to read the last lines of Deuteronomy is called the *Chatan Torah* ("Groom of the Torah," pronounced kha-*tan* To-*rah*), and the reader of the beginning of Genesis is called the *Chatan Bereshit* ("The Groom of Creation"). In communities where both men and women are called to the Torah, there might be a *Kallah Torah* ("Bride of the Torah") or a *Kallah Bereshit*. Traditionally, the entire congregation is called up to the bimah for *aliyot* (to say the prayers before and after Torah readings) on Simkhat Torah.

>> Some synagogues celebrate the yearly cycle of reading by unrolling the entire Torah scroll and forming it into a giant circle so that the end and the beginning of Torah are next to one another for the readings. Children stand in the center of the circle of Torah, as their parents and other adults lovingly hold the scroll, allowing everyone to experience a sense of shared holiness.

>> Everyone is so focused on the joyful singing and dancing that even in many Orthodox congregations the men, women, and children all sit and sing together.

>> People hold Torah scrolls while parading around the sanctuary seven times (called *hakafot*), allowing participants to celebrate and perhaps even dance with the Torah while everyone sings. This part of the celebration can become so frenzied that after the seven circuits, everyone may spill out into the street like a big party.

>> Ask a child what happens on Simkhat Torah and you'll get a definitive answer: "We get candy!" Judaism has a long tradition of associating sweets with sweet occasions. In Reform congregations this holiday is also a time for Consecration, during which young children are formally welcomed into the community as they began their religious education.

REMEMBER

You may remember that the last thing that happens in the Torah is that Moses dies and is buried in an unmarked grave. In some ways, Simkhat Torah honors Moses' death, but the day also clearly ties the death to the first chapter of Genesis: the Creation of the universe. In this way, Simkhat Torah reminds people that life transcends death and that the world is in a never-ending cycle of death and rebirth. Simkhat Torah plants a seed that will germinate all winter, finally blossoming in the spring.

THERE'S ALWAYS MORE TO THE TORAH

Don't Jews get bored of studying the same words, the same stories, year after year? Sure, if reading Torah were like going around a circle it would get pretty dull. However, Torah isn't a circle; it's a spiral. Jews return to the same story at the same time each year, but many rabbis teach that if you see the story in the same way, if you only find what you found last year, then you haven't grown. The Torah doesn't change, of course — people do. Judaism is a path of growth and development, and the Torah (like other spiritual texts) works by drawing a continually deeper part of yourself out in the process of reading and studying. As the first-century sage Ben Bag-Bag said, "Turn it and turn it again, for everything is in it."

Chapter **22**

Seeking Light in Dark Times: Chanukkah

A s the winter solstice approaches, the days get shorter, the nights get longer, and the people begin to wonder if the lost light will ever return. The effect of the winter solstice on people is universal: In every major world tradition festivals of light arise at this darkest time of the year. Ancient pagans celebrated the solstice with wild feasts. The ancient Persians set enormous bonfires on the ground while their rulers released birds into the air, dragging torches of burning grass. Jews have Chanukkah, perhaps the most celebrated of all Jewish holidays (at least in North America).

Shining a Light on the Darkest Night

In the Jewish calendar, Chanukkah's eight-day celebration begins the evening of the 25th of Kislev (which falls sometime during December). The months of the Jewish calendar are based on the cycles of the moon, so the 25th is always four days before the new moon, the darkest time of the month.

More importantly, because Kislev is always close to the winter solstice, Chanukkah takes you into, through, and out of the darkest night of the year. (The solstice is technically the longest night of the year, but it may fall on the full moon, which would make it far from dark.) On the darkest night of the year, wouldn't you want to light a few candles?

REMEMBER

Please don't call Chanukkah "the Jewish Christmas." Jews have nothing against Christmas, but Chanukkah is completely different. Making the comparison is like saying that Cinco de Mayo is "the Mexican Mother's Day," just because these two holidays appear during the same month.

The Good Fight: What Chanukkah Celebrates

Chanukkah celebrates two things: a miracle in which one day's worth of oil burned for eight days, and the victory of the Jewish freedom fighters over the Syrian-Greek forces that tried to wipe out Judaism in the second century BCE. In this way, Chanukkah marks the very first battle fought not for territory, nor for conquest of another people, but in order to achieve religious freedom.

The consequence of that ancient military victory was the right of the Jews to worship as a community. Because of the many times that this right has been threatened over the centuries, the Jewish victory and the rededication to Jewish worship that followed have become paradigms for Jewish renewal across time. In fact, the word Chanukkah means "dedication."

In a larger sense, then, Chanukkah celebrates a reaffirmation of freedom and a recommitment to the spiritual quest.

The two books of the Maccabees

The story of Chanukkah is told in the two books of the Maccabees, written sometime in the first century BCE, about a hundred years after the whole drama happened. Basically, by 325 BCE, Alexander the Great's Greek empire extended all the way to the current-day Middle East, and it was Alexander's policy to allow people to celebrate according to their own religious beliefs. However, after he died, the empire split into smaller pieces ruled by a succession of men who didn't share Alexander's generosity.

Antiochus was such a ruler. After giving himself the surname *Epiphanes* ("god manifest"), he decided to forcibly rid his empire of local religions, including Judaism. He outlawed — upon penalty of death — kosher food, circumcision, and

Shabbat services (see Chapter 18). You have to understand that many Jews at the time were attracted to the great art, philosophies, and culture of the Greeks. So much so that they went along with Antiochus's rule (they were typically called "Hellenists").

On the other hand, some Jews were, well, less happy with the arrangement. One objector, Mattathias (a priestly descendant of Moses' brother, Aaron), was so "less happy" that when one local assimilated Jew tried to follow the king's commandment by making a sacrifice to the Greek gods, Mattathias killed him.

Judah puts the hammer down

Fleeing to the mountains with his five sons, Mattathias gathered an army of other pious believers and began a bloody revolution that lasted three years (from 169 to 166 BCE). After Mattathias's death, his son Judah led the guerrilla warfare against Antiochus's forces and the assimilated Jews. In fact, Judah was so fierce that his family was given the name *Maccabee* (which means "hammer" in Hebrew).

Finally, after a series of terrible clashes, the Maccabees retook Jerusalem, drove out the Syrian-Greek army, and began repairing the desecrated grounds of the Second Temple (see Chapter 13). As it turns out, Antiochus had picked a propitious time to seize the Temple: the 25th of Kislev, which falls near the darkest day of the year. Perhaps in a symbolic gesture of renewal, Judah decided to rededicate the Temple on exactly the same day, in 164 BCE, and pronounced that the nation should henceforth memorialize this rededication with an eight-day celebration.

The story of the oil miracle

History is a funny thing. By the time the later sections of the Talmud were being written (around 500 CE; see Chapter 3), the political situation had changed radically, and the rabbis were less enamored of the Maccabees. First of all, as is so often the case with armed revolutionaries, the victorious Maccabean families later set themselves up as kings over the land and became as oppressive as the previous regime (see Chapter 13). Worse, as time went on, their descendants allied themselves with the Roman Empire, leading to the eventual Roman conquest.

Although the rabbis didn't want to reject the Chanukkah celebration, they decided instead to emphasize a different aspect of the holiday in their commentary. Legend had it that when the Temple was rededicated (see Chapter 13), the Maccabees could only find a single cruse (a small vessel) of pure oil, enough to burn the

Eternal Flame for one night. Unfortunately, it would take eight days to get more oil. God, the Talmud says, performed a miracle and made the oil last for eight nights.

The Talmud's subtle message: People should celebrate the miracle of the oil more than the military victory. Tradition therefore includes these words from the Prophet Zachariah as part of the synagogue readings on Chanukkah: "Not by might, nor by power, but by My Spirit, says the Eternal One . . ."

The Maccabees get their due

For almost 2,000 years, Chanukkah was known as one of the minor holidays of the Jewish calendar. Then, gradually, beginning in the late nineteenth century, Jews began to pay more attention to the story of the Maccabees. And, today, Chanukkah is arguably the most celebrated of the Jewish holidays (or at least it's in a head-to-head tie with Passover). What happened?

Several things changed in the late nineteenth century. First, Christmas gift giving became more popular, particularly in North America. Many Jews, seeing how attractive Christmas was to children, found new meaning and usefulness in celebrating Chanukkah. Plus, the miracle of the burning oil and the victorious story of the Maccabees could easily be interpreted as anti-assimilationist, and so Jews adopted it as a tool for strengthening Jewish identity at a time when that felt increasingly important.

Finally, the Zionist movement (see Chapter 15) began to look more favorably on the military tactics of the Maccabees. Once again, the debate was renewed between those Jews who believed in armed struggle and those who supported peaceful action.

Embracing Chanukkah Customs

ANECDOTE

When David was a child, his family lived in an area of England far removed from other Jewish kids, and his parents felt bad about celebrating Chanukkah when all their neighbors celebrated Christmas. Their compromise: Celebrate both. But Christmas was clearly just a gift giving time to David's family, so it was Chanukkah that he still remembers as a time for stories, singing, candle lighting, and quality family time.

The only essential ritual to perform at Chanukkah is the lighting of the candles, which are held in a *chanukkiah*, which is a candelabra with nine candles or wicks (see Figure 22-1). But families have developed many other traditions that are also meaningful. In this section, we take a look at some of these traditions; who knows, you might just find a few that your kids will someday remember.

FIGURE 22-1: The traditional chanukkiah on the second night of Chanukkah.

REMEMBER

WILL THE REAL MENORAH PLEASE STAND UP?

When most people talk about a *menorah*, they really mean a *chanukkiah* (pronounced "khan-oo-kee-*ah*," with the guttural "kh" sound; the plural is *channukkiot*). The *menorah* is simply a candelabra, and it traditionally holds seven candles (or has seven oil wicks). The seven-candle version is on the official emblem of the State of Israel. The chanukkiah is a candelabra with nine candles or wicks: one for each night of Chanukkah plus the *shammash*, which is the candle that you use to light the other candles. The difference is subtle, but next time you're ordering a "menorah" at some Internet e-commerce site, you'll know enough to look closely.

Lighting the candles

CONTROVERSY

The Talmud (see Chapter 3) says that two great first-century rabbis each teach a different method of lighting the candles. According to Hillel, you should light one candle the first night, two on the second night, and so on until all eight candles are burning on the eighth night. This is the current practice, even though another sage named Shammai encouraged people to light all eight candles the first night and remove one candle each night to reflect the diminishing of the original oil.

The lighting of the candles is traditionally accompanied or followed by a series of prayers (see the following section for more information). After the candles have been lit and blessed, many families open presents, eat special holiday foods, and play Chanukkah games (keep reading for more information on these traditions).

REMEMBER

Several rules govern the lighting of the candles:

>> **Direction:** Insert the first candle farthest to the right, adding candles to the left of the first one each night. However, when lighting the candles, start with the left-most candle (the one that represents the *current* night), and keep going to the right until all the candles are lit (eight candles plus the shammash will be burning on the last day). If you have an oil lamp, then also fill and light the oil cups in this order.

>> **Use:** Don't use the light from these candles to read by. You shouldn't even use the Chanukkah candles to light other candles; so in order to light them in the first place, you use an extra candle, called the *shammash*.

>> **Position:** Place the chanukkiah in a window to publicly proclaim the miracle of the burning oil. Of course, during times when a public announcement of one's Judaism would be dangerous, this rule is relaxed.

>> **Duration:** Allow the candles to burn for at least a half hour — so don't blow them out as soon as you've finished opening presents!

>> **Timing:** When Chanukkah takes place on Shabbat, light the Chanukkah candles before you light the Shabbat candles. Traditionally, you don't light any more candles after lighting the Shabbat candles.

TIP

Some families have a chanukkiah for each family member, others take turns lighting the candles, and in some households, everyone holds the shammash together and lights each candle together. Whatever you do, try to get everyone involved.

REMEMBER

MIRACLES YESTERDAY AND TODAY

Traditionally, the second Chanukkah prayer ends with *bazman hazeh* ("in that time"). However, a prayerbook of Conservative Judaism changes one word: Their blessing says that we bless the Eternal One who worked miracles for our ancestors in those days *u'vaz'man hazeh* ("and at this time") — signifying the continuation of the miracle of light over the ages. For those who tend to see God working in the present tense, this version can be more fitting.

Blessings for the moment

Here are the three blessings recited over the lighting of the chanukkiah:

Barukh Atah Adonai Eloheynu Melekh Ha-Olam, asher kid'shanu b'mitzvotav vitzivanu l'hadlik ner shel Chanukkah.

Blessed are You, Eternal One Our God, Universal Ruling Presence, Who sanctifies us with mitzvot [paths of holiness] and gives us this path of kindling the light of Chanukkah.

Blessed are You, Eternal One Our God, *Barukh Atah Adonai Eloheynu Melekh Ha-Olam, sheh-asah nissim l'avoteynu ba-yamim ha-haym baz'man hazeh.*

Universal Ruling Presence, Who worked miracles for our ancestors in ancient days at this time.

On the first night of Chanukkah, Jews add the following blessing:

Barukh Atah Adonai, Eloheynu Melekh ha-olam, sheh-heh-khi-yanu v'key'manu v'hee-gee-anu laz'man ha-zeh.

Blessed are You, Eternal One our God, Universal Ruling Presence, Who keeps us in Life always, Who supports the unfolding of our uniqueness, and Who brings us to this very moment for blessing.

Remembering the oil: Yummy fried foods

For most Jews, latkes conjure up images of an Eastern European Jewish delicacy: potato pancakes hot off the griddle, moist with oil, and ready to be eaten with applesauce or sour cream (see the recipe for latkes in this chapter).

In fact, Chanukkah is a favorite holiday for some Jews because of the fried food associated with it. Jews are supposed to eat food fried in oil as a reminder of the miracle of the oil burning for eight days! In Israel, the customary special fried delicacies for Chanukkah are jelly donuts called *sufganiot*.

Latkes

PREP TIME: 10 MINUTES   COOK TIME: 40 MINUTES   YIELD: 18 PATTIES

INGREDIENTS

6 to 8 russet (baking) or Yukon

Gold potatoes, grated

1 medium onion, grated

1 teaspoon salt

2 large eggs, beaten

⅓ cup of matzah meal or flour

⅛ teaspoon pepper (white pepper is best)

Vegetable oil for frying

DIRECTIONS

1 In a large bowl combine grated potatoes, onions, and salt. Let the mixture stand in a fine-sieve colander for five or ten minutes before squeezing out as much of the moisture as you can. (You can also squeeze the mixture in a clean dish towel.)

2 In a large bowl combine the eggs, matzah meal or flour, and pepper.

3 Add potato mixture to the matzah mixture and stir together.

4 In a frying pan or griddle, add oil and heat the oil over medium-high heat until it's hot but not smoking; this isn't the time to fret about using too much oil (remember that it's almost a commandment to cook with oil during Chanukkah).

5 Put a heaping teaspoon of batter on the hot pan and spread out the batter so that it's about 1/4 in thick and about 2 to 3 inches in diameter. Cook the latkes until they're golden brown underneath, about 4 to 5 minutes, then flip them over and cook the other side to golden brown.

6 When each latke is done, place it on one or two paper towels and blot off any excess oil. Keep the latkes heated in the oven until ready to serve.

PER SERVING: *Calories 278 (From Fat 143); Fat 16g (Saturated 2g); Cholesterol 62mg; Sodium 415mg; Carbohydrate X30g (Dietary Fiber 3g); Protein 5g.*

TIP: Alternate grating the potato and the onion, mixing the result together as you go (this helps stop the starch from turning that icky brown color).

VARIATION: Some people add scallions, parsley, or other herbs to their latkes before cooking them

SERVING SUGGESTION: Serve the latkes with sour cream, applesauce, jam, powdered sugar, regular sugar, cinnamon sugar, yogurt, or whatever strikes your fancy.

Spinning the dreidel

The official Chanukkah game is called spin the dreidel. A dreidel (pronounced *dray*-del) is a four-sided spinning top with the Hebrew letters *nun, gimel, hay,* and *shin* printed on each side (see Figure 22-2). The letters are the initials for the phrase *Nes Gadol Hayah Sham,* which means "A great miracle happened there."

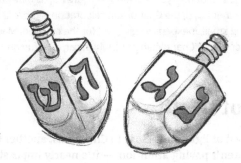

FIGURE 22-2:
Spinning dreidels
is the official
game of
Chanukkah.

Dreidels in Israel are slightly different. The *shin* is replaced with a *pay*, the first letter in the word *poh*. This changes the phrase to "A great miracle happened *here*."

Each person starts with a pile of nuts, pennies, candies, or other small treasures. Before each spin of the dreidel, everyone puts one nut, penny, or whatever into the pot (the center of the table). Next, take turns spinning the dreidel:

>> If your dreidel lands with *nun* side up, nothing happens and the next player (to the left) spins.

>> If your dreidel lands with *gimel* side up, you win all the pieces in the pot, and all the players ante-up (put a nut, penny, or candy in the pot) again before the next spin.

>> If your dreidel lands with *hay* side up, you take half the pieces in the pot. (Or half the pieces minus one, if there's an odd number of pieces.)

>> If your dreidel lands with *shin* side up, you put one more piece into the pot.

Play until the next round of latkes is ready!

The origin of the dreidel is a mystery. Some people believe that the dreidel was a subterfuge adopted by Jews when the authorities forbade studying Torah. To avoid being caught studying, the Jews would pull out their dreidels and pretend that they were gambling.

TIP

A FIRST-TIMERS' GUIDE TO CHANUKKAH

Chanukkah parties are becoming increasingly popular, and they include singing and lots of food. But don't look for a Christmas tree! (Some friends of ours decorate what they call a "Channukah bush," but it's not the same thing, and most Jews find it unfitting.) If you're invited to this kind of party, check to see if people are bringing gifts. If gifts are being exchanged, remember that the typical Chanukkah giftwrap is blue and white, not red and green. If, on the other hand, the Chanukkah celebration is more like a quiet family affair, consider bringing small, inexpensive gifts just for the children. Many stores sell chocolate in the shapes of coins ("Chanukkah *gelt*"), which can be a fun and simple gift.

To gift, or not to gift

Chanukkah, as a festival of light, falls close to Christmas, another festival of light, and — in case you weren't paying attention — it's nearly impossible to avoid the inexorable tug at your pocketbook during this time of year. Jews don't see anything wrong with giving presents to kids on Chanukkah. In fact, unless you're prepared to deal with years of psychotherapy bills for your children, it's probably best to offer them some sort of gift.

For many Jewish children, the question is not, "Do I get a gift?" but "Do I get a gift every night?" Sometimes families give smaller gifts on each night, and sometimes they exchange fewer but larger gifts. However, Chanukkah is much more than simply a time for gifts.

REMEMBER

You don't have to give gifts that cost money. Gifts of service — like helping with chores, serving breakfast in bed, and so on — sound trite, but they can be deeply satisfying for everyone involved. And some families encourage gifts that they make themselves.

Receiving the Real Gift of Chanukkah: Personal Renewal

The Chanukkah lights are to be enjoyed along with the foods and the gifts and the warmth of family and friendship. Yet, you can find deeper meaning in the candles that you light.

Before lighting each candle, you might ask yourself, "What do I wish to illuminate in my world with this light?" Your answer may reflect some personal need or something you know another person needs. You might dedicate a candle to bring greater light into the whole world, to ease the suffering, and to increase the joy.

Try taking some time to simply be with your candles after they are lit. Sit quietly and follow the instructions from the mystical teachers of Jewish tradition: Gaze gently at the flames before you. Let your body and your mind relax, and allow yourself to move into a deeper and more holy space of awareness.

Chapter 23

Celebrating Renewal: Tu B'Shvat

WORDS OF WISDOM

The world is a tree and human beings are its fruit.
RABBI SOLOMON IBN GABIROL, ELEVENTH-CENTURY SPAIN

Like a tree, Judaism began with a seed of an idea: the Oneness of God. Thousands of years ago that seed grew, flourished, and blossomed into a beautiful faith. But the times have changed since then, and — get this — Judaism has changed, too. Judaism's tree branched out, took root in new soil, adapted to new environments, and blossomed again, and again, and again. The tree itself became a central image in Jewish mysticism, and it brought new growth to the holiday called *Tu B'Shvat* (too-bih-*shvat*).

Tithing Fruits of Land and Spirit

The Bible institutes a *tithe* (one tenth of the yearly produce) to support the Sanctuary. When the Hebrews were primarily a society based on agriculture, tithing applied to the "fruit of the land." So if you picked ten apples in the middle of June, you gave one to the Temple.

Just like with any tax, people needed to know when one tithing year ended and the next began. The date was set: Tu B'Shvat (also called *Chamishah Asar Be'Shvat*), literally the 15th of the Hebrew month of Shvat. The holiday usually falls during January or February, on the trailing edge of the rainy season in Israel, when the trees begin to put forth new buds, beginning the fruit of the next year — which helps explain why this holiday is also called *Rosh Hashanah L'Ilanot* (the New Year for Trees).

In the sixteenth century, a group of Jewish mystics in the town of Safed, in the Upper Galilee, attached a much deeper and more mystical meaning to the holiday. By the seventeenth century, the mystics had created a Tu B'Shvat *seder* ("order" of ritual) using wines and fruits as symbols of four major levels of reality (see Chapter 5).

A Seder of Fruit and Wine

The seder is based on the Jewish mystical belief that a Divine spark lives within every being, often hidden beneath an outer shell. Our mission, say the more mystically oriented rabbis, is to become conscious of this holiness within everything, and then liberate these sparks through our awareness, our actions, and our words. All our interactions with the world hold precious possibilities for this liberation, including the blessing and the eating of food. To celebrate both the trees in the natural world and the mystical symbol of the Tree of Life, the mystics of sixteenth century Safed infused deeper meaning in the simple acts of eating fruit and drinking wine on Tu B'Shvat.

The Tu B'Shvat seder is becoming increasingly popular, especially in Reform, Renewal, and Conservative communities. (You can find a Tu B'Shvat *haggadah* — the book that tells the order of service — in any Jewish bookstore. Check out our website at www.joyofjewish.com for more information.) This seder requires red and white wine (or red and white grape juice) and three different kinds of fruits and nuts. The blessings over wine and fruit are divided into the following four sections:

>> **The first blessing:** Made over white wine and fruits with inedible exteriors like oranges, pomegranates, and nuts, this blessing recalls the level of reality on which you live now — where it is winter, and where Divine goodness is often hidden within husks.

>> **The second blessing:** This blessing accompanies the drinking of white wine mixed with a little red, followed with fruit that is soft on the outside with a pit inside, such as dates, olives, and apricots. The wine symbolizes spring (when color begins to return to the land), and the fruit a higher world in which the Divine is more readily accessible, but there is still something hidden within.

>> **The third blessing:** Say this blessing over wine that consists mostly of red mixed with just a little white, and fruit that is totally edible (such as figs, raisins, carob fruit, and apples). The soft fruit relates to the spiritual world where people need no protection and don't have to hide. The almost-red wine symbolizes the fullness of summer growth, when fruit begins to ripen and love is in the air.

>> **The fourth blessing:** Made with fully red wine, this blessing symbolizes the completion of creation. The Jewish mystics taught that the fourth fruit is beyond taste, so rather than eat the fruit (usually an *etrog* [citron] or lemon), you just smell it. The fourth cup celebrates a world of Spirit fully realized, and recalls the rich colors and tastes of the harvest in late summer and fall.

Try This at Home

Whether or not you perform the seder, Tu B'Shvat is a great time for the whole family to participate in activities that bring your attention to the natural world.

TIP

Here are some ideas for celebrating that you can try at home:

>> Read Dr. Seuss's book *The Lorax* out loud and talk about how people can take a stand in ecological matters.

>> Take a walk around your neighborhood or a nearby park. Pay special attention to the sights, sounds, and smells of the nature around you. You might even collect twigs and leaves and use them as a table decoration.

>> Plant parsley seeds in paper cups and turn your windowsill into an eight-week garden experiment. The parsley should be big enough by Passover that you can clip and dip it in salt water during the Pesach seder (see Chapter 25).

>> Give a living plant to someone — a teacher, friend, co-worker, spouse, or parent — who may be underappreciated.

>> Plant a tree! As Ben Ediden wrote in *Jewish Holidays and Festivals*, "A child who plants a tree with his own hands unites himself lastingly with the soil upon which it grows."

Jews traditionally eat at least one type of fruit or nut that they haven't eaten before or haven't eaten in a long time. If you live in a colder climate, there's something truly delicious about having so much fruit at this time of year. The fruit serves as a great reminder of the richness and sweetness of spring, which is soon to come.

LISTENING TO NATURE'S SONG

The story is told of the great Rav Abraham Kook, who was deep in thought as he walked outside with a student. When the student casually plucked a leaf from a branch as they passed, Rav Kook stopped, visibly shaken. Turning, he said gently, "Believe me when I tell you I never simply pluck a leaf or a blade of grass or any living thing, unless I have to." By way of explanation, he continued, "Every part of the vegetable world is singing a song and breathing forth a secret of the divine mystery of the Creation."

Enlightened Gardeners

For hundreds of years, rabbis have pointed out that Genesis specifically states that humans are supposed to tend and guard all of God's creation. Deuteronomy 20:19 goes so far as to say that even if you make war against a city, you must protect the trees that provide food (like fruit trees). From statements like these arose the *mitzvah* (commandment") of *bal tashkhit*, which instructs people not to destroy any living thing unnecessarily (see Chapter 6).

When Zionist settlers in the late nineteenth century in Palestine discovered a deforested desert, planting trees was a crucial step in restoring the country, and Jewish communities around the world began to focus on a single goal: raising money for reforestation. Tu B'Shvat became Jewish Arbor Day, and an organization called the Jewish National Fund collected money to plant hundreds of millions of trees in Israel.

Since then, Tu B'Shvat has become a time to focus not just on Israel but on the whole of the planet's ecosphere. The holiday of the trees calls people to honor humankind's connection to this planet and to work toward the healing of the environment.

An Ever-Living Tree

Tu B'Shvat provides a remarkable opportunity to honor your relation to the natural world. Even though the celebration takes place well before the trees outwardly express their next flowering, you can rejoice in the fullness that they will bring forth.

REMEMBER

Just as you can imagine the sap beginning to rise within the trees, you can appreciate that renewing energy rising within yourself and within all life. From the withdrawal of winter comes the miracle of new life about to spring forth.

Chapter **24**

A Jewish Carnival: Purim

Imagine a holiday that encourages people to reconnect not only to their good side but to their dark side as well. Imagine a holiday on which people dress up, make fun of their leaders, and generally have a great time. And imagine a holiday that challenges people to discover deeper truths about being human. This is the holiday called Purim — the most fun, children-oriented holiday in the Jewish calendar, but ironically, the holiday that memorializes one of the darkest, most sexual, and most violent stories in the Bible.

Purim: Based on a True Story (Sort Of)

Purim celebrates the story told in the biblical Book of Esther, in which the evil Haman plots to exterminate the Jewish people of ancient Persia (now Iran), but is foiled by Queen Esther and her cousin Mordecai, who are Jewish. The story is compelling — of all the Jewish holidays, none would be as good to base a Hollywood movie on as Purim. (We can see it now: *Purim: The Final Conflict*, starring Johnny Deppstein and Keira Knightberg.)

Even though the traditional view is that everything in the Bible is literally true, most Jews tend to agree that the story in the Book of Esther is flat-out fiction. Actually, think of it more like a historical fiction that you may see on the A&E channel, where some of the names are similar, but that's where the facts stop and imagination takes over.

It all starts with a banished queen

Once upon a time, the story goes, a Persian King named Akhashveyrosh (often written Ahasuerus, or translated Xerxes) loved to party. Once, he topped off a 180-day party with a 7-day banquet. Finally, when he was really drunk, the King decided that he wanted to show off his Queen, Vashti, to all his cronies. Some later interpretations suggest that he asked her to dance naked, but whatever the case, she refused. The King, following advice that he must punish the Queen, lest all wives in the kingdom be encouraged to refuse the demands of their husbands, banished her.

Of course, this left him queen-less, so the court held a contest. Jewish parents usually teach their children that this was a beauty contest, but the story is pretty clear: Virgins were brought to the harem, pampered for months in preparation for the King, and then offered to him for an evening to see which woman he would choose as queen. Afterward, each unchosen woman would be "unfit" to marry, so she would just stay in the harem.

Enter Esther, stage left

Meanwhile, a Jew named Mordecai had adopted his cousin Esther after her parents died. Esther was taken to the palace to prepare for a rendezvous with the King, and Mordecai forbid her to reveal that she was Jewish. (Why? No one knows, but it certainly makes for a better story.) Of course, when it was Esther's turn before the King, he was so smitten with her that he crowned her the new Queen.

Mordecai stayed as close to the palace as he could, often communicating with Esther (curiously, no one figured out that they were related). He discovered that two eunuchs planned to assassinate the King. He passed this information on to Esther, who told Akhashveyrosh; the plot was foiled, and the eunuchs were hung. This little event was written in the official court chronicles, and then everyone just forgot about it.

Enter Haman, stage right

Now, every good melodrama has to have a really evil character, and this story's villain is Haman, the new prime minister. He was so full of himself that he became furious when he found out that Mordecai wouldn't bow down to him. (Jews aren't supposed to bow down to anyone except God.) Not content to find a fitting punishment for Mordecai alone, Haman decided to wipe out every Jew in the kingdom. Sort of his own "final solution."

Why Akhashveyrosh went along with Haman's wicked plan is unclear, but the king dispatched a royal decree saying that on the 13th of Adar (which usually falls in March) anyone could kill Jews and take their property. The story says that this fateful date was decided by casting lots (like picking numbers in a lottery). Thus, the name of the holiday: *purim* means "lots."

Mordecai and Esther were understandably upset, and Mordecai urged her to approach the King. Esther was reluctant — the King still didn't know she was Jewish, and what's more, the rule of the land said that anyone who appeared before the King without an invitation could be put to death immediately (even the Queen). Fortunately, Mordecai pressed her with the most interesting lines in the story: "If you persist in remaining silent at such a time, relief and deliverance will come to the Jews from another place, but both you and the house of your father will perish. Who knows? Perhaps you have come to the throne for just a time as this."

Haman's big mistake

Esther and the Jews of the city fasted for three days and nights in preparation for her approaching the King. Fortunately, her fears were allayed, for when the King saw her, he stretched out his golden scepter, and she placed her hand on it. (Oy, what would Freud say?) The King invited her to make a request of him, and Esther invited him and Haman to a special private banquet, an invitation that they both gladly accepted. At that dinner, her only request was that they both come to a second banquet, the following night.

By this time, Haman's ego was as full as it could be, but when he encountered Mordecai the following day outside the palace, he again became enraged that Mordecai didn't bow to him, and ordered gallows to be erected immediately so that the Jew could be hung in the morning.

Unfortunately for Haman, the winds of fate turned that night. The King, unable to sleep, had the court chronicles read to him (insomniacs, take note). However, instead of lulling him, he became curious about one story, that of some guy named Mordecai who helped foil an assassination plot. When he learned that nothing was ever done to honor Mordecai, he called Haman and asked him what should be done for a man who the King wishes to honor.

Haman assumed the King was referring obliquely to him, so Haman suggested that the man be carried on one of the King's horses through the town in fine royal attire, with an attendant yelling, "Here's how the King treats those he wishes to honor."

CONTROVERSY

WHERE IS GOD?

Probably the strangest aspect of the Book of Esther is that God is never mentioned, even when the Jews are in dire straits. The only other book in the Bible that doesn't mention God is the Song of Songs, but many people assume that God is present there as one of the main characters in the love poems. In the Book of Esther, God appears to be entirely absent. Some rabbis teach that the underlying message is that even when life is at its worst and you think you're really alone, God is actually at work behind the scenes. You may not be able to see or even feel this mysterious force, but it's there, nonetheless.

Big mistake, for the King then told Haman to give this honor to Mordecai. What's worse, Haman himself had to attend to Mordecai and lead his horse through the city.

Of course, just when it seemed things couldn't get worse, Haman and the King showed up at the second banquet. Esther revealed that she was Jewish, and that because of Haman, she and her people were about to be killed. The King, in a rage at Haman, took a break to relieve himself. However, when he returned, he found Haman fallen onto Esther's couch. The King didn't realize that Haman was pleading for his life; the King thought Haman was trying to seduce his Queen. The King immediately called for Haman to be hanged on the gallows built for Mordecai.

The final battle

If this were a Disney movie, the King would simply reverse his decree permitting the killing of Jews, and everyone would live happily ever after. But the King insisted that he couldn't reverse his royal edict, so there was only one way forward: Mordecai (who had now become the prime minister) sent out a royal decree that the Jewish people could fight back in self-defense on the 13th of Adar.

The day came, the battle ensued, and when the dust settled, the Jews had won, ultimately killing more than 75,000 of their opponents. And, just to make the point, Haman's ten sons were killed . . . twice — once in the battle and again by public hanging. And the people rejoiced.

Why Purim Survived

If history hadn't taken a rather unpleasant course for the Jewish people, it's unlikely that Purim would be celebrated today any more than the Fast of Gedaliah. (If you've never even heard of that holiday, you see what we mean.) Unfortunately, the story of persecution and Jewish renewal has played out many times since Haman tried to wipe out the Persian Jews.

The persistence of persecution

REMEMBER

Jews themselves often forget that the United States of America was the first country ever to offer full and equal status to Jews. Historically, Jews have been set aside as an "other people," and they rarely had protection under the law. Thus, "Hamans" have been able to rise to power and target the Jewish people time and time again.

Haman has become a symbol of any serious enemy of the Jewish people, whether Hitler or any modern-day terrorist. Celebrating Purim offers an opportunity to remember the persecution Haman symbolizes.

Within you and without you

One of the reasons why the Bible is such an extraordinary piece of literature is that it's filled with stories that didn't just happen a long, long time ago, but are also happening right now, every moment, within people. This may seem like pop psychobabble, but bear with us for a moment and try looking at each character in this story as an archetype, a mirror for an aspect of your own personality.

Everyone has a monstrous bully hidden beneath the surface, as well as a wily and seductive creature, and also a part that just dumbly bumbles along, enjoying the party. Purim is an opportunity to look at each of these roles within ourselves and within others in our communities. The holiday is an especially good time to look at the darker forces, the shady, lustful, perhaps ugly side of your personality — much like the wild masks and floats in the Mardi Gras parade reflect savage and almost nightmarish personalities.

These are the roles that everyone keeps hidden through the year, but if a hundred years of psychology and four thousand years of drama have taught anything, it's that you can't deny this stuff without having it come back and bite you. So Jews let out the monsters on Purim, not to let them run rampant, but to acknowledge them and honor them as part of every person.

Bang a Gong: Celebrating Purim

Take the Christian Christmas pageant, add a down-home Halloween and a couple bottles of wine, and you start to get a good idea of the Purim festival.

TIP

A FIRST-TIMERS' GUIDE TO PURIM

Purim parties are often the most festive events of the year, giving meaning to the phrase "party hardy!" The most important question to ask the hosts before arriving is whether you should wear a costume. People love to dress up on Purim (though sometimes the grownups are too stuffy, and they leave the costumes for the kids). The most popular costumes reflect the characters in the book of Esther: the Queen, the King, and Haman (some folks love playing the villain), but people often dress with all sorts of fanciful and mythical masks and capes.

While you never know exactly what to expect at a Purim celebration, the more traditional the setting, the more likely that many people will imbibe until they don't know the difference between "Blessed is Mordechai" and "Cursed is Haman." Some Jews see this as the one time each year that they can really let down their forelocks and drink freely. We suggest eating something before you get to the party, as often there are only desserts available.

If you go to the reading of the megillah (the book of Esther in this case) at a synagogue or community center, you might want to bring along some sort of noise-maker — perhaps a *grogger* (which clicks loudly as you spin it) or even some pots and pans to bang together. Just watch for the cues around you; you'll pick up the loud game quickly.

Purim is celebrated on the day after the great battle in the Book of Esther, on the 14th of Adar, which is usually in mid-March. However, in Jerusalem, the holiday is celebrated on the 15th of Adar as well because Jerusalem is a walled city, and as the story goes, the Jews had to defend themselves for two days in the capital city of Shushan, which also was walled.

Jews traditionally follow four *mitzvot* (traditional requirements) at Purim:

>> Reading the Book of Esther out loud

>> Being festive and rejoicing

>> Giving gifts of fruits and nuts

>> Offering gifts to the poor

In this section, we explore these basic mitzvot as well as a number of other Purim traditions that have blossomed more recently.

Reading the Book of Esther — the whole megillah

Traditionally, the book of Esther is read out loud at synagogue twice on Purim: once at night and once during the day. This story is one of five books of the Bible that are each written on a single scroll (a scroll wrapped around a single wood post rather than the much longer Torah, which is on two posts). This kind of scroll is called a *megillah*, and if there's one thing you can count on, it's that each year someone will ask, "Do we have to read the entire story?" The answer, of course, is "Yup, the whole megillah."

Even though the whole story is read, you may not actually hear much of it. That's because every time Haman's name is mentioned, congregants boo, hiss, stamp their feet, or twirl noise-makers (the groggers). The idea is to stamp out Haman so completely that you can't even hear his name. Some people write Haman's name on the soles of their shoes or on wood or stone blocks and then stomp and grind on them to help obliterate him further.

Partying and playing dress up

That Purim arrives at the break of spring (at least in the northern hemisphere) is no accident. The air is perfumed with a certain magic that makes you giddy and just a little bit crazy. This time of year just shouts out for a party. In fact, some scholars believe that Purim is based on ancient pagan full-moon spring festivities and myths — the names Esther and Mordecai are eerily similar to the ancient Babylonian Ishtar (goddess of love and fertility) and Marduk (one of several "creator gods").

WALKING THE FINE LINE OF RESPONSIBILITY

The heavy drinking that often goes on during Purim presents a great opportunity to teach older children about the need for limits when drinking. People are far more aware today of the dangers of drinking alcohol. A lot of people are in recovery and can no longer drink at all. Even the ancient sages said that you shouldn't get so drunk that you forget to perform other mitzvot, such as prayers and so on. It's a fine line, but one that enforces the need to be responsible and self-aware. Because the deeper issue involves getting "high" with respect to expanding your awareness, feel free to celebrate this holiday with Spirit but without spirits.

Like the Greek and Roman festivals celebrating Dionysus — god of fertility, wine, and drama — Purim is a sort of Jewish *bacchanalia*, a day when many rigid cultural norms are stripped and people can let off steam in a wild and sometimes frenzied way. Purim has been called the Jewish Halloween, when children — and often adults — dress in costume and enjoy sweet treats.

Walk through any predominantly Jewish area of a large city during Purim and you can see dozens — if not hundreds — of children (and often adults) dressed in colorful costumes and masks. Since the Middle Ages, Purim has been the theatrical season for the Jewish community, when they perform plays (*purimspiels*) based loosely on the Book of Esther. Another custom encourages the community to poke fun at their rabbi, offering satirical parodies of teaching and of sermons.

What's more, Jews traditionally drink wine and brandy heavily on the night of Purim, following the rabbinic commandment of *Ad sheloh yadah*: Drink until you don't know the difference between *Arur Haman* ("Cursed is Haman") and *Barukh Mordecai* ("Blessed is Mordecai").

Giving the gift of sweets

Shalakh Manot (pronounced "shah-lakh mah-*note*") is the practice of sending gifts — traditionally food that can be eaten without further cooking or preparation — to friends, family, and neighbors. Sort of a Jewish meals on wheels, these packages are often chock full o' nuts and fruit. Try to send at least one of these to someone during Purim.

Perhaps the clearest (and sweetest) symbol of Purim is the *hamantaschen*, the three-cornered "Haman's pocket" cookie that is the most popular holiday food eaten during Purim (see the hamantaschen recipe in this chapter). The original name for this confection was *mundtaschen* ("poppy seed pocket"). In Israel, they call it *oznei Haman* ("Haman's ears"). The Jews make their enemy into a cookie and celebrate the sweetness rather than the bitterness of memory.

Hamantaschen

INGREDIENTS

4 ounces poppy seeds (about ½ cup plus 2 tablespoons), ground

½ cup water

½ cup sugar

Juice of half a lemon

¼ to ½ teaspoon lemon rind

½ cup bread crumbs

3 cups flour

1½ teaspoon baking powder

¼ teaspoon salt

⅓ cup oil

¼ cup water

½ cup sugar

2 eggs, beaten

1 teaspoon vanilla

DIRECTIONS

1 In a medium sauce pan add water and bring to a boil. When water is boiling, add sugar and allow it to dissolve. Add the poppy seeds to the sugar water and stir frequently until almost all the liquid is absorbed (about 10 minutes). Mix in the lemon juice, rind, and crumbs. Remove mixture from heat, allow to cool, and chill the mixture, covered in refrigerator, for at least one hour or up to three days, before using as cookie filling.

2 For the dough: In a medium bowl sift together the flour, baking powder, and salt. In a large bowl, mix the oil, water, and sugar, and then fold in the eggs and vanilla. Add the flour mixture to the egg mixture, mix well, and chill the mixture for at least one hour or up to three days.

3 Roll out the chilled dough, using extra flour to prevent sticking, to about a 1/8-inch thickness. Use a 3-inch wide cup (or an empty, cleaned can) to cut out rounds. In the middle of each round, place about 1 tablespoon of filling, and then fold up three sides, pinching the edges together to make the characteristic triangular shape (you should still be able to see a little of the filling at the top). Bake at 350 degrees for about 20 to 25 minutes, or until golden brown.

PER SERVING: *Calories 75 (From Fat 26); Fat 3g (Saturated 0g); Cholesterol 8mg; Sodium 30mg; Carbohydrate 11g (Dietary Fiber 1g); Protein 2g.*

VARIATION: Instead of the traditional poppy seed filling, you can use other fillings, including prunes, cherries, apricots, raisins, and dates.

Remembering the poor

Matanot l'evyonim (prounounced "mah-tah-*note* l'ev-yo-*neem*") is giving to the poor. Although some people find it a suitable time to give to a charity, traditionally people specifically give money to individuals or families. The week during which Purim falls is a time when you don't look away from people asking for money, even if you think they aren't worthy. You may even leave the house with extra dollars in your pocket and make sure you give them away before you get home.

Only have a few bucks in your bank account? Jews consider matanot l'evyonim so important that even poor people must give to those less fortunate than themselves.

Other traditions: The Fast of Esther

The day before Purim is a minor fast day called the Fast of Esther. ("Minor" meaning that you only fast from sunrise to nightfall, and if this day falls on Shabbat, then you move the fast to a day earlier.) Note that the Fast of Esther isn't even mentioned in the Bible or the Talmud; it's just another example of a holiday that sort of developed over time.

Bringing Darkness to Light

REMEMBER

Purim celebrates far more than a particular victory over those who sought the Jews' destruction. And even though Purim reminds us of other terrible times when evil energies attacked the Jewish people, the deeper teaching transcends such battles and finds resolution beyond one side winning and the other losing.

Chapter 25

From Groan to Glee: Passover

W e've always found it ironic that Passover is both the most-celebrated Jewish holiday of the year and the holiday voted most likely to elicit a groan. People groan when they consider the dietary requirements. They groan when they think of all the preparations. They even groan when they remember how much they overate during Passover last year.

But the real irony behind the moaning, groaning, and kvetching is that in some ways this is exactly how you're supposed to feel at this time of year. Don't get us wrong: Passover isn't the holiday of complaining, even if that's the way some Jews tend to celebrate it. Passover is a celebration of spring, of birth and rebirth, of a journey from slavery to freedom, and of taking responsibility for yourself, the community, and the world. However, strangely enough, none of this taking of responsibility gets done without groaning. It was with groaning that the Hebrews expressed the pain of their ancient enslavement in Egypt more than 3,300 years ago. It was with groaning that they called attention to their plight. So groan, already!

Looking at the Reasons behind Passover

On the surface, people celebrate Passover because the Hebrews were redeemed from slavery in Egypt (see Chapter 11). But just as the surface of the ocean belies the deep mysteries beneath the waves, the basic story only hints at the depth of the Passover season.

The Torah states that Jews are to observe Passover for seven days, beginning on the 15th of the Jewish month Nisan (usually in April). You can think of Passover as honoring the renewal of the sun (the first night is always on the first full moon after the Spring Equinox), or a time to step firmly into springtime. You can also think of Passover as celebrating the Jewish people's "birth certificate" and "Declaration of Independence." Or you can think of it as memorializing something that God did for the Jews 3,300 years ago.

However, to make any celebration or ritual truly meaningful, you must find a way to make it personal. Even Moses — and later the rabbis of the Talmud — recognized this when they instructed the Jewish people how to celebrate Passover. The key isn't only to tell the story of the Exodus, or even to compare your life to the story of the Exodus, but to actually personalize the history: feel the feelings and experience the sensations of this journey. In this way, the Jewish people as individuals and as a people move forward. Everything a person does during Passover aids this process.

WHAT'S IN A NAME?

Jewish people love having several names for the same thing. What we call Passover in this book actually has four other Hebrew names, each pointing to a particular aspect of the holiday. The most common Hebrew name is *Pesach*, which is usually translated as "passing over" or "skipping over," as the Angel of Death passed over the homes of the Jews in Egypt. (Killing the Egyptian first-born was the tenth plague, and it convinced the Pharaoh to release the Hebrews from slavery.) *Pesach* is also the source of the word *Paschal*, which refers to the image of the lamb in either Passover or the Christian Easter holiday.

If you really want to sound erudite at your next seder, remember three more Hebrew names for Passover: *Khag Ha-matzot* ("Festival of Unleavened Breads"), *Z'man Kheiruteinu* ("The Time of Liberation"), and *Khag Ha-aviv* ("Festival of Spring").

Edible Do's and Don'ts

Jews do a lot of thinking about food. And perhaps more than at any other time, Jews think about food during Passover. The first night of Passover always includes a special *seder* (ritual dinner; see "The Seder: As Easy As 1, 2, 3 . . ." later in this chapter). Outside of Israel, Jews celebrate a second seder on the second night of Passover. Besides the fact that the Passover seder ritually focuses on food, two commandments during Passover have to do with eating:

>> You must eat *matzah* (unleavened bread) as part of the Passover seder.

>> You should eat no leavened foods during the entire week of Passover.

What exactly is unleavened bread? The Talmud (see Chapter 3) says not to eat any wheat, barley, rye, spelt, or oats if they have leavening—and tradition states that these grains leaven if they're not cooked within 18 minutes of being exposed to water. These five grains (if leavened) are called *khametz*. Traditional Jews, in order to avoid leaven, use other sets of dishes during Passover, and they ritually cleanse their kitchens.

As if this Torah injunction wasn't strict enough, Ashkenazi rabbis ruled that *kitniot* — rice, millet, corn, and legumes such as lentils and beans — were also not to be eaten because of the principle of *ma'arat ayin* (avoiding even the appearance of violating a commandment). The thinking is that ground rice or corn may be mistaken for flour, or that if you mix kitniot with water and cook it, it may rise like leavened bread.

Note that avoiding kitniot is a custom, not a commandment. Sephardic Jews, for example, eat corn, rice, and legumes during Passover without even a tiny pang of guilt. While we're both of Ashkenazic descent (see Chapter 1), we follow the Sephardic tradition in this respect. (Vegetarians especially may find it useful to know about this Sephardic tradition.)

Kosher for Passover

Keeping *kosher* (eating in compliance with Jewish dietary law; see Chapter 4) takes on a whole new level of awareness during Passover, especially if you follow the Ashkenazi tradition. For example, you may notice a "Kosher for Passover" version of Pepsi. What's the difference? Real sugar is expensive, so almost all sodas are made with corn syrup — in other words, kitniot! Kosher for Passover Pepsi uses real sugar, just like soda was made in the good ol' days.

If you look hard enough, each spring you can find many kinds of "Kosher for Passover" products, such as:

>> Coffee (which may ordinarily contain grain additives or have come in contact with khametz-derived ethyl acetate as part of a decaffeination process)

>> Orange juice (which otherwise may have been filtered with bran)

>> Butter (which may contain cultures or color agents derived from khametz)

>> Toothpaste (which commonly contains cornstarch)

Similarly, most alcoholic beverages (except wine and brandy) are made with grains that are khametz. Vinegar (except for pure apple cider vinegar) is often made from khametz. Orthodox Jews simply won't eat any packaged foods during this week unless they are labeled Kosher for Passover.

REMEMBER

Grain flour that you buy at the store is considered khametz, even though it hasn't been mixed with water, because it's typically produced from grains that were washed or soaked before grinding. Kosher for Passover matzah (called *shmurah matzah*, as opposed to regular matzah) is made from flour that is specially supervised from the time the wheat is cut until it is mixed with pure water and flash cooked in under 18 minutes. Even the little holes in matzah are there for a purpose: to make sure air bubbles don't accidentally cause the matzah to rise.

TIP

After matzah has been baked properly, you can grind it up into matzah meal or farfel and use it to cook other dishes, leading to one of our favorite seasonal dishes: matzah ball soup (see Chapter 18 for a recipe).

The symbolism of Passover restrictions

In the Bible, God doesn't just say "Hey, try some matzah this week." No, God makes a really big deal about not eating leavened bread. Why? What's so dang important about avoiding leavened bread?

The Bible says "So you shall tell your children on that day, saying: We eat unleavened bread because of what the Eternal One did for me when I came out from Egypt." In our opinion, this is a perfectly reasonable explanation to tell children. But if you're like us, this answer may not satisfy your own questions regarding this relatively weird practice.

As far as food goes, both matzah and khametz ain't nothin' special. However, as symbols, they both take on great meaning. And, as you can see elsewhere in this chapter, Passover is all about using symbols as catalysts for change.

Khametz is a symbol of the ego. Unlike some forms of Buddhism, Judaism takes no issue with you having an ego — it even encourages a strong sense of individual identity. However, the tradition clearly states that the ego, if allowed to grow and swell for too long, makes you arrogant, sinful, and just plain icky to be around. So Judaism has developed a remedy: matzah (bread that has not leavened or swelled).

Once a year, Jews take a week to deflate themselves, to rid the body and soul of ego puffery, and to remember that none of us is better than the lowest slave. Also, eating only unleavened bread really gets you in touch with what's important. Remember, Judaism can be a practice like meditation or working out at the gym. If every time you drive by a sandwich or burger shop during Passover you think to yourself, "I have a choice between giving in to my desire or eating more simply this week," you soon find yourself becoming more aware of who you are, who you aren't, and who you truly want to be. In fact, the *Zohar* (one of the key books of Jewish mysticism; see Chapter 5) actually calls matzah a medicine when eaten during Passover.

If you do find yourself chomping on the sandwich or with the spoonful of cereal in your mouth, don't kick yourself too hard — it's called a "practice" because almost no one gets it right the first time around!

First Things First: Preparing for Passover

Passover requires more preparation than any other Jewish celebration — not just because of the ritual foods, but because Jews need to clean their houses carefully.

REMEMBER

Unfortunately, too often the extensive preparation falls on the shoulders of "the mama," who ends up planning, cleaning, and cooking until she more than anyone knows in her bones the experience of slavery. This is *not* how it's supposed to be done. Passover is best when you involve everyone in the family.

Cleaning out the khametz

Judaism has made many contributions to Western society: monotheism, written law, a system of social morality . . . and spring cleaning. We don't know if giving your house a thorough cleaning is really a Jewish thing or not, but that's exactly what traditionally happens during the two weeks before Passover begins.

Not only are Jews not supposed to eat any khametz during Passover, they're not even supposed to come in contact with any, own any, or benefit from the sale of any khametz during the holiday. So beginning on the first of Nisan (the *Rosh Chodesh* or new moon of that month), traditional Jews begin to collect and clean away anything in their house that may be considered khametz.

DEALING WITH YOUR KHAMETZ

Most Jews don't actually remove all the khametz from their house for Passover even if they avoid eating or handling it. (Where do you plan on putting that box of Cream of Wheat, anyway?) You shouldn't waste the food by throwing it away if you can avoid doing so. Rather, you might place it in a closet, close the door, and not open it until after Passover. Or, if you do want to rid yourself of it entirely, you might consider giving unopened boxes of food to a soup kitchen or a charitable organization. This would perform two mitzvot, or Jewish religious obligations: clearing the khametz and giving tzedakah (charity).

Judaism strives to be practical, and given that it's really impractical to remove every speck of flour and khametz from your house, a Jewish tradition allows you to ritually sell any remaining khametz in your house to someone who isn't Jewish (because traditionally, you don't have to destroy khametz that you don't own). Different congregations have their own khametz-selling rituals, but typically, you sign a form transferring ownership of your khametz to the rabbi, who then "sells" the entire congregation's khametz. At the end of Passover, the khametz is similarly transferred back to the original owners.

The Ashkenazi tradition of avoiding kitniot says you shouldn't eat those foods (corn, rice, legumes, and so on), but unlike khametz, Jews can still benefit from and possess kitniot during Passover.

You find khametz in products other than food, too, so some traditional Jews often take the injunction further and remove all cosmetics, inks, glues, and medicines that may contain khametz or chemicals derived from khametz.

In Jewish households around the world during the week before Passover, family members scrub floors and sinks, purify pots and flatware by putting them in boiling water, and attempt to vacuum up every last speck of dust, just in case it's khametz. Traditional Jews put away their regular dishes and replace them with special dishes that they only used at Passover time.

ANECDOTE

David has an Orthodox friend who, when remodeling his kitchen, ordered two countertops — one that he installed as usual, and an extra one that he tapes down with duct tape each Passover so that no food touches the unclean khametz–bearing surface.

CAUTION

If you choose to embark on a massive house cleaning, please be careful! Professor Yona Amitai, a senior toxicologist at Hadassah University Hospital in Jerusalem, notes that studies show that "accidental poisonings of children from cleaning fluid triples during the two or three weeks before Passover [in Jewish households], and poisonings from all other causes doubles, compared to the rest of the year."

Many Jews stage an elaborate, last-minute hunt for khametz the night before Passover begins. Best when shared as a family event, the hunt generally takes place with a candle (or flashlight), a feather (or a small palm branch), and a paper bag. Use the feather to sweep every speck of potential khametz you find into a paper bag. (Many parents strategically place little piles of cereal around the house so that their children can find them and brush them up.) The next morning, the whole family ritually burns the paper bag and all the offending particles.

Like many symbols of Passover, this entire process is meant to start people (especially the children) asking questions, such as "Why are we cleaning?" "Why are we using a candle and feather?"

Giving to charity at Passover time

You may have noticed that every Jewish holiday is a time for tzedakah, for giving to charity, which is a key aspect of Judaism. In the weeks before Passover, Jews customarily give *ma'ot khittim* (wheat money) to the less fortunate members of the community so they can afford to buy matzah, which is usually much more expensive than khametz. At Ted's congregational seder, people bring the foods that they're not eating during Passover week, to provide needed sustenance for those non-Jews who are in need.

The Seder: As Easy as 1, 2, 3 . . .

The Passover seder is the heart of the holiday. *Seder* is Hebrew for "order" and refers to the 15-step ritual known as the Passover dinner.

Although some Jews have just a single seder dinner each year (on the first night of Passover), many others have two *sedarim* (the plural of *seder*) — often the first night with family and the second night with their congregation or some other group. We have also heard of Jews celebrating the first night indoors and the second night outdoors, perhaps after a hike with friends.

Clearly, many Jews now celebrate the Passover seder as simply a big dinner party with a few fun (or annoying) prayers and songs added on. But you can make the seder much more spiritually fulfilling than that, depending on how much awareness you bring to the table. The entire seder is designed to use food to symbolize ideas.

The haggadah: Seder's little instruction booklet

The seder is based on the *haggadah*, a book of instructions, prayers, blessings, and stories that lays out the proper order for the ritual. *Haggadah* means "the telling," referring to one of the most important aspects of the seder: the recitation of the Exodus story. The basic text of the traditional haggadah (the one used by most Orthodox families) is almost identical to that used in the eleventh century (though some songs and commentary have been added). However, in the 1960s and 1970s, many different versions began to appear, and now there are literally hundreds of *haggadot* (the plural of *haggadah*) available, each laying out the same basic ritual, but each with a slightly different spin.

Some haggadot provide special material geared toward children, women's issues, the holocaust, vegetarian's needs, and those in recovery programs. Picking a haggadah that speaks to you and the people at your seder is one key to a successful seder.

TIP

Ideally, each person at the seder should have their own copy of a haggadah to use. Some folks even like each person to have a different haggadah, so that as the seder progresses everyone brings something different to the discussion as they share what's in their particular haggadah.

Look who's coming to dinner

Perhaps even more important than choosing which haggadah to use is deciding who to invite to the seder. Everyone who attends a seder must be willing to participate in the prayers, songs, and readings. If you're performing a family seder, you obviously can't pick and choose the guests, but you can help prepare each family member for what you expect them to do. If you're inviting friends over, make sure they're friends who like participating (and it wouldn't hurt to show them this chapter, too). Some of the saddest seders are those where a few people end up "performing" for the rest of the crowd.

TIP

Many Jewish households invite non-Jews to the Passover seder, and we find that frequently the non-Jews at our seders enjoy them the most. While the Jews are busy regressing into traumatic memories of their boring childhood seders, the non-Jews arrive with a clean slate and can really experience the ritual. Sometimes we can be stimulated to greater appreciation of our own rituals when those with us are experiencing them for the very first time. Members of other ethnic or religious groups, like African Americans and Tibetan Buddhists, can identify with the issues of slavery and often find the seder rituals meaningful to their own experience.

A FIRST-TIMERS' GUIDE TO THE PASSOVER SEDER

TIP

Remember these two keys to enjoying a Passover seder: First, educate yourself as much as possible (this chapter gives you most of what you need). Second, eat a snack an hour or two beforehand. We're not kidding! At some seders the meal is served so late that you may pass out instead of passing over.

If you've been invited to a seder, ask your hosts which haggadah they're using. If you can borrow a copy from them in advance, or even buy your own, read through it before the event. Many families share the reading of the haggadah, and they may invite you to read a small section.

Offer to bring a dish or some wine to the seder, but make sure you know how kosher the celebration will be. While you obviously shouldn't bring bread to a seder (see "Edible Do's and Don'ts" earlier in this chapter), the family may or may not care if the dish is absolutely "Kosher for Passover." And although you can't bring regular flour to the seder, you can always bring flowers!

Ultimately, every guest at a seder is a participant, even if you're not asked to do anything. No one cares how well you sing, just as long as you sing. Enthusiasm is the important thing. Also: Remember that asking questions is encouraged; you may even want to think up one or two questions before you arrive.

The prepared table

Before we get to the steps of the seder itself, we want to explain the various ritual foods and other items that you see on almost every seder table. Nothing on the table is selected randomly; each item has its purpose and, often, its specific place on the table or seder plate.

REMEMBER

As with all symbols, each item has a traditional meaning, but that shouldn't stop you from coming up with new ideas that are meaningful for you and the people at your seder.

At a Passover seder, you'll find the following traditional items on the table:

>> **Seder plate:** The seder plate (usually one per table) holds at least six of the ritual items that are talked about during the seder: the shankbone, karpas, chazeret, charoset, maror, and egg (see Figure 25-1). While the booming seder plate industry would like you to buy a beautiful plate made of ceramic, glass,

or silver (and honestly, some really amazing plates are available), you can also use any plate. If you have kids, get them involved by decorating a paper plate with pictures of the events or things that the seder foods symbolize.

>> **Roasted egg:** The roasted egg (*baytsah*) is a symbol in many different cultures, usually signifying springtime and renewal. Here it stands in place of one of the sacrificial offerings that was performed in the days of the Second Temple (see Chapter 13). Another popular interpretation is that the egg is like the Jewish people: the hotter you make it for them, the tougher they get. Don't worry: you don't eat the egg during the meal; the shell just needs to look really roasted.

TIP

If you're going to put an egg in the broiler, hardboil it first. Some people swear that using a blowtorch on the shell provides the best "roasted" look.

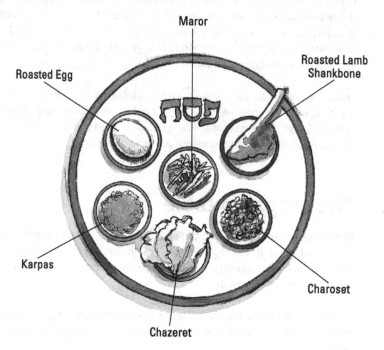

FIGURE 25-1:
The ritual
seder plate.

>> **Roasted lamb shankbone:** One of the most striking symbols of Passover is the roasted lamb shankbone (called *zeroah*), which commemorates the paschal (lamb) sacrifice made the night the ancient Hebrews fled Egypt. Some people say that it symbolizes the outstretched arm of God (the Hebrew word *zeroah* can mean "arm"). You can usually get a shankbone (you can also use a chicken neck) from any butcher; roast it in the oven with the egg until they both appear somewhat burnt-looking.

If you don't like the idea of a bone sitting on your table, you may consider using a roasted beet instead. (That's what vegetarians usually do.) This isn't a new idea; the great Biblical and Talmudic commentator Rashi suggested using a beet back in the eleventh century.

» **Maror ("bitter herb"):** When we think "Passover," we think "horseradish," the bitter herb most commonly used in the seder. Any bitter herb will work, though. Bitter herbs bring tears to the eyes and recall the bitterness of slavery. The seder refers to the slavery in Egypt, but people are called to look at their own bitter enslavements — whether addictions or habits. If you can get your hands on a real horseradish root (make sure it's at least as firm as a parsnip or fresh carrot), cut it in thin slices or grate it up. Horseradish in a jar is okay, too, although it lacks the bite of the freshly grated root.

» **Charoset:** Nothing is farther from maror than charoset (pronounced "kha-*roh*-set"), that sweet salad of apples, nuts, wine, and cinnamon that represents the mortar used by the Hebrew slaves to make bricks. Why would a reminder of slavery be so sweet? Because as much as people like to deny it, there is a sweetness to the security and dependability of any slavery, perhaps especially those enslavements that people create for themselves. Jewish cookbooks offer many recipes for charoset (see the recipes for Ashkenazi and Sephardi charoset later in this chapter); we particularly like Sephardic recipes, which are like a chutney of dates, raisins, almonds, and oranges.

» **Karpas:** Karpas is a green vegetable, usually parsley (though any spring green will do; some folks use celery sticks). For some people karpas symbolizes the freshness of spring; others say that eating it makes them feel like nobility or aristocracy. Some families still use boiled potatoes for karpas, continuing a tradition from Eastern Europe, where it was difficult to obtain fresh green vegetables.

» **Chazeret:** The chazeret (literally, "lettuce," pronounced "khah-*zer*-et") is a second bitter herb, most often romaine lettuce, but people also use the leafy greens of a horseradish or carrot plant. Chazeret has the same symbolism as maror.

» **Salt water:** Salt water symbolizes the tears and sweat of enslavement, though paradoxically, it's also a symbol for purity, springtime, and the sea, the mother of all life. Often a single bowl of salt water sits on the table, and people dip their karpas into the water during the seder. Some traditions begin the actual seder meal with each person eating a hardboiled egg (not the roasted egg!) dipped in the bowl of salt water.

» **Matzah:** Perhaps the most important symbol on the seder table is a plate that has a stack of three pieces of matzah (unleavened bread) on it. The *matzot* (that's plural for matzah) are typically covered with a cloth. (Since three matzot probably won't feed the table, make sure you have extra elsewhere on the table.) Tradition offers all kinds of interpretations for the three matzot. Some say they represent the Kohen class (the Jewish priests in ancient times), the Levis (who supported the priests), and the Israelites (the rest of the Jews). We actually don't care what symbolism you attribute to this trinity, as long as you're thinking about it. During the struggles of Soviet Jewry, Jews added a fourth piece of matzah to the seder plate to symbolize the struggles of Jews who were not yet free enough to celebrate the Passover. Today, some families still use that fourth matzah as a way of remembering all people who are not yet free to celebrate as they may wish.

>> **Wine cups and wine (or grape juice):** Everyone at the seder has a cup or glass from which they drink four cups of wine. Now, before you get any wild ideas about getting trashed, remember that these are usually very small cups of wine. And if you prefer not to drink wine, you can drink grape juice instead. Traditionally, the four cups represent the four biblical promises of redemption: "I will bring you out from under the burdens of the Egyptians, and I will rid you from their slavery, and I will redeem you with an outstretched arm, and with great judgments. And I will take you to me for a people . . ." Others say the four cups represent the four letters in the unspeakable Name of God (see Chapter 2). Besides the wine cups at each place setting, you need one additional cup, called the Cup of Elijah, which we discuss later in this chapter.

Participants don't eat all of the symbols, such as the roasted lamb shankbone and the roasted egg. However, when it comes time to eat the karpas, the charoset, and the other symbols, different families have different traditions. Some eat the symbols from the seder plate; others give each person their own mini-seder plate to eat from; at larger events, hosts may serve the items family style, passing large bowls around so that people can serve themselves.

EMBRACING THE MANY FLAVORS OF CHAROSET

Everyone's favorite dish during the Passover seder is charoset (the "ch" is the guttural "kh" sound), a thick, sweet chutney served with matzah. When you say "charoset" to most Jews in America, they immediately think "apples, nuts, cinnamon, and sweet wine." In fact, for many Jews, a seder without this particular type of charoset just isn't a seder at all. Charoset isn't just for Passover, however. We're charoset-through-the-year kinds of people. And don't let anyone tell you there's only one way to make this dish; after you've tried the basics, allow yourself to be creative with other fruits.

Ashkenazi Charoset

PREP TIME: 15 MINUTES | YIELD: 3 TO 4 CUPS

INGREDIENTS

3 large, firm apples (sweet, tart, or both)

Juice of 1 fresh lemon or 1 teaspoon of reconstituted lemon juice

½ pound coarsely-chopped nuts (walnuts, almonds, pecans, or mix-and-match)

1 teaspoon ground cinnamon

Sweet red wine or grape juice to desired consistency

1 teaspoon sugar or 2 to 3 teaspoons honey (optional)

DIRECTIONS

1   Core and dice the apples. (Some people peel the apples first, but we don't think that's necessary.) If you use a food processor, use the pulse feature to coarsely chop the apples.

2   Mix the apples well with the lemon juice, and then fold in the nuts and cinnamon. Add enough wine or grape juice to achieve the desired consistency, usually about ⅓ cup. Taste to see if you want to add some sugar or honey for extra sweetness.

PER SERVING: *Calories 322 (From Fat 225); Fat 25g (Saturated 2g); Cholesterol 0mg; Sodium 2mg; Carbohydrate 23g (Dietary Fiber 6g); Protein 6g.*

TIP: You can make the charoset up to three days in advance and keep it in the refrigerator.

NOTE: Charoset is a mortar-like mixture that needs be able to sit on a piece of matzah and not fall off before making it to your mouth. So as you add the liquid, don't add too much.

Sephardi Charoset

INGREDIENTS

1 cup pitted dates (¼ pound)

1 cup raisins

1 apple, cored and cut into chunks

½ cup walnuts

1 tablespoon grated orange peel

¼ cup orange juice

¼ teaspoon cinnamon

Dash nutmeg or cloves

DIRECTIONS

1 Combine dates, raisins, apple, and walnuts in a food processor and chop them until the mixture is in small pieces but not minced. Transfer the mixture to a medium bowl.

2 To the fruit mix add the orange peel, orange juice, cinnamon, and nutmeg/cloves. Cover the bowl and chill overnight (it will get a little thicker as it chills). Yields about 3 cups.

PER SERVING: *Calories 249 (From Fat 62); Fat 7g (Saturated 1g); Cholesterol 0mg; Sodium 5mg; Carbohydrate 50g (Dietary Fiber 5g); Protein 3g.*

TIP: Try serving this Sephardi version of charoset at your next seder (or even earlier). It helps those of us who have an Eastern European heritage to more fully appreciate some of the tastes contributed by other segments of the greater Jewish cultural experience.

ANECDOTE: This is the basic recipe that Ruth Neuwald Falcon (Ted's wife) got from her mother, who loved recipes from exotic places. In the Falcon household, Ruth prepares both Sephardi and Ashkenazi charosets each year for all the sedarim they attend.

Steps of the seder

You've set the table, prepared the foods, distributed the haggadot . . . it's finally time for the seder to begin. Each seder needs a leader, someone to orchestrate the proceedings and read key parts of the haggadah. In traditional homes, the leader may wear a white *kittel* (robe), which the individual wears only at special times in his or her life, such as during the seder, Yom Kippur, his (or her) wedding, and burial; wearing the kittel helps create the sense that this is a sacred time.

The 15 steps of the seder (remember that seder means "order") can be broken down into four sections:

» A series of preparatory prayers and rituals, often beginning with a special song listing the 15 steps

» The telling of the story

» The dinner

» The post-meal prayers and songs

The first activity of the seder — lighting candles — isn't included in the 15 steps because this ritual always precedes the evening celebration of any Jewish festival. After you light the candles, the seder proceeds as follows. (Please note that this book is in no way a replacement for a real haggadah, which would go into greater detail and provide the appropriate prayers.)

Step 1: Kadesh (sanctification of the day)

Fill your cup with the first glass of wine or grape juice, lift the cup, say the *Kiddush* (sanctification over the fruit of the vine and over the special energies of the holiday), and drink, leaning to the left. Tradition says to fill the cup to the brim, but it also says that you shouldn't get drunk, so you don't have to drink the whole glass (and the cup may be small). At Purim (see Chapter 24), people drink until they get blurry; but at the seder, people drink to sharpen, to remember, and to transcend.

Step 2: Urkhatz (handwashing with no blessing)

The second step is a ritual ablution — a spiritual cleansing by pouring water over the hands. The water should be warm enough to make the washing pleasant. Traditionally, you pour water from a pitcher over your right and then over your left hand. You can then dry your hands on a towel. In some homes, and in a large congregation, the leader often acts as proxy, performing the urkhatz for everyone in attendance.

REMEMBER

Jews ordinarily say a blessing over the ritual washing of the hands, but not this time!

Step 3: Karpas (eating the green vegetable)

The first bite of food people get is the karpas, the green vegetable, symbol of spring and renewal, which they dip in salt water (purifying tears) before eating. Anyone who forgot to eat a snack before arriving at the seder will be sorely tempted to continue eating the karpas (and any other vegetables lying around) as hors d'oeuvres before the meal. The wise arrangers make sure there is plenty available. Go for it!

Step 4: Yakhatz (breaking the matzah)

Now the seder leader picks up the middle matzah from the matzah plate and breaks it in half. The leader puts the smaller half of matzah back in between the other two pieces of matzah, but the larger half is reserved as the *afikomen* ("dessert"), which is eaten at the end of the meal. In some families, the afikomen is taken away and hidden somewhere in the house, and near the end of the seder the kids are allowed to go looking for it (see Step 12). Another common practice is to place the afikomen near the leader, from whom the kids must steal it during the seder without the leader noticing. In some Sephardic families, each person places a broken afikomen matzah on their shoulder, symbolizing the quick exodus from Egypt.

Step 5: Maggid (telling the story)

Usually the longest of the 15 seder steps, the Maggid is the telling of the Exodus narrative. At this point the youngest child at the table asks the four questions (every haggadah lists them). Actually, any person can read the questions, or everyone can read them together. The four questions all revolve around the basic question, "Why is this night different than all other nights?" (*Mah nishtanah halailah hazeh mikol haleilot?*)

The rest of the Maggid answers this question with the story of the Hebrews' exodus from Egypt, some Torah study, and a discussion of the description of the four types of children: the wise child, the wicked child, the simple child, and the child who doesn't know enough to ask a question (see the Introduction). Many people look around the table to find a good example of each child, but we find it more appropriate to look inside, to find the parts of ourselves that fit each of these descriptions.

Finally, the second cup of wine is poured, but don't drink it yet! Traditionally, participants dip a finger into the wine to transfer ten drops of wine to their plate, one drop for each of the ten plagues in Egypt. After singing songs praising God, pointing out the various items on the seder table yet again, and reciting the blessing over the wine, you can drink the second cup. By this time, you usually need it!

TIP

THE SPIRAL STORY

The Bible speaks of telling the Passover story to your children, but what if you don't have kids or they've grown and moved out? Recite the stories to your partner, friends, or even say it aloud to yourself. According to Judaism, we're each on a path, a journey through life, and we learn incrementally. We like to think of the Passover story as a road marker along this spiraling path, and each year, as we pass this marker, we can see if we've progressed or stayed in the same place. If we're in a different place on the path, then each telling brings new interpretations and new understandings. On the other hand, if we say, "I already know this story; there's nothing new here," then we haven't gone anywhere, and perhaps it's time to work harder to find the places inside us that have become enslaved.

Step 6: Rakhtzah (handwashing with a blessing)

It's time to wash your hands again, but this time you *do* say the blessing (see Appendix B). Note that it's customary not to speak at all between washing your hands and saying the blessings over the matzah. You can use this time for reflection on the sanctification and purification that you're undergoing.

Step 7: Motzi (blessing before eating matzah)

Raise the matzah (unleavened bread) and recite two blessings over the bread: the regular motzi blessing (see Appendix B) and one specifically mentioning the *mitzvah* (Jewish commandment) of eating matzah at Passover.

Step 8: Matzah (eating the matzah)

Blessings said, everyone breaks off a piece of matzah and eats it.

Step 9: Maror (eating the bitter herb)

Ironically, just as your stomach is starting to growl, you get to eat maror, the bitter herbs. Whether you eat a fresh slice of horseradish (which promises to bring tears to your eyes) or a leaf of romaine lettuce (which is pretty wimpy, in our humble opinion), you should be thinking of the bitterness of slavery. Traditionally, you should dip the maror in the charoset (the apple-nut-wine-cinnamon salad) to taste a small amount of sweetness along with the pain.

Step 10: Korekh (the Hillel sandwich)

While the English Earl of Sandwich is generally credited for inventing the snack of his namesake, Hillel (see Chapter 28) may have originated it two thousand years ago by combining matzah, a slice of paschal lamb, and a bitter herb. Jews no longer sacrifice and eat the lamb, so the Passover sandwich is only matzah, charoset, and a bitter herb now (many people use the chazeret [lettuce] instead of horseradish).

Step 11: Shulkhan Orekh (eating the meal)

After the korekh, the real meal commences, usually beginning with a hard-boiled egg dipped in salt water and quickly progressing to gefilte fish with beet-infused or regular horseradish, matzah ball soup, chopped liver, and as much other food as you can stuff down your gullet. Some of this food may be new to you; for example, *gefilte fish* is sort of a fish cake that looks scary if you didn't grow up with it — but try it anyway (it's usually a little sweet and goes great with the horseradish). Even though you drink four ceremonial glasses of wine during Passover, you can have some more during dinner, too.

CAUTION

You can't have beer, though; beer is made from fermented grain, so it's *khametz* (see "Edible Do's and Don'ts," earlier in this chapter).

Step 12: Tzafun (eating the afikomen)

Whether or not your host serves dessert after dinner, the last food that is officially eaten at the seder is a piece of the afikomen matzah (see Step 4), which symbolizes the Pesach sacrifice. If children have hidden or stolen the afikomen, they must return it to the leader by the end of the seder. Some families reward the children who find the afikomen, others reward all the children, and some actually bargain with the children to get the afikomen back. You can't conclude the seder without the afikomen (and tradition says that the seder *must* end before midnight), but the children are usually pretty tired at this point, so both sides have good bargaining positions. Many folks don't actually eat the afikomen itself; any taste of matzah will do once the afikomen has been returned.

The afikomen also represents the part of the self or soul that is lost or given up in enslavement. The seder represents the journey from enslavement to freedom, and at Tzafun, people reclaim the pieces of self that were missing.

Step 13: Barekh (blessing after eating)

Jewish meals traditionally conclude with a blessing, and this meal is no different. At this point, however, the meal may be over, but the seder is not. The third cup of wine celebrating the meal is poured and, after a blessing is recited, everyone drinks it. Now, a curious tradition occurs: A cup of wine is poured in honor of the prophet Elijah, and a door is opened to allow Elijah in. Many folks think the cup is for Elijah. Actually, the extra cup stems from a rabbinic debate over whether we should drink four or five cups of wine during the seder; the compromise was to drink four (the fourth is drunk in Step 14), pour a fifth, and wait until Elijah comes to tell us which is correct.

CHILDREN AT THE SEDER

The seder presents a dilemma: Passover is very clearly set up to be a time to include and educate children, but ultimately the deepest spiritual conversations and prayers/meditations simply can't be performed with children talking, playing, complaining, and just generally being like children. However, you don't have to forsake one for the other. One option is to have two seders, one for the children, and another for adults (while someone else takes care of the kids). You can also work enough children's activities into the seder so that the kids are distracted when you want more serious time.

Here are a few more ideas that can help, too:

- Make sure you get an age-appropriate children's haggadah for the kids.

- Get all the kids involved with making food; children especially like making the charoset. They can even shape it like a pyramid (but it's worth noting that the Jews certainly didn't build the pyramids).

- Remember that children are genetically predisposed to ask "When are we gonna eat?" exactly five minutes after the seder begins. Perhaps kids are enslaved, too — slaves to the present moment and their own desires. Make sure they have a snack beforehand (and maybe at the table, too). The seder is about celebration, not deprivation.

- Some families begin the seder with a short play. After everyone is seated, a knock comes at the door and a "stranger" comes in, looking like someone who has traveled a long distance. The stranger may then lead the seder, answering questions and telling the stories. You can also have your kids practice a play beforehand and then perform it during the seder.

- For young kids, photocopy a fun, age-appropriate picture that reflects the ideals of family on one side of a piece of cardstock, and photocopy a picture of a piece of matzah on the other side (you can use the front of the matzah box). Cut it up into puzzle shapes. Instead of hunting for the afikomen, the kids can hunt for these shapes. When both pictures are complete, you can talk about it.

- Any teenager will appreciate the themes of freedom and empowerment (unless you actually use those terms, in which case they'll just sneer at you). They hunger for freedom without even knowing what it feels like or what to do with it. That's okay; use that energy to discuss these themes. Kids often think they are enslaved, too. You may be surprised to see how engaged they become in the conversation!

- Everyone should remember that there are no dumb questions at a seder; many parts of the seder are "weird" specifically so that people will ask questions. However, don't worry if you don't know the answer to every question. Unanswered questions can stimulate a deeper search for meaning.

An alternative custom invites each person to pour a little of their own wine to fill Elijah's cup, symbolizing each person's own responsibility for bringing about redemption.

Step 14: Hallel (songs of praise)

After closing the door, the final seder ritual includes singing special songs of praise to God, and then filling, blessing, and drinking the fourth cup of wine.

Step 15: Nirtzah (conclusion)

The prescribed rituals and actions end at the 14th step, but like the Havdalah ceremony after Shabbat (see Chapter 18), Nirtzah celebrates a conclusion. The most common prayer at the end is simply *L'shana haba-a bi-Y'rushalayim*, meaning "Next year in Jerusalem!" Then, depending on the hour and the energy level of the participants, you may find yourself singing more songs and possibly even dancing! Some families make a tradition of reading aloud the Song of Songs from the Bible at the end of the seder, though be prepared for sleepy groans if you suggest it.

TIP

Like ballroom dancing, the seder has relatively clear rules and an order, but what makes the evening special are the extra flourishes that you and all the participants add along the way. You have plenty of room to add stuff to the seder: additional songs, prayers, poems, stories, commentary, and so on. The seders David attended growing up always included the song "Let My People Go" (David thought this was a traditional Jewish song until he learned it was a famous spiritual). Ted's seders always include times for silent meditation and a focus on the particular enslavements from which each individual intends to journey in the coming year.

The haggadah is not simply a script to follow, but rather a foundation on which you can build a wonderfully creative seder. It's worth repeating: We believe that if you're not having fun, you're just not doing it right.

New traditions: Miriam's Cup

One of the most popular new additions to the Passover seder is *Kos Miryam* (Miriam's Cup), which sits on the seder table next to Elijah's Cup. This cup is filled with water rather than wine, honoring the Talmudic story of Miriam's Well, which brought life-giving water as the Israelite tribes traveled through the desert, just as the prophetess Miriam (Moses' sister) soothed and nurtured the Children of Israel during the journey. Miriam's Cup honors the motherly spirit of God that works through us all, and it honors all the women in our history who have nurtured and healed our people and us personally.

Like many aspects of the seder, Jews play out Miriam's Cup in a wide variety of ways. Often, after drinking the second glass of wine, the leader invites each person (or sometimes only the women) at the table to pour a little water from his or her cup into the empty goblet. Then, the leader may raise a tambourine and lead the participants in a joyous song. (Any excuse for another joyous song!) This is also a good time to share stories of women who have been important in history and in our own lives.

A Time to Think about Freedom

Every year, it seems, we hear at least one person ask the same question: "Why did God let the Jews be enslaved in the first place?" Although this is a great question, it sort of misses the point. Instead of framing the issue as God letting people do things or not; Judaism teaches that people always have free will (see Chapter 2). In this case, Jacob's family chose to enter Egypt because it seemed like the right thing to do at the time.

Ironically, people's problems almost always begin as a solution to an earlier problem, and what at one time seems like the path to freedom often ends up becoming the next "stuck" place. (Remember that the Hebrew word for Egypt is *Mitzrayim*, which means "from [out of] narrow places.") Think about the really important growth opportunities you've had. Haven't they all come by overcoming a challenge?

Because we learn and evolve best when we're stuck and have to choose to move forward, our enslavements — however minor or overwhelming — offer us precious opportunities for awakening and growing beyond old patterns and beliefs.

Let Passover be a time to think about freedom and independence. If you do nothing else for Passover this year, at least find a friend and discuss these ideas.

WORDS OF WISDOM

We who lived in the concentration camps can remember the men who walked through the huts comforting others, giving away their last piece of bread. They might have been few in number, but they offer sufficient proof that everything can be taken from a man but one thing: the last of the human freedoms — to choose one's attitude in any given set of circumstances, to choose one's own way.

— VICTOR FRANKL

It's all about choice

Everyone loves the freedom to do stuff. We want the freedom to go places, to see and do what we want, and the freedom to say or believe what we want. The "freedom to" is obviously extremely important, but some say the "freedom from" is even more precious. As Dr. Avram Davis writes, "To be free from anger, free from hatred, free from the chains that bind the heart . . . This is what it means to be free 'from' mitzrayim, from the narrow places."

"Freedom from" is fundamentally about the ability to make choices. If every time you visit your parents you turn into a 14-year-old kid inside, you're not free. If you just "have" to have that newest, hottest gadget as soon as it hits the market, you're not free. You may be free to do anything you want, but if you're a slave to the television, or the weather, or the stock market, or getting your way, you're not free.

Unfortunately, it's really hard to get out of our enslavements. Jewish tradition notes that fewer than half of the Hebrews left Egypt after the Pharoah released them. The rest of them stayed because they preferred the familiar routine of slavery to the unknown challenges of the desert. In fact, sometimes we wonder if the ten plagues wrought on Egypt were actually meant as a way to get the remaining Jews to leave, to give them the courage and the trust they so sorely lacked in the state of enslavement.

So, perhaps another interpretation of Passover is celebrating the ability to "pass over," to skip one thing and choose another. After all, that people were made in the image of God doesn't mean that they look like God — it means that they're part of a Greater Awareness, from which they derive their free will. Humans have the freedom to discriminate between right and wrong, and to learn the difference between the spiritual and the mundane. We have the freedom to discover and to choose our paths.

Dayenu: So much gratitude

David's favorite part of the Passover seder is singing the song called *Dayenu*, which means "it is enough" (this usually happens during the telling of the Passover story). Besides the catchy tune and raucous beat, this song captures two other deeply important aspects of this holiday: humility and gratitude.

In short, the song says, "If God just took us out of Egypt, that would have been enough. If God had just given us Shabbat, that would have been enough. If God had just given us Torah, that would have been enough," and so on. The Jews see Dayenu as a call to be grateful for where you are — wherever you are — knowing that it's where you're supposed to be. The song is also a call for humility, balance, and moderation, for not overdoing, overworking, overeating, or even over-celebrating.

Dayenu doesn't mean you should rest on your laurels. Far from it! Dayenu means you must appreciate where you are and what you've accomplished. It also means you need to appreciate others. Each time the Bible repeats the refrain, "Remember that you were a slave in Egypt," think of it as a call to remember humility, to be generous to strangers, and to treat all others as you would wish to be treated.

It's Not Over till It's Omer

The seder is over and you're ready for life to get back to normal, right? Well, don't get too excited yet, because it's time for the 49-day period called the Counting of the Omer (or just the Omer). Many nontraditional Jews tend to ignore the Omer entirely, but it can be a fascinating time for self-reflection and spiritual self-improvement. This period also includes several other specific holidays that we touch on later in this section.

Agricultural roots

The Counting of the Omer, like many holidays, harkens back to the agricultural cycle. In biblical times, the Israelites honored the spring harvest by waving a sheaf of barley (called an *omer*) on what Jews today consider the second night of Passover. Then they counted the next 49 days, until the wheat harvest on the fiftieth day (called Shavuot, see Chapter 26).

Over the centuries, as the agricultural calendar became less relevant to the Jews, the Omer took on more spiritual significance. Although no one knows exactly how long it took the newly freed Israelites to hike from Egypt to Mount Sinai (where they received the Torah; see Chapter 3), tradition dictates that the revelation occurred on the fiftieth day. With this in mind, the omer period reflects the nature of the journey from enslavement (symbolized by Mitzrayim) to freedom and revelation.

(Curiously, the Christian tradition mirrors this seven-week journey: Pentecost — the descent of the Holy Spirit upon the apostles — occurs seven weeks, or 49 days, after Easter. Some say Jesus' "last supper" was actually a Passover seder, so it's not surprising that Pentecost occurs at almost exactly the same time as Shavuot.)

Usually, the first 33 days of the Omer period are a time of semi-mourning, meaning that traditionally no weddings or joyous celebrations take place during this time. Traditional Jews also stop playing musical instruments or even getting their hair cut during this period. Generally, the only exceptions are the two new moons that occur during the Omer and Lag B'Omer (the 33rd day of the Omer, described later in this section).

Because the Bible specifically says to count the days of the Omer, each evening, beginning on the second night of Passover, Jews are urged to say the following blessing:

> *Barukh Atah Adonai, Elohenu Melekh ha-olam, asher kid'shanu b'mitz'votav v'tzivanu ahl s'firat ha-Omer.*

> Blessed are You, Holy One our God, Universal Ruling Presence, Who sanctifies us with mitzvot [paths of holiness] and gives us this mitzvah of counting the days of Omer.

. . . and then read the following line, filling in the blanks with the appropriate numbers (you can leave out the part in brackets during the first week):

> *Today is the ___ day [comprising ___ weeks and ___ days] of the Omer.*

The magical, mystical seven

The heart of Jewish mystical teaching is called *kabbalah*, which literally means "that which is received." By the sixteenth century, the mystics began associating the kabbalistic Tree of Life (see Chapter 5) with the seven weeks of the Omer-counting, so that they could more profoundly honor the specific spiritual energies of each step of the journey.

Rabbis associated the 49-day period with the seven lower *sefirot*, or levels, on the Tree of Life — one for each week. They also associated each day of the week with one of those seven.

Many traditional prayer books include the sefirot of the day along with the order of the counting. More recently, prayer books offer specific meditations and intentions for each of the weeks and even each of the days.

Here, again, is a clear example of how Jewish holidays (with few major exceptions like Rosh Hashanah and Yom Kippur) began as responses to the agricultural cycles, then were associated with historical events, and, finally, received specifically spiritual meaning. Perhaps this reflects the essential nature of Judaism's evolution, moving from a focus on the order of the natural world to the rhythms of the historical world and finally to the spiritual dimension — a Oneness shared by all.

Yom Ha-Shoah

In 1951, the Israeli Knesset (Parliament) set aside the 27th of Nisan (which is the twelfth day of the Omer) as *Yom Ha-Shoah v'Hagevurah* ("Day of the Destruction and Heroism"), usually simply called *Yom Ha-Shoah*. Memorializing the holocaust and the six million Jews killed, Yom Ha-Shoah is clearly a day of mourning and remembrance, and Jews hold events in most cities with large Jewish populations. Often, people publicly read the names of those killed in the Holocaust and recite the kaddish, the Jewish memorial prayer (see Chapter 4).

REMEMBER

Communities around the world take responsibility for remembering the Holocaust in order to increase sensitivities and encourage actions to inhibit such atrocities in the future. In Israel, on this day, the entire country pauses for one minute — all traffic stops — for a shared moment of silent remembrance.

Israeli Independence Day

Jews celebrate Israeli Independence Day on the 20th day of the Omer, which is the fifth day of the Hebrew month of Iyar (although the days of the Omer occur on different days of the English calendar each year, they always are consistent on the Hebrew calendar).

The day preceding Independence Day is called *Yom Ha-Zikaron*, a "Day of Remembrance" of those who lost their lives both in the establishment and the later defense of Israel. However, at sundown (Jewish "days" begin at sundown) that spirit of mourning gives way to celebrations that turn raucous, including the rather unique proliferation of little plastic hammers that children — and adults acting like children — use to bop each other over the head. Emitting a squeak with each harmless blow, the hammers have become as much a part of the Israeli Independence Day celebration as fireworks are in the United States.

Lag B'Omer

The "official" day of respite from the semi-mourning during the Omer period arrives on 18 Iyar, at Lag B'Omer (literally, the 33rd day of Omer). Everyone seems to have their favorite reason for *why* the mourning should stop on this day. Some say you mourn during the Omer because a plague ran rampant among the students of Rabbi Akiba during the early years of the third century of this era, but that the plague let up during the 33rd day. Others say this was the day that manna began falling from heaven during the biblical trek to Sinai.

The Universal Themes in Passover

WORDS OF WISDOM

"Forgetfulness leads to exile, while remembrance is the secret of redemption."
— BA'AL SHEM TOV

The month of Nisan, whose full moon illuminates the celebration of Passover, is the first month of the Jewish year. (This gets confusing, because Rosh Hashanah is actually called the Jewish New Year; see Chapter 19.) Nisan is the beginning of spring, and it signals the reawakening of the natural world that speaks to the human spirit of renewed hope and possibility. The natural world is freed from the constraints of winter and leaps at the opportunity for new expression.

This process of reawakening is universal; this particular celebration of that reawakening is Jewish. We allow the past to be real again so that we can avoid repeating it. We broadcast the enduring messages of that past to create a vision greater than we as yet can see.

Chapter 26

Spring Is Busting Out All Over: Shavuot

The essence of Jewish spirituality isn't an idea, or a rule, or a practice, and it's even deeper than a feeling; instead, it's a change in awareness. Jewish spirituality is that profound *ah-ha!* moment of waking up and realizing that each person is part of something bigger and more unified than any of us can comprehend. The realization may come when you hear an extraordinary piece of music, enjoy a moment of deep silence in meditation, or hold a newborn baby.

These sorts of moments are so rich, so amazing, that Judaism has a holiday just to celebrate them: Shavuot, the Festival of Weeks, which occurs in late May or early June, 50 days after the second day of Passover. *Shavuot* literally means "weeks," referring to the seven weeks of the Omer that lead up to this holiday (see Chapter 25).

Unfortunately, even though this is one of the most important holidays of the Jewish calendar, many Jews ignore it because, unlike Chanukkah, few traditional rituals or practices are associated with it. Many Jewish kids never learn to celebrate Shavuot because it often occurs after religious school has let out for summer. However, as we get older, we find Shavuot increasingly appealing and important in our lives. It doesn't take long to see why.

The Ideas Behind Shavuot

Jewish holidays are generally linked to agricultural festivals, and Shavuot is no exception. Where Passover originally celebrated the harvest of barley and spring wheat, Shavuot honored the shift from spring to summer, the ripening of fruits, and the start of the major wheat harvest. Shavuot is the only festival prescribed by the Bible solely for agricultural reasons, mandating that every family bring their "first fruits" (*bikkurim*) to the Temple in Jerusalem as an offering to God. Thus, the holiday is also called *Khag ha-Bikkurim* ("festival of the first fruits") and *Khag ha-Katzir* ("festival of the reaping").

You can imagine the extraordinary sight of thousands of Jewish families making a pilgrimage to the Jerusalem Temple each year, carrying elaborate baskets of figs, dates, grapes, pomegranates, and olives for the joyous Shavuot festival. In addition, each family brought two loaves of bread made from their best, first-harvested wheat.

Receiving the Torah

Generations later, Jews living in cities asked themselves, "Hey, I don't live on a farm anymore, why should I bother with celebrating Shavuot at all?" Maybe you're asking yourself this same question. For the holiday to survive, Jews had to expand its meaning.

At some point during the time of the Second Temple (see Chapter 13), Shavuot was formally declared as the anniversary of receiving the Torah at Mount Sinai. This gave the holiday a relevance that could persist no matter where Jews lived, even beyond the destruction of the Temple and the next two thousand years of the Jewish exile. To this day, Shavuot is also called *Z'man Matan Torateinu* ("the time of giving of our Torah").

But the pendulum keeps swinging, so perhaps it was inevitable that as Jews settled back in Palestine (and later Israel) in the twentieth century and they began to till the land again, the Shavuot festival returned to its agricultural roots. Today, as townfolk celebrate in cities, non-religious farmers in Israel celebrate this holiday with agricultural festivities.

Meeting at Sinai

If you think that Torah is just a book of history or a set of laws, Shavuot — the celebration of receiving this Book — just isn't going to mean that much to you. Remember, though, that the word *Torah* means much more than just the first five volumes of the Bible; it's the basic Path of Judaism (see Chapter 3). You don't have to agree with every word of the written Torah to celebrate the practice, the spirit, and the "Tao" of Judaism.

Plus, we need to emphasize that Shavuot doesn't just celebrate the books, the oral traditions, or even the whole Jewish path. Shavuot honors the *receiving* of the Way called "Judaism." And when we say "receiving," we don't just mean this happened to a bunch of folks standing around a mountain 3,300 years ago. Judaism clearly views God as giving the Torah every day, every moment.

REMEMBER

Passover challenges people to participate in the transition from slavery to freedom — to make it their own by reflecting on the enslavements in their own lives. Then, 50 days later, Shavuot challenges people to participate in the ongoing chain of Torah transmission through which the essential nature of Torah is deepened. In other words: Get involved!

Tune in today!

Every Jewish holiday has key words that help remind us what is going on. For Passover, you can think of "freedom" and "responsibility." Perhaps Chanukkah can be summed up with "dedication" and "miracles." For Shavuot, the words to focus on are "revelation," "reception," and "commitment." We talk about commitment later in this chapter; for now, we explore the ideas of revelation and reception.

Normal communication can always be pinpointed in time and space ("He said it *there* and *then*"); revelation, on the other hand, is profound spiritual communication that is outside the boundaries of space and time — it's going on everywhere, all the time. Becoming aware of revelation is like tuning in to a radio or television station that you never knew existed. (We can hear the commercials now: "K-G-O-D! All God, All the Time. And now for the weather . . .")

Of course, you can't just dial in this station. You need a particular kind of sensitivity. But where some traditions teach that only certain people can "tune in" and act as a link to God, Jewish tradition encourages everyone to study and become more available for this deeper channel of communication (see Chapter 2).

Go tell it on the mountain

Jewish history, laid out in the Bible, contains plenty of instances in which people have a theophany. (*Theophany* is one of our favorite words; it loosely means "seeing or experiencing God.") Noah, Abraham, Jacob, Ezekiel and the other prophets . . . for whatever reason, these people all received something of enduring significance in the form of words or visions. Similarly, the Bible says that about 3,300 years ago, Moses, leading the Israelites through the desert, had a series of revelations. And those revelations — that which was received — are Torah.

GETTING GOOD RECEPTION ON MOUNT SINAI

If you've ever been to the Sinai desert in Egypt, you know that it feels like the middle of nowhere. Perhaps Jerusalem or some other center of civilization would have made more sense for such an important revelation. However, rabbis over the centuries have taught that the Torah was given in the desert because no one owns the desert, indicating that the Torah is meant for all humankind. If the Torah were received in someone's land, the rabbis reasoned, then one people or another may have boasted that "in my territory, the Torah was given."

Jewish teachers have long used these sorts of stories to teach life lessons. Another rabbinic fable tells of a competition between all the mountains in the region. Each wanted to host the revelation, but Mount Sinai chose not to enter the contest because it felt it was too ordinary. God chose it, say the rabbis, because of its humility.

Shavuot's date marks the day when Moses had his first revelation at Sinai and came down the mountain with the Ten Principles (the stone tablets came 40 days later). They are also called the Ten Utterances, but have come to be known as the "Ten Commandments" for most of Western history (see Chapter 4). Some teachers pun that Shavuot is the "quintessential peak experience."

Telling stories

Shavuot, perhaps more than any other Jewish holiday, has become the focus of many wonderful midrashic stories (see Chapter 3) over the centuries. These tales add to the richness of Shavuot and help describe the range of emotions and themes associated with this day.

For example, some rabbis teach that Pharaoh's daughter pulled Moses from the Nile on the day of Shavuot. Others insist that King David both was born and died on Shavuot, and that the Ba'al Shem Tov (see Chapter 28) also died on Shavuot in the year 1760.

The stories of the giving of the Torah on Shavuot are also wonderfully varied, though few of them have any Biblical basis. Here are just a few samples:

>> Some say that the Israelites only heard God utter the first word of the first principle, *Anokhi* ("I am"). Others insist that the people only heard the first syllable ("Ahh") before sending Moses to receive the rest.

>> One tradition notes that the Ten Principles contain 172 individual words, and that God spoke all 172 of them at the same time so that the Israelites wouldn't consider one principle any more important than another.

>> One often-repeated fable tells that God shopped the Torah around to various other peoples, who each turned it down after hearing what was in it. When God approached the Israelites, however, they replied, "We will do and we will hear," indicating that they would obey even before they heard what the Torah said.

>> On the other hand, according to one sermon, as the Israelites approached Mt. Sinai, God lifted the mountain above their heads, threatening to drop it on them if they didn't accept the Torah. The people shouted, "We accept!" and a myriad of angels swooped down to give each person a crown and a "girdle of glory" (which, by the way, God took back when the Hebrews later built the Golden Calf).

One of our favorite Shavuot stories describes how at midnight on this holiday the heavens open up, all your prayers are heard, and you can experience the whole universe. Revelation is a mysterious thing to capture, but a cosmic open door certainly goes a long way to describing this abstract concept.

Searching for New Rituals

You may be asking yourself "What do we *do* on this holiday?" Good question. Where Chanukkah has candles, Passover has matzah and the seder, and Sukkot has the *sukkah* (the temporary hut), Shavuot has almost nothing in the way of an official ritual, perhaps as a way of encouraging more personal rituals instead. For one friend of ours, eating cheesecake on Shavuot has become an "official" ritual; see the section, "Got Milk?" later in this chapter.

Many traditional Jews visit the *mikveh* (a ritual bath) or any free-flowing river, lake, or ocean on the afternoon just before the beginning of Shavuot (remember that holidays begin at sundown), in order to spiritually cleanse and prepare themselves for revelation.

PENTECOST VERSUS SHAVUOT

If the phrase "50 days later" sounds familiar, perhaps you're thinking of the Christian holiday of Pentecost, which falls on the seventh Sunday after Easter. The Christian tradition says that 50 days after Jesus was resurrected, the "Holy Spirit" or "Divine Presence" descended and filled the small band of Jewish Apostles with inspiration. We find the parallels between the revelation at Mount Sinai and this Christian tradition fascinating; the theme of "receiving" clearly appears to spill beyond Jewish boundaries at this time of year. Interestingly, *Pentecost* was originally the Greek name for Shavuot.

Shavuot begins with a ritual lighting of candles at home (see Appendix B), and often Jewish people then go to a service at a synagogue, where a few special Shavuot prayers and poems are recited. For example, in Ashkenazi synagogues, the eleventh-century poem *Akdamot* is popular, telling of God's love and Israel's devotion to Torah. The opening of the poem is particularly lovely:

> Were all the skies parchment and all the reeds pens, all the seas ink and everyone a scribe, God's grandeur still could not be spelled out.

Often, as an act of rededication, the congregation rises and reads the Ten Principles out loud with a special *trope* (a chanted melody). To emphasize the theme that Shavuot is a symbolic commitment, some Sephardic communities read aloud a special *ketubah* (marriage certificate) that speaks of the love and marriage between God and the Jewish people. Also included may be the Haftarah portion (see Chapter 3) that describes Ezekiel's extraordinary vision of the chariot.

Pulling the mystical all-nighter

Another way to prepare for receiving revelation is "staying awake" to what's going on around you — keeping your mind and heart alert, you're better prepared for "tuning in" to a spiritual dimension. Increasing numbers of Jews take this idea literally and stay awake to study and meditate all night long on the first evening of Shavuot. This custom, called *Tikkun Leil Shavuot* ("Repair on the night of Shavuot"), was started by the mystical Kabbalists in sixteenth-century Safed (see Chapter 5).

The Tikkun, as it's often called, is a ceremony designed to prepare Jews for receiving the Torah again. Traditionally, at a Tikkun, you may read and discuss verses from every portion of the Torah, the books of the Prophets, the volumes of the Mishnah (in the Talmud; see Chapter 3), and the Zohar (see Chapter 5). Foregoing sleep, you attempt to perfect your soul and intellect in anticipation of daybreak and the revelation. Staying focused all night poses a challenge, but as you blearily meet the sunrise, you'll have a definite sense of triumph.

Some congregations don't actually stay up all night; they just have a late-night Tikkun, and then everyone trundles off home.

Deck the halls . . .

For most Jews (those of us who live in cities at least), the only reminder that Shavuot was originally an agricultural festival comes in the form of the beautiful flowers and lush green plants that decorate synagogues and homes at this time of year. Instead of bringing wheat and "first fruits" to the Temple, Jews reconnect to the earth and the beauty around them by bringing roses, fragrant herbs, and leafy plants inside.

After the Vilna Gaon (an important eighteenth-century Lithuanian sage) banned the custom of decorating with trees and plants because he felt it was too pagan, many European Jews instead began decorating their houses and synagogues with paper cut-outs in the shapes of plants, animals, and biblical figures. Now, it's not uncommon to see both paper cutouts (some simple ones made by children, and often some very elaborate ones made by professionals) as well as green plants as decorations.

Got milk?

For many people, "Jewish holiday" can be translated as "food . . . lots and lots of food." So why should Shavuot be any different? Some Jewish teachers say that Shavuot is the best holiday because during Passover you can't eat *whatever* you want, on Sukkot you can't eat *wherever* you want, on Rosh Hashanah you can only eat after saying lengthy prayers, and on Yom Kippur you can't eat at all. But on Shavuot, you can eat what, where, when, and how you want.

However, the traditional food at Shavuot is dairy (which, as we discuss in Chapter 4, could mean almost any vegetarian dish), and often includes cheese blintzes with sour cream and preserves (see the recipe for cheese blintzes in this chapter), cheese pastries, cheese kreplach, and cheesecake. The reasons behind eating dairy are a mystery, though it does tend to remind us of Shavuot's agricultural roots. But when it comes to eating sweet dairy dishes, who needs reasons?

Cheese Blintzes

Cheese blintzes. It's amazing how just two words can start a mouth watering. A blintz is basically a crepe wrapped around some filling, usually sweet and always delicious.

PREP TIME: 1 HOUR	COOK TIME: 40 MINUTES	YIELD: 24 TO 30 BLINTZES

INGREDIENTS

Crepes:

6 eggs, beaten

1 cup water

½ teaspoon sugar

⅛ teaspoon salt

1 cup milk

2 cups flour

Vegetable oil for cooking the crepes and sautéing the blintzes

Filling:

2 cups cottage (or farmer's) cheese, drained

2 eggs

¾ teaspoon salt

2 teaspoons sugar (or to taste)

½ teaspoon vanilla extract

DIRECTIONS

1 To make the crepes, in a large bowl mix the eggs, water, sugar, salt, and milk. Add the flour — just a little at a time — while mixing, until the batter is smooth (it'll be much thinner than a regular pancake batter).

2 Drain the cottage cheese well. You may even want to squeeze out more of the liquid by wrapping the cheese in cheesecloth or pressing it in a fine-mesh colander. (If you're using farmer's cheese, no draining is necessary, but you do want to crumble the cheese finely.)

3 While cheese is draining, heat an 8-inch non-stick pan over medium to medium-low heat and grease the pan with a little oil. When the pan is hot, pour in about a $\frac{1}{3}$ cup of the batter and immediately tilt the pan in circles to spread the batter out as thinly and evenly as possible. Don't flip the crepe over; it's cooked only on one side. As soon as the crepe is set on top and browned on the bottom, turn the pan upside down over a moist cloth towel and gently knock the pan so that the crepe falls out (if you're using a good non-sticking pan, you may be able to just peel the crepe from the pan). Repeat this step until you have finished the batter. You can stack up the crepes separated with wax paper.

4 In a medium bowl, mix 1 egg with the salt, sugar, and vanilla. Blend in the cheese and mix until the filling has a creamy but firm consistency — almost like soft cream cheese. If it's too wet, the filling will run out of the blintzes. (If this happens, you can try adding a little matzah meal.)

5 In a small bowl, beat the second egg with 1 tablespoon of water; you'll use this mixture to help seal the blintzes.

(continued)

6 Place a crepe with the cooked (slightly-browned) side up and drop 2 or 3 tablespoons of the cheese filling on it. Fold the bottom edge up over the filling (it should mostly cover the mixture) and brush a small amount of the egg and water mixture along the exposed, flipped-up edge (this will help seal the blintz). Next, fold in the two sides so that you have a three-sided "envelope." Now, roll the blintz up. Just before the final roll, brush a little more of the egg mixture on the top edge of the crepe to help seal it. Repeat until you've finished the crepes. You can now either cook the blintzes or refrigerate or freeze them to be cooked later. (Put them on wax paper, but don't let them touch each other.)

7 To cook the blintzes, fry them in either butter or vegetable oil, folded side down (to ensure the seal). Fry the blintzes until golden brown, then flip and fry the other side until it's the same color. (Note that it's usually easier to use tongs than a spatula to turn blintzes.) When done, blot off any excess oil with a paper towel and serve the blintzes with sour cream, applesauce, powdered sugar, preserves, fresh berries, or other fun condiments.

PER SERVING: *Calories 150 (From Fat 66); Fat 7g (Saturated 2g); Cholesterol 84mg; Sodium 229mg; Carbohydrate 11g (Dietary Fiber 0g); Protein 8g.*

VARIATIONS: This recipe for cheese blintzes is pretty traditional; some folks like adding nuts, fruits, or spices. Others do away with the dairy filling entirely and use cherry or apple pie filling.

TIP

A FIRST-TIMERS' GUIDE TO SHAVUOT

Shavuot, like all the holidays, is best when celebrated with other people, and as long as everyone honors the same themes, there's no reason those people have to be Jewish. If you're invited to a Shavuot celebration, here are a few suggestions that will help everyone get in the right mood:

- Bring flowers or leafy-green plants. Roses are wonderful if they're not too expensive in your area (some people say that Mount Sinai was covered in roses at revelation, though we have a hard time picturing that).

- If you bring food, consider bringing a vegetarian or dairy dish.

- The all-night Tikkun Leil Shavuot can be great fun and a good educational experience, but do yourself a favor and bring snacks, coffee or tea, chocolate (a good source of caffeine and sugar), and some moist towelettes to wipe your face off occasionally and keep yourself awake.

Once again, there are few rules on Shavuot, and many opportunities for awakening, receiving, and committing yourself to your path. Enjoy!

Reading Ruth

Alongside the green decorations and the vegetarian meals, Jews traditionally read the Book of Ruth on Shavuot. The short tale takes only 10 or 15 minutes to read, but in case you don't have a Bible close by, here's the basic story:

Once upon a time there was a non-Jewish woman named Ruth who married into a Jewish family that had recently moved to her country. When, shortly afterward, her husband and father-in-law both died, her mother-in-law, Naomi, decided to return to her own country of Judah. She urged Ruth to stay behind, but Ruth refused, replying, "Wherever you go, I will go; and where you lodge, I will lodge; your people shall be my people, and your God, my God." In short, she chose to convert to Judaism.

Ruth traveled with Naomi back to Naomi's hometown, married a wealthy relative of her father-in-law, and gave birth to a son named Obed. Obed's grandson, it turned out, was King David, which means Ruth is celebrated as a heroine: great-grandmother of the King and ancestor of the future Messiah. The end.

While the Book of Ruth is a pretty good story, it also happens to resonate with the overall themes of Shavuot. For example, on the topic of commitment: Ruth freely commits herself to Judaism, as the Hebrews committed themselves to the Torah.

REMEMBER

The moral of the story of Ruth is that a non-Jew can not only become an authentic part of the Jewish community, but a crucial part of Jewish history.

The story also touches the theme of "receiving," though with a slightly different meaning than we've been discussing. Naomi and the other Jewish people receive Ruth — that is, they welcome her with open and loving arms. The acceptance that the book presents is a reminder of the ideal that Jews are meant to welcome those who choose to become part of the community.

Nontraditional traditions

Because Shavuot has so few prescribed religious rituals, we see it as a great opportunity to experiment with your own traditions. Here are just a few ideas to get you started.

>> Jewish confirmation ceremonies often happen on Shavuot (see Chapter 8). Confirmation is an opportunity for young people (usually about age 16) to make a conscious, adult choice to continue on their Jewish path and be part of the Jewish community. But why stop at 16? Shavuot is a great time for anyone at any age to confirm or reconfirm. Make up a ritual as simple or elaborate as feels right to you.

>> Sherwin Wine, the founder of the Secular-Humanistic Jewish movement in the 1960s, suggests focusing on the 3,000 years of literary creativity of the Jewish people at Shavuot. Here, the Torah is just the first book in a long history of important Jewish works. As Rabbi Wine notes, "The major harvest of the Jewish people throughout the past two thousand years has not been wheat. It has been the written word."

>> Something about mountains inspires opening to deeper dimensions of reality. Take a day to go hiking or picnicking at a mountain in your area. If you live in Kansas (where the word "flat" doesn't even begin to describe the landscape), you might achieve the same effect while sitting in a really wide-open space.

>> Shavuot and Tu B'Shvat (see Chapter 23) have a similar theme of connecting with nature. Some people even say that Shavuot is the "day of judgment for fruit trees," and encourage people to pray for the trees. Take time to sit in a garden and remember how extraordinary it is that things grow the way they do. If you have a flower garden, Shavuot is a wonderful time to press flowers.

>> Eating a good slice of bread (homemade is best, of course) with some honey while reading a good book (or even "The Good Book") is a heavenly activity on Shavuot. If no one is looking, wave the bread and the book above your head in silent (or not-so-silent) praise and thanks, as the early Jews waved their offerings at the Temple.

Rewakening

Shavuot encourages a greater appreciation of the relationship between the finite and infinite, between the temporal and the eternal. You can imagine the Torah as the form through which the infinite enters the finite world. The cycle of the Jewish year sees the redemption from slavery (Passover) completing itself in the revelation at Sinai (Shavuot). The rest of Jewish history (and year) involves the continuing translation and interpretation of that revelation.

We have an opportunity to consider the unlimited depths of Torah, and to reaffirm its essential messages:

>> There is connection between ourselves and that which is Greater.

>> We live in a universe to which we are intimately connected on all levels.

>> We are individual expressions of a Universal One.

Chapter 27

A Day of Mourning: Tisha B'Av

I n one of the most oft-quoted lines of the Bible, *Kohelet* (the book of Ecclesiastes) says, "To everything there is a season, and a time to every purpose under heaven . . . A time to weep, and a time to laugh; a time to mourn, and a time to dance." These words aren't just some tired cliché. They declare an important truth that many people forget: the profound importance of feeling and expressing a full spectrum of emotions in order to be truly human.

Modern society, in both the East and the West, tends toward a philosophy of "If you're not smiling, then something's wrong." But Judaism has a millennia-old tradition that insists that real strength comes from feeling a wide range of emotions — even the "negative" feelings that many people try to avoid by distracting themselves with frivolous activities.

Tisha B'Av — the "ninth day of the month of Av," which usually falls in late July or early August — is a day to let go of those distractions and feel deep mourning. In fact, Jews traditionally observe the same rites as if a close relative had died (see Chapter 10). On the surface, the day commemorates the destruction of the two

Temples in Jerusalem (see Chapters 12 and 13). However, other tragedies are also associated with this day:

>> Tradition states that on Tisha B'Av, God told Moses and the people of Israel that because they lacked enough faith in God, they wouldn't be allowed to enter the Promised Land for 40 years (until the generation that had been enslaved in Egypt died off in the wilderness; see Chapter 11).

>> Some scholars say it was on Tisha B'Av in 1290 CE that the King of England ordered the Jews expelled (others say it was a week earlier).

>> Tisha B'Av marked the date in 1492 CE when the Jews were expelled from Spain (unless they converted).

>> The Russian army mobilized its armies on Tisha B'Av in 1914, leading to the outbreak of World War I (which many people believe marked the beginning of the end for Eastern European Jewry).

Of course, all these events happened a long time ago, and people rarely get particularly excited about honoring a day of mourning. The result is that fewer and fewer people celebrate Tisha B'Av. But this day raises important themes for today's Jews — loss, exile, and the desire to return home — themes that can help people understand Judaism and themselves more deeply. Tisha B'Av demands that people move through places of personal and communal mourning to deeper hope, optimism, and joy.

Fasting, Reading, and Reflecting

Traditional Jews fast on Tisha B'Av, allowing the day to be one of self-affliction and mourning, with restrictions as exacting as those on Yom Kippur (see Chapter 20).

Evening worship in the synagogue includes the biblical Book of Lamentations (*Eicha* in Hebrew), which the cantor chants to an ancient melody that expresses both personal pain and the grief of the community. The book is a requiem to the destruction of the Temple and Jerusalem, a cry to God to hear the pleas and see the tears of the Jewish people. At this service, Jews often remove their shoes and sit on the ground or on low stools or cushions in a darkened sanctuary.

REMEMBER

These mourning rituals aren't intended to make you miserable. Judaism isn't asking you to wear hair shirts or bang your head against a wall. The idea is simply to be mindful and to create an atmosphere of somberness and deep memorial. Honoring days of sadness reminds you that life is full of ups and downs, and that living fully means taking the bad along with the good.

REMEMBER

A FIRST-TIMERS' GUIDE TO TISHA B'AV

Attending a Tisha B'Av service is unlike any other service during the year, and you may find it to be a fascinating experience if you're willing to open yourself up to the mournful energies of the day. However, remember that this holiday isn't as often observed as it once was, so you may have to search to find a synagogue with a service. Here are a few things to keep in mind if you're going to attend:

- Don't bring food or drinks to the service. In fact, make sure you have a good meal beforehand, as there will be nothing to eat there.

- Don't wear makeup, perfume, or flashy jewelry. Also, don't wear shoes with leather soles (traditional Jews avoid leather entirely).

- Jews at Tisha B'Av services might not greet each other before or after the service, though you should take your cue from the other congregants. Whatever the case, you should keep a somber tone and stay relatively quiet.

- If you don't read Hebrew, make sure that you get a copy of the Book of Lamentations (it's in every Bible) so that you can read along as the cantor recites this fascinating poem; remember that even though the book talks about the destruction of Jerusalem, you should use it to reflect on your experiences of loss.

More liberal Jews might simply spend the day in quiet reflection, going for walks or visiting cemeteries.

Today's Tisha B'Av

Everyone has experienced the loss of personal "temples," like the loss of childhood or of people or things that were deeply important. Even a loss you experienced 30 or more years ago may still require mourning — revisiting a process in which you feel the pain and move through it in order to grow. Tisha B'Av could be the one day of the year when you really let yourself explore these depths as a crucial step in healing.

Similarly, many Jews extend the themes of Tisha B'Av globally, noting that it was around this time of year (August 6 and 9, to be exact) when America dropped atomic bombs on Hiroshima and Nagasaki. Some rabbis also note that humankind is on the verge of destroying the holiest Temple — the earth itself — through pollution, overuse of resources, or global warming.

The ritual of Tisha B'Av calls people to remember pain and to remain conscious in that remembering. The holiday isn't a time of denial, but rather an invitation to taste grief and pain deeply. Ultimately, Jews think of Tisha B'Av as a time of affirmation, in which that grief and that pain promote capacities for experiencing and sharing greater joy, compassion, and caring.

Tu B'Av: Releasing into Joy

The first Shabbat after Tisha B'Av is called *Shabbat Nachamu*. The name comes from the first words of the week's *Haftorah* passage: *Nakhamu nakhamu ami* ("Comfort, comfort my people"). The service is a welcome comfort, like being held in your mother's arms after crying. Then, a few days later, comes the joyous celebration of Tu B'Av ("the 15th of Av"). The full-moon festival of Tu B'Av is exactly six months after Tu B'Shvat (see Chapter 23), and while most Jews haven't even heard of this holiday, it's an increasingly popular time to celebrate weddings. Where Tu B'Shvat offers a hint at the coming spring, Tu B'Av provides the first glimpse of autumn, when the temperature drops and the weather becomes more moderate.

5

The Part of Tens

We introduce you to our favorite Jewish thinkers and leaders — after all, as they say in baseball, you can't tell the players without a program! And we serve up answers to the most commonly asked questions about Judaism, from what it means to say that Jews are the "chosen" people to the serious matter of Jewish humor.

Chapter **28**

Ten People Who Helped Shape Judaism

I n this chapter, we take you on a quick tour of ten of the most important and influential Jewish thinkers over the past two millennia. These ten were not only great Jews and great thinkers, they were also great thinkers about Judaism itself.

REMEMBER

These are not *the* ten great thinkers, just ten from a very long list, organized chronologically. Because of space, we limited ourselves to post-Biblical thinkers, and we had to omit many others who deserve to be recognized.

You may notice another omission here, too: the relative lack of women (only one of these ten is a woman). Clearly, women have been an important part of Judaism. However, women in the past have unfortunately not been encouraged to study and write about Judaism, and those who did weren't widely recognized. You can find rare exceptions, such as Bruriah (the wife of the Talmudic sage Rabbi Meir) and the nineteenth-century Hasidic teacher Hannah Rachel (known as the Maid of Ludomir). Given the number of women who are currently becoming rabbis and writing about Judaism, we trust that the ratio of men to women on such lists will be more equal in the future.

Hillel

Rabbi Hillel (70 BCE to 10 CE) was known for his enigmatic questions and answers that required deep reflection by his students. But his rabbinical decisions, and his focus on the spirit of the law over the letter of the law, truly distinguished him as a great Jewish thinker.

Rising to become the leader and greatest sage of the rabbis during the time of Herod the Great and the second Temple (see Chapter 13), Hillel's rules for interpreting the Torah laid the foundation for all future analysis of the Bible. He always stressed practical and ethical interpretations over a strict regard for the rules and rituals.

Hillel taught that the most important goal in Judaism is *tikkun olam*, the bettering of the world through moral and ethical action. In a teaching that has resonated for 2,000 years in both Jewish and Christian circles, he asked, "If I am not for myself, then who is for me; But if I am only for myself, then what am I; and if not now, when?"

Several of Hillel's famous descendants were also named Hillel, which makes deciphering Jewish history quite a challenge. To help distinguish Hillel from his progeny, people often refer to this great teacher as "Hillel the Elder."

Rashi

When you think of the eleventh century, you probably think of people living in hovels and slinging mud to eke out a living. After all, that's what the movies would have you believe. However, in Troyes, France, a young man, named Shlomo ben Isaac (1040 to 1105 CE), became the greatest Medieval teacher of Judaism and forever changed people's understanding of the Torah and the Talmud. Rabbi Shlomo ben Isaac is better known by an acronym built from the first letters of his name: Rashi.

Rashi's special skill was in translating and commenting on the meanings of Torah and Talmud passages. He wrote in an uncommonly clear and concise manner, bringing a layperson's perspective to an incredibly dense body of work. Fluent in many languages and an accomplished poet, Rashi owned several vineyards in which he worked the grape harvest, and imagery of everyday work and winemaking appear throughout his writing.

Rashi's commentaries on the Torah and Talmud helped ordinary people decipher the texts, and some years later it became mandatory for Jews to study the weekly Torah portion along with Rashi's commentary.

Today, 900 years after Rashi died, every printed Talmud still includes Rashi's commentary. Rashi's legacy wasn't limited to this accomplishment: Opposite Rashi's notes are the commentaries called the *Tosafot*, which were written in large part by five of Rashi's descendants (two sons-in-law and three grandsons).

Maimonides

Rabbi Moses ben Maimon (1135 to 1204 CE) — better known as Maimonides or simply as "the Rambam" — was an intellectual, a theologian, and a philosopher. He was born in Spain, but after Muslim persecution there, his family fled first to Morocco and then to Egypt, where Maimonides later became the leader of Cairo's Jewish community and the physician to the Sultan of Egypt.

Did this guy go bowling in his spare time? No, but somehow on top of all his work, he managed to write numerous medical books as well as the *Mishneh Torah* (Repetition of the Torah), the ultimate compendium of all Jewish law, culling the essence from the Bible, the two Talmuds, midrashic literature, and even the *Gaonic Responsa* (see Chapter 3). His goal was to take these incredibly difficult texts, which require years of scholarly research and study, and distill them into something that almost anyone could read. He even threw in a generous dose of medical advice for good measure. The book was a boon to the common man, who might be committed to Judaism, but not enough to spend his whole life in study. You might say it was the first *Judaism For Dummies*.

Maimonides went on to write a more dense philosophical tome called *The Guide for the Perplexed*, in which he argues that there are no contradictions between Judaism and science. Maimonides strongly believed in the importance of reason, and that nothing in the sacred Jewish writings should require people to take anything simply on faith.

Joseph Caro

Rabbi Joseph ben Ephraim Caro (1488 to 1575) was a brilliant legal scholar who admired Maimonides' work but felt that he could improve upon it in some ways. Born in Spain, Caro grew up in Constantinople (Istanbul), where he studied Torah and Talmud. In 1537 Caro emigrated to Tzfat (in modern-day Northern Israel; also called Safed in English), where he was quickly recognized as a brilliant legalist, and he became the leader of the scholars there.

In Tzfat, he finished his magnum opus, the *Beit Yosef* (House of Joseph), in which he clearly discusses each Jewish law, tracing it from its source, through various diverging Ashkenazi and Sephardic interpretations, finally arriving at a decisive ruling. The book was, and is, a magnificent work of scholarship, but was still so dense and intimidating that he had to distill it into a smaller version called the *Shulkhan Arukh* ("The Arranged Table"). It's this work for which he's best known, and it's this version that most rabbis today first consult when asked to rule on a question of Jewish law.

Before you get the idea that this Caro guy was just some stuffy lawyer, you should know that he seemed to live a double life: one life compiling the code literature (how Judaism should be observed), and another life as a mystic. Caro said that an angel would regularly visit him and speak through him, revealing mystical truths and deeper legal arguments.

Isaac Luria

Of all the prophets, scholars, and teachers in Jewish history, only one man was given the title and name "divine" by his contemporaries. In sixteenth-century Tzfat (in what is now northern Israel), a young man named Yitzchak (Isaac) Luria (1534 to 1572) was given the name Elohi Rabbenu Yitzchak ("Our Divine/Godly Rabbi Isaac"); he is also known by the acronym "The Ari" (which means "lion").

Born in Jerusalem, Luria's family moved to Egypt when he was young. He was regarded as a child prodigy, and he studied under some of the great Jewish teachers of the time. After meditating alone in a hut by the Nile for two years, he moved to Tzfat in 1570 and was soon accepted as a great master.

Luria taught that in the beginning of the universe, a cosmic accident shattered vessels holding divine energy, and sparks of divine light became hidden in shells of matter. The function of the Kabbalist (Jewish mystic), he said, was to redeem the hidden sparks, to actualize the *yichud* ("unification of being").

Luria was considered by his contemporaries to be so great that his practices were taken as legally binding rules. His teaching is still seen by many to be as important as the *Zohar* (see Chapter 5). Unfortunately, his untimely death at age 38 cut short a life rich with mystery and divine inspiration.

Ba'al Shem Tov

Rabbi Israel ben Eliezer (1700 to 1760) was a highly charismatic leader whose legendary miraculous works led people to call him the Ba'al Shem Tov ("Master of the Good Name of God"), or simply by the acronym "the Besht."

The Ba'al Shem Tov lived humbly as a teacher of children until his thirty-sixth birthday, when he revealed that he was a healer and began to gather a group of disciples. The Ba'al Shem Tov taught a path of joy and love, of hope and exuberance, and he became extremely popular almost overnight.

Rumors of his miracles, especially healing the sick and driving out evil spirits, contributed to his fame. However, Rabbi Israel ben Eliezer mixed his magic with beautiful lessons on life, emphasizing a joyful — even ecstatic — connection with God through dance, song, and celebration. These lessons and ideals survived to help form the basis of Hasidism (see Chapter 1).

At a time when deep mystical spirituality was practiced only by an elite group of people, he taught that an intimate connection with God was available to everyone (of course his definition of "everyone" was probably only men). He taught that prayer shouldn't be restricted to certain times of the day, but that people could be in constant prayer, and that all life — even business transactions — could be performed with devotional joy.

Henrietta Szold

Henrietta Szold (1860 to 1945) wasn't your typical Jewish scholar. The eldest of eight daughters born in Baltimore, Maryland, in the latter half of the nineteenth century, she used her knowledge of Torah and Talmud to write books and also to support a lifetime of social action, including an instrumental role in the creation of the Jewish state of Israel in 1948.

At a time when women were rarely given more than a nominal education, Szold's father, a renowned rabbi, believed in a proper education for his daughters. His eldest daughter was an eager and accomplished student, becoming fluent in Hebrew, German, and French, and later becoming the first woman given permission to study at New York's Jewish Theological Seminary (on the condition that she wouldn't try to become a rabbi).

But it wasn't until Szold took a trip to Palestine near the turn of the century — when she was over 40 — that she began the most important work of her life.

Seeing the terrible health conditions of both Jewish settlers and Arabs in Palestine, Szold proposed to a small group of New York women that they create a new organization that would send medical help to the area. The group took the name Hadassah (the Hebrew name of Esther, the heroine in the Biblical book of Esther), and later became the largest Jewish organization in the world, with over 400,000 members.

Szold, a devoted Jew and a staunch Zionist, ensured that the health needs of both Jews and Arabs were a priority to Hadassah. She firmly believed that the future of Zionism lay in Jews and Arabs working together. In 1942, six years before the creation of an Israeli state, Szold joined the Unity movement, which supported the forming of a binational Arab-Jewish state in Palestine.

Moreover, Szold helped organize a group (called Youth Aliyah) that would help over 10,000 Jewish children and teenagers escape certain death in Nazi Germany.

Abraham Isaac Kook

Listening to the acrimonious rhetoric between religious and secular Jews in Israel, you'd think it impossible to bridge the gap. However, in the early days of Zionism, before the founding of the State of Israel, Rabbi Abraham Isaac Kook (1865 to 1935) did just that, preaching compassion and tolerance among various Jewish groups. His overwhelming love of humanity was infectious, and remarkably, he was as at home in a traditional Orthodox setting as he was in the context of a secular *kibbutz* (see Appendix A).

Born in Latvia, Kook received a traditional education and became an Orthodox rabbi. At that time, most Orthodox Jews were opposed to the idea of a Jewish state. They felt, as some still do, that only God — not people — could or should create a Jewish state. Rabbi Kook differed, moved to Palestine in support of Zionism, and later became the country's first Chief Rabbi.

Rabbi Kook felt that simply following the strict religious laws without constantly returning to the spirit of the law was untenable. Recognizing the holiness in every person, no matter whether religiously observant or not, he wrote that there is "nothing totally secular in this world," and that all human attempts at holiness "are secular in comparison to the exalted light of holiness that emanates from the *Ain Sof* (the "Without End")."

Martin Buber

Do you remember a time when, perhaps just for a moment, you had a deep connection with another person? A connection in which you felt the whole of your soul make contact, along with an inexplicable sense that it was all profoundly meaningful? You may have later brushed the encounter off as irrational or even silly, but internationally renowned Jewish philosopher Martin Buber (1878 to 1965) would certainly not have called it silly. In fact, much of his philosophy and sense of religion was based on exactly this phenomenon.

Probably the greatest Jewish philosopher of the twentieth century, Buber wrote extensively on the theme of this kind of intense, intimate encounter, which he dubbed the "I/Thou" relationship. Through his poetic, though somewhat dense, writing, Buber linked elements of psychology, religion, and mysticism, pointing to a deeper underlying motif of finding meaning in life.

By 1930, Buber had worked extensively in academia, and he became a professor at the University of Frankfurt. Unfortunately, in 1933 the Nazi party, coming into power, forced German universities to fire all Jewish faculty members. In 1938, Buber finally emigrated to Palestine, becoming a professor of social philosophy at Hebrew University in Jerusalem, where he lived and worked until he died.

One of the most fascinating aspects of Buber's work was his focus on Hasidism (see Chapter 1) and on the rich tradition of Hasidic stories. In these marvelous stories, Buber discovered the I/Thou relationship unfolding between teacher and student and between person and God. The irony is that while Buber was responsible for making these stories known to so many people, he was nonobservant himself and actually felt strongly that the traditional rituals stifled spontaneity.

Ultimately, Buber's ideas — especially that meaning itself unfolds through deep and true relationships so that "all real living is meeting" — inspired an entire generation of Jews and non-Jews.

Abraham Joshua Heschel

The writings and actions of Abraham Joshua Heschel (1907 to 1972) remind people that spirituality transcends the boundaries of practice, religion, and race.

Heschel was born in Poland but studied in Germany until, three weeks before he completed his doctorate, the Nazis rose to power and deported all Polish natives. Finally, he was hired by Hebrew Union College in Cincinnati, the main rabbinical school of the Reform movement.

But Heschel was no Reform rabbi. He was an Orthodox Jew and was often ridiculed at the college for keeping kosher and following the other Jewish laws. He then moved to the Jewish Theological Seminary in New York, which was the primary rabbinical school for the Conservative movement, where he taught until his death some 30 years later. Sadly, he was the butt of many jokes there, too, because of his interest in spirituality and mysticism rather than strict rationalism and scholarship.

Although Heschel was in many ways a traditionalist, he focused on spirituality and meaning, which he felt were the most important aspects of Judaism. He understood that some Orthodox Jews followed the laws but had no connection with God, and that some Reform Jews were intensely spiritual while ignoring many of the laws. Like Martin Buber, Heschel believed that each person could have a profound relationship with God, and he taught that there was a give and take, an interaction in which both God and human are transformed. "Revelation," he wrote, "is nothing less than the sense of awe we feel when we become aware of being confronted by God in one of these moments of wonder and mystery."

Heschel's theology led him to a deep involvement in social activism. He was concerned with issues of human dignity and worth, a concern no doubt increased by his own experiences with Nazi atrocities. He was an early and vocal opponent of the Vietnam War, and was a good friend of Dr. Martin Luther King, Jr., who called Heschel "One of the truly great men of our day and age, a truly great prophet."

IN THIS CHAPTER

» **Jews, Jesus, and Islam**

» **Israel and the "Chosen People"**

» **The role of women in Judaism**

» **The sounds of Judaism: music and laughter**

Chapter **29**

Answers to Ten Common Questions about Judaism

O ur Jewish and non-Jewish friends alike have always asked us questions about being Jewish. Perhaps that's why we wrote this book in the first place. Over time, we've heard a lot of questions, but some arise more than others. Here are ten of our favorites. We span a lot of ground here, from feminism to the relationship between Judaism and Islam, from Jewish humor to Jewish law. So fasten your seatbelt — it'll be a wild ride!

Why Don't Jews Believe in Jesus?

Probably the greatest point of difference between Jews and Christians is their perception of Jesus. For Christians, Jesus is the *Christ* ("anointed one"). While many Jews believe Jesus to have been a great teacher, Jews don't believe he was the Messiah for several reasons.

Jews believed that the Messiah was supposed to herald the dawning of a new age of peace, compassion, and love. This clearly didn't happen (see Chapters 13 and 14). Also, Jews don't believe that any person (even the Messiah) can be a God, or even the only "son of God." The Jewish view is that all people are "sons" and "daughters" of God.

While Jews can't accept the Messiah-ship of Jesus, many Jewish teachers have acknowledged his great importance. Maimonides (see Chapter 28) said that Christianity was a way in which God brought important parts of Judaism's message to the rest of the world. Certainly similarities exist between Jesus's teachings and the rabbinic literature of his time. For example, his emphasis on "Thou shalt love the Eternal One your God . . ." and "Love your neighbor as yourself" are totally congruent with rabbinic teachings and are direct quotes from the Hebrew Bible. In this way, Jesus translated the monotheism of Judaism to a larger community.

By the way, neither the Hebrew nor Aramaic languages have a "j" sound, so this person was clearly not called "Jesus" during his lifetime. Rather, he was likely called *Yeshua*, a variant of the Hebrew name *Yehoshua* ("Joshua").

What Does It Mean to Be the "Chosen" People?

Perhaps no aspect of Jewish belief has caused as much consternation among non-Jews, or as much perplexity among Jews, as the notion that the Children of Israel are "the chosen people." Certainly, proclaiming yourself as "special" is one great way to create enemies — whether you're declaring to your sibling that you're the parents' favorite, or whether you're the spokesperson for a country announcing superiority over other nations.

However, being "chosen" is in no way meant to imply superiority over anyone else. Judaism doesn't teach that the "non-chosen" people can't go to heaven or anything like that. The Jewish people are "chosen" for the Path called Torah, just as all peoples are chosen for their own unique and special Paths. Reconstructionist Jews change the wording from "the chosen people" to "the choosing people," so that the choice comes from each person rather than from God.

"Chosenness" is both a blessing and a heavy responsibility for both ethical and spiritual action in the world. The prophet Amos translates God's word to the people of Israel: "You alone have I singled out from all the families of the earth. That is why I call you to account for all your iniquities."

Why Is Israel So Important to the Jews?

To understand the importance of Israel to the Jews, consider that traditional Jews have included a mention of the centrality of Jerusalem and the land of Israel in their prayer services every day for almost 2,000 years. During the many centuries when the Jewish people were denied their homeland, Israel provided a focus for prayer and identity.

Religious Jews point first to the Biblical stories in which God gives them the land. When Abraham first received his call to leave his father's house, God promised him the land of Canaan as an inheritance forever. Later, after the Hebrews were freed from slavery and had wandered for 40 years, God once again gave the land to them.

The Israelite kingdoms developed in this region 3,000 years ago, under Kings Saul, David, and Solomon. This is the land from which the people were again driven into exile in 586 BCE, only to return half a century later to rebuild the Temple and reconstruct their culture. This is the place that the Romans destroyed in 70 CE, driving the greater part of the Jewish community into exile.

When the remnants of the European Jewish community, released from the horrible tortures of the Nazi era, were refused entry into country after country, the establishment of the State of Israel guaranteed them a place where they could live. To this day, the Law of Return guarantees all Jews citizenship in Israel should they choose to live there.

Why Are So Many Doctors, Lawyers, and Entertainers Jewish?

A surprising number of doctors, lawyers, and celebrities are Jewish, given that Jews make up less than 2 percent of the American population and less than a quarter of 1 percent of the world's population! So why have over 20 percent of Nobel prizes been awarded to Jews or people of Jewish descent? Here are just a few ideas that help explain the disparity:

>> The Jews have long been called "the People of the Book," not just because the Bible is central to the religion, but because study of texts and education in general are among the most important values passed from generation to generation. So many Jews enter professions where study is central.

>> Jews have a long tradition of studying law or medicine. For over 1,000 years medicine has been considered a highly noble profession for a Jew. Law, medicine, and science can make the world a better and more just place, which is as important in Judaism as spiritual study.

>> Antisemitic policies over the centuries have forced Jews to live in urban centers and become good at jobs that can be done there (finance, medicine, law, retail, entertainment, and so on). In the 19th and 20th centuries, American urban areas like New York, Philadelphia, Cleveland, Boston, San Francisco, Los Angeles, and Chicago — areas that had a much higher percentage of Jews than the rest of the country — became increasingly influential. So, Jews were already living in the midst of the most powerful media centers and best universities in the world.

>> Many Jews report a general sense that they have to succeed more than most people, though few can really explain why. Some say they feel the burden to prove that Jews really are "just as good" as everyone else.

>> Some fields were virtually created by Jews. For example, all the major Hollywood studios — Universal, MGM, 20th Century Fox, and so on — were started by Jewish immigrants from Eastern Europe.

What Is the Role of Women in Judaism?

Traditionally, women have been exempt from performing any time-based positive *mitzvot* (commandments like going to services at specific times) because women were in charge of the home and the children. Unfortunately, the word "exemption" has become a code word for "prohibited" in most Orthodox communities.

For the vast majority of Jewish history, all rabbis (and priests before them) were male; only men counted when gathering a *minyan* (a quorum; see Chapter 4 for details); if women were allowed in a synagogue at all, they had to be behind a barrier called a *mekhitzah*; women weren't allowed to read the Torah (at least, not in public) or study the Talmud; they wouldn't recite the daily kaddish for a dead parent; they weren't allowed to wear prayer shawls or tefillin (see Chapter 4); and so on.

Most Orthodox Jews see women as equal in importance to men and deeply respect their contributions to Judaism. However, traditional Judaism believes that men and women have different roles to play. As in many other conservative religions, traditional Judaism sees women as the key to raising children properly and keeping the spirit of the home.

In the early 1970s, women began to challenge and change their traditional roles. The Reform movement ordained the first woman rabbi, Sally Priesand, in 1972. Now hundreds of women are rabbis in Reform, Reconstructionist, Renewal, and Conservative synagogues. As of this writing, several women have been ordained by Orthodox rabbis, but they have not yet received acceptance by the wider Orthodox community.

Most non-Orthodox synagogues have done away with the mekhitzah and count women in a minyan. Many congregations have changed their Hebrew translations to be more gender-neutral and less sexist, and some have even altered the Hebrew liturgy itself to make it more egalitarian. Some women who want a more traditional observance have created smaller community groups (independent *minyanim*) or have joined Jewish Renewal congregations that offer women a chance to worship more traditionally but with equality.

What Is "Jewish Humor"?

By some reports, as many as 80 percent of popular American comedians in the past 60 years have been Jewish, including Milton Berle, Mel Brooks, Lenny Bruce, Sacha Baron Cohen, George Burns, John Stewart, Billy Crystal, Rodney Dangerfield, Groucho Marx (and his brothers), Sarah Silverman, Jackie Mason, Ben Stiller, Adam Sandler, Seth Rogen, Jerry Seinfeld, the Three Stooges, and Henny Youngman.

Jews have a long history of making humor a part of their lives. Some insist that it's their sense of humor that enabled the Jews to survive for so long. Others even say (only half-jokingly) that a person's sense of humor is itself the determining factor in whether or not someone is Jewish.

To say that Jews have a peculiar sense of humor would be wrong — Jewish humor clearly strikes a chord with an enormous number of non-Jews. Yet, there does appear to be something called "Jewish humor," which is different than other humor, though perhaps subtly so.

Self-examination: Try it at home!

A clear and lucid definition is a marvelous thing, but unfortunately Jewish humor defies clear and lucid definition. Scholars have tried for years to pin down exactly what Jewish humor is and is not, but they've succeeded primarily in giving themselves (and their readers) headaches. Nonetheless, here are a few fundamental notions of Jewish humor.

Self-critical

While Jewish humor is usually self-critical and often self-deprecating, it's almost always told in a spirit of fun and even celebration.

> A German, a Frenchman, and a Jew are walking through the desert. The Frenchman says, "I'm tired, I'm thirsty, I must have a glass of wine." The German says, "I'm tired, I'm thirsty, I must have a glass of beer." The Jew says, "I'm tired, I'm thirsty, I must have diabetes."

Anxious

Jewish jokes often focus on areas in Jewish life where there is anxiety: assimilation, antisemitism, financial success, religious dogma, education, and so on. Jewish humor is typically pessimistic and resigned about the immediate future but optimistic about the longer run. The result is an anxious humor, or what some call "distressed optimism."

> Two Jews are walking down an alleyway at night when they see two tough-looking guys. "Let's run," says one of the Jews, "There are two of them, and we're alone."

> Typical Jewish text message: "Start Worrying. Details to follow."

Rarely cruel

While Jewish humor may not always be kind, it's rarely cruel. Jews, so long the underdog themselves, avoid attacking the weak or the infirm. Jews won't stop themselves from taking a stab at their colleagues or those in power, however.

> Yiddish curse: May your enemies get cramps in their legs when they dance on your grave.

Democratic

Jews often side with the "common man," and tend not to trust anyone who displays too much power or appears too pretentious. Jewish humor, then, is often anti-authoritarian and feels free to mock anyone — even God.

> A man goes to a tailor to have some pants custom made. After a week, the pants aren't ready. After two weeks, they're not ready. After six weeks they're finally done and to the man's pleasant surprise, they fit perfectly. Nonetheless, he teases the tailor, saying "It only took God six days to make the world, and it took you six weeks to make just one pair of pants!" "Ah," replied the tailor, "but look at these pants, and look at the state of the world!"

Instructive

Jewish humor almost always exposes something about Jews or Jewish sensibilities. The point of many Jewish jokes isn't to make someone laugh but, as authors William Novak and Moshe Waldoks have noted, to provoke "a bitter nod or a commiserating sigh of recognition."

Mrs. Levy finds Mr. Levy sitting in the parlor, naked, wearing only his fedora.

"So, nu? Why are you sitting here naked?" she asks.

" 'tsall right, Mama, nobody ever comes to visit."

"So why the hat?"

"Well, maybe someone will come."

While there is much scientific and religious controversy over when, exactly, the moment of life begins, the Jewish tradition is clear: The fetus isn't considered viable until after it graduates from medical school.

Characters

Many Jewish jokes aren't about Jews in general, but rather about certain types of Jewish characters. For years, the *schnorrer* ("beggar") and the *schlemiel* (see Appendix A) were popular personalities in Jewish humor. In the 1980s a rash of "Jewish American Prince/Princess" jokes focused on those Jews who had become caught up in material possessions. Jewish mothers (once called *yiddishe mamas*) are a constant staple of Jewish humor. Of course, stereotypes can be dangerous and are often used to pigeonhole people who don't deserve it.

What's the difference between a Pit Bull Terrier and a Jewish mother? Answer: Eventually the Pit Bull lets go.

Jewish mothers are so notoriously picky at restaurants that the story is told of one waiter who asks, "Is *anything* all right?"

Resigned

Jewish humor recognizes that sadness and happiness always come hand in hand, like the intertwining double helix of DNA. As author Harry Golden notes, "At the core of Jewish humor is the belief that God made it hard to be a Jew for His own reasons." These jokes often mirror both a Jew's resignation to his or her lot in life and the deep belief that life can be better. As the saying goes, "God gave us shoulders, and God gave us burdens."

> Mr. Fischer enters the offices of the burial society to inquire about funeral arrangements for his wife.
>
> "Your wife?" asks the secretary. "But didn't we bury her last year?"
>
> Sighing, Fischer notes, "That was my first wife. I'm talking about my second wife."
>
> "Oh, I didn't know you remarried. Mazel tov!"

Dress British, think Yiddish

Turning tears to laughter is often an essential element of Jewish humor, and has long been the basis of stories by Yiddish writers such as Isaac Bashevis Singer, Sholom Aleichem, and I.L. Peretz. Somehow being clever and funny can be more powerful than the oppressor's thumb. As Leo Rosten once wrote, "Humor . . . serves the afflicted as compensation for suffering, a token victory of brain over fear."

The twentieth century brought Jewish humor to the masses, in part because Hollywood was invented by Jews from the old country who were raised in the midst of Yiddish theatre and vaudeville. Jewish humor has so impacted American (and world) comedy — whether it be movies, standup comedy, radio, or television — that it has become difficult to tell what is Jewish and what is not anymore.

What Role Does Music Play in Jewish Culture?

Asking about "Jewish music" is like asking about "American music" or "English music" — it's just too big a category. That said, when many non-Jews talk about "Jewish music" in America, they're often talking about klezmer music, the music brought over from Central and Eastern Europe and played on instruments like accordion, violin, and clarinet. Klezmer music can get you up and dancing in no time, or it can break your heart with sadness. As Ari Davidow notes at his excellent site klezmershack.com, "It's Balkans and blues, ancient Jewish culture and prayer and history, spirit and jazz all mixed together."

Klezmer music was rediscovered in the folk music revival of the 1970s, and it quickly became a staple of Jewish weddings, bar/bat mitzvah parties, and other social events. More recently, klezmer groups such as the Ellis Island Band and the Klezmatics have become highly popular.

When Jews talk about Jewish music, they are often thinking of folk songs from summer camp, Israeli songs, or traditional liturgical melodies. Often, these categories blend in the compositions of popular American Jewish songwriters like Debbie Friedman and Shefa Gold.

Contemporary Jewish liturgical music has been greatly influenced by people like Shlomo Carlebach, David Zeller, the late Lubavitcher Rebbe, and Zalman Shachter-Shalomi — who revitalized the use of song and *niggun* (wordless melodies that use syllables like "dai, dai, dai; bai lai, lai, bai," and so on). Curiously, some Jews today complain when synagogues use "nontraditional" music — even though what they consider "traditional" was likely written in the 1930s or 1940s and was radical for its day.

Because Jews tend to incorporate aspects of their cultural environment, the prayers and songs of Arab or North African Jews have distinctly "oriental" melodies, and the Ashkenazi Jews use Eastern European-sounding melodies.

Who's In Charge of Judaism?

Judaism has no Pope, no patriarch, and no committee to hand down decisions through an accepted hierarchy to all Jews. And yet, Judaism does have a very large body of rules and laws, and they're not all thousands of years old or from the Torah (see Chapter 3). Who makes these rules?

Traditional Jews say that the answer to every question is hidden in the Torah, but study and scholarship is required to extract it. With that in mind, Jewish law is based almost entirely on more than 2,000 years of rabbinical interpretations and re-interpretations of Torah, beginning with the many arguments posed in the Talmud (see Chapter 3). The sixteenth-century *Shulkhan Arukh* ("The Arranged Table") distilled these arguments into legal decisions, and that book is still the basis for authoritative judgments.

Today, individual rabbis make religious decisions for their communities based on all these texts and their own interpretations. Of course, questions still arise, and since the time of the Babylonian Talmud, there's been a tradition of a *bet din* ("house of judgment"), a panel of three qualified rabbis who decide on matters of civil and religious law within each Jewish community. These laws have always evolved slowly and organically, with decisions making their way around the international Jewish community and either being accepted in other locales or not. For example, while Rabbi Gershom's eleventh-century ban on polygamy was widely accepted, Sephardic Jews ignored it, and some continued marrying multiple wives as late as 1948.

You may have heard that "chief rabbis" sometimes announce legal decisions, but it's still up to the community to agree or not. The chief rabbis may serve as spokespersons for their own communities, but no individual is a spokesperson for all Jewry. Ultimately, Judaism teaches that each person is responsible for his or her own acts and beliefs.

In Hasidic communities, the authority is vested in the *rebbe*, the rabbinical leader who carries authority for that particular community. Remember that there are many Orthodox communities, and many rebbes, and — to put it politely — they don't always agree with each other's policies. It's not uncommon for an Orthodox Jew to decide to switch from one rabbi to another saying, "I like his policy on such-and-such better." The other major Jewish movements have rabbinical organizations through which decisions are often made.

Can You Convert to Judaism?

Jews have a very long history of welcoming converts. The Book of Ruth says that King David himself was a descendent of a woman (Ruth) who chose to join the Jewish people. Today, over 200,000 Jews in America are Jews by choice.

REMEMBER

If you're Jewish and someone you know is thinking of converting or has converted, the best thing you can do is be loving, open, and welcoming. Remember that someone who has converted is no more or no less Jewish than anyone else. Also, note that some people find the term "convert" offensive and prefer "Jew by Choice."

If you're thinking of converting, first read about Judaism, and also experience it by going to synagogues and Jewish lectures and beginning some practices (like lighting Shabbat candles; see Chapter 18). Also, check out books and websites about conversion (like www.convert.org). Don't go hog wild and try to do and learn everything at once; that's a surefire way to burn out.

Next, find a rabbi who will teach and sponsor you. When looking for a rabbi, ask the following questions:

>> **What denomination is the rabbi?** Orthodox Jews will only accept somebody who was converted by an Orthodox rabbi. But unless you're planning to emigrate to Israel or marry an Orthodox person, this might not be an issue. Reform, Reconstructionist, and some Conservative Jews tend to accept each other's converts (See Chapter 1 for details on Jewish denominations.)

>> **Do you feel comfortable with this rabbi?** Rabbis are like therapists or managers — even a really good one might rub you the wrong way, so it's worth looking around. Some traditional rabbis test the resolve of potential converts by turning them away three times, so don't be discouraged.

Usually, people need to study for a year or so (many synagogues have conversion classes), though it may take longer for an Orthodox conversion. Often, you have to learn basic Hebrew, Jewish history, the prayer service, and the religious practices. This book isn't a study guide for conversion, but if you know everything in this book, plus learn some Hebrew, you're way ahead of the game.

Finally, when the rabbi decides that you're ready for conversion, you appear before a *bet din*, a religious court usually comprised of three rabbis. Although you may be nervous, remember that the rabbis aren't trying to trick you, and you're not being graded. The bet din simply needs to assess your sincerity, that you're converting of your own free will and that you studied well. Often, rabbis ask a candidate to recite an oath of allegiance to the Jewish people, too.

Once the bet din accepts your conversion, you go to the *mikveh* (ritual bath; see Chapter 4) for an immersion (both men and women do this, though many Reform Jews omit it). If you're a man, your penis needs to be circumcised by a mohel (if you're already circumcised, you still have to give a drop of blood as a symbolic circumcision; see Chapter 7). Some rabbis will conduct a conversion ritual without requiring circumcision.

What's the Relationship Between Judaism and Islam?

Judaism and Islam are more alike than perhaps any other two religions. Islam is based on the teachings of Muhammad, a seventh-century Arab businessman who had learned a great deal about monotheism from his Jewish and Christian associates. The Quran, the holy book of Islam, includes many stories of Abraham, the flood, Moses, the virgin birth of Jesus, and so on. However, Muslims believe that Muhammad was the final prophet, the one who corrected the "errors in transmission" that crept into the Jewish and Christian texts. Although Jews don't believe this final point, the two religions do have a surprising number of similarities:

>> Jews and Muslims (and Christians, for that matter) all believe in the same One God (the Arabic word for God is *Allah*) and strictly condemn worshiping idols.

>> Both Islamic and Jewish traditions trace back to Abraham: Jews through his son Isaac, and Muslims through his son Ishmael. Muslims claim Abraham was the first Muslim (insofar as he was the first person to submit to the will of the One God). Remember that Arabs and Jews are both considered Semites (descendents of Shem, the son of Noah).

>> Where Christianity is based primarily in faith or belief, both Judaism and Islam are based on comprehensive legal systems that cover every aspect of life, including eating, drinking, ethics, civil law, criminal law, family law, purity, and so on. In Judaism, this set of laws is called *halakhah*, in Islam it's *shariah*, both of which mean "a path that is walked." Similarly, these laws are based on legal decisions and interpretations of scholars (where a rabbi makes interpretations in Judaism, the Ulama or Ayatollah makes them in Islam), and these interpretations are often the cause of great arguments.

>> Many of the laws are similar, including those regulating marriage and divorce, prayers, hygiene, and purity of food. The Islamic version of kosher food is called *hallal*, and though they're not exactly the same, they do have similarities.

Basically, when it comes right down to it, there is very little that is directly antagonistic between the two religions, other than whether Muhammad was a true prophet of God. And for most of the past 1,400 years, the relationship between Muslims and Jews has been relatively good. Although Jews still weren't accorded equal status under Muslim rule, Islam tended to treat them better than Christianity did. Certainly, while Palestine was under Turkish and British rule, Jewish people lived side by side with Muslim neighbors in peace and, usually, goodwill. Still, Muslims, like Christians, tended to resent the fact that the Jews didn't fully agree with them.

Perhaps these two religions are like two siblings in the same family who are so similar that they forever squabble and compete for the attention and love of a parent. Between Ishmael and Isaac, who did Abraham love more? Who did God love more? We are saddened by the fact that monotheism has, in some regards, turned into a game of "There's only one God and it's *my* God" rather than "We're all on our own paths to the One God."

Appendixes

When you need information fast, you can turn here to
get it, from the definitions of important words to the
proper blessing for seeing a rainbow.

Appendix A

Oy Vey! and Other Words You Should Know

In this appendix, we focus on words that you might hear from folks talking or writing about Judaism — words which you might want to know in order to carry on your side of the conversation.

A Primer of Basic Words

REMEMBER

When you're reading through the following list of words, remember that the "ch" sound in Hebrew is *not* the "choo-choo" sound (see the Introduction). When you see "ch" in a Hebrew word, you should always read it as a "kh" sound made in the back of the throat, as though you were clearing your throat, or trying to sound Scottish or German. We usually use "kh," but some words are so commonly spelled with a "ch" that we leave them as is.

Bagels. After vacations, Ted often brought back bagels from Cleveland to his small state college in Ohio, and many of his non-Jewish friends would gape, never having seen such a food before. How times have changed! Over the past 20 years, ring-shaped, doughy bagels have transformed from a Jewish delicacy into part of mainline American culture. Bagels are traditionally served with a *schmeer* of cream cheese (see "Yiddish, Yinglish, Oy!" later in this appendix), red onions, and a pile of smoked salmon.

Chabad (pronounced kha-*bahd*). Several sects grew out of the original Hasidic movement founded by the Ba'al Shem Tov (see Chapter 28) in the late 18th century, but the one you're most likely to run into is the Chabad Lubavitchers. The Chabad movement is Ultra-Orthodox and tends to be intellectually focused; the movement has had a major presence on college campuses for many years.

Ellis Island. Most Jews in America today had ancestors who came from Europe in the late 19th and early 20th centuries, and almost all these brave immigrants traveled into New York Harbor (past the Statue of Liberty) and were processed by government officials on Ellis Island. Perhaps the most significant aspect of Ellis Island is that this is where many Jews were given new family names. Unable to spell or understand the strange-sounding names they heard, officials often assigned names that sounded right to them.

Golem. Form some mud into a human shape, say the right incantations, and you may find yourself with a *golem* on your hands: a "living" creature with no soul. The idea of a golem was first discussed in the Talmud (which says that Adam was a golem before receiving his soul), but the most famous of these imaginary creatures is the 17th-century Golem of Prague, who became the superhuman protector of the Jews, bringing anti-Semitic criminals to justice.

Hatikvah. Written as a poem in the late nineteenth century by Naftali Hertz Imber, *Hatikvah* ("The Hope") was set to music and sung by many of the early Zionists. In 1948, *Hatikvah* was adopted as the Israeli national anthem.

Kibbutz. A *kibbutz* (don't confuse this with the Yiddish *kibbitz*, which we discuss later in this appendix) is a collective farm supporting a democratic and socialist ideal of shared responsibility and benefit from the land. Immigrant Jews founded the first kibbutz in Palestine in 1910, and there are now over 200 *kibbutzim* (the plural form of the word) in Israel. Even though only 5 percent of Israelis live on a kibbutz, the kibbutz movement's ideals and attitudes have been extremely influential in Israeli culture and politics.

Ladino. Where the Ashkenazim of Eastern Europe mixed and matched languages to form Yiddish (which we talk about later in this appendix), the Sephardim of Spain and the Mediterranean countries built a completely different language, called *Ladino*, based on Spanish and Hebrew, with some Turkish, Greek, French, Italian, and Portuguese mixed in. Here are two Ladino phrases you can use to impress people: *Dos Judiyos, tres kehilot* ("Two Jews, three opinions") and *Buen moed* ("Good holiday").

Magen David. The six-pointed star that appears on the Israeli flag is called the Magen David, and it has become a symbol of everything Jewish. Often translated as "Star of David," Magen David really means the "Shield of David." There's actually no connection between the star and King David at all, and it wasn't until the seventeenth century that the Magen David was linked specifically to Judaism. In the late nineteenth century, the star became the official symbol of the Zionist movement. In the twentieth century, the Magen David became a symbol of humiliation as Jews were forced to wear a "yellow star" to identify themselves as Jews. The star is also a symbol of comfort, in the form of the Magen David Edom (the Jewish version of the Red Cross).

Pilpul. If you really believe that the Torah and the Talmud are true word-for-word revelations from God, then each detail deserves extraordinary scrutiny. *Pilpul* is a form of study in which the minute details of the oral and written texts are deconstructed and debated. Note that *pilpul* means "pepper," and it's meant to add spice to Talmudic discussions.

Righteous Gentiles. While thousands, and perhaps millions, of non-Jews were either active in the killing of Jews during the Holocaust or passively let it happen, there were some who, during the dark days of the Nazi era, risked their own safety to support, shelter, and protect Jewish members of their communities. These people are called *righteous gentiles,* a phrase taken from the Talmud: *Chasidei Ummot ha-Olam* ("Righteous ones of the nations of the world"), a term of honor and respect. Perhaps the two most famous examples are Oscar Schindler, whose story was told in Steven Speilberg's film *Schindler's List,* and Raoul Wallenberg, a Swedish diplomat stationed in Budapest who is credited with saving as many as 100,000 Jews by giving them Swedish citizenship. Denmark is sometimes considered a "nation of righteous gentiles" because of its peoples' heroic efforts to save the Danish Jews during World War II by sending them to Sweden, a neutral country that accepted many thousands of Jews.

Shalom aleikhem. If someone says *shalom aleikhem* to you as you walk down the street, the appropriate response is *aleikhem shalom.* Both phrases are generally translated as "peace to you," but *shalom* means something deeper than just "peace." *Shalom* comes from a root which means "to make whole," so the wish is for "peace" in the sense of wholeness and completeness.

Shammos. The word *shammos* is a Yiddish pronunciation of the Hebrew word *shammash,* which literally means a servant, an attendant, or a waiter. *Shammos* generally refers to either the "helper" candle in the Chanukkah menorah (see Chapter 22) or the caretaker of a synagogue.

Six-Day War. In May of 1967, the governments of Egypt, Syria, Iraq, and Jordan each announced that they intended to attack Israel. After Egypt closed the Strait of Tiran (in the Red Sea) to all ships carrying strategic materials to the Jewish state, and the Arabs began to ready their armies, the Israeli government made a decision: On June 5th, Israel launched a preemptive strike and in a single day destroyed the majority of both the Egyptian and Syrian air force. After six days of fighting,

Israel dealt a humiliating defeat to the Arabs and captured the Sinai peninsula from Egypt, the Golan Heights from Syria, and the West Bank (including East Jerusalem) from Jordan.

Tikkun. *Tikkun* literally means improvement, repair, or correction. However, the term is at the core of an important Jewish teaching: that the greater purpose of Jewish identity and observance has to do with the healing of both our planet and ourselves. The phrase *tikkun olam* is sometimes translated as the "healing of the world," and refers to world peace, global security, social justice, or — in the more mystical tradition — the completion of all of God's creation.

Western Wall. The most sacred site in Judaism isn't a synagogue or the home of some important relic, but rather an enormous stone wall in Jerusalem that originally had no religious purpose. The Western Wall (in Hebrew, *Kotel ha-Ma'aravi*) is the only structure still standing from the Temple Mount, which was completely destroyed by the Romans in 70 CE (see Chapter 13. Even though this was only a section of an outer retaining wall, so many people cry and pray fervently here that it's also known as the "Wailing Wall." If you visit the Western Wall, you will see people praying, reading from the Torah (this is a popular place for boys to have their Bar Mitzvah ceremony; see Chapter 8), and stuffing written prayers into cracks in the wall.

Yad Vashem. Yad Vashem is Israel's Holocaust memorial. The dignity and holiness of the memorial helps new generations to remember atrocities beyond words and often beyond understanding. Recent redesign and an online database of those killed in the Shoah provide even greater access to the realities of that terrible period. The memorial strives to accurately present what occurred hoping that this information will inhibit such a tragedy in the future.

Yeshivah. A *yeshivah* (literally, a place for "sitting") is a general term for a school for Jewish study, but the term refers more particularly to traditional institutions for higher education. The focus of most *yeshivahot* is Torah and Talmud study, though some — including the progressive Yeshivah University in New York City — encourage secular studies as well. A Kollel is traditionally a *yeshivah* for older, married students, sort of like a graduate school for Jewish study.

Yom Kippur War. On Yom Kippur (see Chapter 20), 1973, when the vast majority of Israeli soldiers were at home or in synagogue, Egypt and Syria launched a massive surprise attack on Israel, beginning what is now known as the Yom Kippur War. Syria invaded the Golan Heights, and over 70,000 Egyptian troops crossed the Suez Canal into the Sinai, where they met fewer than 500 Israeli soldiers. However, after three weeks of fighting, Israel won the war and drove both countries out.

Yom Tov. Each Jewish holiday is called a *Yom tov* (Hebrew for "good day"). This phrase got shortened in Yiddish to *yontif*, and people commonly greet each other on holidays with, "Güt yontif," which actually means "good good day."

Zion. Zion (from the Hebrew *tzion*) is another name for Israel, though it also refers to Jerusalem and even the whole of the Jewish people. A Zionist is someone who believes in the necessity of a Jewish state of Israel.

Yiddish, Yinglish, Oy!

Yiddish has deep roots. Its history reaches back to Germany in the Middle Ages, though it really came into its own around the fifteenth century. For most of the past 500 years, it was common for Jews in Eastern Europe to read Hebrew during religious teaching or prayer; speak Polish, German, or Russian to their non-Jewish neighbors; and to speak Yiddish to each other.

Yiddish is a mongrel language, a mixture of Hebrew, German, Polish, Slavic, and Russian. To the untrained ear, Yiddish sounds a lot like German.

We don't speak Yiddish fluently, but like many Jews today, we grew up hearing our parents and grandparents sprinkle Yiddish words into their English sentences. Yiddish simply captures a tone that is hard to find in English alone.

Many people think that Yiddish is a dying language. But the irony is that Yiddish, which survived for hundreds of years by borrowing words from other languages, is now thriving in part by being incorporated into English. An increasing number of universities are now teaching Yiddish — and the first ever Japanese-Yiddish dictionary was recently published.

The following is a list of Yiddish words that are increasingly common, even in English conversations. If your interest is sparked, get a copy of Leo Rosten's *The Joys of Yiddish*, a book we consider essential for every Jewish household.

REMEMBER

Where Hebrew doesn't have a "ch" sound (like the word "chewy") and instead uses a guttural "kh" sound (see the Introduction), Yiddish uses both sounds. However, in the following list, you can assume the Hebrew pronunciation unless we note otherwise.

Alter kahker. Yiddish has little tolerance for fancy gentility. *Alter kahker* literally means an old pooper (though "pooper" is still not brash enough). The term refers to any old man who just sits around all day and is meekly ineffectual. We don't recommend calling someone an *alter kahker* to his face.

Apikorus. Ancient Greek culture was seductive to many Jews around the Eastern Mediterranean, many of whom dropped their Jewish ways and assimilated. The term *apikorus* (from the Greek philosopher Epicurus) developed in Talmudic times to describe a non-observant Jew. The term was later generalized to mean any skeptic or non-believer.

Baleboosteh. While any woman who keeps house or runs a business can be considered a *baleboosteh* (pronounced "bah-leh-*boo*-stah"), the term is usually reserved for a woman who excels in organization, cleanliness, and homemaking. While some might use the term to mean "a bossy woman," it's usually said with high praise. The male counterpart is called a *balaboss*.

Boychik. Pronounced "*boy*-chick," this word means almost exactly what it sounds like: a young boy. Of course, a grandmother might call her grandson her *boychik* even if he's 40 years old.

Bubeleh. While *bubeleh* (pronounced "*boo*-balah") really means "little grandmother," it is used in place of almost any endearment. Mothers call their children (both male and female) *bubeleh*, and adults call each other *bubeleh*. You'll also hear a shortened version, *bubbe* (pronounced "*booh*-bee"), often between friends.

Bubkes. While *bubkes* (pronounced "*bub*-kiss") stems from the Russian word for "beans," it means something trivial or of no value. Leo Rosten writes, "*Bubkes* must be uttered with either scorn, sarcasm, indignation, or contempt. The expletive takes over where 'Nonsense!' 'Baloney!' or 'Bushwa!' stop for a rest." What are they paying you? *Bubkes!*

Chazzer. Anyone cheap, slovenly, vulgar, or greedy is a *chazzer* (pronounced "*khazzer*"), but usually the word describes someone who eats a lot. Instead of calling someone a "pig" you could call them a *chazzer* (and, in fact, *chazzer* is the Hebrew word for pig). While you might use *chazzer* affectionately to a little child, we think it sounds best when accompanied by scowling. One of David's favorite Yiddish words is a close relative: *chazzerai*, meaning junky items or trashy stuff. David's office is filled with *chazzerai* and *tchotchkes* (see the listing later in this list). *Chazzerai* can also mean junk food; the kind of food a *chazzer* would *fress* (also later in the list).

Chutzpah. It's easy to understand why *chutzpah* (pronounced "*khutzpah*") would be so commonly used, even by non-Jews: There just isn't another word (at least in English) that so well captures a sense of brazen arrogance, guts, presumption, or gall. It's just gall to telephone the president of a large company and ask her to lunch in order to get a job in the mail room. It's *chutzpah* to actually get her to take *you* to lunch, where you talk yourself into a title like Vice President of Mail Operations.

Dreck. We grew up at a time when it was unfashionable (to say the least) to use four-letter words in front of our parents, so when it came time to describe something trashy or worthless, we relied on the Yiddish word *dreck*. Quite literally meaning "excrement," *dreck* might describe the excruciating movie you saw last week, the food at that new restaurant, or the opinions of certain well-known radio talk show hosts. *Dreck* is a great word, but don't overuse it; like a fine bottle of wine, it should be reserved for just the right time.

Fress. We'll use psychic powers to look into your past: If you're Jewish, your grandmother thought you didn't eat enough, and when you sat down to eat, she didn't tell you to eat, she said *fress*, meaning eat *a lot*. Of course, if you grabbed a bite out of the refrigerator and ate it quickly on the way out the door, she complained just as loudly, "Slow down, already! Don't *fress*." It's a subtle difference that perhaps only a grandmother could understand. Also note that someone who eats a lot, or who eats quickly, is a *fresser*, as in "Oy, look at that guy at the table over there; is he ever a *fresser!*"

Gay gezuntaheit. If only Lawrence Welk had ended his classic television show, amid bubbles, with "Goodnight, *auf wedersein, au reviour, gay gezuntaheit!*" Meaning "go with health," (and pronounced "gay geh-*zoon*-tah-*hite*") this Yiddish phrase is said when parting from someone you like.

Goy. A *goy* is any non-Jew (plural: *goyim*). Like *gaijin* in Japanese, *goy* simply means someone from another nation. However, also like *gaijin*, it has unfortunately taken on a somewhat negative undertone. The result is that it's hard to know if someone is saying the word in a derogatory fashion or not. We both grew up saying *goy*, and we like to think we weren't being nasty about it. However, we now try to use "non-Jew" because it's less ambiguous and loaded a word.

Hokn a cheinik. When confronted with someone babbling about something (you gave up listening five minutes ago), you can say, "Please, stop *hokn a cheinik*" (Yiddish has the more familiar "ch" sound, so here the "ch" is anglicized, as in "China": "hok'n a *chai*-nik"). Although *cheinik* refers to any yammering or incessant talking, the phrase more or less literally means, "Stop banging on the teapot."

Kenahora. Don't you feel silly when you say "knock on wood" (glancing around for the nearest piece of wood)? And yet superstition has such a firm grip on the human mind that you almost feel more uncomfortable *not* saying it after uttering some positive statement. Fortunately, you can use the phrase *kenahora* instead (meaning "no evil eye," a slurring of three Yiddish words: kein (no), ayin (eye), hara (evil); maybe if you sound ethnic, no one will notice that you're superstitious). This is pronounced in various ways: "ken ah-*hor*-ah" or "kine ah-*hor*-ah." "My son is graduating in June, *kenahora*." "I haven't had a cold all year, *kenahora*." "You should live, *kenahora*, to see that day."

Kibbitz. Here's another Yiddish word that has worked its way into the English language: To *kibbitz* means to butt in, to give advice, or to comment on, especially when it's none of your business. For example, it's almost impossible for a Jewish chess player to refrain from *kibbitzing* while watching two other people playing. The person doing the *kibbitzing* — whether from across the room or from the back seat of the car — is a *kibbitzer*. Note that if you're asked to make suggestions, you're an adviser, not a *kibbitzer*.

Kishkes. On the one hand, *kishkes* is a culinary delicacy involving stuffing a cow's intestines with vegetables, spices, and chicken fat. (Look, we didn't say we eat this stuff; just that it exists.) On the other hand, *kishkes* is another word for "guts," as in the stuff in your abdominal cavity. When your airplane or an elevator suddenly drops slightly, you can feel it in your *kishkes*. An evangelical minister (with a sense of humor) might ask in a sermon, "Can you feel that spirit right down in your *kishkes*?"

Kvell. When your child comes back with a straight-A report card, you can't help but *kvell*. When your son marries a doctor, you *kvell*. *Kvelling* is filling with pride and pleasure, to the point where you've got to tell someone. When someone gives you *nakhes* (see later in this list), you *kvell*. *Kvelling* is a parent's favorite pastime.

Kvetch. One of the best Yiddish words ever invented, *kvetch* means to complain or gripe. (It can also refer to the person who is *kvetching*, as in "He's such a *kvetch*.") Making a clear statement about a complaint you might have is not *kvetching*; whining about it, kicking clods of dirt, or writing 15 e-mails to the editor is *kvetching*. You can procrastinate for at least half a day by *kvetching*, and then you can *kvetch* about the time you've wasted.

L'chayim. When raising a glass to make a toast, Americans say "Cheers," Germans say "Prost," the Japanese say "Campai," and someone (we can't figure out who) says "Here's mud in your eye." The Jews say *L'chayim*, literally "to life."

Lokh in kop. Sometimes Yiddish phrases get translated into English before becoming part of the everyday language. A good example is *lokh in kop*, meaning "a hole in the head." You need a tax audit like a *lokh in kop*. Try this phrase out a few times; for some reason we find it's more satisfying to say than the English version.

Makhetunim. Your spouse's family is *makhetunim* (pronounced "makh-eh-tu-num"), and it always seems that your *makhetunim* is twice as big as your own family. Some people also use the word referring to their children's in-laws. For example, if your son is married, your daughter-in-law's family are your *makhetunim*.

Maven. Some people don't even know that the word *maven* — meaning a connoisseur or an expert — is Yiddish; it has simply become part of English common usage. *Maven* (*may*-ven) implies more than just great knowledge, however. Someone who works on cars is a mechanic; a *maven* not only knows cars inside and out, but can tell you what's wrong with your car by just listening to your engine.

Mazel tov. Every major step along life's path, like a graduation or wedding, is punctuated by the words *mazel tov*. While this literally means "good planet," it's used more like "good luck" or "congratulations." Something good happened to you today? *Mazel tov!* Some people mistakenly use *l'chayim* when they mean *mazel tov*; but we know you wouldn't do that.

Mensch. While the Germans use *mensch* to refer to any human being, Yiddish ascribes much more meaning to the word. To be a called a *mensch* (or better yet, a "real *mensch*") is perhaps the greatest compliment and sign of respect. A *mensch* implies more than just a successful person; it implies that someone is morally and ethically upright, someone of noble character. Being rich or beautiful or even popular doesn't make you a *mensch*. It's something richer than money. It doesn't have to be grand, though: Someone who finds a wallet and returns it intact to the owner is a *mensch*.

Meshuggeh. *Meshuggeh* (pronounced "meh-*shug*-ah") means "crazy," but it might mean "foolish," "absurd," or even truly "mentally ill," depending on the context and how forcefully it's said. A related word is *mishegass* ("mish-eh-*gahss*"), meaning insanity or foolishness. The difference? A particular congressman might be a *meshuggeh* (or a *meshuggener*), but politics (like sausage) is a *mishegass*. David now knows that the idea of remodeling a house is *meshuggeh*, primarily because of the *mishegass* he had to deal with last year. Basically, *meshuggehs* with all their *meshuggener* ideas cause a real *mishegass*.

Mishpokhah. Your family is your *mishpokhah* (pronounced "mish-*pokh*-ah"). No, we're not talking about just your immediate family; *mishpochah* implies *all* your family. In fact, the term is often extended to the entire Jewish family. When a Jew sees someone he doesn't know but suspects is also Jewish, he or she might quietly ask, "*Mishpochah?*" Of course, recent DNA tests seem to indicate that we're all *mishpochah* anyway, if you go back far enough.

Nakhes. Like *kvell*, the word *nakhes* means proud or joyous; however there's a subtle difference between the two words. *Nakhes* is the reflected light that falls on you when someone else (typically your child) does something great. For example, you might *kvell* because your son is a doctor, but the fact that he became a doctor reflects well on you, giving you *nakhes*. (For some reason, you always *get* nakhes. Who are we to question Yiddish grammar?) After your child strikes a home run, you might say, "Oy, you give me such *nakhes!*"

Nebbish. Yiddish has a wonderful ability to describe personality types, and one of our favorite types is the *nebbish*, that sadsack loser who, no matter how sorry you feel for him (nine out of ten *nebbishes* are men), just makes your teeth itch. Leo Rosten recalls the saying that when a *nebbish* leaves the room you feel like someone just came in.

Nosh. There are few pleasures as great as *noshing*, eating little snacks. In fact, we're certain that Jews invented *hors d'ouvers* as a good excuse to *nosh* at parties. You might also say, "I'm just going to get a little *nosh*." But watch out: Your friends might start calling you a *nosher*.

Nu? One of the most used of all Yiddish words is *nu*. Almost always asked as a question, "*Nu?*" can mean two dozen different things, depending on context, the telling, the raising of the eyebrows, and the tone of the voice. For example, "*Nu?*" might mean "How are you," "I'm waiting for you," "Isn't that obvious," or "What could I do?"

Oy! The epitome of Yiddish is *oy!* (It really deserves to be spelled with an exclamation point.) Like *nu*, saying *oy!* can mean so many different things that it's hard to pin down. It can be a cry of surprise, pain, frustration, joy, contentment, or dismay. It can be an exclamation, a question, or a sigh. For emphasis, you might say *oy vey* ("oh, woe!"), or draw it out with *oy veyzmir*.

Pisher. A *pisher* is someone who is inexperienced or just young and "wet behind the ears," like a "little squirt." While a *pisher* is literally someone who urinates, no one uses it in this sense; rather, people say *pisher* either affectionately ("What a cute little *pisher* you are!") or derisively ("You can't trust what he says, he's just a *pisher* around here").

Plotz. You know those cartoon strips where someone is so surprised or aggravated that you see them flip over, legs in the air? Have you ever wondered what they're doing? They're *plotzing*. *Plotzing* in the real world often happens when someone tells a really funny joke ("I laughed so hard, I thought I'd *plotz*.") or when bad news is imminent ("Don't tell your grandmother that; she'll *plotz*.").

Putz. Every 14-year-old knows that you can judge the efficacy of a language by the number of euphemisms for the male genitalia. Yiddish, in this respect, excels. *Putz* (pronounced like a golf swing: "Moishe putts next") is one such word, and it was once considered vulgar enough to avoid using in mixed company. However, no one really uses *putz* to describe a penis; instead, a *putz* is a fool, a jerk, or almost anyone who is a pain in your *tukhis*: "That *putz* couldn't get himself out of a paper bag if he tried."

Schlemiel. A *schlemiel* (pronounced "shleh-*meal*") is an incompetent, socially maladjusted, foolish person, who constantly makes mistakes. A well-known Yiddish phrase says that when a *schlemiel* falls on his back, he breaks his nose.

Schlep. To *schlep* something is to carry or drag it. For example, "Help me *schlep* the groceries in from the car." or "Oy, I don't want to *schlep* this stuff all over town." However, sometimes *schlepping* refers to your own body: an hour-long commute is a major *schlep*. On the one hand, a *schlepper* is someone who *schleps* things. However, the term has connotations of anyone who drags his or her heels, acts inefficiently, or is lazy. When he was a teenager, David's mother was forever telling him to brush his hair before going out so that he wouldn't look like a *schlepper*.

Schlemazl. Almost every Yiddish word that begins with "sch" belittles someone or something, so perhaps it's no surprise that a *schlemazl* refers to someone with chronic bad luck. When a *schlemazl* finds a 50-dollar bill on the street, the first person she runs into is the guy she owes $51. The *schlemazl* is the one the *schlemiel* drops his soup on.

Schlock. When you drive around town and see household items on the sidewalk with a sign that reads "Free, take me," that stuff is *schlock*. *Schlock* can be anything junky.

Schmatta. A *schmatta* is a rag or something sullied. A Jewish woman can spend a week finding the perfect dress for the New Year's ball, but when you compliment her on it, she'll answer, "Oh, this old *schmatta*?" Soon after author and meditation teacher Ram Dass (who was born a very Jewish Richard Alpert) had a stroke, a doctor had to determine how well his mind was still functioning. The doctor held up a pen and asked, "What is this?" Ram Dass answered, "A pen." Then the doctor held up his tie, and Ram Dass answered, "A *schmatta*."

Schmeer. One of the side effects of the increasing popularity of bagels in America has been the simultaneous increase in the usage of the word *schmeer*, meaning a spread, or as a verb, to spread or smear. You can't just eat a bagel; you have to *schmeer* on some cream cheese (or at least some raspberry preserves). Note that some people also use *shmeer* to indicate a bribe ("Do we need to *schmeer* the maitre'd here?"), though that's much less common. Additionally, *schmeer* can mean "beaten badly," as in, "He really got *schmeered*!"

Schmuck. Okay, confession time: When David was eight years old, he found a badge that read "Super Schmuck" (a friend had given it to his father as a gag). As proud as any super-hero, he bounded around the house, yelling "I am super schmuck!" He was so disappointed when he found out that *schmuck* actually meant penis. (It's from the German word for "jewels.") *Schmuck*, like *putz*, has evolved over time and entered common American usage to mean a dolt, a fool, or a jerk.

For example, "Any *schmuck* knows that!" Back when *schmuck* was a more loaded and vulgar term, Americans shortened it to *schmo* (like, "Who is that schmo, anyway?" or "I feel like such a schmo.").

Shiksa. A *shiksa* is any non-Jewish woman, though it primarily refers to a young woman, and especially one who has eyes for your Jewish son. Remember that the Jewish lineage is traditionally passed from mother to child, so a non-Jewish woman marrying into a family has long been considered a special kind of threat. Obviously, the word *shiksa* is generally tinged with a bit of tension. The corresponding word for a male non-Jew is a *shaygets*.

Tchotchke. A *tchotchke* (pronounced "tsa-tskeh" "chotch-keh," or chotch-kee) is literally a child's doll, but it describes any small toy or bauble. Key chains, fun pens, and those squishy foam toys that help relieve hand stress are all examples of *tchotchkes*.

Tsuris. As the song goes, "Nobody knows the *tsuris* I've seen!" Well, that could be the Yiddish version. *Tsuris* mean heartaches, troubles, or woes. It's what your kids can give you when they're not giving you nakhes. "Don't give me *tsuris*," a mother might scold her misbehaving child.

Ungepotchket. A casserole made by throwing together last week's leftovers is *ungepotchket* (pronounced "ung-geh-*potch*-ket"). Some modern art (the stuff that is copied from the brilliant works of five-year-olds) is *ungepotchket*. Blindly grabbing whatever clothes are clean (maybe) and at hand when you dress in the morning ensures you'll be dressed *ungepotchket*. Anything Martha Stewart makes or designs is, almost by definition, the opposite of *ungepotchket*.

Yente. Pronounced either "yen-tah" or "yen-teh," *yente* refers to a vulgar or gossipy woman. Calling a woman a *yente* to her face is considered bad form, to say the least. We keep hearing people mistake "Yentl" for *yente*. Careful! *Yentl* is a woman's name, and the title of a Barbra Streisand movie. Interestingly, in recent times *yente* is becoming a positive term, as in the "Rent-a-Yente" company, which hires out people who are willing to help with tasks and projects.

Zaftig. In today's world of supermodels the shape of toothpicks, it's hard to remember the definition of *zaftig*, which literally means "juicy," but is most often used to refer to a body type which you can really wrap your hands around (usually female). The opposite of *zaftig* is *svelte*, which we always thought was Yiddish, but is not. *Zaftig* is a sensual word, and may also be used to describe fruit ("Oy, this plum is so zaftig, I can't wait to eat it!") or even ideas ("His lecture was full of zaftig ideas."). Yes, men can be zaftig, too. It's an equal-opportunity adjective.

Zayde. Your *zeyde* ("zay-dah" or "zay-deh") is your grandfather, and many Jews refer to their grandparents as "*zayde* and *bubbe*." You may also hear people affectionately and respectfully referring to any older man as *zayde*.

Appendix **B**

A Sampler of Jewish Prayers and Blessings

Prayer is a way of expanding your awareness, allowing a deeper appreciation of life. Blessings remind you of the sanctity contained even in the rather ordinary moments of each day. This appendix includes a few central prayer texts and some blessings you might find useful to help you focus through the day.

All these prayers and blessings are taken from a traditional *siddur*, or prayerbook, though several of them are selections from much longer texts. If you're not familiar with the prayers, practice with these, then later you can move up to a full siddur. Many different siddur versions are available today, and you can find them at any Jewish bookstore or on the Internet.

You can say the prayers in English until you feel more comfortable trying the Hebrew. When you get ready for the Hebrew, remember that the *kh* transliteration is pronounced like the guttural, clearing-the-throat sound in "loch ness." When you see the letter *i*, it is to be pronounced "ee," and where you see *e*, it sounds like "eh." The *o* is meant to be a long "o."

Jews usually recite their prayers and blessings out loud; for instance, at a Jewish home, the blessing over the food is said before anyone eats (either by each person or by one person who does it for everyone). You don't have to say the words loudly; Jews often mutter them quietly, but with intention.

The Central Focus: Sh'ma and V'ahavta

What might be called the basic affirmation of Jewish faith is taken from the Book of Deuteronomy. When Moses retells the journey of the Children of Israel, he calls upon the people to awaken to the deeper love and compassion of their beings and hear the deeper message that all is One.

> *Sh'ma Yisrael: Adonai Eloheynu Adonai Ekhad.*
>
> Listen, Israel: The Eternal is our God, the Eternal is One. (Deuteronomy 6:4)

The Sh'ma is like a "mantra" that can be said anytime throughout the day (see Chapter 4 for more on the Sh'ma). These are the last words a Jew is to speak before dying, and these are the words contained in daily prayers and included (see the following sections) in the prayer upon retiring for the night. They are the most famous of all Jewish prayer words; they are the "watchwords" of this faith.

The words that follow the Sh'ma in the Torah are called the *V'ahavta*. You hear these chanted at any synagogue service. David found all the "weird" mixtures of syllables overwhelming at first; fear not, after 20 or 30 times it'll roll trippingly off your tongue.

> *V'ahavta et Adonai Elohekha, b'khol l'vav'kha, uv'khol naf'sh'kha, uv'khol m'odekha. V'hayu had'varim ha-eleh, asher Anokhi m'tzav'kha ha-yom, ahl l'va-vekha. V'she-nan-tam l'vanekha, v'debarta bahm, b'shiv-t'kha b'vay-tekha, uv'lekh-t'kha va-derekh, uv'shokh-b'kha uv'kumekha. Uk'shartam l'ot ahl ya-dekha, v'hayu l'to-tafot bayn aynekha. Ukh'tavtam ahl v'zuzot baytekha, u-vish-arekha.*
>
> Then you will love The Eternal One your God with all your heart, with all your soul, and with all your energy. Let these words, which I command you today, be upon your heart. Repeat them to your children, and speak of them when you sit in your house, when you walk on the way, when you lie down and when you rise up. Bind them as a sign upon your arm and let them be for frontlets between your eyes. Write them on the doorposts of your house and upon your gates.

While some people read these words as commands ("you *will* do these things, or else"), others — like us — see them more as the logical outgrowth of the Sh'ma: awakening to Oneness always leads to the expanded capacity for love and compassion.

First Thing in the Morning

The first words a traditional Jew recites upon awakening each morning express gratitude, setting a tone for whatever is to be that day.

[Men:] *Modeh* [Women:] *Modah ani l'fanekha, Melekh khai v'kayam, sheh-heh-kheh-zarta bee nishma-ti b'khemlah — rabah emunatekha.*

In Your Presence I give thanks, Living and Sustaining Ruler, for You have returned my soul within me with Compassion — abundant is Your faithfulness.

Last Thing at Night

The Jewish day is framed with prayer. Here is one of our favorites, a prayer of forgiveness that precedes the bedtime recitation of the Sh'ma. Repeating this prayer not only helps you sleep but puts you in a good mood when you once again awaken.

Ribono shel olam ha-rayni mo-khail l'khol mi sheh-hikh-is v'hik-nit oh-ti, oh she-khatah k'neg-di – bayn b'gufi, bayn b'ma-moni, bayn bikh'vodi, bayn b'khol asher li; bayn b'o-ness, bayn b'ratzon, bayn b'sho-gaig, bayn b'ma-zir; bayn b'di-bur, bayn b'ma-aseh, bayn b'mah-khah-shah-vah, bayn b'hir'hur; bayn b'gilgul zeh, bayn b'gilgul a-kher – l'khol adam, v'lo yai-anais shum adam b'sibati. Y'hi ratzon mil'fanekha Adonai Elohai vai-lo-hai avotai v'imotai, sheh-lo eh-kheh-tah od. U'mah sheh-khah-tah-ti l'fanekha m'khok b'ra-khameh-khah ha-rabim, ah-vahl lo ahl y'dai yisurim vah-khah-lah-yim rah-im. Ye'h'yu l'ratzon imrai fi v'heg'yon libi l'fanekha, Adonai Tzu-ri v'Go-ah-li.

Ribono shel olam, Ruling Presence of the Universe, I hereby forgive anyone who angered or antagonized me or who sinned against me, whether against my body, my property, my honor or against anything of mine; whether done accidentally, willfully, carelessly, or purposely, whether through speech, deed, thought, or intention, whether in this incarnation or in any other. I forgive everyone. May no one be punished on my account. May it be Your will, Eternal One, my God and the God of my ancestors, that I sin no more. May You blot out whatever sins I have committed before You in the abundance of your Mercy, that they may not manifest through suffering and illness. May the words of my mouth and the meditations of my heart be for good before you, Eternal One, my Source and my Redeemer.

You can recite the Sh'ma (see above) after this nighttime prayer, just before going to sleep.

Various, Sundry, and Otherwise Useful Blessings

Saying a blessing offers the opportunity to celebrate the moments of your life. Tradition teaches that each Jew should say a minimum of 100 blessings each day. That's a lot of celebrating! While reaching this goal really is no problem if you worship three times a day, reciting the entire liturgy at each service, it does present a challenge for those who don't observe in that way.

The blessings in this section will help you work toward your daily 100. But remember that tradition also teaches that you can find your own words for blessing things and events, too.

REMEMBER

When you hear another person recite a blessing, you should say, "Amen" at the end. Doing so allows the blessings you hear to count toward your own 100! You usually don't say "Amen" to your own blessing.

Blessings for food

Like saying "grace" before meals, these blessings encourage us to be aware throughout the day instead of just shoveling food into our mouths.

Before drinking grape juice or grape wine

Barukh Atah Adonai, Eloheynu Melekh ha-olam, boray p'ree ha-gafen.

Blessed are You, Eternal One our God, Universal Ruling Presence, Who creates the fruit of the vine.

Before eating bread

Barukh Atah Adonai, Eloheynu Melekh ha-olam, ha-motzee lekhem min ha-aretz.

Blessed are You, Eternal One our God, Universal Ruling Presence, Who brings forth bread from the earth.

Before eating other products of wheat, barley, rye, oats, spelt, or rice

Barukh Atah Adonai, Eloheynu Melekh ha-olam, boray minay m'zonot.

Blessed are You, Eternal One our God, Universal Ruling Presence, Who creates various kinds (grains) of nourishment.

Before eating fruit that grows on trees

Barukh Atah Adonai, Eloheynu Melekh ha-olam, boray p'ree ha-etz.

Blessed are You, Eternal One our God, Universal Ruling Presence, Who creates the fruit of the tree.

Before eating produce that grows directly from the earth

Barukh Atah Adonai, Eloheynu Melekh ha-olam, boray p'ree ha-adamah.

Blessed are You, Eternal One our God, Universal Ruling Presence, Who creates the fruit of the earth.

Before eating or drinking other foods

Barukh Atah Adonai, Eloheynu Melekh ha-olam, sheh-ha-kol nih'yeh bid'varo.

Blessed are You, Eternal One our God, Universal Ruling Presence, through Whose Word everything comes to be.

After the meal

The traditional blessing after the meal is called the *Birkat Ha-Mazon* ("The Blessing for Nourishment"), though some people refer to it simply as "the Birkat." This blessing is much longer than those that precede meals (the following blessing is the central paragraph of the traditional version).

The Birkat talks about the experience of being filled, nourished, and supported by food and by the Universe in which the food grows and seeks to universalize this experience and affirm that it might finally be available to all.

A side effect of the Birkat is that it encourages families or communities to end the meal together, instead of just drifting away as soon as people finish.

Barukh Atah Adonai, Eloheynu Melekh ha-olam, ha-zan et ha-olam kulo, b'tuvo, b'kheyn b'khesed uv'rakhamim, hu notayn lekhem l'khol basar, ki l'olam khas'do. Uv'tuvo ha-gadol, tamid lo khasar lanu, v'al yekhsar lanu mazon l'olam va-ed. Ba-avur sh'mo ha-gadol, ki hu ayl zahn um'farnes la-kol, u-may-khin mazon l'khol b'ree-yo-tav asher bara. Barukh Atah Adonai, ha-zahn et ha-kol.

Blessed are You, Eternal our God, Universal Ruling Presence, Who nourishes the entire universe in Goodness; Who with Grace, with Lovingkindness, and with Mercy, provides nourishment for all flesh, with everlasting Lovingkindness. In that Great Goodness we have not lacked and may we never lack nourishment evermore. For the sake of God's great Name, because God nourishes and sustains all, and prepares food for all creatures which God created. Blessed are You, Eternal One, Who nourishes all.

Blessings making moments special

To bless is to affirm the beauty and the rightness of a moment, even if that moment is less than joyful. To bless opens you to a fuller awareness, and with that awareness, a greater freedom. Here are some blessings to brighten your day.

Celebrating first-time experiences

The following blessing, usually just called the *Sheh-heh-khi-yanu*, is probably our favorite blessing. You can say this anytime you acquire or use something new, or when you do something for the first time.

> *Barukh Atah Adonai, Eloheynu Melekh ha-olam, sheh-heh-khi-yanu v'key'manu v'hee-gee-anu laz'man ha-zeh.*

> Blessed are You, Eternal One our God, Universal Ruling Presence, Who keeps us in Life always, Who supports the unfolding of our uniqueness, and Who brings us to this very moment for blessing.

Experiencing the awe of nature

Tradition says this is the prayer to say when you experience an earthquake, or see lightning, a lofty mountain, or a large river. But honestly, it works with any awe-some natural event.

> *Barukh Atah Adonai, Eloheynu Melekh ha-olam, oseh ma-asay v'rayshit.*

> Blessed are You, Eternal One our God, Universal Ruling Presence, Who makes the works of Creation.

Going to the bathroom

Jews have a blessing for every moment, including using the toilet. While this sounds silly to some folks, it's actually a wonderful opportunity to bring your awareness to the amazing fact that your body actually works so well. This blessing is usually recited after the event. (Don't forget to wash your hands!)

> *Barukh Atah Adonai, Eloheynu Melekh ha-olam, asher yatzar et ha-adam b'khokhmah, u-vara bo n'kavim n'kavim, khalulim khalulim. Galu-i v'yadu-a lifney khisay kh'vodekha, sheh-im yipa-tay-akh ekhad may-hem, oh yi-sa-taym ekhad may-hem, ee ef-shar l'hit-ka-yaym v'la-amod l'fanekha afilu sha-ah akhat. Barukh Atah Adonai, Rofey khol basar u-maf-lee la-asot.*

> Blessed are You, Eternal One our God, Universal Ruling Presence, Who fashioned people with wisdom and created within them many openings and many cavities. It is clear and known before Your Throne of Glory that if only one of them were to be

open [when it's supposed to be closed] or only one of them be closed [when it's supposed to be open] it would be impossible to survive and to stand before You even for a moment. Blessed are You, Eternal One, Who heals all flesh and acts wondrously.

Blessings for ritual acts

Performance of traditional *mitzvot* ("commandments," or "acts that allow us to connect to God") require special focus, and these blessings provide that focus. They help transform what in some cases might just be an automatic act into a moment of holiness.

Lighting candles on Shabbat or a festival

Jews light candles at the beginning of every *yom tov* ("good day" or "holiday"), including Shabbat on Friday night (see Chapter 18). The light of the candles on Shabbat evokes the first act of Creation, which was light. On Shabbat as well as on festivals, the lights speak to the specialness of the moment.

> *Barukh Atah Adonai, Eloheynu Melekh ha-olam, asher kid'shanu b'mitzvotav v'tzivanu l'hadlik ner shel shabbat (or shel yom tov)*

> Blessed are You, Eternal One our God, Universal Ruling Presence, Who sanctifies us with *mitzvot* [paths of holiness] and gives us the mitzvah of kindling Shabbat (or festival) lights.

Note that the final words of this blessing change slightly depending on what's being celebrated. For example, if it's Chanukkah, you say ". . . *l'hadlik ner shel Chanukkah . . .*" (see Chapter 22). Or, if it's Yom Kippur *and* Shabbat, then you say ". . . *l'hadlik ner shel Shabbat v'shel Yom ha–Kippurim . . .*" (see Chapter 20).

Before the study of Torah

> *Barukh Atah Adonai, Eloheynu Melekh ha-olam, asher kid'shanu b'mitzvotav v'tzivanu la-asok b'div'ray Torah.*

> Blessed are You, Eternal One our God, Universal Ruling Presence, Who sanctifies us with mitzvot and gives us the mitzvah of engaging ourselves in words of Torah.

Putting on a tallit (prayer shawl)

> *Barukh Atah Adonai, Eloheynu Melekh ha-olam, asher kid'shanu b'mitzvotav v'tzivanu l'hit-atef ba-tzi-tzit.*

> Blessed are You, Eternal One our God, Universal Ruling Presence, Who sanctifies us with mitzvot and gives us the mitzvah of enwrapping ourselves with the fringed garment.

Upon affixing a mezuzah

The mezuzah is attached to the doorpost on the right side of the door as entering, with the top tilted slightly toward the room entered. (See Chapter 4 for more information.)

Barukh Atah Adonai, Eloheynu Melekh ha-olam, asher kid'shanu b'mitzvotav v'tzivanu lik'bo-ah mezuzah.

Blessed are You, Eternal One our God, Universal Ruling Presence, Who sanctifies us with mitzvot and gives us the mitzvah of affixing a mezuzah.

Blessings as reminders and as teachers

The following blessings help celebrate moments not only of joy but of difficulty and of grief as well.

Upon hearing unusually good news

Barukh Atah Adonai, Eloheynu Melekh ha-olam, ha-tov v'ha-may-tiv.

Blessed are You, Eternal One our God, Universal Ruling Presence, Who is Good and bestows Goodness.

Upon hearing unusually bad news, such as a death

Barukh Atah Adonai, Eloheynu Melekh ha-olam, dayan ha-emet.

Blessed are You, Eternal One our God, Universal Ruling Presence, the True Judge.

Upon seeing exceptionally beautiful people, trees, or fields

Barukh Atah Adonai, Eloheynu Melekh ha-Olam, sheh-kakha lo b'olamo.

Blessed are You, Eternal One our God, Universal Ruling Presence, Who has this in the Universe.

Seeing a person or animal that is disturbing to you

Barukh Atah Adonai, Eloheynu Melekh ha-olam, m'shaneh ha-b'ri-ot.

Blessed are You, Eternal One our God, Universal Ruling Presence, Who creates variety among living beings.

Appendix C

Go Now and Learn

WORDS OF WISDOM

Around 2,000 years ago, the great sage Rabbi Hillel was asked to explain the meaning of Judaism while standing on one foot. Hillel replied, "What is hateful to you do not do unto others. That is the whole of Torah, all the rest is commentary — go now and learn." We offer the following list as an aid for your journey to go and learn.

Of course, the Web is one of the best places to start gathering information about Judaism. To make your Web surfing experience even easier, we've gathered a list of the best links at our webpage at www.joyofjewish.com.

Books for The People of the Book

Between the two of us, we've got hundreds of books about Judaism on our shelves. Fortunately, you don't need this many books to gain a deep feeling for Judaism. Here's a list of just a few of our favorites, the sort of books that we think should be part of any Jewish person's library.

These books are all available at bookstores (we encourage you to visit your local Jewish bookstore, if you have one). We also provide links to them at our Web site:

>> *The Bible (Tanach,* Stone Edition): Many people think that if you've seen one Bible you've seen them all. Not so. We recommend the Stone Edition of the Tanach (the Hebrew Bible; see Chapter 3), published by Artscroll. This version

contains both Hebrew and a very readable English translation as well as some helpful and traditional commentary.

>> *Etz Hayim: Torah and Commentary:* This is Rabbi Ted's current favorite, produced by the Conservative Movement and including the Jewish Publication Society's latest translation. The commentary honors tradition but often transcends it.

>> *Entering Jewish Prayer,* by Reuven Hammer: Prayers and blessings are important elements of Jewish practice (see Chapter 4). This wonderful book offers a deeper consideration of the inner and outer dimensions of Jewish worship, including an introduction to the liturgy.

>> *God Is a Verb,* by David A. Cooper: Jewish mysticism (see Chapter 5) is all the rage these days, and for good reason — it provides a deeply satisfying approach to life. Unfortunately, many books on the market simply make mysticism more mystifying. Not so with this gem, which explains things clearly and makes the esoteric relevant to each person's life.

>> *Jewish Literacy,* by Joseph Telushkin: When writing *Judaism For Dummies*, we've often been frustrated that we couldn't (because of the introductory nature of this book) delve more deeply into a topic. Telushkin's book is a great "next step" down the Jewish path.

>> *Jewish Meditation,* by Aryeh Kaplan: If you found the idea of Jewish meditation intriguing in Chapter 5, rush out and get a copy of this excellent introductory book.

>> *The Handbook of Jewish Meditation Practices,* by Rabbi David Cooper: Here is a more modern take on some ancient practices. Rabbi Cooper communicates clearly to support the inner journey.

>> *The Joys of Yiddish,* by Leo Rosten: We've included many of the most important Yiddish words in Appendix A, but Rosten explores and explains Yiddish idioms better than anyone. This is a must-have volume.

>> *The New Jewish Wedding,* by Anita Diamant: Don't buy this book as a wedding gift; give it to the couple on their engagement! Diamant offers a wonderful vision of weddings and how they can be deeply meaningful events (for Jews and non-Jews alike).

>> *Seasons of Our Joy,* by Arthur Waskow: Want a deeper understanding of the history and interpretations behind the Jewish holidays? We find ourselves referring to this book throughout the year, finding good reminders and great lessons.

>> *A Short History of the Jewish People,* by Raymond P. Scheindlin: Jewish history is so long and rich that most Jewish histories are overwhelming and take months to digest. This book lays the history out in significantly more detail than we were able to in Chapters 11 through 16, but in an easy-to-read and to-the-point manner.

>> *A Treasury of Jewish Folklore,* by Nathan Ausubel: We don't know anyone who has read this classic (and enormous) collection of Jewish stories and humor from cover to cover, but it provides a great opportunity for browsing and reading out loud to children and partners.

On the Newsstand

Magazines and journals are a great way to keep up with current issues relevant to Judaism. Here are several of the best periodicals in print:

>> *Commentary:* This magazine offers a wide range of political articles and opinion pieces with a conservative angle and a Jewish slant. (165 East 56th Street, New York, NY 10022 USA. Telephone: 800-829-6270. Web: www.commentarymagazine.com.

>> *International Jerusalem Post:* Keeping up with the news in Israel is a challenge without getting the news directly from the inside. (Suite 334, 401 North Wabash Avenue, Chicago, IL 60611, USA. Telephone: 312-321-3247. Web: www.jpost.com.

>> *Moment:* Each issue of this bi-monthly magazine seems to include something to rejoice in, something to get upset about, and something to learn. What more could you ask for? (4710 41st Street NW, Washington, DC 20016 USA. Telephone: 800-777-1005. Web: www.momentmag.com.

>> *Sh'ma:* This independent-minded journal has been publishing articles on a wide variety of religious, social, and political issues since 1970. (PO Box 1019, Manchester, NH 03105-1019 USA. Telephone: 877-568-SHMA. Web: www.shma.com.

>> *Tikkun:* This bi-monthly journal of culture, politics, and social issues also delves deeply into the importance of spirituality in everyday matters. (2107 Van Ness Avenue, Suite 302, San Francisco, CA 94109 USA. Telephone: 800-395-7753. Web: www.tikkun.org.

Some Jewish Organizations

Whether you want more information about a particular religious movement in Judaism or about how to donate money to plant a tree in Israel — the following organizations can help. We've also got links to each of these at our website at www.joyofjewish.com.

Education and social action

Here are service organizations dedicated to strengthening the bonds within the Jewish community:

>> American Jewish Committee: 165 East 56th Street, New York, NY 10022. Telephone: 212-751-4000. Web: www.ajc.org.

>> American Jewish Congress: 15 East 84th Street, New York, NY 10028. Telephone: 212-879-4500. Web: www.ajcongress.org.

>> Anti-Defamation League: 823 United Nations Plaza, New York, NY 10017. Telephone: 212-885-7970. Web: www.adl.org.

>> B'nai B'rith International: 1640 Rhode Island Avenue NW, Washington, DC 20036. Telephone: 202-857-6600. Web: www.BBInet.org.

>> Hillel: The Foundation for Jewish Campus Life: 1640 Rhode Island Avenue NW, Washington, DC 20036. Telephone: 202-857-6560. Web: www.hillel.org.

>> InterfaithFamily: 90 Oak Street, Fourth Floor, P.O. Box 428, Newton Upper Falls, MA 02464. Telephone: (617) 581-6860 Web: www.interfaithfamily.com.

>> United Jewish Communities: Suite 11E, 111 Eighth Avenue, New York, NY 10011. Telephone: 212-284-6500. Web: www.ujc.org.

Charities

Because tzedakah is such a crucial part of Judaism (see Chapter 4), here are some places to discover how you can contribute:

>> Hadassah: 50 West 58th Street, New York, NY 10019. Telephone: 212-303-8093. Web: www.hadassah.org.

>> Jewish National Fund: 42 East 69th Street, New York, NY 10021. Telephone: 800-542-TREE. Web: www.jnf.org.

>> Mazon: 12401 Wilshire Blvd., Suite 303, Los Angeles, CA 90025. Telephone: 310-442-0020. Web: www.mazon.org.

Judaism on the Web

Many great Jewish websites provide a wide spectrum of information about Judaism. Here are just a few sites you should check out:

» Maven Jewish Web Directory: www.maven.co.il

» MyJewishLearning: www.myjewishlearning.com

» Judaism 101: www.jewfaq.org

» Jewish Virtual Library: www.jewishvirtuallibrary.org

» Joy of Jewish: www.joyofjewish.com

Index

Gut Yor, 268
Gut Yuntoff, 268
Gute voch, 254

H

Hadassah (website), 408
Hadrian, Emperor, 187
Haftarah, 37, 40, 56, 251
haggadah, 4, 326
Hagganah, 211
Hag ha-Asif ("Festival of Ingathering"). *See* Sukkot
Ha-Kadosh Baruch Hu, 30
hakafah, 59, 251
hakafot, 291
halakhah, 43, 48
hallal, 382
Hallel (songs of praise), 56, 338
hamantaschen, 316–317
Hamantaschen recipe, 317
Hammer, Reuven (author)
 Entering Jewish Prayer, 406
hamsa, 68
The Handbook of Jewish Meditation Practices (Cooper), 406
hands, washing, 247
Haredi. *See* Ultra-Orthodox Jews
Ha-Satan, 32
Ha-Shem, 28
Hasidic movement, 18, 78, 201
hatafat dam, 110
hate, origins of, 227–228
Hatikvah ("The Hope"), 386
Havdalah
 about, 252
 spices for, 253–254
 wine and candles, 252–253
healing, 235
Hebrew Bible (Tanakh), 37, 39–40

Hebrew vowels, 3
Hechalot, 75
hekhsher, 63
Henry IV, King of England, 193
hermeneutics, 40
Herod the Great, 182–183
Hertz, Naftali (poet), 386
Herzl, Theodore (journalist), 205, 211
Heschel, Abraham Joshua (rabbi), 369–370
hesped, 145
High Holidays. *See* Rosh Hashanah; Yom Kippur
Hillel (rabbi), 42, 364, 405
Hillel: The Foundation for Jewish Campus Life (website), 408
Hinduism, 219
hitbodedut, 79–81
Hitler, Adolf (leader of Nazi party), 206–207, 210, 227. *See also* Holocaust
Hod, 85–86
Hoda'ah, 56
hokn a cheinik, 391
Holocaust, 207–211, 215–216, 227
Holy Scriptures, 39
homes, Jewish, 68–69
homosexuality, 100
hooves, cloven, 60
"The Hope" (Hatikvah), 386
hora, 135
host, desecration of the, 231
House of Joseph *(Beit Yosef)*, 366
humane slaughter, 60
Humanistic Judaism, 21–22
Human Potential Movement, 217
Hyrcanus II, King of Judea, 182
Hyrcanus, John (Maccabeean leader), 182

I

icons, explained, 6
images and symbols
 about, 81
 five levels of soul, 88–89
 Four Worlds, 87–88
 sefirot, 84–87
 Tree of life, 81–84
Inner Presence, 78
Inquisition (Spanish), 194, 227
instructive humor, 377
interfaith challenges, 97
InterfaithFamily (website), 408
interfaith marriages, 132
International Jerusalem Post (magazine), 407
The International Jew (Ford), 230–231
"in that time" (bazman hazeh), 299
intrafaith challenges, 97
intrafaith marriages, 132
invitations to Passover seder, 326
Isaac (Bible character), 159–160
Isabella, Queen of Spain, 194
Islam
 Jews under, 189–191
 relationship with Judaism, 381–382
Israel. *See also* Kings of Israel
 anti-Semitism and, 233
 birth of, 216
 importance of to Jews, 372–373
Israeli Independence Day, 343
Israeli pronunciation, 3
Israelite kingdom, 173–174
Israel, Richard (Rabbi), 267
Italy, 226

J

Jacob (Bible character), 159–161

Jannaeus, Alexander (King of Judea), 181

Jefferson, Thomas (U.S. president), 200

Jesus Christ, 228–229, 371–372

Jew (word), 69

Jewish Arbor Day. *See* Tu B'Shvat

Jewish celebrities, 22

Jewish Holidays and Festivals (Ediden), 307

"Jewish Humor," 375–378

Jewish Literacy (Telushkin), 406

Jewish Meditation (Kaplan), 406

Jewish National Fund (website), 408

Jewish Renewal Movement, 220

Jewish state, 211–213

Jewish Virtual Library (website), 409

Jewish words, pronouncing, 2–3

Jews. *See also specific topics*
  about, 12–15
  under Islam, 189–191
  as spiritual teachers of other traditions, 218–219
  war against, 208–209

Jew Slaughter, 235

John Paul II, Pope, 229

John the Baptist, 183

John XXIII, Pope, 229

Joseph (Bible character), 161–165

Josephus (Jewish general), 184

journals, 407

Joy of Jewish (website), 7, 122, 132, 134, 306, 405, 409

The Joys of Yiddish (Rosten), 389, 406

Judah, 295

Judaism. *See also specific topics*
  about, 12
  blessings and prayers. *See* blessings and prayers
  branches, 15–22
  Christianity and, 188
  converting to, 13, 194, 226, 380–381
  defined, 15
  dietary laws, 60–63
  garments and clothing customs, 64–68
  homes, 68–69
  mitzvot, 48–52
  questions about, 371–382
  relationship with Islam, 381–382
  rites and rituals. *See* rites and rituals
  role of women in, 374–375
  Synagogue, 57–60
  who's in charge, 379–380

Judaism 101 (website), 409

Judea, exile from, 178

judgments, making, 258–260

K

kabbalah, 72–74, 342

Kabbalat Shabbat, 251

Kaddish, 56, 148–150

Kadesh (sanctification of the day), 333

kadosh, 147

kallah, 129, 134

Kallah Bereshit, 291

Kallah Torah, 291

Kaplan, Aryeh (Orthodox rabbi), 74, 406

Kaplan, Mordecai (rabbi), 120, 233

kapparah ("atonement"), 274

Kapparot, 268–269

Karaites, 191

Karpas (eating the green vegetable), 328, 329, 334

kashered, 61

kashrut, 52, 60, 250

kavvanah, 52, 77

kenahora, 391

Keter, 84

ketubah, 130, 133–134, 350

Ketuvim (writings), 39–40

Khag Ha-aviv ("Festival of Spring"). *See* Passover

Khag ha-Bikkurim ("Festival of the First Fruits"). *See* Shavuot

Khag ha-Katzir ("Festival of the Reaping"). *See* Shavuot

Khag Ha-matzot ("Festival of Unleavened Breads"). *See* Passover

khametz, 322–325

khatan, 129

khet, 273

Khiyah, 89

khos'n, 129

kibbitz, 392

kibbutz, 386

Kiddush, 333

kiddushin, 127, 130–131. *See also* weddings

Kingdoms, 173–174

"Kingship" (Malkhiyot), 264

Kings of Israel
  about, 167–168
  fall of first Temple, 174–175
  finding, 168
  Kingdoms, 173–174
  Lion of Judah, 170–173
  Lost tribes, 174
  prophets, 168
  wars, 169–170

Nirtzah (conclusion), 338
Nisan, 259, 344
nissuin, 131
Noahide Laws, 49
nontraditional traditions, 355
Northern Kingdom, 173–174
nosh, 394
Nu?, 394
Numbers (BaMidbar), 36, 37
numbers, in mysticism, 87
Nuremberg Laws, 207

O

oat products, blessing before eating, 400
oil miracle, 295–296
Oneg Shabbat ("Delight of the Sabbath"), 251
online resources, 409
Oral Torah, 41–46, 181
orange juice, 322
organ donation, 144
organizations, 407–408
origins of hate, 227–228
Orthodox Jews, 16–18, 135–137, 242, 374
Ottoman Empire, 206
OU, 63
Oy!, 394
oznei haman, 316

P

Pale of Settlement, 201
Palestine, 205, 226, 382
Palestinian Talmud, 189
parashah, 37, 122, 251
pareve, 61, 250
parochet, 57
parshiot, 37
parting words, reciting, 142

Passover
about, 231, 319
charoset, 329–332
children at seder, 337
Counting of the Omer, 341–343
first-timers' guide, 327
food, 320–325
freedom, thinking about, 339–341
giving to charity, 325
khametz, 322–325
kosher for, 321–322
Miriam's Cup, 338–339
names for, 320
preparing for, 323–325
reasons behind, 320
seder, 325–339
symbolism of restrictions on, 322–323
universal themes in, 344
Path of Awakening, 83
peace, 101–102
Pentateuch, 37
Pentecost, Shavuot compared with, 350
"Peoples of the Book," 190
persecution, 191–193, 313
personal renewal, from celebrating Chanukkah, 302–303
Pesach. See Passover
Pharisees, 181–183, 187
Philip Augustus, King of France, 226
phylacteries, 67–68
Pidyon Haben, 117
"pigs" (marranos), 194
pikuakh nefesh, 100
Pillar of Balance, 83
Pillar of Mercy, 83
Pillar of Severity, 83

pilpul, 387
pisher, 394
Pius X, Pope, 205
planning for death, 140–142
planting trees, 308
plotz, 394
pogroms, 204, 227
Poland, 198, 235
Pompey, Roman Emperor, 182
poor, remembering the, 318
position rule of lighting menorah candles, 298
prayers and blessings
about, 52–53
bathroom, 402–403
Chanukkah, 299
community workship service, 54–56
early morning, 398–399
first-time experiences, 402
for food, 400–401
last thing at night, 399
nature, 402
private worship, 54
as reminders and teachers, 404
sample, 397–404
Shabbat, 244–248, 403
Sheh-heh-khi-yanu blessing, 262
Sh'ma, 397–399
Tu B'Shvat seder, 306–307
V'ahavta, 398
Yom Kippur, 278
yom tov blessing, 262
prayer shawl (tallit), 51, 66, 77, 144, 251, 276, 403
premarital sex, 99
Priesand, Sally (rabbi), 374
private worship, 54
produce, blessings before eating, 401

S

"Sabbath Peace!" (Shabbat Shalom!), 248

Sabbath Sanctification (Shabbat Kiddush), 246–247

Sadducees, 181–183, 229

Safed, 76–77

Salome, Queen, 182

salt water, for Passover seder, 329

same-sex ceremonies, 137

Samuel, Book of, 170

sandek, 111

Sarah (Bible character), 157–159

Satan, 32

Saul, King of Israelites, 169–170, 373

Scheindlin, Raymond P. (author)
  A Short History of the Jewish People, 406

Schindler, Oscar (industrialist), 387

schlemazl, 395

schlemiel, 395

schlep, 395

schlock, 395

schmatta, 395

schmeer, 395

schmuck, 395–396

Schulchan Aruch (The Arranged Table) (Caro), 50

Schwartz, Richard H. (animal rights activist), 93

Seasons of Our Joy (Waskow), 406

seating area (Synagogue), 58

Second Temple
  about, 177
  after destruction of First Temple, 178–179
  Greeks, 179–180
  Herod, 182–183
  Israel in strife and combat, 180–181

Rome, 181–182

sects and violence, 183–184

Secular-Humanistic Jewish movement, 355

sedarim, 42

seder
  children at, 337
  Passover, 325–339
  Tu B'Shvat, 306–307

seder plate, 327–328

seder zeved habat, 14

seed, spilling of, 98

seeking forgiveness from God, 272

Sefer Ha-Bahir, 75

Sefer Ha'Mitzvot (Book of the Commandments), 50

Sefer Ha-Mitzvot Ha-Kitzur (The Concise Book of the Commandments), 50

Sefer Torah, 37, 38

Sefer Yetzirah, 75

sefirah, 82

sefirot, 84–87, 342

Seleucas, 179

self-critical humor, 376

self-examination, in humor, 375–378

Sephardi, 15, 201, 321

Sephardi Charoset recipe, 332

Septuagint, 39, 179–180

services
  morning Shabbat, 251
  Musaf, 262, 264–266
  Rosh Hashanah, 268
  Shabbat evening, 251
  S'lichot, 261

seudat havra'ah, 144, 147

seudat mitzvah, 112, 123

seven blessings, 131–132

Severus, Emperor, 226

sexuality
  about, 98–99
  birth control and abortion, 99–100
  homosexuality, 100
  mystical visions of sexual union, 99
  prohibited relationships, 100–101
  prohibitions on, 226

Shabbat, 244–248
  about, 240, 243
  attending evening services, 251
  blessings, 244–248, 403
  breaking rules, 242
  celebrating for first time, 245
  discovering what's enough, 241–242
  doing what you can, 243
  Havdalah, 252–254
  lighting the candles, 244–245
  Matzah Balls recipe, 249
  meals, 248, 250, 252
  morning service, 251
  redefining rules, 242
  spices for Havdalah, 253–254
  universal aspects of, 255
  what to avoid, 241
  wine and candles for Havdalah, 252–253

Shabbat Kiddush (Sabbath Sanctification), 246–247

Shabbat Nachamu, 360

Shabbat Shalom! ("Sabbath Peace!"), 248, 250

shadchan, 128

Shaddai, 30

Shakharit service, 54

Shalakh Manot, 316

shalom aleikhem, 387

Shammai (rabbi), 42

shammash, 297, 298

About the Authors

Rabbi Ted Falcon, Ph.D., one of the pioneers of Jewish spirituality within the Reform Jewish context, was ordained in 1968 from the Hebrew Union College–Jewish Institute of Religion, in Cincinnati, Ohio. He received a doctorate from the California School of Professional Psychology in 1975. He is a nationally recognized lecturer and teacher, and the author of *A Journey of Awakening: A Guide for Using the Kabbalistic Tree of Life in Jewish Meditation*. Since 2001, Rabbi Falcon has worked with Pastor Don Mackenzie and Imam Jamal Rahman, together known as the Interfaith Amigos. With them he has authored *Getting to the Heart of Interfaith: The Eye-Opening, Hope-Filled Friendship of a Pastor, a Rabbi, and an Imam,* and *Religion Gone Astray: What We Found at the Heart of Interfaith*. Rabbi Falcon founded Makom Ohr Shalom, a Synagogue for Jewish Meditation in Los Angeles, and Bet Alef Meditative Synagogue in Seattle. He is a speaker, a writer, and a spiritual therapist in private practice.

David Blatner is an award-winning, best-selling author of 15 books on a wide range of topics—from aviation to digital imaging to the number pi (π). Known for his easy-to-read and humorous style of writing about difficult subjects, Blatner is a Seattle-based writer whose books have sold over a half-million copies and have been translated into 14 languages. He has presented seminars in North America, Australia, Asia, the Middle East, and Europe, and can be found online at 63p.com. Mr. Blatner has been a Jew his whole life.

Dedication

Ted: For my grandchildren, Ezra and Veronica, with much love.

David: To my mother, Barbara, who always encouraged me

Authors' Acknowledgments

Remember the adage "Never trust a book by its cover"? Well, this cover has our names on it, but that only tells part of a much bigger story. We'd like to thank our many teachers, friends, family, and supporters (some of whom fall into more than one of those categories).

First, we've got to give a hand to our wives, Ruth Neuwald Falcon and Debra Carlson, whose patience and love made this grueling process bearable. Thanks, too, to the lead technical reviewer from the first edition, Rabbi Harry Zeitlin, whose wise and kind availability never failed to offer two interpretations when we had room for only one. We also relied on the wise and helpful comments of Rabbi Yossi Liebowitz and Arielle Vale.

Similarly, dozens of others — such as David Morgenstern and Gabe Harbs — contributed facts and figures that helped immeasurably. Thanks, too, to Rabbi Rami Shapiro and Aaron Shapiro, our great technical editors for this second edition. This book couldn't have been produced without considerable caffeine (Ted drinks decaf) from Seattle's Third Place Books in Lake Forest Park. Many thanks to our agent, Reid Boates, and to the folks at Wiley, including Tracy Boggier and our excellent editor, Jennifer Moore.

David: I'd like to thank David Weinstein (and his family) for dragging me to shul as a child to eat great food, as well as Lawrence Horwitz, Mordy Golding, and Glenn Fleishman for their inspiration, kind words, and help along the way. Thanks, too, to my sons Gabriel and Daniel, who love learning alongside me. And great thanks go to my coauthor, Ted, whose profound, open-hearted teaching helped me see Judaism in a new way.

Ted: I would like to thank my teachers and my students (who are often the same people) over the years, and especially my communities in Seattle and in Los Angeles, who taught me what it means to be a rabbi. My work as one of the Interfaith Amigos has deepened my appreciation for the wisdom of Judaism while at the same time celebrating the truths of other traditions, and I am grateful for the presence of Pastor Don Mackenzie and Imam Jamal Rahman in my life. And I continue to be deeply grateful for the expertise, the humor, the wisdom, and the friendship of my coauthor, David Blatner.

Publisher's Acknowledgments

Project and Copy Editor: Jennifer Moore
(*Previous Edition: Mary Goodwin*)

Acquisitions Editor: Tracy Boggier

Technical Editors: Rabbi Rami Shapiro and
Aaron Shapiro

Production Editor: Siddique Shaik

Cover Photos: © D. Hurst/Alamy Stock Photo

Take dummies with you everywhere you go!

Whether you are excited about e-books, want more from the web, must have your mobile apps, or are swept up in social media, dummies makes everything easier.

Find us online!

dummies.com

dummies
A Wiley Brand

PERSONAL ENRICHMENT

9781119187790
USA $26.00
CAN $31.99
UK £19.99

9781119179030
USA $21.99
CAN $25.99
UK £16.99

9781119293354
USA $24.99
CAN $29.99
UK £17.99

9781119293347
USA $22.99
CAN $27.99
UK £16.99

9781119310068
USA $22.99
CAN $27.99
UK £16.99

9781119235606
USA $24.99
CAN $29.99
UK £17.99

9781119251163
USA $24.99
CAN $29.99
UK £17.99

9781119235491
USA $26.99
CAN $31.99
UK £19.99

9781119279952
USA $24.99
CAN $29.99
UK £17.99

9781119283133
USA $24.99
CAN $29.99
UK £17.99

9781119287117
USA $24.99
CAN $29.99
UK £16.99

9781119130246
USA $22.99
CAN $27.99
UK £16.99

PROFESSIONAL DEVELOPMENT

9781119311041
USA $24.99
CAN $29.99
UK £17.99

9781119255796
USA $39.99
CAN $47.99
UK £27.99

9781119293439
USA $26.99
CAN $31.99
UK £19.99

9781119281467
USA $26.99
CAN $31.99
UK £19.99

9781119280651
USA $29.99
CAN $35.99
UK £21.99

9781119251132
USA $24.99
CAN $29.99
UK £17.99

9781119310563
USA $34.00
CAN $41.99
UK £24.99

9781119181705
USA $29.99
CAN $35.99
UK £21.99

9781119263593
USA $26.99
CAN $31.99
UK £19.99

9781119257769
USA $29.99
CAN $35.99
UK £21.99

9781119293477
USA $26.99
CAN $31.99
UK £19.99

9781119265313
USA $24.99
CAN $29.99
UK £17.99

9781119239314
USA $29.99
CAN $35.99
UK £21.99

9781119293323
USA $29.99
CAN $35.99
UK £21.99

dummies.com

dummies
A Wiley Brand